Praise for *The War Behind the Wire*

'Lewis-Stempel describes our prisoners as the lost men of the Great War ... In writing this moving, harrowing account he has done them a noble service'   Colonel Richard Kemp, former
Commander British Forces Afghanistan, *The Times*

'Fantastically well-written, thoroughly researched and full of surprising facts'   Chris Short, *History of War Magazine*

'[Lewis-Stempel] has performed a notable service by telling the story of 1914–18's prisoners, a sad but significant epic'
Max Hastings, *Sunday Times*

'The author's enthralling narrative describes the new horror of the First World War as well as any account from the frontliners'
Louis Rive, *Military History Magazine*

'[An] excellent study of British and colonial prisoners of war . . . What makes *The War Behind the Wire* important, however, is John Lewis-Stempel's destruction of two widely held beliefs. First, he reveals that some 90 per cent of the 420 successful escapers were not elite officers. Second, and even more importantly, Lewis-Stempel proves that the Germans were animated more by the Kriegsbrauch (which allowed for the killing of POWs) than by the humanitarian values of the Hague Convention'
Nathan M. Greenfield, *Times Literary Supplement*

'Lewis-Stempel recreates life behind the wire for British servicemen, looking at how they kept their sanity, maintained their health, and sought to survive an often very grim existence. Readable and absorbing'   *Good Book Guide*

'An entertaining read, and one characterised by the authenticity of the prisoners' own testimony   *BBC History Magazine*

Praise for *Six Weeks*

'One of the most important new studies of the Great War'
Contemporary Review

'A superb study ... Lewis-Stempel's marvellously evocative book is full of throat-catching moments ... The result is the most moving single book on the First World War that I have ever read'
Literary Review

'A harrowing but engrossing meditation on a national tragedy ... This book could not demonstrate more vividly how those ideals which inspired such bravery were shattered'   *Daily Mail*

'A valuable addition to the vast literature of the First World War'
Daily Express

'Lewis-Stempel is excellent on life in the trenches ... for all the horror and pity of their struggle, their legacy is our freedom'
Andrew Roberts, *Mail on Sunday*

'Compelling'   Julian Fellowes

'Superb'   Professor Sir Michael Howard OM, MC

'Wonderful ... hugely moving'   John Simpson

'It is only rarely that a book deserves to be recommended unreservedly but John Lewis-Stempel's *Six Weeks* falls firmly into that category ... This is a book that should be read by every young man who aspires to serve as an officer in the Army; it will educate him about how to behave in command of soldiers and about how to face the perils of war'   *Guards Magazine*

John Lewis-Stempel is an historian and author, predominantly known for his works on military and natural history. His *Six Weeks: The Short and Gallant Life of the British Officer in the First World War* has been widely acclaimed as one of the outstanding recent books on the 1914–18 conflict. He lives on a farm in Herefordshire with his wife and two children.

THE WAR
BEHIND
THE WIRE

The Life, Death and Glory
of British Prisoners of War, 1914–18

JOHN LEWIS-STEMPEL

PHOENIX

A PHOENIX PAPERBACK

First published in Great Britain in 2014
by Weidenfeld & Nicolson
This paperback edition published in 2014
by Phoenix,
an imprint of Orion Books Ltd,
Orion House, 5 Upper St Martin's Lane,
London WC2H 9EA

An Hachette UK company

1 3 5 7 9 10 8 6 4 2

Copyright © John Lewis-Stempel

A CIP catalogue record for this book is available
from the British Library.

ISBN 978-1-7802-2490-9

Typeset by Input Data Services Ltd, Bridgwater, Somerset

Printed and bound by CPI Group (UK) Ltd, Croydon, CR0 4YY

The Orion Publishing Group's policy is to use papers that
are natural, renewable and recyclable products and made
from wood grown in sustainable forests. The logging and
manufacturing processes are expected to conform to the
environmental regulations of the country of origin.

www.orionbooks.co.uk

CONTENTS

I wonder if the people at home ever realize that the prisoners in Germany number amongst their ranks some of the greatest heroes of this war. On the battle-field the hero, or at least some of them, are recognized, and rewarded accordingly; but the exile is never known, though he fights against far more hopeless odds; for him there is no chance – all is at an end. Fine deeds are done in the heat of action, when the excitement of the moment gives the spur to many a noble act; but it takes a braver and more steadfast spirit to pass smiling and cheerful through the endless stunted and hopeless days of a prisoner's life, to cheer up those of our comrades who have for the moment fallen into the slough of despondency, and to harass the German guards at every turn in the matter of attempted escape, since if the prisoners were peaceably quiescent the number of their guards would be reduced, thus freeing so many more men to go and fight against their brothers on the front.

Captain Horace Gilliland, Loyal North Lancashire Regiment.
Taken prisoner at Ypres, 1914. Escaped Germany, 1917.

Note on Terminology

Where individuals are identified by rank, the rank stated is that held by the individual at the time. Where battalions are identified, I have generally rendered the 2nd Battalion Royal Welch Fusiliers as 2/Royal Welch Fusiliers and so on. Place names are as 1914–1919; where they have changed I have endeavoured to show this.

PROLOGUE: THE ESCAPER

In the tomb darkness of the tunnel he hauled himself along, hoisting on his forearms, scrabbling with his boots. There was barely enough room to squeeze through (what was it – eighteen inches high, twenty-four inches wide at best?) and the collar of his coat kept catching the roof, bringing down little cascades of soil. He had to fight the rising fear of being buried alive; it did not help that the flow of air was blocked by the bulk of Sammy Jenkins to his front, and the boy Roberts to his rear. The effort required to move along was hellish, and despite the cold of the winter earth that January 1917 night he was sweating like the proverbial pig.

Along with six other PoWs he had dug this thirty-yard tunnel in the heart of Germany, inch by inch, for six months, equipped with nothing other than a trowel stolen from a camp workman and spoons 'liberated' from the canteen.

Oh God! There was no air. He frantically tried to speed up, but in his mole blindness he of course failed to see Jenkins' boot, which hit him square in the face. So parched was his mouth from anxiety, that the resultant trickle of blood from his gums was, funny to say, almost refreshing.

He pushed on, groping and crawling. The abrupt dip in the tunnel floor told his hands that he had come to the stone foundations of the *Kommandantur* that had almost finished off the project. They had tried to dig under, but to no avail, because every time it rained the water had risen up and threatened to drown the man working the face. In the end, they had picked their way through the wall with the ends of the spoons, stone by stone; his hands still bore the weals of that desperate labour, and if they hadn't had Pearce – a Yorkshire miner back in the time of peace – with them, they'd have given it up. But with those shoulders Pearce could hack away for three—

A commotion ahead of him. A small chain of whispers. 'Guard! Stop moving.'

In the sudden stillness he could hear his heart beating; the noise of it seemed to cannon off the tunnel walls.

He prayed: Oh God! Please don't let me die in here. He was no miner, he for heaven's sake was a clerk in a solicitor's office on the High Street, which now suddenly seemed like the airiest place in the world.

Someone coughed. That would be Stephens, whose lungs had been no good since he was gassed at Hill 60. 'Ssshhhhhhhsssss, for Christ's sake.'

The thump, thump of the guard's boots, just three feet overhead, came closer.

The tunneller held his breath. The boots stopped. Had the guard heard something?

The tunneller said another silent prayer to God. He had been in one PoW camp or another in Germany for going on two years, ever since the counter-attacking Germans had picked him up concussed in that shell hole at Loos. He had tried escaping by impersonating (badly) a German soldier and walking through the front gate of Dülmen *Lager*, and he had tried climbing the wire (only to bump into the camp's canteen NCO on the road outside). Third time lucky. He needed this tunnel to be third time lucky. He hadn't volunteered in August 1914 to sit out the war in Germany.

Or work like a slave in one of Fritz's factories. Last week they'd brought into the camp a gang of Tommies who'd been working in the coking plant at K-47. They looked like the walking dead. And they were the survivors; they said four lads had been left dead by the wayside.

There was something else, if truth be told. He had to rid himself of the shame of being a prisoner. He needed his self-respect back. Oh, he had done his bit in battling the Boche in the camps – he'd refused to salute German officers in the way they wanted, which had earned him a rifle butt to the head and a week in cells – but only a 'home run' would truly restore his reputation. In his own eyes as much as anyone else's. Besides, he was aware that after nearly two years of being cooped up he was beginning to exhibit symptoms of 'mouldiness', that overwhelming apathy that came over prisoners. In the barbed-wire camps when all spirit left men, sometimes they just died. He'd seen that more than once.

The rivulets of sweat crept down his face onto his moustache.

A stamp of feet above his head. Then, at last, the drum-beat of footsteps making their mechanical march into the distance.

Someone behind, panting desperately: 'He's gone . . . Get a move on boys, for fuck's sake.'

The tunnel was at its tightest here, and only by exerting all his strength could he haul himself forward. His damned knapsack, tied to his leg, dragged like a malevolent anchor. But he couldn't do without the rucksack. A rucksack was an essential prop for every escaper intent on passing himself off as a German civilian.

Haul. Scrabble. Haul. Scrabble. Just when, in a pure panic, there seemed to be no exit, that the tunnel was going on for ever, he was aware of fresh air on his face. Old Jenkins, a Regular taken captive in the 'retirement' from Mons ('We never retreat, we Regulars,' Jenkins used to tell anybody unwise enough to ask how he ended up in the cage), must already be out. Yes, there was no shuffling sound ahead.

Then he too was out into the night, popping up like a startled jack from the box. The stark arc lights of the camp were behind him, and there to the front across the frosted field was the road, its stone surface lit by moonlight. He could see no one else; those ahead of him had already disappeared into the shadows.

There was no sense in hanging about. From his pocket he extracted a black, peaked workman's cap, which – and he was quite proud of this, being an office man – he'd fashioned himself from discarded uniform trousers and dyed with India ink. He set it at a jaunty angle on his head.

He was free!

With his rucksack swung over his shoulder, the escaper walked quickly off towards the road.

Everyone had their own 'Cooks travel plans' to get to neutral Holland, a hundred miles away. His was simplicity itself. He was going to steal a bicycle from the village over the hill and pedal to the frontier. He had a mini-compass, secretly made by some clever bod in the barrack hut with a magnet, needle and watch case, hidden in the heel of his shoe, but he did not really need it. He had spent two hours every week in his last camp attending a class on astronomy run by a sergeant in the Warwicks who had been a science professor at the Victoria University of Manchester in civvy life – it was funny the chaps you met in the *Lager* – so he could steer by the stars, navigate by the sun.

Ten days later Corporal Thomas Perry of the 2/Worcesters succeeded in crossing the border into neutral Holland. He had indeed cycled all the way to the border zone, before dumping the bike to walk the final stretch at night, doing so as craftily as any cat burglar. There had been a nasty moment though, right at the last when, bitter cold from wading through a dyke, he stumbled over a frontier tripwire. German guards had come shouting, screaming, firing wildly, but he'd kept on going and they had been unable to get him.

On his return to Blighty, his home town of Ledbury turned out to welcome their local hero. He gave evidence to the Government Committee on the Treatment of Prisoners of War, some of which was used later in the Leipzig War Crimes Trials. To his annoyance, however, the War Office dithered about allowing him back to the front, so it was not until August 1918 that he was allowed to rejoin the Battalion in France.

He ended the war with the rank of sergeant, winning a Distinguished Conduct Medal on the Hindenburg Line in September 1918. And there was another honour too, of which he was prouder really, because when you got down to it the guts he'd shown then were greater than the mad dash with the Lewis gun he'd got the DCM for. He received a Mention in Dispatches for his successful escape from Hunland, the notice of which was posted in a special supplement to the *London Gazette* in 1920.

Thomas Perry was one of over 600 British PoWs who made successful 'home runs' in the Great War.[1]

INTRODUCTION

They are the lost men of the Great War. There are no tears for their suffering, no quickenings of the heart at their valour. They are not part of the 'Memory' of 1914–18, which is now the sole province of the sacred dead who fell in France and Flanders.[1]

Some 171,720 British officers and other ranks were taken prisoner by Germany and her Allies in the First World War.[2] In wartime Britain, the fate of the prisoners caused national anguish; a Government Committee was set up to investigate their maltreatment. The names of star British escapers were said with reverence. When the prisoners were repatriated after the Armistice, they were given a hero's welcome, their homecoming ships met by cheering flotillas of boats. The King shook their hand.

But who today knows the name of arch-escaper Second Lieutenant Harold Medlicott?

Who today knows that the death rate in the Kaiser's prisoner-of-war camps – from brutality, starvation and disease – was sometimes higher than that on the Western Front?[3] In other words, in certain phases of the First World War a Tommy had a better chance of survival in a Flanders trench than in a German prisoner-of-war (PoW) camp.

But who today knows *anything* of what befell Britain's prisoners of war in those four years of total war?

The reasons for the historical amnesia are not hard to fathom. Prisoners were, after all, men who had surrendered – which was hardly glorious, was it? Hardly Rorke's Drift, 'Fix bayonets and die like British soldiers do!' stuff – and often felt a burden of shame about their capture. More, their official status as 'war casualties' seemed growingly questionable, paltry, pathetic when compared to those 702,410 British dead buried in corners of foreign fields. Even more than other veterans of the Great War the prisoners tended not to speak of their experiences. So, the prisoners were silent, out of shame for themselves and respect for the fallen.[4]

They did not even speak to each other. A national organization of PoWs shrivelled on the vine.[5]

There was convenience in forgetting the prisoners too. Prisoners were away for longer than other veterans; they understood less of home, and home understood less of them. A spate of memoirs by officer escapers probably did more harm than good, since in their standard style they were penned in that Henty-esque, stiff-upper-lip manner of the era, with chaps trying to 'score off the Germans' by achieving escapes to neutral countries. Making light of misfortune is an excellent quality in a soldier-leader; in a memoirist it sadly fails to convey the truths needing chronicling. The public was left with the distinct impression that PoW life was all a bit of a game, and anyone who did open their lips about 'Boche brutality' was being economical with the *Wahrheit* or making an embarrassing fuss about very little. Really, it was all so much easier to deal with by being forgotten.

It must be admitted too, that it seems to be human nature (or at least the nature of old British soldiers) to forgive and forget. In 1918 Sapper George Waymark, taken captive at Le Cornet Malo in Flanders on 12 April 1918, ended the secret diary of his captivity:

> Now I can rest and try to imagine what I should do if I met some of those guards whose one aim in life seemed to be to make our existence a hell. I wonder.[6]

By 1977, when interviewed, he considered: 'Most (guards) were decent sorts.'

All these are 'honest' causes for the loss of the prisoners in the national remembrance of the First World War. The other reasons are more invidious. By the late 1920s, that decade of disillusion, the Great War was being re-written by pacifists and politicians as an immoral, avoidable conflict caused by the great powers', principally Germany and Britain, divvying of the globe. (The influence of a Marxist 'curse on both your imperial houses' was forensically detectable.) In the new moral equivalence, the treatment meted out to

British prisoners in Germany was held to be no different from that meted out to German prisoners of war in Britain. Or, indeed, any PoWs, anywhere. By 1932 the writer J.R. Ackerley, a former PoW himself but never a reliable witness, could blithely state in a collection of escape stories, 'Prisoners of war were treated the same in every country that took part in the war.'[7] Wartime accounts of atrocities committed against British PoWs – which had once so troubled the nation – became dismissed as propaganda. In his influential book *Falsehood in Wartime* (1928), the Labour MP and pacifist Sir Arthur Ponsonby claimed 'Stories of the maltreatment of prisoners have to be circulated deliberately in order to prevent surrender. This is done, of course, on both sides.'[8] 'Stories.' 'On both sides.' Ponsonby was the man who gave the world the motto, 'When war is declared, truth is the first casualty.' Alas, the first casualty of peace was the truth about crimes committed by the Kaiser's wartime regime against British PoWs.

In blunt sum: the experience of the British prisoner of war became, in the popular view, either unremarkable – or, if direly awful, a politically fabricated falsehood. And so much better if ignored.

Nobody was keener to forget the prisoners than the selfsame government that had once championed their cause. The 1920s were not only the years of disenchantment, they were the years of diplomatic and commercial re-engagement with Germany. To treat with Germany in peacetime demanded a Realpolitik in which British PoWs, with their grievances and horror stories, were conveniently lost in the shuffle of papers in Whitehall in-trays.[9] No one could be beastly to the Boche any more. This willingness to sacrifice the prisoner on the altar of diplomacy was evident as early as 1921 during the War Crimes Trials at Leipzig – set up, in part, precisely to bring those who had maltreated British prisoners to justice. In the event, the British government made a half-hearted deposition and risibly allowed the Germans to sit in judgement on themselves. To no great surprise, convictions were few, punishments mild.

But what of historians, the professional analysers and 'rememberers' of the past, what have they made of Britain's captives in the

Great War? With a handful of exceptions[10] in almost a hundred years they have not found the prisoners a fit subject for study. Field Marshal Haig's navel is usually so much more rewarding to gaze at. History, like Nature, abhors a vacuum; in the absence of proper historical study two small, persistent myths about First World War PoWs have emerged, burrowed and lodged. The thickest-shelled of the fables, and one which is usually given an injection of 'classist' genes, is that escape was the prerogative of officers. Thus the sociologist Joan Beaumont can confidently assert: 'Escape plans . . . are largely the experience of a privileged elite, not of the many millions of prisoners of war from the other ranks.'[11] And the military historian Neil Hanson can state, without so much as a qualifying blush:

> Breakouts by other-ranks prisoners were comparatively rare, partly because they usually lacked the financial and other resources available to officers, including the time, with which to plan and carry out escapes.[12]

A mere second's glance at one sole set of figures should be enough for extreme caution in advancing such a claim. Before chucking it over the side. Of the 420 British soldiers listed in the official record as having escaped German clutches and reached neutral territory, only 49 were officers.[13] Put another way: other ranks made up 88 per cent of the British Expeditionary Force's 'home runners'. More figures: of the Canadians who made successful escapes to neutral territory in the Great War 99 per cent were enlisted men. (I should make plain here that this is a book about British soldiers, though with some reference to Empire forces,[14] incarcerated in Germany and on the front line in the West; the story of British prisoners held by Turkey runs to a different tune, and is worthy of its own volume.) Actually, the whole scale of British 'escapology', whether perpetrated by officers or other ranks, is woefully underestimated.[15] As for why men escaped, the mischievous J.R. Ackerley set the trail false in his introduction to *Escapers All* in 1932, suggesting that escape was a form of 'self-expression'. In other words, men only escaped because it was their personal 'free-spirited' nature to find life behind bars unbearable. Actually, the reasons men escaped were several and varied; Private George Hall wasn't alone in escaping because he feared the casual sadistic beatings of German guards, just as Lieutenant F.W. Harvey of the Gloucestershire Regiment was in good company in believing escape was necessary so that men could rejoin 'that dreadful and glorious fight for England and her liberty' on the orthodox battlefield.

Then there is the pernicious myth that captured British soldiers were uniformly 'glad to be out of it', joyously relieved to be taken captive and so safe from the fighting on the Western Front. Perhaps some were. Most weren't. To be captured was a bewildering humiliation for proud men who had, after all, signed on to be *fighting* men, to be soldiers. If any Tommy *did* think he was evading Death's shadow by surrendering he was in for a rude and possibly fatal surprise. For a bloody start he had to survive the moment of capture by German troops – the odds of which ran, say, 80:20.[16] German troops fired up to kill did not always find it easy to change down a gear to accept surrender in its stead. Neither did they always want to. Execution of surrendered Tommies by Germans was far from unknown.

And there was no peace in the PoW camps of Germany for those soldiers who surrendered. The Kaiser's army was institutionally brutal to its own men, so what could be expected of it when put in charge of enemy soldiers? Systematic violence and crushing nothingness were givens in the *Lager*. There was disease which rampaged through camps with Goya-esque fury. Then there was the lack of food, which caused men to die of starvation, and others to become skeletally thin in a way that is uncomfortably reminiscent of another, later Germany. British prisoners were worked to death in German factories, pits and salt mines. *Literally* worked to death.

The Enlightenment's search for civilized principles to govern conduct in war had resulted in international conferences, notably those at The Hague in 1899 and 1907, which laid out, among their many promulgations, agreed rules on the treatment of the PoW, from capture to camp. Regarding the prisoner The Hague Convention stipulated, *inter alia*:

Chapter II:

Article 4. Prisoners of war are in the power of the hostile Government, but not of the individuals or corps who capture them. They must be humanely treated . . .

Article 6. The State may utilize the labour of prisoners of war according to their rank and aptitude, officers excepted. The tasks shall not be excessive and shall have no connection with the operations of the war . . .

Article 7. The Government into whose hands prisoners of war have fallen is charged with their maintenance. In the absence of a special agreement between the belligerents, prisoners of war shall be treated as regards board, lodging, and clothing on the same footing as the troops of the Government who captured them.[17]

These rules were flouted, ignored, trampled on by the Kaiser's regime. The long march of European liberal decency stopped at the reactionary Prussian doorstep of the *Stadtschloss* and the *Kriegsministerium*. A Red Cross commissioner, after observing the PoW camps in Wilhelmine Germany wrote in exasperation:

Neither treaty nor humanitarian consideration induced the German Government to treat its prisoners of war as human beings, or make much effort to preserve their lives . . .[18]

Carl Dennett did not lie. Of the British incarcerated by Germany, 11,147 are officially listed as having died in captivity.[19] There were thousands more. On the war memorials that stand agonized and proud into the skies of Britain, France and Flanders are the names of the missing; we presume these to be the dead lost in the mud of the battlefields of Ypres, the Somme and wherever the thin khaki line held the Western Front. But some of these 'missing' were actually captured troops made to labour for the enemy behind the front and who, unregistered by the Germans, died of starvation after being deprived of the Red Cross parcels that were their right. As many as 50,000 Allied troops and civilians perished as slaves behind the German front line in the West.[20] The number of unregistered British

PoWs among them is unknown and unknowable, but an estimate of 2,000 would be reasonable. By any measure, their deaths constitute a war crime. By any measure, the Kaiser's vast slave army prefigured that of Hitler's.

For prisoners the war was eternal, because there were demons in the head to battle too. The war was within as well as without. Boredom, the lack of privacy, loneliness, hopelessness all sapped the spirit. The resultant depression, considered Lieutenant Alec Waugh, incarcerated in the officer's *Lager* in Mainz and the brother of the more famous Evelyn, was 'far and away our worst enemy: whole days were drenched in an incurable melancholia'.[21] Waugh constantly tormented himself for having surrendered. By the honour code of the British Army, soldiers – especially officers – did not put their hands in the air and wave white flags, they died fighting heroically in last stands. Such as Rorke's Drift. Regimental traditions and Victorian patriotic history books, however, were no match for the realities of the 1914–18 battlefield. Twenty-four hours of pounding by 'Jack Johnsons' and *Minenwerfer* often left men – those still alive, that is – so battered and enfeebled they could not bear arms even though they wanted to. Few British surrenders in the Great War smacked of cowardice; confusion, accident, incapacitation yes, but yellowness no. Alas, *ex post facto* justifications by an historian are cold comfort for Waugh and all the other PoWs who spent their prison days in turmoiled humiliation for having surrendered.

Humiliation was hottest on Sunday afternoons in the camps. On Sunday afternoons German civilians, in a favourite entertainment, came on sightseeing trips to view the captured specimens of *Britannicus militarius* displayed behind the wire. Schools organized visits. Financially astute commandants charged the gawpers and pocketed the Marks.

Small wonder, then, that Lieutenant F.W. 'Will' Harvey, a veteran of seven camps and the PoWs' unofficial laureate, began one of his most famous poems with the lines

Walking round our cages like the lions at the Zoo,
We think of things that we have done, and things we mean to do . . .

Harvey's choice of leonine metaphor was precise and apposite. They were lions, the captured soldiers of the British Army, officers and other ranks alike. Because they fought back. 'When we realized we were prisoners,' recalled one soldier, 'we decided to buck the Germans any way we could.'[22] British prisoners were more than happy to carry the war into the camps, where they fought the national cause as certainly as any khaki-clad soldier in the trenches. In the barbed-wire war of the camps only the weapons differed; here British soldiers fought with taunting humour (the British were, all Allied PoWs agreed, beyond compare in the parodying of Prussians), by putting a sabotaging spanner in the works of the factories they were forced to labour in, by singing songs of defiance, by arson, by escape . . . by living. Because in circumstances where people are killing you, whether deliberately or by neglect, to struggle to live is an act of resistance. To survive is a victory.

Any prisoner who *did* want a quiet life was unlikely to get it. By 1916, 80 per cent of British prisoners were in forced labour, and the German need for workers was only getting bigger, more desperate. As prisoners found out all too quickly the German interpretation of 'not excessive' work, as per Article 6 of the 1907 Hague Convention, was generous – such as a twelve-hour shift in a Hameln salt mine. 'If you could only see the boys here,' wrote one private soldier in a smuggled letter from a white pit, 'they all look like dead men; they are all worked to death.'[23]

No act of resistance behind the wire was inconsequential or without consequence. Whatever smoky, silky lies the German authorities put out about 'shot trying to escape', they executed Second Lieutenant Medlicott and his friend Captain Walter in cold blood that 1917 day in the morbid shade of Pfaffenholz forest. Medlicott and Walter were murdered because they were unstoppable 'jug-crackers' – escapers – whose refusal to bow to German military authority irked unbearably. And had to be snuffed out. A luckier escaper, Lieutenant Peter Anderson, on making his 'home run' was invited to Buckingham Palace by George V. Amid his congratulations, His Majesty added the opinion that he considered the bravery involved in escaping was, if anything, greater than that required on the battlefield, which was usually the product of the heat of the moment.[24] Who can gainsay him? An escape might take weeks of preparation, weeks in which to fret, weeks in which to factor the chances of fatality. If you want to see pure, distilled courage, look no further than the life and death of the Kaiser's most unwilling guest, Harold Walter Medlicott. A man – a boy, really – of serial *sang froid* and outrageous daring, whose fourteen escape attempts included sliding down the outside of a nearly perpendicular sixty-foot tower at Wesel fortress and, in a magnificent moment, climbing the perimeter wire at Holzminden in broad daylight.[25] He was everything the British were reputed and hoped to be. So was Corporal John Brady, King's Own Yorkshire Light Infantry, who refused, time and time again, to do work that would aid the German war effort, suffering beatings and solitary imprisonment for his Bulldog guts.[26]

But there were so many forms of courage in the war behind the wire. To occupy the endless day in a godforsaken place like Strohen Moor, to maintain personal integrity amidst hunger so desperate men would fight each other for pig scraps, to nurse comrades through the typhus epidemic at Wittenberg, to keep the national faith under constant '*Gott strafe England*' taunts – all required forms of courage beyond the physical. Having looked at the memoirs and records of over five hundred British prisoners in the Great War, I can only conclude that theirs was the glory. British prisoners of war did so much more than suffer silently. They founded camp libraries, refused to salute German NCOs, dug escape tunnels, held dignified Communion services in leaking huts, made skeleton keys from sardine cans to raid German stores, went on strike, skived work by pretending to be Hottentots on Sabbath, escaped, escaped again, played football, wrecked German munitions trucks by putting sand in the axles, mocked the goose step long before John Cleese, put on little variety shows in their barracks, made pets of stray dogs, held study classes, and dreamed and dreamed of food.

This is the war the prisoners knew.

Map of the Main Prison Camps in Germany and Austria

Reproduced from 'Map of the Main Prison Camps in Germany and Austria' (Una Pope-Hennessy, 1920)

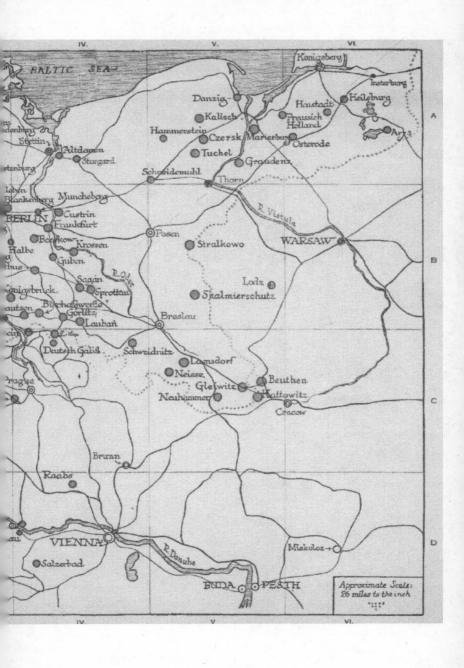

IN THE BAG: CAPTURE

Surrender? Was it then to come to this, after all?

Lieutenant Gilbert Nobbs,
London Rifle Brigade, at Leuse Wood, 1916

Somewhere outside the French hamlet of Audencourt on 26 August 1914, that fateful month in which the world separated from peace to war. The sun is shining, as it seems to have done every day of that perfect summer. Lieutenant Malcolm Hay's platoon of the 1/Gordon Highlanders, after retreating for days, is ordered to make a stand against the advancing Germans. Hay tells his exhausted men to throw up a trench in a stubble field. Hay knows – almost – what to expect; Number 13 Platoon has already met the figures in *feldgrau* at Mons.

Soon German shells start landing in front of Hay's trench, the shrapnel breaking over the top in waves. Shells upon shells.

Then, unreal moment: Germans emerge from the woods into the shimmering haze above the wheat stalks and come on in overwhelming numbers. Between shell-bursts, the Lee Enfield rifles of Number 13 Platoon shoot off two rounds before their owners duck down again. Their aim is good and true, even at 900 yards, and they slow the grey advance. But they cannot stop it. A German machine gun opens up, its bullets flicking along the trench top. Through his field glasses, Hay directs the platoon's return fire as best he can . . . until a bullet hits him in the head.

A voice says, 'Mr H. has got it.'

Not quite. Hay is bandaged up by Private Sinclair and when darkness falls his men, as gently as they can, move him out of the trench, using a greatcoat and rifle as stretchers, to a safer place in the lee of a sunken road. Hay is intermittently conscious. When he is awake, one fear wells up: 'to be left behind and taken prisoner'.[1] Although the battalion is instructed to retire at midnight, two of the platoon remain with Hay; only when Hay directly orders them himself will they leave him.

A straggler from the Royal Irish Rifles appears, and makes Hay as comfortable as he can, before disappearing into the orange-grey gloom. Audencourt is burning.

Later, Hay hears foreign, guttural voices on the road. Small parties of German soldiers pass by, staring sympathetically. Nevertheless:

> For some inexplicable reason I tried to get away. By seizing a tuft of grass in the left hand I could move along a few inches at a time. After advancing in this manner for about a foot . . . I collapsed from exhaustion and drew the greatcoat over my head. I do not know how long I had been thus covered up when I heard a shout and, peeping through one of the holes in the coat, saw a German soldier standing on the top of the bank. He was gesticulating and pointing to his revolver, trying to find out if I was armed! But he soon saw that I was past any further fighting.
>
> He offered me a drink from his water bottle and pointed to the Red Cross on his arm. I can never hope to convey to anyone what a relief it was to me to see the cross, even on the arm of an enemy.[2]

The Red Cross orderly calls him 'Kamerad'. A German officer arrives on the scene, expresses his sympathy for Hay, offers him a piece of chocolate and the information that the German Army will be in Paris in three days. Hay is loaded onto a stretcher, taken to a field hospital run by the French under German supervision, where his condition becomes so serious that Extreme Unction is read over him not once but twice. Hay, though, is made of tough stuff and survives to become a prisoner of war in Germany.

In understanding why British soldiers became prisoners of war between 1914 and 1918 the capture of Lieutenant Malcolm Vivian Hay is pregnant with explanation. Of the 165,055[3] British troops captured by Germany on the Western Front over the course of the war, over 80 per cent surrendered in just two four-month periods at the bracket ends of the conflict. These were August–November 1914 and March–June 1918, when there was movement on the battlefield in the shape of gargantuan offensives by the German Army. In his little stand in the sunlit stubble field at Audencourt, a corner of the bigger battle of Le Cateau, Hay was outnumbered three to one; British troops facing the make-or-break German Spring Offensive of 1918 faced a similar imbalance in men. The month of Black March 1918 saw 100,000 British soldiers taken captive, 20,000 of them on 21 March alone, the worst day of surrender in British military annals until Singapore in 1941. In contrast, when the war was static and stuck in the trenches British surrenders were a trickle. Up to the end of November 1914 18,500 British troops were, in the parlance of the day, put 'in the bag', including 1,400 from Le Cateau; the total of those who surrendered in December 1914, the first month of proper trench warring, was 369.[4] Between January 1915 and November 1917 only 20,000 British troops were bagged by the Germans on the Western Front.

If these numbers seem large, they are not. Of the British Army 1914–18 vintage only 6 per cent would end up as prisoners of war, compared to 9 per cent of German forces and 50 per cent of Russians.[5] The British Army of 1914–18 was tightly bound, between officers and men (witness the tender care of Hay by his troops), and men and men. They were often from the same town or village, and until 1916 they were either prideful professional Regulars or idealistic volunteers. They had a patriotic commitment to a war of justice and defence. Surrender was an unthinkable taboo, like those other dishonourable means of exiting a battlefield, self-inflicted wounds and desertion. The men saw it like the Army saw it. Surrender, without damn good reason, was an evasion of duty, a betrayal of comrades, Regiment, family, school, country – everybody on 'our side'. There was also the whole weight of Army tradition, with all its storied last stands. Who wanted to let down glorious tradition? No one.

No information was given to troops leaving for France and Flanders on how to surrender because it might make surrender as opposed to fighting to the last round a not dishonourable option.

On the contrary, the 1907 Manual of Military Law declared it to be a court martial offence under the Army Act to 'display the white flag in the presence of the enemy' without specific orders from HQ or indeed to be 'taken prisoner, by want of due precaution'. Officers, in a less than subtle aid to doing the right thing, were informed that, should the unspeakable occur, they would have to write a report on their surrender for the information of the War Office. Surrender came trailing the distinct odour of, at worst, cowardice, at best incompetence.[6]

So, why did British soldiers surrender? Woeful crimson, as with Malcolm Hay, played its part. A wound rate of over 70 per cent occurred with some units in the battle of Le Cateau; overall, about 25 per cent of British prisoners taken in the Great War were taken wounded and *hors de combat*.[7] The sight and sound of the wounded could have a knock-on effect; in a trench, with the moaning tide of wounded comrades rising around them, some men suffered a collapse of spirit. Incapacitation of an officer – Malcolm Hay again – led to lack of leadership, lack of fighting will, since even the best regiments of the British Army needed an officer to make the men stand.[8] Men without officers were particularly prone to capture. There is a whiff too, that British units left officerless would actually heed the orders of a German officer in locum. Lance Corporal Thomas Higgins, 3/5 North Staffordshire Regiment, a former steelworker and no shrinking violet, tellingly recalled about his surrender at Lens in 1915:

> A German officer then shouted in English, 'Surrender'; so we threw our rifles down, and put up our hands.[9]

Of course, there were other things to run out of in battle, apart from blood. Without ammunition continued resistance was impossible, though the frequency with which 'lack of ammo' appears in prisoner memoirs suggests a request for absolution[10] rather than a statement of fact; no one can be expected to fight without the wherewithal. The 'heat of battle', however, is no misnomer; excruciating thirst was an unrecognized and unlikely cause of incapacitation.[11] More common was the ending of proper mental and physical functioning, either brought on by exhaustion, gas or heavy shelling. The really big catches of British prisoners in the Great War were invariably preceded by artillery poundings – Le Cateau was the first major artillery attack of the conflict – or barrages which boxed soldiers in. Both tended to cause catatonia. Unlucky Private C. Sharpe, 2/8th Lancashire Fusiliers, sat through the immense opening salvo of the infamous German Spring Offensive of March 1918, with all its *Sturm und Drang* Wagnerian intensity. He thought

> such HELL makes weaklings of the strongest and no human's nerves or body were ever built to stand such torture, noise, sorrow and mental pain.[12]

They weren't. And when the survivors looked out of their ruined trenches, the cries of the wounded shrieking around them, their head-ringing befuddlement was only exacerbated by the sight in front of them. Private Sharpe again:

> As far as the eye could see, on what a day ago were flat green fields scarcely pitted with shell holes, was nothing but the blue grey uniforms of German troops advancing in well ordered company formation.

Those grey men were alarming in their appearance as they marched in on the back of the artillery maelstrom. Often the first German a British soldier saw up close was the one lumbering towards him with his 'butcher's blade' (as the fearsome German MI898/05 sword bayonet was known) ready to gut a Tommy stomach. With their animal hide backpacks, their pickelhaube hats or science-fiction storm-trooper helmets the Germans were alien beings.[13]

Those grey men were alarming in their numbers too. In autumn 1914 and spring 1918 they were able to overrun British positions, leaving units shocked, encircled, out of communication, out of orders and left to cope as best as they could with regiments of the enemy between them and the main British line. Malcolm Hay's Samaritan straggler from the Irish Rifles was only an extreme case of the fragmentation and isolation that occurred in the great German attacks. Incapacity, absence of leadership, shellshock, impossible odds,

encirclement all created the indispensable condition for the surrender of British soldiers in the First World War, which was not
fear but confusion. Time and time again, those who surrendered
described the experience as though it was a bewildering dream.
For Private Percy Williams, 1/5 Northumberland Fusiliers, gassed,
shelled, wounded by shrapnel in his leg as he tried to crawl along
the road to British positions, the noise left him 'in all of a muddle'.
Many of his unit were eighteen-year-olds with no battle experience.
He 'never saw a British officer'. Rifleman Victor Denham sat under
a *Minenwerfer* bombardment ('those earthquakes in miniature')
at Arras:

> 'I watched and waited in a state of mental numbness or apathy . . .
> When I took a further interest in matters I was a prisoner.'[14]

So perplexed was Lieutenant Archibald Bowman, Highland Light
Infantry, by his surrender in spring 1918 that, despite being a professor of Logic, he believed it best explained in poetry. He would
spend most of his seven months in German captivity at Hesepe and
Rastatt writing sonnets examining the impossible experience:

> How it befel? — The overreaching arm,
> Bombs; and he was among us. In his plan
> Surprise completed what surprise began.
> The treacherous shelter of a too-near farm,
> A ditch along a road, a false alarm.
> Thirty yards of the open; in the van
> A desperado running – How he ran! –
> And the pack had us. Hands up and disarm!
> – It is the end of all, the bitter end.
> The unpardonable, though ineluctable,
> A breach in life no living now will mend;
> The sin that sinned not; fell not, yet a fall.
> One thought burned in the brain: How dear it cost
> England to gain what I this day have lost![15]

The instinctive reaction of soldiers, in confusion and chaos, and a
German suddenly right THERE! was to prefer the uncertainty of

captivity to the certainty of death from a bullet or a bayonet. Life over death.

Some, should the occasion warrant it – an occasion such as covering the retreat of a unit or plugging a front-line hole on which the destiny of a battle might depend – and should the mind be clear enough and the heart stout enough might choose a fighting death. In the situation of impossible odds most soldiers, when and where they were capable of rational thought, tended to go through the same mental process as did Captain George Foley, 7/Somerset Light Infantry, during the March 1918 offensive. And come to the same conclusion:

> Further concealment was useless, and we were in one of those plights when a soldier has to consult whatever conscience he may possess, and choose between a death of doubtful glory, but obvious futility, or surrender.
>
> At twenty yards' distance the leading Hun raised his rifle and aimed it with dispassionate care at my head. It seemed to me that to be shot like a pig in a poke was in no way furthering the cause of the Allies. Consequently, and in rather less time than it takes to tell . . . I indicated that we were willing to capitulate . . . With all those grey figures round us, I had the sensation of being swallowed alive.[16]

The surrender of Captain Foley's company of West Countrymen is a reminder that at least half of British prisoners had no say in their capitulation. The British Army of 1914–18 was a disciplined army in which men obeyed the orders of their officers and NCOs. If ordered to surrender they did. Generally.

Officers of the British Army were caring of their men, and would not have wanted them to die in vain. In charitable light the notorious surrender of Lieutenant Colonel Mainwaring, 2/Royal Dublin Fusiliers, at St Quentin on 27 August 1914 was because of compassion for his men, lying in the town square barely conscious following their scorched march from Mons. He wrote of his surrender order:

> The fact is that the men could do no more for the time being. Their

limit of endurance was reached. I considered it my duty to protect
these men, who so nobly had done theirs.[17]

Mainwaring himself was so far mentally and physically collapsed
he could only walk with the aid of a stick.

What a plethora of ways there was for men to become captive
outside their will! There was the naive subaltern on night patrol
who had not yet learned when a German star shell lit the wire-and-
mud landscape with its stark white light to *stand still*; instead he
dived to earth, the movement attracting the eye of a nearby enemy
patrol who snatched him away to their line. Then there was Captain Robert Dolbey, Royal Army Medical Corps (RAMC), running
a field hospital in a farm at La Bassée when Germans loomed
through the mist on a foggy morning in October 1914. His job was
to stay with the wounded. Duty saw him put in the bag.[18] Private
J.T. 'Tanner' Milburn, a native of the Northumberland pit village of
Ashington, was buried by a shell-burst as he attacked the German
lines at La Boisselle on 1 July 1916. He was underground for six hours
until disinterred by the enemy:

> After being dug out, there was about five Germans standing around
> me. I thought my time had come because one wanted to put the bay-
> onet through me but the others would not have it.[19]

Perversely, as with Tanner Milburn, it was emphatically possible to
be captured for doing deeds of bravery. The trench career of Lieutenant Will Harvey, Gloucestershire Regiment, is proof enough of
that:

> To put it baldly, I was taken alone in a German front line trench,
> which I had entered unseen yet in broad daylight, and was proceed-
> ing to explore . . . it was up to a point the prettiest piece of patrolling
> I ever did. Certainly it was the identical rashness which got me a
> decoration that got me taken prisoner in 1916.[20]

He was 'collared' by two large Germans emerging from a dug-out.
One of them so looked like a labourer on his father's Gloucestershire farm that Harvey burst out laughing – 'which possibly saved

my life!'[21] The decoration Harvey had been awarded for his previous solo patrol was the Distinguished Conduct Medal. A move up to the ranks of the commissioned had also been the reward for Corporal Will Harvey.

Musing later on his 1916 capture, Harvey concluded:

> It is a strange thing, but to be made prisoner is undoubtedly the most surprising thing that can happen to a soldier. It is an event which one has never considered, never by any chance anticipated.[22]

They were good men, the Glosters, everybody said that, being one of those unflashy but solid county regiments England could always put in a breach and be certain they would fill the wall with their dead. There was none finer in the Glosters than smooth-faced Second Lieutenant Claude Templer, former pupil of Wellington College, who had been commissioned in August 1914, aged barely nineteen. Like Will Harvey, Templer would turn out to be a poet (though not such a fine or famous one), and like Harvey he was nabbed by the Germans while he reconnoitred a trench alone ahead of his platoon. This was December 1914 at La Bassée. Alas for the Germans, they didn't kill him when they knocked him from behind with the butt of a rifle. With the exception of Harold Medlicott, no one would prove a more resolute, troublesome escaper than Claude Francis Lethbridge Templer. And in the end, he beat them.

There were other ways in which courage could put a man on the road to a prisoner-of-war camp. Lieutenant Gilbert Nobbs, a Territorial in the London Rifle Brigade, was captured because he did what British officers did: he led a charge. At Leuze Wood ('Lousy Wood') in 1916, he told his men, 'My lads! It's for England!' Up from the flat ground they rose, machine-gun rounds and shells pouring into them ... The attack faltered, men took refuge in shell holes. Nobbs ran from shell hole to shell hole, urging the men on. The line reformed. They pressed forward. Nobbs got to a shell hole within 20 yards of his objective. And decided to finish matters with a bayonet charge. He jumped out of the shell hole:

> I wanted to kill! Kill!

But:

I was blind.[23]

A rifle round had entered the side of Nobbs' head and exited through his right eye. He drifted in and out of consciousness for two days in the shell hole where he fell. His head bloated massively. Just as he was about to embrace death he heard a voice say, 'Englishman! *Kamerad*!' Like Lieutenant Hay he was torn between joy at hearing a human voice and wanting to shrink to avoid discovery: 'Surrender? Was it then to come to this, after all?'[24] It was.

There were numerous other officers and men brought in from the wire fronting the German trenches, where they lay following wounding in an attack and made captive. But who could have done more?

The first Victoria Cross of the Great War awarded to a private soldier went to Sidney Godley, Royal Fusiliers, a latterday Horatius, for holding the railway bridge at Nimy, Mons, with a machine gun for two hours. He held off six German divisions before being captured seriously wounded. But who could have done more?

Whereas in the contemporary collective mind the Western Front of 1914–18 is a set of distinct trenches running in continuously parallel lines from the North Sea to Switzerland, the reality was fuzzier. After heavy actions such as the Somme and Passchendaele, the front would turn into a pitted landscape as featureless as the Moon. It was ridiculously easy to get lost on this bleak muddy planet. In other words, men could stray mistakenly into becoming prisoners of war. Even an old hand like Lieutenant Hugh Durnford did it. Trying to find Battalion HQ at Hell-Fire Corner in the Ypres Salient, Durnford and his orderly approached a pillbox on roughly the right map coordinates, where they spotted a Tommy buggering about wearing a pickelhaube hat. Only when Durnford was about to hail the pillbox a hearty welcome did the awful truth dawn. By then the Germans had him covered with their rifles and there was no running away. Not in that mud:

I stammered out a few words in bad French to their officer and then asked leave to sit down, I was exhausted and quite overwhelmed. So this was the result of my fourteen months cumulative experience. What a culmination! To walk over No-Man's land on a bye-day in broad daylight into a German nest. Such a thing had never come into our ken that I could remember. And if it had I should have been the first to pass uncharitable comment.[25]

He blamed himself. Or did Battalion give him the wrong coordinates? A round of who-was-responsible set up in his head. Many would recognize that mental whirlpool.

After a heavy shelling almost anyone might capitulate and be 'glad to be out of it'. The sense of relief was nearly always transient, after which the soldier would join his comrades in the predominant feelings of the First World War Tommy on surrender: shame and anger. When, at Lys in April 1918, Private Tucker's commanding officer ordered a surrender:

His order was received with angry imprecations and yells of defiance. It was the one and only occasion I have ever heard British soldiers directly voice disobedience and insubordination to their officer's command.[26]

Tucker's officer had been shown by the Germans the hopelessness of the British position. And could not bear to sacrifice his men.

Jack Evans, 16/Canadian Mounted Rifles was 'wild with anger over our helplessness' when captured in the German attack at Zillebeke in June 1916. The 'Fritzes' jabbed him with a bayonet, then kicked him; in the heat of it all he stupidly retaliated. His life was saved by a German officer intervening.

Thomas Spriggs, 55th Division Machine Gun Corps, would have understood Evans' fury. Above his trench at Cambrai there appeared a German officer waving a bomb who ordered him to surrender. Spriggs thought, 'No, I'll be damned if I am going to hold my hands up for you . . . Surrender to a bloody German, no fear.' No fear. Having gone through Passchendaele, Spriggs was immune to death. Such carelessness of life was common in veterans, men who had served in the trenches for a year or more. Only the insistent

echoing of the order by a British officer made Spriggs throw down
his equipment and capitulate.[27]

On being told '*Hände hoch!*' Corporal Arthur Speight, 7/Durham
Light Infantry, considered:

> Disappointment seemed to be the great thing. Here we were – cap-
> tured without a chance of hitting back. We had the satisfaction of
> knowing that our hands did NOT go up! They went into our trouser
> pockets instead.[28]

He was kicked, thumped and jabbed by German rifle butts for his
impertinence.

Taken after capture to an enemy dug-out for interrogation, Captain Geoffrey Phillimore was told '*Für Ihnen der Krieg ist fertig*'.
For you the war is over. Phillimore thought nothing could have
been better calculated to infuriate a soldier, 'though it was probably
meant in kindness'.[29]

Lying in a shell hole after a brigade attack on Malt Trench near
La Barque, William Cull, 22nd Battalion Australian Imperial
Force (AIF), worried what 'the Battalion would think of me if they
knew that I was taken prisoner. The thought was so bitter that for
a moment I cared little whether I lived or died.'[30] He had a grenade
splinter in his hip and was unable to walk. He resolved to live for
the sake of his family.

Ernie Stevens, 20/Middlesex Regiment, his platoon attacked from
behind ('How did they get there?') was told by his subaltern, 'new
out to France and looked very worried', that it was impossible to
make a fight of it and suggested surrender by tying a handkerchief
to the end of a bayonet: 'It made me feel as if I was a coward. I was
letting my country down, I was letting my unit down, I was letting
my family down . . . Being taken prisoner, oh what a disgrace!'[31]

In almost all cases in the First World War the capitulation of
British soldiers was forced. There was no great breakdown of morale
and 'going over' to the enemy as other armies suffered.[32] The number
of British troops who stole over No Man's Land to the German lines
was vanishingly small, no more than a few hundred out of an army
of five million. Few of these, if any, were attracted to the German

cause. The motivation of those who crossed the line was to leave the travails and troubles of the battlefield. Similarly, in a treason of a lesser degree, there were isolated instances of demoralized men in the midst of battle sometimes letting themselves be captured.

British soldiers did not want to surrender, and they did not do so lightly. Not least because their experience of the passions and uncertainties of battle would have led them to know a fundamental truth of war: Surrender was not a safe thing to do.

*

In the dreadful moment when surrender was decided upon or groped to, there emerged a mundane yet vital question: how to signal the actual act of capitulation? No corporal at Aldershot or instructor at Sandhurst gave classes in surrender or showed the correct drill for presenting submission, Sah! As a reflective Lieutenant Alec Waugh, Royal Artillery (RA), wrote,

> the etiquette of surrender is not included in Field Service Regulations, and as it is not with that intention that one originally sets out for France, the matter had not bulked largely in the imagination.[33]

Holding hands high in the air was not taught but seems to have been universal and instinctive.[34] A sergeant in Fred Hodges' cut-off battalion, when the matter became unavoidable, settled on hand-raising plus a loud and judicious use of German, saying: 'You can't do anything, lads. Put up your hands and cry "*Kamerad*".'[35] Although waving a white flag actually indicated intention to parlay, it became the more or less accepted signal for surrender, which left everyone scrabbling in a mud-infested trench for something white, or sufficiently pale to pass. All the Canadian platoon of Captain T.V. 'Tom' Scudamore could find at Ypres was a bandage – not that his father would have approved, whatever material was hoisted. A veteran of the Afghan Wars, Scudamore Senior later wrote to his imprisoned boy assuming he'd been captured unconscious, the implication being – and it was all the worse for being entirely sincere – that the scion Scudamore would have fought to the death otherwise. When surrender came, most soldiers who waved a white 'flag' flapped a pocket handkerchief, like Ernie

Stevens' platoon, which made the act all the more pathetic and poignant.

However signalled, surrender was not always given. Prisoner-killing was explicitly proscribed by the Hague Convention, the international agreement setting out the rules of warfare. Regulation 23(c) stated that it was forbidden to kill or wound a prisoner who had surrendered by laying down his arms. But the well-meaning deliberations of men in civilized rooms in Den Haag were meaningless on the bloody battlefield of Hooge; there was no afterlife appeal to Regulation 23(c). Prisoner-killing was committed by all combatant armies, although somewhat less often than sensationalist historians would suggest, since between 6.6 and 8.4 million men were taken alive during the war.[36]

No national armies on the Western Front operated prisoner-killing as a matter of policy, although the Kaiser's army came closest, since it was the only one in which prisoner-killing was sanctioned by the head of state.[37] Also, the German manual of military law, the *Kriegsbrauch,* showed markedly less restraint on the subject of prisoner-killing than international equivalents, stating:

> Prisoners can be killed . . . in cases of extreme necessity when other means of security are not available . . . exigencies of war and the safety of the State come first . . .[38]

More, when Wilhelmine Germany crossed the borders of Belgium and France in August 1914, it also crossed a moral Rubicon in ordering the mass execution of civilian prisoners, announcing to the world its *Schrecklichkeit* ('frightfulness'). Of the combatant armies on the Western front the Kaiser's was the most culturally committed to prisoner-killing. Yet, the real problem with the German Army was not policy or culture, it was hate. There was the ordinary hate of all soldiers for the enemy when berserk in battle, when prisoner-killing comes out of quick, blind violent passion. As the German infantry officer Ernst Jünger explained:

> The defending force, after driving their bullets into the attackers at five paces' distance, must take the consequences. A man cannot

change his feelings again during the last rush with a veil of blood
before his eyes. He does not want to take prisoners but to kill.[39]

Death of a friend, a desire to avenge comrades might well inculcate
a bloodthirsty frame of mind. However, German hate towards the
British became fanatical and collective from the end of August 1914.
And the fault lay with Malcolm Hay and the men who fought at
Le Cateau and in all those other little engagements that put span-
ners in the wheel of the German juggernaut as it rolled into France
and Flanders. The Kaiser is alleged to have described the British
Expeditionary Force (BEF) as a 'Contemptible Little Army' to be
dismissively brushed aside. The BEF was small, contemptible it was
not, as Walter Bloem, a Reserve Captain in the 12th Brandenburg
Grenadier Regiment, confirmed from the German side of the line
at Le Cateau:

'Our first battle is a heavy, unheard of defeat, and against the English
– the English we had laughed at.'[40]

August Schmidt, a German soldier escorting British PoWs to
Hameln in October 1914, caught the frustration of his countrymen
perfectly in a letter home: 'The English soldier may be a dangerous
enemy and a good shooter in the field and that is probably why there
are so many resentments against him.'[41]

The lethal consequence of this hatred was confirmed by Major
Koebke, of Imperial Artillery Regiment 3. Koebke noted in his diary
on 20 November 1914:

The anger at the British was enormous. Very few prisoners were
taken according to statements from the front and where there was
the occasional one he had nothing to smile about during his trip to
the rear.[42]

Guards escorting British prisoners were the subject of indigna-
tion, their progress ringing with shouts of 'shame on you for taking
prisoners'.[43]

Hatred of Britain for spoiling the Kaiser's plan for a *Mitteleuropa*
empire would bitterly colour German attitude to British soldiers for

nearly two years. Also, wild autumnal stories about British troops firing 'dum-dum' bullets (bullets with flat noses, designed to maim) and using their jack-knives to gouge out the eyes of German wounded put Imperial troops into a highly febrile state. The consequence for Tommy Atkins was that he was more likely to be murdered on surrendering than his French or Belgian Western Front counterparts. Prisoner-killing of British soldiers, however, was not constant over the course of the war: the rate was low in August 1914, rose steeply from October to December of that year, plateaued until 1915, then went into a declining curve until the Armistice. Within this general delineation there were blips caused by outrages real and imagined, such as the *Baralong* incident,[44] but the broad topography of murder stands. By 1917 war weariness had taken over and the Kaiser and all his men came instead to be blamed for the debacle that was Deutschland's putative war of conquest. There was another reason for the diminishing hostility towards the British soldiery; in front-line service German troops found the Tommies to be soldiers much like themselves, not the blood-dripping staring-eyed demons of the Berlin patriotic press. A bogeyman is easy to kill. A fellow human being, suffering the same hardships and anxieties who just happens to be wearing a different colour uniform, is not.

What a difference four years made! Around Ypres in the first autumn of the war prisoner-killing by *feldgrau* men was commonplace. In the great German 'Michael' Offensive of March 1918 the surrender of British troops was accepted without demur and almost without violation. Taken in the German attack of 11 April 1918 at Ploegsteert ('Plugstreet' to proudly monoglot Tommy), Lieutenant Cust, Royal Artillery, considered that 'the treatment met with was almost without exception most courteous: we all agreed that this seemed studied and intentional on the part of the enemy'.[45] To Cust's bemusement he was captured in almost exactly the place in the wood where he had been picking cowslips in a felt hat three days before.

Alas, for the individual British soldier with his hands high to heaven, there were bastard variables in the general contour of prisoner-killing. By these variables he would have his surrender accepted, or he would be slaughtered.

Youth helped. Sergeant Arthur Gibbons, Toronto Regiment, spent two days beating off German counter-attacks before succumbing on 24 April 1915 at St Julien. His head bleeding and his thigh shattered, Gibbons closed his eyes and screamed as a *feldgrau* figure lunged towards him with a bayonet. A German officer suddenly intervened. On finding that Gibbons was only nineteen he said: 'Why you are only a boy. This is a man's war: You should not be here.'[46] Gibbons was dragged four hundred yards to the rear. As we shall see, other Germans took a less benevolent view of his callowness.

Native wit was good too. No sooner had he surrendered and was making his way towards the German rear than Private Thomas Bickerton, 2/Essex Regiment, was confronted by a German flourishing a dagger: 'Fortunately I had the presence of mind to whip out my pocket wallet which I thrust into his hand, and whilst he was looking at it, I ran on.'[47] Bickerton had also had the forethought to remove his Lewis gun badges. Those who operated bogey weapons like Lewis machine guns, sniper rifles, or flame throwers held the short straw in surrender survival.

Anyone conspicuously appeasing his captors was likely to boost his odds in the lottery of life. Ernst Jünger, that hardbitten *über*warrior, gave the perspective from the other end of the bayonet on the successful etiquette of surrender: 'Most of them showed by their confident smiles that they trusted in us as human beings. Others held out cigarettes and chocolate in order to conciliate us.'[48]

Oh, but the divide between pleasing appeasement and displeasing subservience was so thin. One British officer recorded of his surrender in October 1914:

> Seeing the position was hopeless, I ordered the men to kneel down, put down their arms and hold up their hands. They did so. I stood up and held up my hands. A German soldier fired at me and shot me in the hand. They then came and shot down all the men [about twenty] who appeared to be alive.[49]

Psychologically, genuflecting reduces humanness. In all probability, the anonymous officer would have done better to have his men stand and face the foe as equal fellows.

Anyone fighting to the last round could expect no quarter when the ammunition ran out. And yet even here there was caprice. Private J. Parkinson was changing belts on his machine gun when a German officer put a pistol in his back and said, 'Come along, Tommy, you've done enough.' Parkinson rightly commented that 'the officer must have been a real gentleman'.[50]

Surrendering soldiers were generally more leniently treated at the beginning of a battle or offensive than the end of the affair, when tempers were worn down. Which was another reason for the good humour of Malcolm Hay's German officer on the sunken road at Audencourt: the Germans had not yet realized their offensive was running out of steam. Equally, in March 1918 when Lieutenant Alec Waugh surrendered to the all-conquering troops of the Spring Offensive, so happy were the Germans to be on the final road to victory that they presented him with a cigar.[51]

Unsurprisingly, any soldier looking defiant, troublesome or who was still armed was unlikely to be tolerated. In March 1918 William Easton, 77th Field Ambulance RAMC, was standing in a surrendering group next to a man who, out of unthinkingness, was still carrying his rifle:

> I don't know who the lad was who'd kept his rifle, but he didn't seem to understand that we were already prisoners. The Germans were using a loudspeaker, calling on pockets of resistance to surrender. However, he'd still got his rifle knocking about when the Germans surrounded us, and they promptly shot him. I thought it was such a pity, but it was his own fault, he ought to have known when to give his weapon up.[52]

On occasions there seemed to be neither reason nor rhyme why one prisoner was killed as he raised his hands, and the man next to him was not. Only the strange Fate who ruled soldiers' lives could be responsible. His Sacred Majesty, Chance.[53]

A wholly explicable danger in surrender came from one's own

side. Private H.J. Clarke's colonel in the 1/Suffolks decided to make the best of a bad thing as the grey tide surrounded his little remnant of fighters at Frezenberg Ridge, Ypres. He ushered everyone into a dug-out and handed round the cigars. They hardly had the 'steam up' when the Germans appeared at the door and shouted down '*Hände hoch*'. On emerging, Private French, standing next to Clarke, was shot dead instantly by a bullet fired from the British line.[54] Possibly the shootist was aiming at the Hanoverians taking the surrender, but one unit's honourable capitulation could be another unit's version of dishonourable submission, and it wasn't unknown for British troops to fire angrily on others in khaki if they thought them yellow. Across the dismal mud of Passchendaele Captain W. Tickler of the 5/Lancashire Fusiliers saw a German officer taking the surrender of a British sergeant and his men in that long wet autumn of 1917:

So I screamed across at this bloke, 'What the hell are you doing giving yourselves up?' I didn't wait for him to answer me, I just let fly with my revolver. I was aiming at the German officers, but they were all mixed up together.[55]

Clarke thought the 77th Hanoverians taking his surrender 'good fellows all round'. They must have been, since on approaching an enemy dug-out the stock German action was to throw in a bomb, as was witnessed by a young private taken prisoner in March 1918. When the stormtrooper was told there were British wounded in the trench dug-out:

He took a stick grenade out, pulled the pin and threw it down the dug-out. We heard the shrieks and were nauseated, but we might have done the same in the circumstances.[56]

In the dark recesses of a dug-out any danger or trick might be lurking. To bomb first and ask questions afterwards was only wise.

Proportionately, British officers were marginally more likely to be taken prisoner – or at least taken prisoner alive – than other ranks. Precise figures are impossible to ascertain now, though the

official *General Annual Report of the British Army 1913–1919* pro-
vides a crude guide:

Percentage missing and PoWs of Army	Officers	Other Ranks
1 October 1914–30 September 1915	3.7	2.9
1 October 1915–30 September 1916	1.3	1.3
1 October 1916–30 September 1917	1.5	1.1
1 October 1917–30 September 1918	3.4	3.4
1 October 1918–30 September 1919	0.1	0.1[57]

The British Army was an army in which officers led, men followed. A general rule of bloody thumb in His Majesty's land force
was: officers headed attacks, officers were the last to retreat. Unlike
other major combatant services, in the British Army officers also
led out patrols, wiring parties – and any other dangerous job going.
Accordingly, the casualty rate for officers was higher than other
ranks across the board, from deaths to wounds to capture.[58]

Only in two experiences of the Great War was the mortality of officers lower than that of other ranks. One was the act of
surrender, and the other was the subsequent incarceration in the
Kaiser's prisoner-of-war camps. Numerous testimonies indicate
that German officers routinely interceded to stop their troops from
killing British soldiers wearing pips and crowns. Although invariably ill-founded, the German assumption was that British officers
were a likely source of military information. (Actually, anyone
below the rank of major in the British Army knew sweet zero about
anything regarding dispositions or 'shows'.) A suspicion lurks too
that some Wilhelmine officers, with their acute sense of class, considered British officers fellow gentlemen and therefore deserving of
protection from the proletariat in uniform. Lieutenants Cull and
Ahnall of the 7th Brigade Australian Infantry Force (AIF), lying
in a German hospital, had a simpler answer for why they had been
spared when their surrendered men had been bludgeoned to death
by rifle butts. They concluded they were human 'Souvenirs'.

*

To the captor the spoils. After the moment of successful surrender there were no certainties, save that the prisoner would be pillaged of his possessions. And of his dignity as a man and as a soldier.

Seizing the spoils of war from defeated warriors is an ancient rite. On slaying Pallas in *The Aeneid* (Book X), Turnus took the young prince's sword-belt and put it on, so confirming his victory. While few Britons went into action on the Western Front wearing swords, they wore military paraphernalia that would serve equally well as 'souvenirs' for their German captors. To take a man's medal ribbons, his buttons, his cap badge was to strip him of his military pride and identity. He was de-soldiered. More: a Briton thus robbed was walking evidence of his submission to the authority of the German Army. For the perpetrator, the 'zooveneers' he demanded confirmed his power, and were proof that he had seen front-line service. In the plundering of the Scots Guards at Gheuvelt in October 1914 the balance of power in looting was made manifest. Corporal Green of the 1st Battalion wrote in his diary:

> I shall never forget the search and the ensuing few hours. The ever gallant Huns made us go on knees, and proceeded to take our money, tobacco, cigarettes etc from us and make away with them.[59]

Personal items such as wedding rings, photos, watches and letters were also stolen from the numbed captives. This could be a particular hurt, because it severed the soldier from his civilian self, from his family and friends; it cut him emotionally adrift. Lance-Corporal Tommy Higgins had 'to beg and pray as well as I could to make them understand me' to keep the photo of his wife and child, his father's card and his tobacco box.[60]

Souvenir-hunting was against the Hague Convention of 1907 which declared that a soldier's property should remain in his possession following capture. The German Army only honoured the proscription in the breaching of it. Souvenir-hunting was ubiquitous on the Western Front, as common as and prevalent as the mud. Sage British soldiers who understood the rules might place cigarettes and chocolate handy in their tunic to appease the enemy should the worst happen. An exceptionally far-sighted Tommy might go into battle with his valuables hidden, as did Sapper George Waymark, who had the prescience to hang his watch on the back of his braces. He managed to keep the chronometer throughout his eight months of captivity in 1918.

The wounded, who might be left lying around for days, could be robbed at leisure.

Sergeant Arthur Gibbons, Toronto Regiment, was incapacitated with a wound in his right thigh in a field four hundred yards behind the German trench for four days:

> the whole of the time I was lying upon that field they played with me as a cat plays with a mouse. A German soldier would come up to me, curse me, kick me a few times, and then pretend to run his bayonet through my body. They took away everything I possessed, even to my boots, buttons and shoulder straps. I had a small gold ring on one of my fingers. I had worn the ring for several years and it could not be removed.
>
> Several Germans tried to take it off but failed. One of them attempted to cut off the finger to get the ring, but was prevented from doing so by others standing near.[61]

Untreated, humiliated, frightened, in agonizing pain Gibbons added with justification: 'How I managed to live through those four days I don't know.'[62]

If the Germans hated the British, they had a particular loathing for Canadians, who had inexplicably come from across the ocean to interfere with Teutonic hopes. They hated the Canadians yet more when they discovered they were paid one dollar and ten cents a day to fight. This was the equivalent of four Marks; the basic pay of a German private was half a Mark. Henceforth Canadians were always 'Geldsoldaten'. Moneysoldiers. Mercenaries.

Greatcoats were favourite objects for plunder, and whole companies of the BEF were forced to divest themselves of the outer garment at the crudely persuasive point of a 'butcher's blade'. Looting, on the other hand, might be accomplished with a light-fingered cunning a Fagin would admire. Soon after falling into German hands in October 1914, the wounded Captain I.M. Henderson of the London Scottish was asked by a German NCO for his Burberry so it 'might be disinfected'. This 'seemed a reasonable request' at the time; the coat was purloined. When the hapless Henderson was then put on a hospital train to Ghent, the stretcher-bearers 'slipped quietly away with my boots and spats'.[63] On finally reaching Brussels military hospital, his kilt was stolen. 'I was sent to Frankfurt,' he glumly recalled, 'without any belongings except such items as a brush and comb which I had bought in Brussels.' Clearly, spatterdashes, boots and coats were low on valour-laden military symbolism. Such looting mostly humiliated the victim and charged up the ego of the perpetrator. Items of clothing also had utilitarian value. They could be sold, or they could be used, and by 1917 the direly kitted German soldiers were scavenging like beggars. By 1917 the Germans would almost have the shirt off your back if you were a British PoW. Lying in a shell hole at Malt Trench in February 1917 desperately injured by grenade splinters, Lieutenant William Cull, AIF, was discovered by a German patrol. One of the men felt him over:

'Where is your revolver?' he asked, and I told him that I hadn't got one.

'Where is your watch?' was his next question. It was on my wrist, and, with the contents of my pockets, soon disappeared. My Sam Browne belt, which he next examined, had little interest for him, and he tossed it out into No Man's Land, but he took my compass and another souvenir.

The German party then carried Cull in a waterproof sheet to their trench (ironically enough, the very one he had been wounded trying to capture), and placed him in a dug-out:

The first act of the Huns was to strip me of my clothing, one of them with great eagerness pulling off the heavy pair of riding boots that I wore. He looked them over, patting them approvingly, and then smiled at me as though in appreciation of a gift . . . They took all my clothes, excepting a shirt.[64]

On the Craonne Plateau in the shocked dawn of 27 May 1918, Private Ernest Thornton, 1/Northumbrian Field Ambulance, was one of many Tommies to be divested of his boots ('They simply made us hand things over'),[65] his robbers being troops on the way to the trenches who fancied something better than the substandard German issue. A Tommy thus plundered might be tossed the boots of his pillager, as was Thornton. Or, equally, he might be left to tear his shirt up and bind it around his feet as best he could.

One souvenir in the Great War was parted with willingly. When a German seized Captain Tom Scudamore's Ross rifle as a trophy, 'I told him he was welcome to it.'[66] The Ross rifle had badly let down the Canadians in their stand at Second Ypres, 1915, because of its tendency to jam. Since the Ross Model 10's other idiosyncrasy was to blow the bolt back into the face of the firer with lethal effect, the soldier who took Scudamore's Ross rifle may well have come to regret his choice of souvenir.

*

Schnell, schnell.

Where the state of battle allowed it, prisoners would be fleeced immediately. Otherwise, if they could walk, they would be escorted off the battlefield quickly, to flurries of incomprehensible German commands and all too comprehensible rifle butts and robbed in the relative quiet of the rear lines.

The Hague Convention required that prisoners be promptly removed from danger. This invariably occurred. By default. In the mind of the German soldier ordered to escort British prisoners to the rear, the injunctions of international treaties would weigh less heavily than the sanctity of his own skin. A battle is a live beast, and it snarls to the end. Often there would be a barrage falling between the high-tide line of the German attack and the home trench, while the reach of British machine-gun and rifle bullets meant they could take life at the end of their life, at a range of a thousand yards or more. Conveying prisoners across a battlefield was plain hazardous for the German escort. It was dangerous for prisoners too. Captain Esler, RAMC, Medical Officer with 2/Middlesex, captured on the night of 27 May 1918, marched off in a group towards the German line thinking, 'that is the end of the war for me, I am alive and shall not be shot at any more'.

His optimism was premature. As they proceeded to the German rear they passed through

> a pretty heavy barrage by our own people on the German reinforcements coming up. A few [British] were wounded and killed which was certainly a bit tough after escaping enemy action for so long, and then to be hit by our own side.[67]

Jittery German escorts, on the lookout for escapes or belated retaliations, could fatally misinterpret the actions of their charges. Exhausted from battle and an average of an hour a day's sleep for a week, James Farrant and a small group from the Royal Naval Division's October 1914 Antwerp attack were stumbling along under guard when they were fired on:

> Our guards made a dive for the hedges on either side of the road. So did we, with disastrous results, as a German officer screamed out we were trying to escape, whereupon our guards opened up at point blank range or used their bayonets. A man next to me was bayoneted, and was left, as were others, in the ditches.[68]

The lurking killer of poison gas almost did for Private Reginald Morris, Northumberland Fusiliers, as he threaded his way across No Man's Land. (Morris, a stretcher-bearer, had been captured at La Fontaine with 'so many dead and dying around me that I was bewildered'.) His escort, his own lungs uppermost in his estimation, had sensibly stolen Morris' gas-mask. Hence for Morris 'it was no joke trying to avoid the gas-infested areas' lying like malevolent low clouds. The gas was worst in the shell holes into which they would need to dive should a barrage start up.[69] Not that Morris was beyond a little looting himself; the night was so cold he later quietly robbed a dead man of his coat.

If the German escort considered taking prisoners to the rear was simply too dangerous, the likelihood of them being shot upped. A live prisoner is a problem, a dead one is no trouble. Prisoners also posed a logistical problem; men from the German attack force needed to be detailed off as escorts. In favourable circumstances a guard would escort up to half a dozen PoWs rearwards. On that dread day of 21 March 1918 so many British soldiers surrendered that they were merely shown the direction to take, and they set off in trickles of ones and twos, joining others to form rivers, to finally make a sea of docile humanity flowing eastwards.

Few Germans would have seen a British soldier close-up. Prisoners wending to the rear would be stared at and usually abused, verbally and physically. On reaching the German reserve line at Bapaume in the Somme summer, Tanner Milburn, Northumberland Fusiliers, was greeted by German soldiers who 'made a football of me'.[70] Being an amateur soccer-player he well understood what a booted ball might feel like.[71] He had already been stoned, hit with sticks and used as a target for lumps of dirt, and had a revolver waved in his face by an officer. At least he was alive.

Unwounded prisoners would invariably be ordered to carry German and British wounded off the field of battle. Rarely were there stretchers, so waterproof sheets or duckboards from the bottom of a trench were used. William Tucker had the unhappy experience of a 'long carry':

> The combined weight of a wounded man and the heavy trench duckboard was far too much for only two men with four hands, so four prisoners were assigned to carry each 'stretcher' – on their shoulders. Before barely 100 yards were covered over the shelled, torn-up and muddy ground, the sharp rough corners of the duckboards began to cut into our shoulders which soon bled profusely. Although we did not know it, we were to be forced to endure about nine miles of this really tortuous ordeal.[72]

To make the prisoners move faster the guards prodded them with bayonets and incessantly growled 'los, los', much as herdsmen yell 'girrup-pp, g-i-r-r-u-p'.

There were other tortuous ordeals for the newly captive. Sapper George Waymark, captured on 12 April 1918 at Le Cornet Malo – 'Had no chance. Completely surrounded.' – was put to work burying the dead of both sides:

Dug a hole about 9' wide and 14' long and 6' deep. Into this we had to place dead bodies, head toward the outer edge. Four or five rows like this, and we had to stand on the dead to lay them evenly ... No burial service, nothing to mark who or what they were English, German and a civilian [an elderly woman] all together, poor devils.[73]

The covering layer of soil was only a foot deep. He was then ordered to help to carry wounded on stretchers to Marquilles, where there was a prison camp. He was shelled en route by his own side.

Burials of comrades without ceremony, and likely without marker, were deeply upsetting to the prisoners who dug their shallow graves. On the Western Front, where death became so commonplace, marking the passing of the killed assumed an extraordinary significance.[74] Soldiers would do their utmost to identify the fallen and sign their resting place, even if it was just a Huntley & Palmers biscuit-tin lid with a name scratched on, or a broken rifle shoved barrel-end down with *Pte. T. Hargreave, West Yorks 17.6.16* etched on the butt with a jack-knife blade. To leave fellow Britons nameless and unheeded in that rich earth upset an established order, and was a real pity of war.

The newly captured Tommy, not yet properly off the battlefield, might well find himself forced at bayonet point to perform yet more tortuous tasks. In contravention of the clauses of the Hague Convention banning the employment of new prisoners at the front and in work directly related to the war effort, new prisoners were forced to dig gun emplacements and bring up ammunition – all within range of British shot and shell. Private A. Wood, 7/Cameron Highlanders, captured on the 28th of March 1918, lamented:

As soon as we were taken prisoners, Private Tulloch, Macpherson, myself and another man whose name I do not know, were made to work for two hours serving a field gun with ammunitions and digging a position for it under British fire![75]

And yet, when danger had died down and the red-mist of killing evaporated, German soldiers were known to show exemplary consideration to British prisoners. One German NCO at High Wood mopped up British resistance with a consummate professionalism then, the fighting done, led the prisoners to the rear. In a gesture of magnificent humanitarianism and true soldierly respect:

> About two miles back he halted them at a canteen, went in and bought a box of cigarettes and a bottle of brandy; each prisoner was given six or seven cigarettes and a pull at the bottle.[76]

An Australian officer at Pozières recalled:

> Struggling along the muddy trenches to company headquarters a German officer lent me his stick; he himself picked up a shovel. I thought this rather an act of decency. I have no complaint to make of our treatment by the Germans while in the lines.[77]

Such kindnesses were golden shafts in clouds of black hopelessness. Lieutenant Bowman likened his straggly groups of fellow prisoners leaving the battlefield to a funeral procession:

> Never wound cortege more exceeding slow,
> Nor mourners to more melancholy tones,
> Than that wan wending, musicked by the moans
> Of wounded men, whom pity bade us show
> That much of tenderness. Nor friend nor foe
> Spoke in the heavy language of these groans,
> But stark mankind, whose utter anguish owns
> A common nature, in a common woe.
> Full many a mile of weary footing sore,
> By miry side tracks, not unkindly led;
> And each unwounded man his burden bore
> On stretcher or in blanket, ransacked bed.
> Duck-board uprooted, hand-cart, unhinged door.
> We left behind the dying and the dead.[78]

The 'musicked moans' of the dying left behind were a never-to-be-forgotten sound. As Lieutenant Horace Gilliland, Loyal North Lancashire Regiment, involuntarily departed the Ypres battlefield in December 1914 he could see the Germans finishing off the

wounded with their bayonets.[79] He himself had lain wounded in
the bottom of a sodden trench wondering what it would be like to
have his 'brains bashed out with a rifle butt'. Fortune, or at least a
good-hearted German, had taken him alive instead. The squeals of
the murdered unlucky rang in his ears like a terrible tinnitus.

As they stumbled along, men carrying any papers potentially
useful to the enemy would try to lose them. Walking under heavy
guard Second Lieutenant Joseph Lee, King's Royal Rifle Corps, sur-
reptitiously put his into his tunic pocket, and 'succeeded in tearing
up and scattering over the land, sundry military papers'.[80] A Dundee
journalist, and one of the war poets, the forty-one-year-old Lee also
had in his pocket the proofs of one of his books. This contained
some very 'uncomplimentary references to the Kaiser'. And was
thus best rendered into white confetti to lie among the detritus of
war. So was the pamphlet on machine-gunning Private Jack Evans
had in his pocket. That too was conveniently lost in Flanders mud.

When the weary walk to a place of safe assembly was concluded,
prisoners would sit and wait in silence for a large enough group to
be formed to march off to a holding pen. In that waiting time, the
full recognition of all that had occurred sank like iron into the soul.
When he looked back on his experience of being a prisoner of war,
Alec Waugh considered 'Nothing could exceed the depression of
that evening'.[81]

*

The wounded prisoner had his own special journey of pain off the
battlefield.

The German system of treating the battlefield wounded was the
nearly mirror image of the British one, in that the wounded would
progress through a chain of medical facilities stretching from the
front-line trench (or just behind it) to the base area; in order, these
were the regimental aid post, the advanced dressing station, casualty
clearing station, hospital.

In theory British wounded were treated as German wounded.

In practice, German stretcher-bearers and medical staff prior-
itized their own kin. After being taken a mile to the rear Captain I.M.
Henderson lay out in a field next to a Bavarian battery of field guns,

where 'I was passed over again and again in favour of any German they could find, however recently they had been wounded'.[82] Unfortunately for Henderson, the Bavarian artillery was spotted and came under fire from the British, making his resting place dangerous as well as uncomfortable. Eventually Henderson was picked up, unlike the unfortunates who featured in an Australian official report on prisoner mistreatment, *How the Germans Treated Australian Prisoner of War*. One anonymous Antipodean officer stated that ranks of his countrymen were left helpless on the screaming, moaning battlefield at Bullecourt with nothing done for them:

> I have no hesitation in saying that hundreds must have died through sheer exposure and neglect.[83]

A German major, either particularly dense or dragged from the very rear echelons, apparently still believed at this late stage of the war – April 1917 – the Grimms' fairy tale that British Empire forces were using 'dum-dum' bullets. In retaliation for the imagined atrocity, the 'Fritz' officer, recalled the anonymous Australian, poured paraffin down the mouth of a wounded lance corporal, killing him. There are other and innumerable testimonies detailing the brutality with which German troops dispatched wounded prisoners, the bayonet being the preferred weapon, rather than paraffin.[84]

Yet, midst the storms of shot and shell, some recalled acts of exemplary compassion and courage by the enemy. Second Lieutenant Ernest Warburton, 1/5 Sherwood Foresters, nearly got as far as the German parapet at Arras when he was hit by bomb splinters and fell into the wire. He lay there, unable to move, for twenty-three hours, bullets whizzing overhead until dusk the next day when

> four German soldiers crawled out and carried me on a ground sheet into their trench. They treated me with the greatest kindness and gentleness. I was given some coffee, etc, in a front line dug-out, and some of my wounds were dressed there.[85]

Walking British wounded would be escorted to a dressing station, usually at a fair clip by guards anxious to get out of the line of fire.

To the intense agony of Captain T. Kidson Allsop, bearing a bullet wound in the chest sustained during the charge of the 1/London Scottish at Messines in October 1914, his guard repeatedly hit him in the back with his rifle butt to hurry him up. Kidson Allsop complained to the first German officer he saw. To Kidson Allsop's bemusement, the cavalryman replied that he would not forgive the British for using black troops against German forces. Too exhausted to discuss the matter, Kidson Allsop stumbled on, helped by a private in his regiment who vainly tried to ward off the sentry's blows.[86] Impatient with the progress of Corporal Peter Thornton, 4/Canadian Mounted Rifles, his officer escort simply shot him, leaving Thornton collapsed in the mud. A pair of German stretcher-bearers, clearly made of more humane stuff, picked up Thornton and took him to a casualty clearing station (CCS). He survived.[87]

Since Thornton had been shot in the back, jaw and leg, the German medical officers must have worked wonders. They often did; the experience of the British wounded prisoner when finally in the hands of medics in dressing stations and field hospitals was infinitely better than feared. Staff in these enclosed spaces of dug-outs and tents seemed to be more cognisant of Hippocrates than others in the German medical profession. Richard Griffiths, 3/Royal Welch Fusiliers, remembered all his life that a German doctor in a casualty clearing station took the trouble to ask him his civilian occupation. When Griffiths replied he was a master tailor, the doctor said he would do his best to make sure he still had movement in his wounded arm.[88] He succeeded. Another soldier taken prisoner in spring 1918, Second Lieutenant C.E. Carr, wrote to his fiancée about his sojourn in a CCS: 'There was a very sporty nurse there who seeing that I had rather a tiring time eating arranged for porridge for me.' And a young doctor was so helpful that Carr gave him his Fusilier collar badges as a souvenir. Carr left the devastating detail of his injury until the last paragraph:

> One point I did not mention, although the bullet went in my neck and came through my cheek my face was not torn nor my eyes and nose. Jolly lucky n'est ce pas, ma chere?[89]

Lieutenant J. Harvey Douglas, seized at Hill 60 in June 1916, passed along the German medical chain without complaint. At the first dressing station, an enormous state-of-the-art concrete dug-out (German dug-outs were always a wonder to British prisoners), the desperately dry-mouthed Douglas was given coffee and had his wounds dressed. At the next post Douglas was given a tetanus jab and full details of his treatment were appended to him. And on he went.[90] He had been taken prisoner by a German who had been a waiter in an English hotel before the war.

After putting up a resistance so brave yet so forlorn that the Germans took pity on his company of cyclists at Lys, William Tucker took an injured mate to a German dressing station, a shell-blasted brick farmhouse of three remaining walls:

> It was full of injured German soldiers but my maimed and bleeding British charge was accepted gently and almost amicably by the German orderly looking after the outfit.[91]

Sadly, well-meaning German doctors and orderlies in the dressing stations frequently lacked the means to match their morality, with trained medics and supplies all too few in number. British PoWs were flabbergasted to be treated with paper bandages – but the German wounded were bound the same way. In anything approaching a battle, German medical officers were overwhelmed by wounded, whether wearing *feldgrau* or khaki. At Neuve Chapelle Sapper George Waymark, saw the wounded laid out in rows in a paddock with no tents for cover, only one doctor and one Red Cross man to attend to them all. It was 'absolute chaos'.[92] Even the most idealistic, non-chauvinistic adherent of the Hippocratic oath was likely to be extremely clinical and his work fast but crude in such circumstances. Corporal Ernie Stevens captured (to his chagrin) on 8 April 1918, only his second day in the trenches, helped carry a wounded platoon member, Sam Simpkins, to a German aid post, a three-walled tent:

> As we put Sam down, a German medical officer came out. He looked at Sam, returned to the tent and immediately came back with a

scalpel and he just cut Sam's forearm off and threw it on a heap of
other arms and legs and what have you, some in German uniform,
some in khaki, they were easy to distinguish.[93]

The heap was knee deep. Stevens felt sick.

In all probability, the fatigued silence of the medical officer
who amputated Simpkins' arm was a boon. The babble of alien
German in aid posts unnerved prisoners whose nerves were already
stretched. As an apprehensive Norman Cowan waited to be operated on at a casualty clearing station, the doctor told him, in perfect
English: 'Well don't worry, I've spent two years before the war at
Guy's Hospital in London.' This was comfort indeed.

His Sacred Majesty Chance also smiled on British prisoners who
were put 'in the bag' with RAMC personnel. By the rules of warfare
Medical Officers were to be returned to their own side at the earliest
opportunity. This the Germans did not do, but the glorious upshot
is that British lives were saved and pain eased. Put in a requisitioned
freezing church with other wounded, Captain Baird-Douglas received no medical treatment for five days except what a captured
RAMC medical orderly and several unwounded men were able to
do for him. When Lieutenant Basil Willey's small party of West
Yorkshires staggered off the battlefield to a German first-aid post at
Sapignies, the company's own MO dressed his wound with the aid
of a German orderly.[94] This brought physical relief, but on looking
round Willey saw a young officer, 'a particularly nice fellow', stumble towards the doctor with a large hole in his abdomen and gasp
out 'Oh, Doctor, is there any hope?' There was not.

Another man, lying next to Willey, breathed mechanically with a
'peculiar dog-like snuffle' having been shot through the head.

Though Willey was 'dazed and half-benumbed' these images registered for a lifetime. But the good work of the West Yorkshires' MO
that day gave lifetimes where none might otherwise have existed.
The wrongful incarceration of RAMC medics would continue to
save British lives when the prisoners took the iron road to prison
camp in Germany.[95]

There was little RAMC staff could do, however, to improve

the transportation of the wounded, a matter in which the Germans would brook no interference. British PoWs proceeding from a first-aid post to a base hospital had a rough ride; at the sound of incoming shells or small-arms fire, the stretchers carrying the wounded would be dropped as the bearers took cover while the standard vehicle for the carriage of the wounded from a casualty clearing station to a base hospital was an ambulance, sometimes a motorized one, usually a horse-drawn one. This was actually a euphemism for a springless farm cart, the jolting of which was torture for the wounded. The journey of Corporal Alexander Fyfe, 1/Cameron Highlanders, by cart to Laon hospital was hardly improved by the driver calling out 'Engländer hier', resulting in Fyfe being constantly threatened by *Soldaten* along the route.[96]

It was not unknown for German medical officers to commit cruelty against British PoWs directly and personally. Waiting at Brussels railway station for the hospital ambulance, Lieutenant T.J. Dobson, Royal Naval Volunteer Reserve (RNVR), who had a bullet from the Antwerp action lodged in his elbow, had the temerity to ask the medical officer on the platform dressing station for morphia.

> This he curtly refused, muttering something about English swine. While we were waiting to be taken to hospital, he walked up and down the line of stretchers, and every time he passed mine managed to get in a skilful kick on the handles with the object of jarring me.[97]

Arthur Gibbons fared much worse. After his four days out in the open, Gibbons was taken to the military hospital at Handzaeme, about fifteen miles from Ypres, where he was put in a stable to lie on straw. His mud- and blood-encrusted clothes remained on him. All he received in the way of medical treatment was morphine. Finally, fourteen days after first being wounded he was taken to the operating theatre. Before administering the ether the doctor – another who spoke faultless English – told him he was a murderer and an assassin, his only motive as a Canadian to fight in the war being gold. When he came round, the German nurses shouted at him, '*Schwein Engländer*'. Visiting Belgian nuns slipped chocolate and

fruit under his bedclothes. He needed it. A single bowl of soup was
the quotidian ration of food for hospitalized prisoners per day.

The operation left Gibbons with one leg shorter than the other.
The opinion of Canadian surgeons post-war was that the operation
to set Gibbons' leg was so inept as to be deliberate. That is, the operation was intended to cripple him.[98]

Memoirs constantly affirm that British prisoner patients received
less food and nursing than their German equivalents in base hospitals. Aside from being tormented by crowds of Germans gathering
around his bed shouting 'Now, you British swine, show us how you
make dum-dum bullets' ('I have associated Germans with shouting
ever since those days'), young Brian Horrocks, Middlesex Regiment, was forced to endure filth and festering wounds:

> It was a nasty hospital. The whole time I was there, which was nearly
> a month, neither our shirts nor our blankets were changed, and
> we were still wearing the blood-soaked garments in which we had
> been wounded. As our wounds were suppurating we soon became
> unpleasant.
>
> The most degrading thing of all, however, was the fact that, as
> a refinement in beastliness, we were not allowed to use bed-pans
> or bottles, but were forced to heave ourselves out of bed and crawl,
> because none of us could walk, along the floor to the lavatory which
> lay at the end of a stone passage. The sight of our bare anatomy as
> we crawled laboriously along always excited loud jeers from the rest
> of the ward.[99]

Treatment for British PoWs in base hospitals did not appreciably
improve over the course of the war. Captain Alan Binnie, Royal
Flying Corps (RFC), captured on 14 April 1917, was given nothing
to eat for seven days. In his ward there were 'practically no sanitary
arrangements'. There was one commode for everybody. Binnie at
least had a bed. After lying for days on the floor of St Quentin hospital the blind Gilbert Nobbs, ravaged by thirst and hunger, managed
to whisper hoarsely, 'Hauptmann!' to get attention. The stretcher-
bearers picked him up and took him to a room reserved for officers.
Where there were beds.

*

Between the battlefield and cage, interrogation of prisoners was standard, but mostly cursory. The reason for the dilatory nature of the German inquisition was simple: the questioner invariably knew more than his subject. As Alec Waugh's interrogator explained outside Bapaume in Black March 1918, with just a touch of gleeful patronizing: 'It is no good my asking you any questions. You'd be sure to answer the wrong way, and besides, I don't think you could tell me so very much.'[100] He then proceeded to give Waugh a most detailed account of the Division, down to the number of stretcher-bearers. Meanwhile, the young Basil Willey found the charm of his questioner 'irresistible'; this quality was no help, of course, in extracting information from Willey because, being a mere subaltern, he was not in the information loop. The German Intelligence officer was, and so Willey and colleagues ended up asking the Teutonic charmer about the progress of the great 'Michael' Offensive.

Interrogations rarely involved rough stuff to extract 'gen', although one British officer went on record to complain:

> After being captured I was asked for information. I refused to give it. A German officer ordered me to be placed against a wall, and fell in a firing party. Some of the men fired but I was not hit. He had previously placed a revolver against my body and threatened to shoot me if I did not give information.[101]

RFC pilot Gerald Knight, captured on 9 November 1916 after being shot down on a bombing run to Douai, decided on a policy of obmutescence when interviewed at the local Germany Army HQ. The 'politesse' of the interviewer – a general no less – quickly vanished, to be replaced by cardiac-inducing anger, though he limited himself to words, before storming off. Knight, incidentally, was a rare bird. He made an attempt to escape soon after capture, and got quite close to the front line before recapture. Although the chances of escape were best when first apprehended – because the prisoner was at that stage closer to the British lines – initiative was at its worst, because it was stalled by feelings of inferiority, bewilderment and exhaustion.

Silence was one thing; anything that could be construed as 'cheek' was likely to beget a definitely violent retaliation. So when the Canadian Tom Scudamore was asked, 'What right have you to come over here and kill our good Germans?' and he sarcastically replied that he had come for the fun of it, the cursing blows from the officer's riding whip were perhaps inevitable.[102]

Any prisoners misunderstanding their inquisitor's English were also likely to get short shrift. William Quinton, a Newfoundlander, assumed the answer to the question 'What is your Reegaumen?' was 'Church of England'. It was in fact 'Newfoundland Regiment'. A kicking was the painful result.

Taken after street-fighting in Lens, the exhausted Lance-Corporal Thomas Higgins found that his interrogator was as much propagandist as inquisitor: 'He told us Germany was bound to win in the end. We let him have his say, as we were fed up with war at any rate.'[103] The former employee of the Etronic steelworks would soon discover that captivity was war's equal in pain.

Although German Intelligence staff usually knew best, they resolutely interviewed all and sundry in the hope of uncovering a military secret. This zest for gold nugget information actually handed power to the victim. At La Bassée, Lieutenant Horace Gilliland had seen one of his men bayoneted to death and others denied proper medical attention. So, steeped in the Sandhurst tradition of 'the men first', he refused to be interrogated until they had received treatment. It worked.

Sometimes, just sometimes, the tables were turned, and the interrogators received an unpleasant surprise. Private Henry Clarke, 1/Suffolk Regiment, captured in 1915:

We were questioned by a number of officers, trying to pump us for information. If they had not asked so many questions they would not have had so many untruths. They all thought we were Kitchener's men, we told them they were still in England and didn't they look shocked. They had the impudence to tell us our Regular Army was absolutely wiped out during the latter part of 1914; they were more surprised than ever when they were shown some of our paybooks proving we were Regulars, we told them there were also lots more to come from India.[104]

In cases where German Intelligence genuinely thought they might discover useful information, they resorted to sophistication. Captured flyers were sometimes taken to German aerodromes and shown the latest magnificent machines in the hope that the RFC men would be drawn into uttering technical indiscretions. Similarly, a good meal and fine wine in the German mess might be laid on for the soon-to-be-caged-birds with a view to loosening their tongues. Second Lieutenant H.T. Champion, RFC, and his observer Newbold, downed in February 1916, received the absolute works – cigarettes, wine, food and civilized conversation with a minor royal who had been educated at Eton: 'We were treated as guests.' But the two aviators were not fooled, and at the earliest convenient moment asked for the conveniences, where they destroyed passes and papers. Which was just as well; later the mask came off and their coats were rifled.[105] Shot down while flying a single-seater Nieport Scout in April 1917, Hamilton 'Flossie' Hervey, RFC, also requested the latrine during interrogation, where – in a somewhat flustered moment – he ate his pass rather than flushing it. As Hervey dolefully noted, 'This was to be my last square meal for some weeks!'[106]

Technology was also employed in intelligence-gathering. Targeted British soldiers would have their progress as a prisoner lined with hidden microphones; many a British officer, before entering Karlsruhe distribution camp, would spend a few days locked with others in a room at a nearby three-storey suburban *Gasthof*, the interior walls of which were studded with listening devices. This was the infamous 'listening hotel' at leafy Ettlinger Strasse 39.

By 1918 the German Army wanted to divine more than military information from captured Britons. The acuteness of the country's manpower shortage required the putting of prisoners into permanent forced labour, often with immediate effect, often in occupations that directly aided the war effort and transgressed international agreements. Agreements the Germans had signed on the dotted line. Private William Tucker was barely off the battlefield before he was taken to a shell-ruined street at Salome, where a German officer walked along the line of exhausted, red-eyed prisoners examining their paybooks. The hundred or so men were then divided by trade. As Tucker was an 'Artificer' he was sent to a motor depot. (In fact, he had done a course in bicycle repairs; the Germans would rue the day they put Tucker into slave labour, because he would be both an intentional and unintentional saboteur.) On Tucker's back a guard scrawled '71' in big green paint: 'This numbering ritual had a humiliating effect that had to be experienced to be appreciated. Nothing like being a walking number to cut one down to size.'[107] One thing, though, cheered Number 71 a little; his pal Private Lacey darted out of the line into a ruined clothes shop, snapped up a top-hat, put it on his head and rejoined the parade. The German officer moving along the line doing the quizzing 'was moved to smile, as we all did, and the episode lightened our ordeal'.[108] Tommy humour. It would be needed again and again in the ordeals to come.

*

Aufstehen!

After battle, after being stripped for souvenirs, after interrogation there came a ritual that would make a memory as indelible as the first time under shellfire, create an image that would define the Western Front. This was the forced march to the cage, the temporary holding facility where prisoners would await their forwarding to Germany or to a labour camp behind the lines. A ritual the Germans liked to dress up with full martial, all-conquering pomp by putting mounted Uhlans at the front and rear of the column of prisoners.

With their lances, glorious fluttering plumes and prancing horses the Uhlans made an imposing spectacle. They had little capability as escorts, other than to awe with ancient symbols of power – any really large or possibly troublesome contingent of prisoners would merit accompanying guards on foot or bicycle. Naturally the German guards gave their packs to the Tommy prisoners to carry.

Uhlans. Dead straight French roads lined by cloned poplars. Flat landscape. Everything about the march on the unyielding *pavé* only served to depress the PoWs yet more. Every French village they traipsed through had *Mairie* crossed out and *Kommandantur* in its place, as if grotesquely reminding prisoners of their severance from their own side. On the route inland from Cambrai in April 1918 Private George Gadsby saw the corpses of British dead lying by the side of road, left there since the battle of the previous November; he thought the German failure to bury them constituted a lack of respect for the fallen which made for 'a stain on a civilised country'.[109] And, oh God, the thirst! Since stress speeds up the metabolic rate, prisoners, having come through battle and capture, were desperate for drink and food, in that order. In summer heat, thirst tormented almost beyond endurance. Captured on 2 June 1916 at Sanctuary Wood in a Somme still arcadian, Frank MacDonald, 1/Canadian Mounted Rifles, marched towards Coutrai in blistering sun: 'We were suffering terribly from thirst ... Again and again I thought it would be better to die there than try to make another hundred yards.' What kept him going? A determination 'to show the German brutes that we were British and that British soldiers had the nerve and stamina to endure anything without being broken'.[110] The wellspring of patriotism would keep countless Britons off their knees in captivity.

The thirst. Men broke ranks to scoop water from the ditches; those unlucky enough to be caught were certain to get a rifle butt from a guard in the head, chest or shoulders. In rain, men put their faces to the sky to try to catch the drops; in the mornings they tried to lick dew from the grass. Prisoners, though, found succouring friends on the march – which could take hours, even days – in the angelic shape of French and Belgian civilians who rushed from their houses to line the road and slip cups of water, apples, bits of bread and potatoes into the hands of the shuffling captives. Or leave these things on the pavement. Edward Edwards, a Briton serving with Princess Patricia's Canadian Light Infantry, was lucky enough to be thrown that indispensable of British soldiering, a 'gasper'; if the British Army of 1914–18 marched on its stomach, its lungs were powered by cigarette smoke. The smokers – almost everybody in the Army – were already beginning to feel a desperate craving for nicotine.

Lucky too were the prisoners shivering in the winter cold who were thrown caps and jackets from the second storey of road-hugging French and Flanders houses.[111] Such aid was given at risk, because the stock response of the German guards to the gift-giving was to beat the civilians – boys, girls, men, women, it was indiscriminate – with the flats of their swords or the sides of their lances. (The lances of Uhlans proved good for hitting civilians or prisoners about the head.) On his weary way to the cage, Private William Tucker, to his horror, witnessed guards setting Alsatian dogs on the civilians lining the streets.[112]

The civilians of the occupied lands gave more than *matériel* to the prisoners passing by. They gave cheer and encouragement. As his column made its way through the streets of St Quentin, Captain Phillimore found the French behaving 'in a very kind and plucky manner', edging up and murmuring sympathetic noises, or shouting from the other side of the street '*Vivent les Allies*' despite curses and threats from the guards.[113] Gifts of food and the shouts of '*Hurrah les Anglais*' had a 'terrific' effect on the morale of William Tucker's column: 'Our rather shambling, humiliated and dejected gait became sprightly, almost martial.'[114] They started whistling.

It was a war of surprises. One German soldier passing William Tucker's motley column shouted 'Up the Spurs' in perfect English; a weak but welcome April sun came out shortly afterwards in seeming celebration of a note from home so strange.

In his memoir of service with 11/King's Royal Rifle Corps, Benjamin Muse recorded an incident on the march to the cage which deeply affected him, and the poignancy of which is undimmed a century on:

> In one small village an old French gentleman came out into the street and raised his tall silk hat to us. Instinctively the boys in the front of our column responded with a salute, and their example was followed by each section of fours in its turn, as they marched past. Three or four German officers came up, cursing and shaking their fists to drive the old man away, but he remained defiantly bare-headed and motionless until the last of his country's allies had filed past.[115]

Lance-Corporal Muse was an American volunteer with the British Army, signing up, as he saw it, to fight a dictatorial militarism that besmirched humanity. A man of an unquenchable longing for justice, Muse would become a senator and a campaigning journalistic voice against racial segregation in the US Southern states.

There were foes on the *pavé* road too, as well as *amis*. As the prisoners tramped exhausted, thirsty and anxious about the future, away from the front – and towards what? – they encountered the German Army marching the other way. So, more abuse. One British officer recalled his greeting by the marching men in *feldgrau*:

> On the way we passed through a battalion of German infantry, who were halted and formed up on each side of the road. With the exception of one company (where the officer stopped it) both officers and men abused us, using such expressions as 'English swine' and 'sons of bitches'. They spat at the men.[116]

In emotionally charged times, when the war was not going the German way or rumours of war crimes were flying in the air, British PoWs would walk a gauntlet. After an incident in 1915 when the British allegedly shot German prisoners holding a white flag, armed German troops lined both sides of a road for four hundred yards, and set about the Tommies with sticks and rifles as they passed along. Two Scottish soldiers were killed and Captain Lancelot Robins, 2/Welsh Regiment, already concussed and suffering heat exhaustion, had his eye knocked out:

> I can recollect being assaulted when walking in front of several prisoners. The man struck me on the chest, and I know I hit him in the face. I was knocked down either by a German or by the rush of the other men behind me all of whom I heard afterwards were hit or kicked. On getting up, I picked up my water bottle which had fallen over my head, and seeing a German running at me with his rifle held up in both hands, I swung my water bottle, which was full, clean into his face. I was then knocked down and struck over the face, and this blow I believe destroyed my eye.[117]

After being captured in street-fighting in Lens, Lance-Corporal Thomas Higgins was forced to march through the city in what was part gauntlet-run and part parade of the vanquished:

> There were thousands of German soldiers all around us. We had to march with our hands held up in the air. I did not think we should get through alive even then. The Germans were cuffing, and kicking us along the way. Some rushed at us with their bayonets – it was the German Officers who stopped them – and I noticed those who seemed most bitter had not been in the scrap with us.
>
> The officers could not stop all the violence. Some of the lads got jabbed in the arms and legs by bayonets.[118]

What a difference four years made! In 1914 British prisoners marched to captivity against the mighty tide of the German Army. Captain Robert Dolbey recalled:

> I had come from an army where the horses were all skin and bone and sore backed and foundered and here were young animals, fresh and in excellent condition. How could one compete I thought, with such as army as this?[119]

For all its seeming success, the German Army of the spring 1918 offensives was nothing like the same animal. No Tommy prisoner, no matter how dejected or benumbed, failed to cheerfully notice the ramshackle state of the Kaiser's men, their transport and their kit in this otherwise cheerless time. 'We could not but raise a smile,' recalled Private George Gadsby; 'The Germans' transport reminded us of a travelling circus.' Tramping to St Quentin in 1918 Captain G.D.J. McMurtrie, Somerset Light Infantry, cast a professional eye over the deficiencies of the German Army on the other side of the road:

> One was the extraordinary absence of enthusiasm on the part of the German troops ... The second thing was the deplorable state the transport was in. There were bony horses, looking starved, with ribs sticking out, awful old wagons, which might fall to pieces at any moment without the slightest warning. It looked like a procession of

farmers with their wagons and not soldiers with the transport of a great army. The third thing was the extraordinary mixture of young boys and old men who seemed to make up the Reserves ... We passed a great many dead and crossed the original frontline from which they had driven us. All the dead, both our and the enemy's, had been stripped of their boots and sometimes of their clothes. Germany wanted leather, Germany wanted clothes and badly.[120]

So badly, indeed, that a 'Fritz' passing a Tommy on the bitter road to the front in 1918 was quite likely to barter cigarettes and bread for clothes, sealing the deal in pidgin French: 'La Guerre fini pour vouz. Gut, eh Tommy?'

But these were still only small and occasional brightnesses on the journey to the cage, which might be twenty miles away or more, an exhausting march for men already fatigued from battle and drained dead by mental anguish. Although fit, young and twenty-one, Lieutenant Archer Cust became so tired on his march through the night ('the most appalling twelve hours') that he kept falling asleep as he walked, 'waking up again with a start'.[121]

Walking, walking until, after an eternity of walking, the column of prisoners arrived at their holding facility. Entering an unknown village at night, Benjamin Muse's attention was caught by the church: 'The edifice loomed beautiful before us in the mellow moonlight and reflected a feeling of peace and reverence in us warriors fresh from the trenches.'

Little did Muse think the church was his place of incarceration. Or did the village's curé think his sacred space would be turned into quarters for prisoners of war. When the curé tried to protest the desecration, a German officer seized him by the shoulders and threw him down the church steps.[122]

Usually the Germans erected barbed-wire pens or 'cages' to hold prisoners, but where these could not be built or built quickly enough they pressed into service barns, derelict factories, civilian prisons and churches galore – for, with the pews ripped out, churches were ideal gaols. After all, they had solid walls, only two or three doors requiring guarding, and few if any opening windows. Into these churches men were crammed tighter than cords of wood to sleep. By the estimate of James Farrant, Royal Naval Division (RND), he shared a small church near Exarde with at least a thousand other prisoners, British, French and Belgian. There were two pails 'for urinal purposes'.[123] Being a prisoner of war was a dirty and embarrassing business; wire cages had an open trench as a midden.

No longer places of contemplation and choirs, these church prisons resounded with the screams and sighs of the wounded, while the light of lanterns caught the painted murals of Passion and Crucifixion, strange in themselves to men used to the plain walls of Anglican establishments. Placed in the Roman Catholic church at Bertincourt along with other badly wounded, an Australian officer considered: 'It was a veritable chamber of horrors, and gave me a grotesque idea of what Dante may have imagined when he limned his inferno.'[124]

Regardless of the stench and noise, men would sleep this night from sheer exhaustion, though it was fitful because of the cold ground and gnawing anxiety about the future. If they were fortunate, they would have received a minute meal of a piece of black bread and a bowl of 'ersatz' coffee made from acorns to help them on their way. Such was their introduction to the black bread and acorn coffee that would become the dismal staples of prisoner life, sometimes the only food and drink prisoners would get for days on end.

The food was not to Tommy's taste, as Lance-Corporal Thomas Higgins explained:

> The bread was made of rye and potatoes and tasted dreadfully sour. It was mouldy as well. I was hungry. I had not tasted food from Saturday night [it was Tuesday], but I could not face it . . . Later on when hunger grew worse we did not think of taste.[125]

Reginald Morris, 2/5 Northumberland Fusiliers, incarcerated in a barbed-wire enclosure, did not even get that:

> In this cage I found many others, perhaps about 500 prisoners. We stopped there, exposed to the weather all that day and the following

night, and with nothing whatever to eat or drink. Here we were searched by an interpreter who tried to frighten us. He warned us we should be shot at sight if we attempted to escape. We were not to communicate with the inhabitants of the occupied area, or to receive food from them.[126]

Food. For hungry men it was already becoming the motif of life behind barbed wire. Next morning a German transport driver offered a piece of coarse black bread to a prisoner in front of Morris in exchange for a leather jerkin: 'The exchange made, the prisoner tore the bread into pieces and gulped it down. Such an incident cannot easily be forgotten; it is stamped into the memory.'[127]

A guard at the Le Cateau factory which held Lieutenant Joseph Lee saw the chance of fat profit and auctioned a tin of sardines 'to the provocation almost of a riot'.[128] After two, three, four days in a cage, men would barter anything they had left for food, be it coins, wedding rings, boots. Who could blame them? Alec Waugh bought with some francs a little humble bread and lard and 'It seemed like a banquet'. Waugh had learned one of the first rules of PoW life: find a bribable guard. There were many.[129]

To starve men of food was to do more to them than cause them physical discomfort. It altered the patterns of civilized behaviour, it set comrades against comrades. It was an assault on dignity.

*

Willkommen an schwierige Zeiten.

Some prisoners, especially from 1917 onwards, were put straight to *Arbeit* instead of being transported to Germany. Along with *verboten*, *Arbeit* was the word soonest learned by the prisoners. After reaching the cage at Ramecourt at midnight Private Ernest Thornton fell into the sleep of the dead. He was awoken at 4 a.m. next day for *Arbeit*, and kept at it 'very hard' from 6 a.m. until 8 p.m. The guards, stone-faced old *Landsturmer*, long pipes permanently hanging from their mouths, 'used to beat us with sticks' as Thornton and his fellows repaired roads and laid railway track.[130]

Attached to an *Arbeitskommando* (work gang) at Peronne railhead in 1918, Sergeant S.W. Poulton, London Regiment, also found his guard 'to be free with a stick', not to mention his whip and rifle-butt too. Indeed, so free was the guard with the butt end of his Mauser that he killed Private Baker by smashing it into his skull.[131]

And yet, here too there were individual German guards who were unheeding of official strictures and the exigencies of war, whose humanity could not be restrained. Rifleman Victor Denham, London Rifle Brigade, captured on the chaotic, incomprehensible morning of 28 March 1918, stumbled into the Kommando cage where a German soldier 'no doubt pitying my bandaged head and my youthfulness' gave him his ration of coffee. 'This action impressed me very favourably at the time, as we were conjecturing on the treatment we were going to receive.'[132]

Belying their reputation for textbook efficiency, the Germans marched some PoWs from holding cage to holding cage until their destiny was sorted. Reginald Morris spent nearly a week being moved from one barbed-wire enclosure to another barbed-wire enclosure. He was nearly bombed by his own side's planes. He became weaker and weaker, his feet transmogrified into shapeless blobs of burst blisters:

> The guards paid no attention to my pitiful state. They just pushed me along or hit me with the butt-end of their rifles when my legs began to give way or the pain of walking became too great. There were many other prisoners like me.[133]

For those inside the cage awaiting *Arbeit* or Germany there was boredom. There was nothing to do save sit round and wait, though nobody knew for what. Old and wise hands did best, because they always carried a book tucked in a tunic pocket to deal with the many *longueurs* of service life. Out the book now came. In Joseph Lee's group of prisoners in a discarded factory at Le Cateau someone had a Testament, another a Book of Common Prayer, both were 'in continual demand'.

In the meantime they waited. For who knew what?

Sometimes prisoners were given a postcard to send to Britain via the Red Cross to announce their capture. This was a relief, because an uppermost worry in the prisoner's head was that he would be reported 'missing' and his worried family would presume him dead. In a little vicious vortex, worry begat worry and sapped the prisoner's spirit.

As did the body lice that spread from man to man with a speed that beggared belief. 'Every man jack of us was lifting with lice,' wrote Tanner Milburn in a memoir pencilled for his family after the war. 'It was awful.'

In the holding cage there was another search, this time for any sharp object that might be used to escape or retaliate. Naturally anything valuable would disappear into the pockets of the German searcher. But by now anyone wise had hidden away anything of worth. William Tucker managed to keep the francs he'd won playing Crown and Anchor by stuffing them between his underpants and breeches.

And the prisoners waited. A minor variation on bread and coffee came with the arrival of 'soup', which turned out to be ground maize in water. Some wit called it 'Sandstorm' and the nomenclature stuck. Maybe if His Sacred Majesty was in benevolent mood the prisoners would get 'bean soup' – or, more accurately, horse beans boiled in water. Soldiers out of smokes – which was pretty much every man jack of them, because cigarettes were eminently lootable – followed the guards like sad sheep hoping to pick up the discarded ends of their cigars and *Zigaretten*. They might be lucky; equally the guard might flick the cigarette butt over the wire to lie tantalizingly close, yet deliberately unobtainable. Anyone with a cigarette could hardly call it his own, because they would be followed by a flock of soldiers asking, 'Short end, after you?'

There would be a winnowing out of any officers, although they may have already been separated off from other ranks, destined for officer-only camps in Deutschland. The Hague Convention confirmed the traditional social distinction between officers and men, and they would have different wars behind the wire.

In quiet periods on the Western Front a British officer taken prisoner was more likely to be held temporarily in a military fortress – the foul casernes at Douai and Cambrai especially – than in a cage. Airmen almost always ended in a fortress, as did Lieutenant 'Flossie' Hervey, RFC. Put alone in a room, he made a valiant effort to pass the lonely hours by making a draughts board on a table, using coins as checkers, and playing himself. His cell was:

> A room, 10 ft by 5 ft in one corner a straw-filled palliasse covered with a filthy, moth-eaten blanket, a floor littered with straw thick with dust, a rickety table and chair, one small window, closely barred, overlooking stables occupied by Hun artillery – this comprised my quarter during five of the most miserable days I have ever spent.[134]

He was then, to his happiness, transferred to a room with three other RFC men. Alas, this quadrupling up was not done out of kindness or restrictions on space; the pilots found a microphone, placed there by their captors in the hope of hearing indiscretions. Any Germans eavesdropping on Gerald Knight and his pals in Cambrai fortress would have been dismayed at their combativity, which was also evidenced in artwork: 'we amused ourselves by carving our names on the tables, or by drawing regimental crests or pictures of Hun aeroplanes descending in flames'.[135]

Solitary confinement was perhaps hardest on the gregarious. Captured after the RFC plane in which he was being given a lift was downed, the altogether earthbound infantry officer Captain Lyall Grant was imprisoned in Douai:

> Today has been one of the hardest, a continual fight against depression. I never knew that a heart could be so heavy and it mustn't be carried on the sleeve. To my guards I appear the most cheery of mortals and greet them all in French, but to myself I'm in the depths of despair. Solitude was never pleasing to me, and when one has nothing to read, nothing to see, and nothing to do but think of 'this time a week ago!' and the like, it takes all one's time to keep back an ever-rising lump and I never realized before how nearly mental sickness could make one physically sick.[136]

He worried about his family. A German pilot, 'who proved to be quite nice', promised to drop a note over British lines to say Grant and his pilot were okay. In the diary he started that day, Grant wrote with regard to the note: 'I hope that it is picked up all right so that those at home may know I am safe; I believe worrying about them is one of the worst parts of the whole business.'[137] He hid the diary in the waistband of his kilt. Like other diarists he used the diary as a psychological prop – a paper friend – as well as a record of what befell him. Grant's diary remains one of the fullest records of the British officer experience in German captivity in the First World War.

Since the German Army used solitary confinement as punishment, one can only conclude that the lengthy periods some PoWs were held solo before transportation to Germany was intentional cruelty. Certainly, numerous depositions and memoirs attest to officer prisoners in the fortresses being taunted and maltreated. Lieutenant J.S. Poole put through a mock execution, was lined up against the wall, the guards assuming the position of a firing squad. 'It may have only been horseplay,' considered Poole later, 'as they were quickly told off by a German officer.'[138] But frightening enough at the time. One of those larger-than-life types magnetically attracted to the Edwardian army, John Poole would achieve the thankfully rare distinction of becoming a prisoner of the Germans in both World Wars.[139] His other call on national record was to make a 'home run' escape in the First of them.

Lieutenant Will Harvey, farmer's son turned solicitor, was among those thousands of men who went into khaki in 1914 and became a better soldier than anyone might have expected. (One of Harvey's men memorably described him as looking as though 'he stuffed birds in civil life . . . a small, dirty, nearly middle-aged man wearing glasses and an apologetic air'.) This son of Gloucestershire found his ten days 'banged up' in solitary confinement tough going. On the one hand capture seemed unreal, 'a green dream world', as though he had dropped in to see a 'lot of rather eccentric strangers, and would presently go back to my friends to laugh over my experience'.[140] On the other hand his torment over allowing himself to be captured was all too real. To cope with depression during the day he read the volume of Shakespeare he carried with him:

'I learned several of the sonnets by heart, forgetting for a while the lice which bothered me.'[141]

To cope with the nights in 'the lousy little room' Harvey doped himself with morphia from the field first-aid kit in his tunic. The morphia came in a tube of quarter grains; one grain was enough to cause semi-insensibility. Shakespeare for the light, morphia for the night. On the flyleaf of an old French book Harvey found in his cell he wrote 'Solitary Confinement' and began his career as 'Dear Poet', the most loved of the PoW poets of the Great War:

> No mortal comes to visit me to-day,
> Only the gay and early-rising Sun
> Who strolled in nonchalantly, just to say,
>   'Good morrow, and despair not, foolish one!'
> But like the tune which comforted King Saul
> Sounds in my brain that sunny madrigal.
>
> Anon the playful Wind arises, swells
> Into vague music, and departing, leaves
> A sense of blue bare heights and tinkling bells,
> Audible silences which sound achieves
> Through music, mountain streams, and hinted heather,
> And drowsy flocks drifting in golden weather.
>
> Lastly, as to my bed I turn for rest,
> Comes Lady Moon herself on silver feet
> To sit with one white arm across my breast,
> Talking of elves and haunts where they do meet.
> No mortal comes to see me, yet I say
> 'Oh, I have had fine visitors to-day!'[142]

And then it was time to go to Germany.

*

Für Ihnen der Krieg ist fertig.

On capture British officers and men were routinely told by the Germans 'For you the war is over' (yes, that immortal phrase dates from the First, not the Second World War) but nothing could be further from the truth. The British soldiers taken prisoner in 1914–18 had merely exchanged one war for another war. As they were about to find out.

THE IRON ROAD:
THE JOURNEY TO THE GERMAN BABYLON

It is the truth that nearly all British soldiers taken prisoner and
sent to Germany during the first months of the war were made
the object of special contempt, neglect, or cruelty.

Lieutenant Malcolm Hay, Gordon Highlanders

In December 1914 the magnificently monikered Major Crofton
Bury Vandeleur, 1/Cameronians, broke out of Crefeld camp and
made a home run to Britain. He was the first British officer to do so.
There was much interest in his escapade, which was effected with a
panache that was all that could be hoped for from a British Regular.
Having 'borrowed' a German uniform, Vandeleur had walked out
through the camp's front gates (he was a fluent German speaker),
taken a train, puffed cigars in his carriage with Imperial officers,
then sneaked across the border to Holland, turning up at his club
in St James's still dressed in *feldgrau*. What increasingly caught the
attention of the press, the public and eventually Parliament, however, was Vandeleur's account of the mistreatment of British PoWs
at the hands of the Germans, especially in the transportation of the
prisoners to Germany. Vandeleur's sworn statement became part of
an official HM Government report. He testified:

At the station [Douai, 17 October 1914] we were driven into closed-in
wagons from which the horses had just been removed, 52 men being
crowded into the one in which the other four officers and myself
were. So tight were we packed that there was only room for some of
us to sit down on the floor. This floor was covered fully 3 inches deep
in fresh manure, and the stench was almost asphyxiating. We were

thus boxed up for thirty hours, with no food, and no opportunity of attending to purposes of Nature. All along the line we were cursed by officers and soldiers alike at the various stations, and at Mons Bergen I was pulled out in front of the wagon by the order of the officer in charge of the station, and, after cursing me in filthy language for some ten minutes, he ordered one of his soldiers to kick me back into the wagon, which he did, sending me sprawling into the filthy mess at the bottom of the wagon. I should like to mention here that I am thoroughly conversant with German, and understood everything that was said. Only at one station on the road was any attempt made on the part of German officers to interfere and stop their men from cursing us.[1]

The German authorities loudly decried Vandeleur's account and published an official response in the international press in June 1915, insisting that all officers were transported east in second- or third-class passenger carriages, with other ranks conveyed in cleaned horse trucks. Any defiling of the carriages with urine or excrement was due to the British yobbishly relieving themselves.[2]

The Germans did protest too much. In truth, Vandeleur's experience on the iron road to Germany was only moderately awful in comparison to what other British prisoners endured. Many, many fared worse. The journey to Germany could be purgatory on wheels. For apprehensive and exhausted men, even the unfolding Teutonic landscape, with its startling red rooves and pine forests seemed threatening. Peering through cracks in the slats of horse carriages at the strange scenery, men could see only too clearly that they were getting further from home. One prisoner believed that the very rattle of the wheels on the track seemed to tap out a message: 'Further-from-home, Further-from-home'. Travelling to Kamstigall-bei-Pillau in East Prussia, the thoughtful, sensitive Lieutenant Basil Willey passed through mountain scenery which, had it been in England, would have 'made my heart leap up'. But here the mountains were 'only protuberances in a hostile and alien land'.[3] Packed in a horse carriage, with not even a slit for fresh air, Private Jack Evans, another Briton for all of his enlistment in

4/Canadian Mounted Rifles, considered that his encasing black box had a silver lining: he could not see Germany outside. 'We did not want to see it.'[4]

A hostile and alien land. Hostility was encountered at almost every station the train stopped at, and these were many. PoW trains went on side lines and were constantly halted because military traffic had priority. There was trouble from the outset. Since the Germans blamed the British for frustrating their war of conquest, they standardly gave preferential treatment in transportation to French and the Belgian PoWs.[5] Captured after the fall of Antwerp, Able Seaman James Farrant, RND, noticed, ominously, on entraining in wagons at the railhead:

> The Belgians had straw in theirs, and 20 men to a truck. We had 40 men and no straw. A further distinction was made with the aid of chalk on the Belgian trucks, where someone had written 'Belgian gut, Francoses gut, aber English Schwein'.[6]

Sometimes as many as sixty 'English Schwein' were packed into the horse trucks. The air became so fetid and depleted of oxygen that the men 'banged away continually on the wooden sides of the van', fearing they might be suffocated.[7] The men were packed standing up, like skittles. They would steam with sweat in summer, and become maddened with thirst. Conversely, in winter – and the Great War saw some of the worst winters of the century – the men grew despairingly cold. Hot or cold, they travelled in the dark, barely able to move. One prisoner recalled:

> It's practically dark most of the time, you can't see where you are or where you're going, you can only hear the reverberation of the music of the wheels on the lines as they're going along, rackety bang. Well, as a matter of fact I think you wouldn't be sorry if you died. If that isn't enough to drive anybody mad, I don't know what is.[8]

A British officer, travelling in a mixed party of officers and other ranks (so much for German guidelines) stated in a smuggled report to the British government:

Five officers, fifteen rank and file and thirty-two French civilians were hustled into a goods van which was labelled '40 men and 8 horses'. The van had recently been occupied by horses, and the floor was deep in dung and urine. The doors were closed and the heat and stench were appalling. At the first station a man who said he was station commandant came and took away all the great coats which had not already been taken, saying he had orders to take them for use of the *Landsturm*. The doors were opened at every station to allow the crowds of soldiers to come and insult us. French civilians were given food and water. They were occasionally allowed out for purposes of nature, but we were not until the afternoon of the following day. [9]

To be deprived of lavatory facilities was a form of torture. Either men had to piss and crap in corners (where corners could be got to) like animals, or soil themselves. For proud men it was dehumanizing.

It was not a gentlemanly war; a constant complaint of officers was that instead of being placed in decent carriage accommodation they were put in trucks with the men. From the point of view of twenty-first-century sensibilities this seems like rank snobbery; from the point of view of Edwardian proprieties, mixing with the men or travelling fourth class entailed a vertiginous, disorientating loss of social position for officers.[10] In all likelihood, the Germans, who were earnest adherents to class stratifications, intended the insult and the hurt. There are enough occasions when French officers travelled in swanky Pullmans and British officers did so in equine excrement to suggest that. A German government statement published in the international press denied that the French were given preferential treatment in transportation, yet only in a way that tacitly confirms the opposite was true:

If the English pretend that they were attended to during the journey after the French, the reason is to be found in the quite comprehensible bitterness of feeling among German troops who respected the French on the whole as honourable and decent opponents, whereas the English mercenaries had, in their eyes, adopted a cunning method of warfare from the beginning, and, when taken prisoners, bore themselves with an insolent and provocative mien. That any such distinction in treatment was ordered by superior officers is an untruth.[11]

Whether officer or enlisted man, the prisoner heading east would suffer Biblical thirst and hunger. On his sixty-hour train journey to Döberitz near Berlin, James Farrant was given one bowl of soup and one slice of bread. Private Edward Page, Royal Marines Light Infantry (RMLI), fared a little better; his journey to 'Hunland' from Antwerp took from 5 a.m. Tuesday, 3 November 1914 to 12 noon Thursday, 5 November 1914 (sixty-one hours) during which time he received half a pint of coffee, four ounces of bread and half a pint of soup. Some journeys to the German Babylon took up to four days, on a ration of one piece of bread and coffee per day.[12] The length of the journey to captivity was not caused solely by the vagaries of German railway timetabling; prisoners were the responsibility of whichever regional army corps that captured them. Anyone made captive by the German II Army Corps, garrisoned in Stettin and environs, was in for a very long haul.

If the conditions on the trains were appalling for the non-wounded, they were worse for the wounded. On hearing that he was to be transported east on a 'Zug Lazaret' Malcolm Hay fondly imagined a comfortable, sterile hospital train. Instead he was put in an ordinary third-class carriage, packed with English and French wounded; his bed consisted of wooden boards nailed over the seat, with a covering of straw. He was refused help entraining, and had to crawl to the compartment. When he complained to the German officer in charge he was told, 'Das ist schön für einen Engländer'.[13] An Australian officer, captured at Pozières in 1916, the year of the Somme, told how:

> Officers and men prisoners were packed into the guard's van to lie upon shavings: the German wounded rode in the carriage. We were all badly wounded, and this nine hours railways 'jaunt' proved a very trying journey indeed for us.[14]

Put on a freezing hospital train to Bochum a fellow Australian,

Lieutenant William Cull, asked for his blanket to be pulled up; the orderly refused. There was one thing left to warm Cull: 'pure, primitive resentful rage'.[15] Horace Gilliland, his wounds jolted by the jarring motion and ravaged by hunger, found merciful release in a stupor that made him oblivious for pleasant interludes. His journey had begun so well too, from a Lille station brightly illuminated and full of decorated Christmas trees. Meanwhile, on the putative *Zug Lazaret* transporting Captain Henderson, London Scottish, incapacitated by an exposed sciatic nerve, there was no bed bottle; all that could be found was a rusty tin, which the Germans affirmed was the only suitable utensil on the train. There were no beds either. Henderson:

> On 28th May I was moved by motor-ambulance to the station and placed in the train. I protested to a German officer, because, although I stated that I had never left my bed since August 1914 and that I was extremely weak and thin, he nevertheless made me travel lying on a narrow wooden bench, causing me great pain during the 24 hours' journey into Germany.[16]

A female Red Cross doctor refused to dress his wound because it 'smelled'. Lack of medical treatment on the journey east led to wounds becoming infected, although Private Peters, Loyal North Lancashire Regiment, whose wound became 'crawling with maggots' was luckier than he knew.[17] Maggots were visually loathsome yet clinically wonderful, because they actually cleaned wounds; the phenomenon was observed in the war by W.S. Baer, physician with the American Expeditionary Force, who later pioneered the use of 'maggot debridement therapy'.[18] Other men were not lucky. Men died on the journey east because of the lack of medical treatment.[19]

Even allowing for the over-stretched state of the German transport and military medical service, Captain Henderson was convinced that the treatment British PoWs received was 'deliberately designed for our discomfort'. Certainly, British prisoners were made to travel with black troops in the absolute hope that the proximity of racial inferiors (as the Germans saw it) would be unpleasant for them. Placed in a fourth-class carriage with a couple of badly gassed Algerian privates, Lieutenant Peter Anderson, 9th Battalion Canadian Expeditionary Force (CEF), was told by the gleeful officer commanding the train, 'Now travel with your black friends you like so well.' The Germans thought this a great joke.[20] As if to confound Teutonic expectations, Lieutenant C.E. Wallis, 1/ Loyal North Lancashire Regiment, was delighted to be travelling with Senegalese troops, since they generously shared their provisions with him, giving Wallis the only sustenance he received on his journey to Mainz: 'If it had not been that the blacks were very decent fellows, we should have had absolutely no food the whole time.'[21] These Senegalese troops, *Tirailleurs* (skirmishers) brought from France's African colony to fight on the Western Front, were assuredly more kind than the women of the German Red Cross.

At every railway station, German Red Cross women dispensed coffee, biscuits, sandwiches, soup and other comforts to the travelling soldiery. British prisoners expected ministering angels; they got Furies. In the words of *The Quality of Mercy*, an abridgement of the British government's official investigation into the transport of British PoWs to Germany between August and December 1914, the behaviour of the Red Cross women was 'so vile as to be almost incredible'.[22]

Red Cross women routinely spat at British Tommies. Their favourite two words when they caught sight of men in khaki desperate for water and food, any food, any water, were '*Nein! Engländer!*' Captain A.J.G. Hargreaves, Somerset Light Infantry, recalled:

At Liege I tried personally to get the German Red Cross officials to give our wounded men water. They refused. I saw some German Red Cross nurses actually bring water in cans up to our men, show it to them, and then pour it on the platform. This also happened to me personally. At Aix-la-Chapelle there was an elaborate Red Cross dressing station. All water and food was rigorously refused us. The German wounded in the train had their wounds dressed. This was refused us.[23]

Captain T. Kidson Allsop remembered: 'The Red Cross women who passed through our carriage at different stations with trays laden with comforts for the wounded did not offer us any.'[24]

Given a pair of French soldier's trousers in a Brussels hospital because his own were beyond repair, Lieutenant T.J. Dobson, RNVR, passed for a *poilu* and was happily handed sandwiches by a Red Cross nurse at Cologne. 'However, she soon found out her mistake and warned her fellows.'[25] Poor Drummer Joseph Dawson, 2/Northumberland Fusiliers, captured at Ypres (with shrapnel in his head), on his way to Munster, got water, but not in the way he wanted: 'A Red Cross nurse asked us in broken English if we would have anything to drink. Of course, being very thirsty we asked for water. She bent over me and spat in my face!'[26]

German Red Cross nurses went beyond expectorating and contemptuous refusals to dispense food and drink. Private Edward Page was unfortunate enough to encounter a female Red Cross nurse who borrowed a bayonet from the train guard and tormented the prisoners – almost all of whom were wounded – with it.[27] At Bouvigny frontier station, L.J. Austin, a British surgeon working for the Belgian Red Cross recalled: 'At this particular station quite little girls of sixteen and seventeen wearing their Red Cross would come and mock us through the window, and with unmistakable gestures indicate that we should be hanged.'[28]

In all likelihood, British PoWs sometimes confused the Red Cross with the *Vaterländische Frauenverein* – a German patriotic organization that served treats to the troops, the insignia of which was also a blood-red cross.[29] Not that the fine distinction mattered when, after hours of deprivation in a suffocating, banging black box, they were desperate for kindness, food and drink. Such high hopes the prisoners had when they saw the Red Cross badges, so cruelly dashed. That women, who were meant to be comforting creatures like mothers and wives, did such deeds made it all the worse. 'I could not believe that women could behave so cruelly,' lamented Major H.W. Long, RAMC, on his way to Torgau in Saxony and wearing a Red Cross armband himself. He had been refused even water.[30]

On the iron road east, there were plenty of others who wanted to abuse British prisoners aside from girls with Red Cross armbands.

Peering out of the carriage window Malcolm Hay considered the vine-clad cliffs of the Rhine (a sight even the most apathetic, downhearted prisoner was roused by) quite remarkably pleasant under the circumstances. The natives were another matter; they got in at every station to loot the helpless, injured prisoners, and only stout action by Hay's sentry prevented his greatcoat from being stolen. Arriving at Aschaffenburg station, PoWs were greeted by civilians making throat-cutting gestures. The burghers of other towns made more of an effort. One common welcome sign was a mannequin dressed in khaki swinging by its neck from the station roof.

On occasion the abuse went beyond words and signs to sticks and stones. At Aix-la-Chapelle injured PoWs, lying on stretchers on the station platform, were stoned by civilians, among them the much suffering Arthur Gibbons, Toronto Regiment.[31] No one stopped them. So vicious was an attack by drunken Uhlans and railway-workers on the truck carrying Captain Beaman to Torgau that he genuinely went in fear of his life. On his passage to captivity, Horace Gilliland meanwhile was repeatedly stoned at stations through the trap door of the cattle-truck:

'By "stones" I do not mean small pebbles; I mean large stones, heavy enough to knock a man senseless.'[32]

Prisoners on the trains came to dread the sound of squealing brakes as the locomotive slowed down for the stations. Every station stop brought the potential for fresh torment, primarily because they were thronged with German civilians seeing off soldiers going to the front, their trains garlanded with green boughs and flowers for victory. Looking out through the narrow aperture slat in his cattle truck (it was his turn to stand), all Sergeant George Wells could espy at stations 'was the vast array of flags in celebration of the great German offensive'. Stations were iron-and-glass cauldrons of tension and emotion.

Cologne. There was something about Köln. At Cologne Austin and his small group of British doctors had to be protected by a squadron of mounted police, who used the flat of their swords to keep baying crowds back. At Cologne Lieutenant John Caunter witnessed British privates being hauled out of a cattle truck and placed on the platform so that a mob, 'largely comprised of women', could bait them. Sergeant R. Gilling, Scots Greys, experienced this baiting up close: the crowd 'amused themselves by throwing buckets of water over us ... even urine was used'.[33] At Cologne Horace Gilliland watched Red Cross nurses feed the French – but not the British; fortunately for Gilliland the French 'very liberally shared' the food they received. Gilliland got two inches of raw sausage. At Cologne there was a twenty-foot-square cell under the station platform where British prisoners were sometimes stored while awaiting a connecting service; they were packed in so tight they could hardly breathe. Inevitably, it was dubbed 'The Black Hole of Cologne'.

Spat at, jeered at, robbed, stoned ... and still maltreatment had not finished for the British prisoners. It is the ancient lot of the captive to be shown the power of the conqueror. On arriving at the Belgian university town of Louvain, the guards of Sergeant R. Gilling's train threw open the sliding doors of the horse trucks so that the prisoners could look upon the ruins wrought by German *Kultur*, telling them 'that was what we should see on our return to England!'[34]

Another antique rite was perpetrated on the travelling prisoners. They were ceremonially, publicly humiliated in front of the conqueror's citizens. Men from Scottish regiments were officially paraded on station platforms and, at bayonet point, made to lift their kilts to music-hall laughter.[35] PoWs using station latrines would find the doors suddenly opened by the guards so the prisoners were exposed in the process of 'completing necessities' to a gathered mob.[36] One British officer declared in a sworn statement:

> We were then marched to ... station, where we were partially stripped and searched on the public platform. Our breeches were taken down to the knee and our shirts pulled up, while we were compelled to hold our hands above our heads ... [37]

Another British officer, travelling alone with forty German soldiers, was made to stand to attention in the open doorway of the truck at every halt for the delectation of the *Volk*. The soldiers 'struck me with their rifles if I moved and on one occasion I had to stand in this way for four hours'.[38]

Disgusted by the treatment of British PoWs travelling through Germany, James W. Gerard, the US ambassador in Berlin, read with interest and relief an article in the *North German Gazette* which ran:

> The following inhabitants (naming a small town near the border of Denmark), having been guilty of improper conduct towards prisoners of war, have been sentenced to the following terms of imprisonment and the following fines and their names are printed here in order that they may be held up to the contempt of all future generations of Germans.

Gerard thought this action 'splendid', assuming that the German authorities had at last decided to protect PoWs from abuse by the population. Actually, the good people of that small town in northern Germany had been punished for generously giving the PoWs food and drink.[39] By the unflinching rule book of the German War Ministry, their punishment was just and right; the *Kriegsministerium* had issued an edict on 13 August 1914 that unwounded captives were to receive no sustenance at stations. It was unpatriotic.

What made the journey east endurable were those qualities that made the trenches bearable: inspirational pluck, comradeship, and humour. When Captain Gerald Knight, RFC, was put in a carriage with other officers, they sang defiantly 'Pack up your troubles in your old kit bag and smile, smile, smile' as their train departed.[40] This small act of collective resistance doubtless raised morale in the moment; it also steeled Knight's spirit for the longer term. His 'career' as an escaper was born in that clanking carriage. During his twenty-four-hour sojourn in Cologne's Black Hole, Flossie Hervey noticed that some Brit had scrawled a patriotic rhyme on the damp walls. True to Tommy form, the words were 'unprintable'.[41] That raised a smile too.

In reading over a hundred accounts of British officers taken prisoner, I found none that expressed anything other than profound admiration for the bearing of other ranks during transportation.

And for their unstoppable sense of humour. Lieutenant Brian Horrocks watched a long train packed with British PoWs pull in at a station in Germany:

> Dirty, unkempt, many of them wounded, their morale should have been at its lowest. But when the German general walked across to have a look, there was a cry down the train of: 'All tickets, please!'[42]

There was another pleasant and enduring memory for Horrocks and others on the way east: the kindness of individual German soldiers. Whenever the train transporting Captain Robert Dolbey arrived at a German railway station his two guards pulled down the blind of the compartment so the Red Cross nurses would not spy him; in this way they were able to procure him food and drink. Otherwise it was *'Nein! Engländer!'* The sentries also 'slyly' offered him shares of their own black bread and sausages, as long, of course, as no officers were about, in which circumstance they put on faces of 'studied ferocity'.[43]

Robbed of his Burberry and boots, paralysed by his injury, Captain Henderson shivered with cold but:

> I have to record an act of kindness on the part of a wounded German who sat at my feet; he put his overcoat over me, in spite of my protests, and, turning up his collar, went to sleep. I . . . was most grateful for the kindness, which stands out more in memory as it was such a rare occurrence.[44]

Later he struck up a friendship with his guard, who gave him and his travelling companion, Lieutenant T.J. Dobson, RNVR, a postcard as a memento. It was as well received as given.

Travelling third-class to Karlsruhe in February 1917, Second Lieutenant Ernest Warburton, 15/Sherwood Foresters, was only given bread to eat on the fifteen-hour journey. However:

> The whole of the journey the carriage was quite full of German privates, who all treated me most kindly and several times obtained free coffee for me at the stations where it was served out.

At one station I do not know the name of, my guard took me to
the railway restaurant and I bought coffee, and sat with him in the
restaurant.[45]

On his way to the same destination a year later, Alec Waugh found
his two guards 'a delightful couple', although not quite so pleasant
that they could take his mind off the lack of food and the excruciating tedium of forty-eight hours confinement in a carriage.

Warburton and Waugh were both beneficiaries of the abatement
in hostility towards the British from 1916, and Warburton's journey
is a reminder that some prisoners had an easier ride east. His *Zug
Lazaret* was, he acknowledged 'very comfortable', the food and attention on the train was 'very good'.[46]

Anger against the British abated, it never entirely disappeared.
Few truly recalled the journey east with pleasure or entirely avoided
unpleasantness. Flossie Hervey considered his moonlight journey
along the Rhine in April 1917 wondrously 'unforgettable'; one other
memory that stuck was a woman spitting in his eye at Frankfurt.
As late as April 1918 the injured Basil Willey was surprised that his
accompanying nurse, a girl, hated the British on principle.[47] One of
life's gentlemen, Willey doubtless caused the Germans some surprise himself; on Hamburg station platform he shook hands with
Grabenhurst, the German clerk who had been so kind to him in the
city's Altona hospital. German officers did not shake hands with
mere privates.[48]

Invariably, kindnesses towards British prisoners, whatever the
date in the war, were only performed in the absence of German
officers. Captain A.J.G. Hargreaves remembered: 'The German soldiers gave us water at night (when they thought they would not be
seen doing so).'[49] On the way to Lille a German guard tried to cover
Gilliland and the sleeping British men with straw:

This was a small act of kindness which I shall always remember . . .
We noticed that any little act of kindness . . . was never done by a
German soldier when one of his officers or N.C.O.'s was at hand.[50]

Such individual kindnesses may have been prompted by plain

humanity or Christian compassion, but generally they came from Germans who had served at the front and saw British prisoners as brothers in uniform. The sentiment was expressed perfectly by Brian Horrocks' *Feldwebel* escort, who had himself fought in the trenches as a member of the Imperial Guard. Horrocks wrote in his autobiography:

> On another occasion we went to the station-master's office to find out about trains. As there was no one in the room, my Feldwebel pushed forward a chair for me to sit on. Suddenly the door burst open and in came a typical fat, German railway official.
>
> 'Why is this English swine seated in my office?' he shouted. 'Get up!'
>
> The Feldwebel walked slowly over to him, bent down towards the little turkey-cock and said: 'This is a British officer who was wounded fighting, which you are never likely to be. He will remain seated.'
>
> And I did.
>
> Afterwards he apologised for his fellow countryman, saying: 'All front-line troops have respect for each other, but the farther from the front you get, the more bellicose and beastly the people become.'
>
> How right he was. I have always regarded the forward area of the battlefield as the most exclusive club in the world, inhabited by the cream of the nation's manhood, the men who actually do the fighting. Comparatively few in number, they have little feeling of hatred for the enemy rather the reverse.[51]

Horrocks was as good as his written word, and became firm friends with his *Feldwebel*. To Horrocks' dismay he received a letter after the war from the man's father saying his boy had been killed in his second year of fighting.

Captain Dolbey, RAMC, assuredly agreed with Horrocks' *Feldwebel* on the definite relationship between distance from the front and increased race prejudice:

> Even then I noticed that the frightfulness of the German officers and soldiers varied in direct relation to their distance from the trenches. The further away they were from the front, and judging by their

uniform the less likelihood of their ever having been under fire, the more savage did they appear.[52]

This did not bode well for British PoWs because the guards manning the 170 camps they were to be incarcerated in were, almost to a man, taken from the *Landsturm*, the German home guard. Who had never seen war, and never would.

III

THE WIRE WORLD:
LIFE AND DEATH IN THE KAISER'S CAMPS

I don't know how much longer I can stick it; my strength has
just about given out . . .

Able Seaman James Farrant, RND,
Reiskatte Reprisal Camp, East Prussia, Winter 1917

Every picture tells a story. There they are, British prisoners in
their black prison uniforms or, for the lucky ones, their familiar
khaki. They are posed with guards, who stand nearby, resem-
bling stern but concerned foremen. The huts the prisoners live in
are clean, wooden and passable in the spartan manner one would
expect, given wartime exigencies. Some prisoners are working in
fields, almost indistinguishable in the June sun from the peasant
haymakers they are assisting.

Look again. The absence of pictures tells its own story. Trawl
any military photographic archive for a sepia snapshot of British
PoWs up to their knees in water cutting peat in November in the
wind-whipped north, or down a Hameln salt mine covered in sup-
purating blisters, or forced at bayonet point by the suddenly less
remote guard to work in the Zeppelin factory at Friedrichshafen,
and you will be hard-pressed to find a single image. Germany was
the leading camera manufacturer in Europe, the land of Huttig-AG,
Zeiss and Agfa, and hundreds of peripatetic photographers plied a
trade taking 'snaps' of prisoners in a commerce as lucrative as it was
dishonest. Only the best face of prisonerdom was to be captured,
and many of the images ended up as government-blessed 'Feldpost-
karten' or were reproduced in the international press to reassure the
world of the decency of captivity under the Kaiser.

The photographic record of British prisoners in Germany is not half the story. Not even a tenth. When Private Arthur Lapworth, 12/London Regiment, was persuaded to have his photograph taken as a 'memento' (and for a price), he allowed his true feelings out in two poignant words scribbled in pencil on the reverse: 'In exile'.

British prisoners arrived in their exile hungry and exhausted after two or three days cooped up in a horse truck, and wondering what the future held.

The question was soon answered. More pain.

Generally, *Lager* were situated on the outskirts of railway towns. All too often to walk from station to camp was to perambulate a gauntlet of malevolent locals. The reception accorded Lieutenant-Colonel R.C. Bond, King's Own Yorkshire Light Infantry, on his arrival at Torgau stuck in his mind almost as well as the townsfolk's sputum stuck to his face:

> ... the mass of people seemed to be trying to get at the prisoners ... There was one very old woman who distinguished herself by the violence of her denunciations and the direction of her aim ... with three well-delivered spits! Old German women can spit![1]

In the art of spitting, German women practised strict egalitarianism regarding rank, as well as showing admirable stamina. Private William Easton arrived at Friedrichsfeld in 1918, the last year of the war and reported: 'women started spitting at us and calling us swine, and goodness knows what'.[2]

To the bemusement of British soldiers, the most hostile among the *Wilkommen* committees numbered the well-heeled as well as the distaff. Major E. Jones, Royal Field Artillery (RFA), recalled:

> The town was well lighted, and the crowds immense. All the house fronts, hotels, etc., were filled with well-dressed, well-fed people. We had great difficulty in getting through a hostile crowd, which abused us, spat at us, and threatened violence. They were drunk with wine and with hatred for us. Most of them were well-dressed people from the middle classes.[3]

The housing of the enemy nearby was of understandable alarm

and provocation to the local citizenry. Not that such an explanation was consolation to British prisoners beaten with sticks or, in
the case of those marching to Klein Wittenberg in the Mark of
Brandenburg, iron bars. For Corporal R. Burrows, Royal Scots
Fusiliers, who tramped to Süderzollhaus in freezing Schleswig
Holstein, the hostile attitude of the town's burghers was likely the
last thing on his mind: 'Many of us had no boots but we had to
march 10 kilometres. Many fainted on the way but were kicked up.'[4]

Corporal Burrows was hobbling to a *Mannschaftslager,* a camp
for NCOs and other ranks. By the articles (not always observed
by the Germans)[5] of the Hague Convention, officers and men were
socially segregated in captivity. Only in scale and accommodation
did *Offizierslager* and *Mannschaftslager* truly differ. Whereas the
average officers' camp housed 500–600 men, *Lager* for NCOs and
enlisted men were of Brobdingnagian proportions, with the capacity of the standard *Mannschaftslager* reaching 12,000 men by
1916. Some *Mannschlaftslager* were great grey cities; Schneidemuhl
Mannschaftslager housed up to 50,000 men. Whether *Offizierslager* or *Mannschaftslager* the camps were managed by the regional
army corps. While the Prussian War Ministry laid down central
standards, the commanders of the twenty-five districts had great
autonomy, and were answerable to God and the Kaiser in that order.
Likewise, the commandant of each individual camp enjoyed a free-
ish reign. *Alles hängt vom Kommandant ab* – 'All depends on the
commander' – was the watchword of the German PoW system. The
life of the British prisoner would depend much on the personality
of the *Lager* commandant. Ultimately, though, all commandants
were steeped to the core in the Prussian way of discipline, which
required instant obedience and considered brutality ordinary. All
commandants would bow to the rapacious needs of the German
war economy.

Officer camps were established in country houses, universities, forts and, as the war progressed, in cavalry barracks, since
horse-warfare was blindingly outmoded. Crefeld *Lager* had previously been the home of the 11th Hussars. The *Offizierslager* at
Clausthal in the Harz Mountains was a former '*Kurhaus*' beside a

lake – although *Kommandant* Heinrich Niemeyer was decidedly not running a health resort. Perhaps only his twin brother, Karl, the commandant of Holzminden, was a bigger bully.

Old castles made popular conversions; the Bishop's Castle at Beeskow dated to the thirteenth century, while Celle Schloss was formerly home to the kings of Hannover. Lieutenant Alec Waugh thought the interior walls of Mainz Citadel unprepossessing as they were daubed with human shapes for shooting practice; on the other hand the Citadel, which dated from 1660, offered unparalleled views over the Rhine. Like Mainz, Karlsruhe *Lager* (along with Rastatt, the main distribution camp for British officers) was unusual in being located plumb in the centre of a town. In the case of Karlsruhe, British PoWs were of the unshiftable belief that inmates were human shields and the camp precisely located to deter RFC raids. Or as Lieutenant Lee versed, Karlsruhe was:

> Umpteen huts in umpteen rows,
> Dumped in a spot where the bomber goes,
> A wooden fence and strands of wire,
> A few odd Sentries with orders to fire,
> That's our Camp![6]

When Captain Lyall Grant and his companions set eyes on Schwarmstedt on Lüneburg Heath they 'nearly threw a fit'.[7] After a seven-kilometre walk along a sandy track through woods they were confronted by hastily built, leaky, draughty huts ringed by barbed wire. There was no room in the huts for even a small table between the straw mattress beds. Inmates nicknamed it 'Swamp Camp' because no less than three pumps failed to keep it dry. A favourite pastime recorded Lieutenant Will Harvey was catching lice, beetles and cockroaches; each morning 'exhibits from the inter-barracks bug-hunting competition were pinned to the doors of the rooms'. Perhaps inevitably, this 'sporting and scientific event' became *verboten* because it was deemed insulting to the Kaiser.[8]

All British officers were convinced that Schwarmstedt was the most uncomfortable of *Offizierslager*, until they ended up in a *strafe* or punishment camp like Strohen-Moor – another chicken-run set-up, but with the added disadvantage of being on wind-chilling open moorland. The sanitation system leaked into the well. Fort 9 at Ingolstadt in Bavaria was a semi-underground casement whose internal walls oozed water. In winter the rooms gave the appearance of being inside an igloo. While Lieutenant Horace Gilliland sojourned there the temperature in the cells reached 32 below. With fuel rationed, he did the only sensible thing and made repeated requests to see the commandant in his office. At every audience Gilliland stole large black lumps from the *Chef*'s coal box ('Ah! That was a little job worthy of the daring'). Lieutenant Gilliland, on his forced tour of the Kaiser's *Lager*, also landed in Munden, a former oil factory. Thanks to the *Kriegsministerium* policy of deliberately mixing Allied nationalities together – in the hope they would fight and fall out – he shared a thirty-foot-square room with sixteen Russians and one tiny air vent. No eating utensils were provided. 'One was forced to dip one's hand into the pail, take out some of the frightful food, or go without and starve.'[9] At Fort Zorndorf, 'a sort of penal camp', Brian Horrocks and other confirmed officer escapers 'lived in dark galleries underground'.[10] There was no light for days on end in winter. Magdeburg *Lager* was a former warehouse; there were few internal divisions. The abiding impression of Magdeburg in the mind of medical officer L.J. Austin was 'the entire impossibility of getting away from one's fellow creatures for even a minute, and the perpetual noise in the rooms'.[11] In a pathetic attempt at privacy officers at Crefeld forfeited their shared rooms and made individual cardboard or wooden 'huts' in the passageways. Lieutenant Colin Campbell, Argyll and Sutherland Highlanders, did such a good job of partioning off his corner of Hut C at Torgau that it was known as 'Chateau Campbell'. The secrecy offered by the partitioning was advisable. An escape tunnel started under his bed.

Very few *Mannschaftslager* were converted fortresses, barracks or other buildings; most were austere purpose-built enclosures on heathland and fields. To the apprehensive prisoners trudging to their main gate, they all looked the same: sentry boxes with black-and-white down-pointing chevrons. Horizontal strands of barbed-wire on pine-tree posts making a perimeter fence nineteen feet high, an inner barbed-wire fence behind it. Looming wooden watchtowers at the four corners with machine guns. Spindly arc lights reaching into the sky. Guards with dogs patrolling the perimeter. A sign with the wingspread black Imperial Eagle, 'the Carrion Eater', under which the prisoners entered.

Private Edward Page, arriving at Munster in Westphalia on Bonfire Night 1914, was put in a canvas shelter which had been used for temporary stabling of horses; the straw for the prisoners' bedding had been permanently ruined by soaking up equine urine and faeces. The proper camp accommodation and its wire-walls were being built; the unwounded like Page were compelled to assist in their construction. Private Page built his own prison.

At Döberitz, where the Germans again failed to provide any shelter aside from ragged tents, PoWs excavated dug-outs. A group of Royal Navy boys, either suffering a pang for things maritime or overflowing with 'We'll show 'em pride' (or maybe even both), dug an underground hut that perfectly resembled the inside of a submarine.

When the age of tents was over, other ranks prisoners generally slept in hastily made, thin-wood barrack huts about 300 feet long and 35 feet wide. The huts were on stilts, and arranged in rows. Uniform huts in maddening uniform rows. The 'average prison barrack' was described by one observer thus:

> Low long rows of double-tier bunks take up the central floor space of the barrack. Long tables for serving food are placed next to the walls. Bags filled with straw, sea grass or paper serve as mattresses. Every available space is used for food packages and clothes. The place has a dim, confused, unkempt appearance on account of the crowding of men, the arrangement of the bunks, food packages, clothes etc.[12]

Huts generally held two hundred prisoners. Sometimes a German NCO was placed in charge of the huts, sometimes a British sergeant, referred to as *Dolmetscher* (translator) by the Germans. To Tommies he was always a 'dumb-major'. His was a thankless task, being both buffer and go-between, but in general British prisoners preferred one of their own in charge of the hut.[13]

New arrivals had to endure a lengthy medical procedure before they got to see the inside of a barrack hut. Camp regulations in the majority of districts required prisoners to be de-loused, inoculated and quarantined on arrival. When the *Lager* gates closed on Corporal John Brady, King's Own Yorkshire Light Infantry, captured at Le Cateau on 26 August, he had his 'hair cut like a convict'.[14] A still closer shave awaited Corporal L.G.B. Eastwood, Border Regiment, at Worms:

> When we arrived there, we had to be disinfected. They had great tubs filled with disinfectant, and you had to climb right inside them – you'd see a chap with his head sticking out. Then they'd shave all the hair off your body – the Russians did that under instructions from the Germans.[15]

Prisoners were also relieved of any francs or shillings still somehow in their possession. These were sometimes exchanged for Marks, though more commonly they would be issued with escape-unfriendly camp tokens. The rate of exchange, one prisoner lamented, was 'abysmal'.[16] Troublemakers, such as those officers detailed for Holzminden, a bad boys' camp for officers, might expect what Douglas Lyall Grant euphemistically termed a body search of 'the most rigorous nature'. That is, they were stripped naked and orifices examined.

Well-run camps, particularly as the war went on, had 'lousoleums', which were delousing huts where clothes as well as men were fumigated. In here too, men were quarantined for fourteen days and inoculated. Lance-Corporal Thomas Higgins was alarmed to be vaccinated five times when he passed through the barbed-wire doors of Dülmen; a year later Frank MacDonald was inoculated with no less than 'seven doses providing against every known disease'. The jabs were straight to the chest, one after the other.

The delousing regime was no respecter of military status. Where facilities existed officers had their hair cropped close, and were treated with anti-lice preparations. Archer Cust was discontented to be unceremoniously daubed at Rastatt 'with some sulphuric substance'. 'What treatment for British officers!'[17]

Lucky were the arrivals whose clothes were fumigated, and who were treated for body lice. Luckier still were the prisoners whose camp had an attached fumigator. Everyone else was condemned to a life with lice. Corporal John Brady, King's Own Yorkshire Light Infantry, had 'millions' of them at Sennelager: 'I was three months and never had a wash with soap I only had one shirt never was washed for three months all that time we had to go out to work if we were sick.'[18] There were camps – Döberitz among them – where two taps had to serve thousands of men.

Scratching at lice, which lived off human blood, caused impetigo and nephritis. Some prisoners became sensitized to each body-louse, each bite, making sleep impossible. Whole hours were given over to sitting nude – one soon lost inhibitions in the Kaiser's camps – and crushing grey scuttling *pediculus vestmenti* between thumb and forefinger. In summer the prisoners at sandy Sennelager put their shirts in ant heaps and 'the enterprising insects would hunt most carefully through shirts spread out upon the ground near their nests and carry off the louse and her eggs in triumph'.[19] But even ants were not multitudinous enough to defeat lice. Until the Germans consented to the inclusion of safety razors in parcels from Blighty, British prisoners grew lousy beards to rival Rasputin and Robinson Crusoe. Or took the painful course followed by Lance-Corporal Thomas Higgins, who found a jack-knife in the rubbish and sharpened it up on a stone. Some men were tougher yet, employing honed tin lids as cut-throats.

To the inconvenience of the Germans, and the perplexity of the Russians and French, the British were wedded to washing and bathing. On tipping up at Koningsberg penal fortress, Flight Lieutenant L. Dalzell McLean, RN,[20] was horrified to discover the bathing habits of his fellow Allies:

On arrival I found that the Russian officers only had a bath once in three weeks, and I demanded to have a hot one once a week and a cold each morning. The German officer was extremely offensive when I asked for this, but we got our bath once a week, and, after some weeks' continual rowing, also the cold ones.[21]

Cold baths were in vogue in Edwardian and Georgian Britain, and were an essential part of the popular health-and-physical fitness regime propounded by guru Lieutenant J.P. Muller.[22] The British love of bathing gave any bloody-minded commandant an effortlessly easy punishment. He turned off the taps. The 'brutish' Karl Niemeyer at Holzminden ('Hellminden' to all who attended) went one better and gave the shower block over to his Alsatians as a kennel. One of the Buggins who ran Mainz *Offizierslager* was infinitely more sly; he made bathing compulsory, which subtly suggested he believed the British to be behind Teutonic standards of cleanliness. 'This was enforced by means of bath tickets, which had to be handed in to an NCO,' recalled Lieutenant T.J. Dobson, RNVR. 'It was a form of insult in which the authorities took delight.'[23]

Prisoners wore what they were captured in, until luck or a parcel brought replacements. Any man who had come through hard battle or wounding lived in shreds and ribbons. According to Lance-Corporal Thomas Higgins:

> Our clothes were in rags, we had only what we were captured in. My shoes were completely worn off my feet. They gave me a pair of wooden sabots to wear, they were awful to walk in, the wooden sides rubbed my feet raw. I had to wrap my feet in old rags. When I had nothing else, I ripped part of my shirt off to wrap round them.[24]

Sabots or clogs were usually made in the camp; as jobs went, it was deemed 'cushy' and it was long a complaint of the British prisoner that this sitting-down occupation in the dry was invariably given to the French.

The problem of footwear was compounded by the German tendency to confiscate a prisoner's boots as punishment, leaving him to wear the ubiquitous ill-fitting clogs or to go barefoot. Private W. Butcher, 1/Queen's Regiment, was tied to a post in snow for three hours for stealing a loaf of bread at Güstrow, and as an additional punishment had his footwear permanently removed. He developed frostbite and several of his toes had to be taken off; the German doctor used a penknife and a pair of scissors to perform the operation. No chloroform was given.[25]

Tommies who had been relieved of their greatcoats on capture – the vast majority – wore blankets as a covering for head and shoulders in winter. James Farrant and his fellows at Güstrow found some oilskins, which they tied over the top of the thin blankets, giving them the appearance of lifeboat-men. Whatever the prisoners decked themselves in, thick identifying stripes of bright red or yellow paint were daubed along sleeves and the side of trousers, and 'bad boys' had the letters KG (*Kriegsgefangener*) painted on the back of their jackets. If the Germans could be persuaded to dole out clothing, it came from plunder and off the bodies of dead PoWs, leaving the men in a hotchpotch of British, French and Belgian clothing, a sort of walking sartorial statement of Allied unity.

From spring 1915 the Red Cross began to ship a 'prisoner uniform' to Germany, which consisted of a dark bluey-black serge jacket, trousers and cap, along with underclothes and shirts. Since, for would-be escapers, the Red Cross uniform handily lent itself to a perfect imitation of a working man's clothing, the Germans had camp tailors insert wide coloured strips into sleeves and trouser legs. In the better-run camps the Red Cross uniform became well, uniform. Elsewhere prisoners remained in rags; the American naval attaché noted on a visit to Geissen in December 1915 that: 'A very large majority [of British PoWs] were without overcoats, a great number without suitable shoes and many without underclothing and socks.'[26]

British officers generally had an easier time than other ranks over clothing due to Prussian insistence they be correctly attired on parade. Accordingly, on capture, they were allowed to write home for additional and replacement clothing to be forwarded in parcels. Alternatively, officers could contact their London tailor direct.

Whether a prisoner was commissioned, non-commissioned or enlisted, wearing the same clothes for months on end, with little or no opportunity to wash them, was uncomfortable, unhealthy and demoralizing. Lieutenant Archer Cust's pleasure on receiving a parcel of clothing from home is tangible: 'Oh the joy of getting a change after the same boots, breeches, and tunic for three and a half months.' In the first parcel was his Eton OTC shirt and old staff hat. 'So funny to see these old friends again.'[27]

*

The wrath of winter was unforgiving on the sandy plain at Klein Wittenberg in December 1914. A wind whipped in from Siberia, sending temperatures plunging to minus 20 and freezing the water troughs in the newly built *Lager*, which occupied a 10.5 acre site adjoining the railway line to Berlin. Rather than venture outside, the 17,000 prisoners squeezed into the fetid wooden huts.

Body against body did little to keep out the cold, because most of the PoWs' greatcoats had been pilfered and rations of fuel were too paltry to keep the two stoves per cavernous barracks running. The men – most of them Russians captured at Tannenberg, but including around seven hundred British as well as a number of French – were underfed. Each man received a daily ration consisting of one cup of black acorn coffee, 100 grams of black bread, thin soup from potato and horse beans for lunch, and a thinner soup containing grease, usually margarine, in the evening.

The lying together of overcrowded, starving prisoners at Wittenberg produced a disaster as great as if God himself had come down and smitten the land. By order of the *Kriegsministerium* each mattress in the camp was shared by a Frenchman, a Briton and a Russian. This forced mingling of the nations condemned hundreds of British and French prisoners to death as certainly as putting them before a firing squad. Because their Russian bedmates carried lice which harboured the typhus bacterium *Rickettsie prowazekii*; the Russians had a level of immunity to the disease, British and French did not.

On Christmas Eve men started dying at Wittenberg. Instead of devoting proper resources to treating the sick, the German staff, led by the commandant, General von Dassel, opened the internal gates to allow the healthy and the diseased to freely mix. Then the Germans evacuated the camp. Utterly, totally abandoned it, setting Alsatian dogs to patrol outside the wire to make sure the diseased could not leave. Supplies for the prisoners were thrown over the wire, or pushed through on a trolley running on a twenty-yard

railroad, all so there was no actual physical contact with the pari-
ahs. Not until the Fleck typhus epidemic had been running amok
for over a month were six British RAMC doctors (detained at Halle
despite the Geneva Convention rules on non-combatants) sent to
Wittenberg. The six were Major Fry, Major Priestley, Captain Sutcliffe, Captain Vidal, Captain Field and Lieutenant Lauder.

On entering Wittenberg the good doctors happened upon scenes
of suffering so appalling that Major Fry broke down. Dead and
living were lying next to each other in the crammed dim-lit huts;
since there were no stretchers, the sick were moved around on table
tops on which the men ate. These could not be cleaned because
there was no soap. Some who had survived typhus had succumbed
to gangrene because there were no blankets, socks or shoes to keep
them warm. Almost everyone was grey, pallid and running with
lice. According to the subsequent official British report, the appo-
sitely named 'The Horrors of Wittenberg':

> Major Priestley saw delirious men waving arms brown to the elbow
> with faecal matter. The patients were alive with vermin; in the half-
> light he attempted to brush what he took to be an accumulation of
> dust from the folds of a patient's clothes, and he discovered it to be a
> moving mass of lice.[28]

Those patients who had been moved to the so-called camp hospital
were on a diet of half a *petit pain* and half a cup of milk per day.
There were no bedpans or toilet paper, and no more than half a
dozen beds for a hundred men.

Through tireless work and incessant seeking of supplies, the
British doctors, aided by fifty volunteers from among the inmates,
eventually triumphed over the disease. By July 1915 the cases had
dwindled to zero. The cost was high. Of the 1,975 typhus cases recorded between 15 January and 23 July 1915 at Wittenberg, 185 men
died, 60 of them British. The fatalities included three of the six
RAMC doctors – Major Fry, Captain Field, Captain Sutcliffe – along
with ten of the volunteers: Lance-Corporal E. Long, Loyal North
Lancashire; Lance-Corporal P. Almond, LNL; Lance-Corporal
Alfred McDonald, RIR; Private P. Wright, LNL; Private J. Gormley,

LNL; Private W. Jackson, Middlesex; Private George Ramsay, Camerons; Private W. Rennell, S. Lancashire; Private J. Ward, LNL.

Alfred McDonald was well known to Malcolm Hay, as the two had convalesced together at No. 106 Hospital in France. Of young McDonald, Hay wrote: 'he died a hero's death in Wittenberg'. The Government Committee on the Treatment by the Enemy of British Prisoners of War was similarly moved to praise the volunteers of Wittenberg:

> The Committee feel that every one of these officers and men as truly offered his life for the sake of others as any soldier on the battlefield, and they venture to hope that the devoted service of such of them as survive will be duly remembered at the proper time.[29]

A number were indeed awarded medals and Mentions in Dispatches in 1919, among them Sergeant Thomas Miller, Highland Light Infantry, whom Major Priestley described thus: 'He was of the greatest possible use to me as regards discipline and further he distributed parcels and clothing and I placed him in charge of this when I left the Camp. I consider his conduct worthy of the highest praise.'

A black obelisk memorial, paid for by the British survivors of the epidemic, was erected in 1921 'in honour of those who died during the Typhus Epidemic 1914–1915'. It was moved to its present position in the local church graveyard in the 1960s.

Along with the sinking of the *Lusitania* and the shooting of Nurse Cavell, the typhus epidemic at Wittenberg sealed the hearts of the British into bitterness against Germany. Only once during the entire epidemic did the official German camp physician, Doktor Aschenbach, enter Wittenberg. He did so, recalled Captain Vidal, 'in a complete suit of protective clothing, including mask and gloves'. His inspection was 'very rapid'. Aschenbach was instrumental in refusing the request of the RAMC doctors ('*Englische Schweine*') that the British prisoners be segregated from the Russians on the inevitable and sarcastic grounds that the British should get to know their allies better. Improbably, Aschenbach was awarded the Iron Cross for his dutiful 'gallantry' at Wittenberg.

Typhus smote at least thirty major German camps between December 1914 and July 1915, among them Gardelegen, Kassel (7,000 cases), Cottbus (1,765), and Schneidemuhl (where every British prisoner save eleven was hospitalized). At Minden the commandant provoked uproar among the British PoWs by refusing to allow the Anglican chaplain to visit the sick and dying. As at Wittenberg, the local populace cheered when the British coffins were wheeled out through the gate. Wittenberg. The cradle of the Reformation.

Historians have generally amnestied the Imperial regime for the terrible typhus epidemic of 1914–15, accepting the argument of, among others, the German Inspector General of PoW Camps of IV Army Corps that typhus was almost unknown in Germany before 1914. In fact, the link between poor hygiene and typhus was accepted by German scientists before the war's beginning. And Austrian military regulations of 1911 identified lice as the most likely carrier of the disease. There was, of course, no excuse other than blatant self-preservation for abandoning the camp.

What a devil's delight of diseases the Kaiser's camps incubated! Sent to Sennelager, Captain Robert Dolbey, RAMC, encountered 'almost every infectious disease' known, headed by scarlet fever, tuberculosis, pneumonia, typhoid, dysentery, cerebro-spinal meningitis, mumps and measles. Sewage dumped above the camp seeped into the stream which was the sole source of water for washing, including food bowls. The lack of hygiene extended to the camp hospital or lazaret:

In the hospital there were no sanitary conveniences, no nursing utensils of any kind; men who were actually ill had to go 50 yards in the coldest weather to the latrines. There was only one clinical thermometer in the whole camp; this was passed indiscriminately from mouth to mouth without any attempt at disinfection. One large bucket in the corner of each room was the only sanitary article.

Our men had to bring their lousy blankets with them from the camps and place them on still more verminous palliasses in the hospital; they slept and were nursed in their clothes. There was no hospital linen whatever, not one sheet or shirt or bed-gown or pillow. A man would come into hospital gravely ill with pneumonia, for instance, and pass the whole weeks of his disease in the same shirt, tunic and trousers, with which he had come out to France four months before.[30]

Dolbey complained to the *Chef-Arzt* about the lack of sanitation, who replied 'Shut your jaws'. Dolbey was perhaps more fortunate than he knew; Captain Vidal at Wittenberg was physically attacked by an NCO for his temerity in complaining about the dearth of Imperial hospital provision. With the doggedness that defined the men of 1914–18, Dolbey prepared a comprehensive written report on the deplorable death rate among the British. This time the German response was to throw him in a cell; British other ranks stole food for him.

Expecting German doctors to treat enemies as well as they treated their fellow countrymen was always a high moral expectation, especially when patriotic emotions ran red. A doctor at Güstrow consistently refused to help the English, saying 'if they had not come into the war they would not be there'.[31] Exiled and helpless in this alien land prisoners could assume maltreatment, up to and including amputation of limbs – not just toes or fingers – without anaesthetics as happened to an Australian officer at the Würzburg lazeret : 'I shouted out and struggled violently, breaking the operating table.'[32] He had had both his legs sawn off.

The butcher of Würzburg lazeret was hardly unique in his medical cruelties towards prisoners. And where there was not violence, there was often poor practice, with bedsheets unchanged for weeks and bandages swopped from patient to patient. Of the 11,147 British PoWs officially recorded as having perished in captivity, the fate of hundreds of individuals can be attributed to medical negligence and sadism. But disease was the main reaper of British lives. In the teeming wire world, disease was a constant companion. Captain Dolbey's personal survey of bacilli and viruses missed those which caused smallpox – from which one luckless Briton perished – relapse fever, cholera, and rigid cramp. A bare minimum of 2,735 British PoWs died from communicable diseases, with tuberculosis

(485 deaths) and pneumonia (1,389 deaths) the biggest killers.[33] Following a dip in the death rate between 1915–17 due to improvements in the sanitary conditions of the main camps, the rate rose sharply in 1918 when the German Army put tens of thousands of prisoners in impromptu labour camps behind the front line. Medical supplies by then had almost run dry. A British government report described the tragic conditions at Flavy-le-Martel in the Aisne in summer 1918:

> Into sheds capable of accommodating at the utmost 450 men, over 1000 were crowded. The sanitary and washing arrangements were so primitive as to be practically non-existent . . . In a very short time the men were starving, verminous and in a filthy condition with the inevitable consequence that dysentery appeared almost at once and men began to die with appalling regularity.[34]

All that could be had by the way of medicine was a potion of nettles boiled in water. Between 5 April and 10 June 1918 seventy British prisoners at Flavy-le-Martel died of dysentery.

Flavy-le-Martel earned itself a small footnote in the history of ignominy. For his failure to maintain hygienic conditions at Flavy-le-Martel the commandant, Emil Müller, was charged with war crimes at Leipzig in 1920. During the trial it emerged that Captain Müller, a giant of a man, habitually kicked and thrashed the dying prisoners. Unlike other Germans, he was a keen photographer of depravity in the camps. His favourite snaps were of diseased, incontinent men using the latrine.

*

In the quarantine compound, the prisoners received their introduction to the starvation diet of the German *Lager*. Any prisoners fortunate enough to have concealed valuables now lost them in bartering for food – any food – tossed over the wire or pushed through a window. Canadian survivors of Ypres, with no valuables between them, sold their boots and shirts for handfuls of bread or a ladle of soup.[35] They had no bowls for the soup, so had to use their helmets.

According to the Hague rules, a prisoner was to receive the same rations as troops of the detaining Army. In a refinement, the *Kriegs-ministerium* in April 1915 undertook to ensure that a 'plentiful diet' was the happy lot of its uniformed guests. British prisoners only remembered hunger as their allotment from the German authorities. At Güstrow, Private E. Caine, 1/Dorset Regiment, recalled:

> The food ration was barely sufficient to keep one alive; Breakfast: Soup (rice water). Dinner: Cabbage water or foul-smelling soup made from boar's head. Supper: Soup, and sometimes raw herring ... Every four days a loaf weighing about a kilo was served to each man. This bread was very hard and heavy, sometimes almost uneatable; we frequently found whole potatoes embedded in it.[36]

The great dilemma was whether to scoff the bread or try to make it last, one hour's glorious satiety versus a minuscule edge taken off gnawing hunger over a day or several. During his 'hungry days' on arrival at Mainz, Lieutenant Alec Waugh received one proper meal a day, which was lunch: 'Life simplified itself into an attempt to spread out a small loaf of bread over four days. It did not often succeed.'[37]

Thievery had to be factored in as well, as Lance-Corporal Higgins explained:

> When you got your daily piece of bread you had to eat it at once, or it would get stolen off you by your hungry mates. You would steal food off your best friend. Hunger knew no law.[38]

Anyone caught stealing 'rooty', as bread was universally known to British troops, was likely to receive rough justice. At Döberitz one such malefactor was offered, after a court martial by Royal Navy petty officers, the choice of being reported to the Germans or running the gauntlet. He chose the gauntlet, two rows of men whipping him with knotted wet towels.

Men who rationed their bread dole on the little-but-often basis slept with it under their heads, or carried it around with them in a trouser pocket. Since loaves of bread needed to be divided among barrack-room inmates, this was done under watchful eyes. Corporal

L.G.B. Eastwood at Worms: 'We used to weigh each portion on a pair of home-made scales. You had to eat your bit quickly otherwise somebody'd pinch it.'[39]

No knives were allowed in the *Lager*. James Farrant at Döberitz used a spoon handle sharpened on stones to cut bread. Not that knives were really necessary because, with the exception of the war-economy black bread ('KK bread', meaning 'Kleie und Kartoffeln', bran and potato, but usually made from sawdust and potato), the German rations could all be consumed with a spoon. Private A.W. Green, Lancashire Fusiliers, lamented in his diary: 'Soup, soup, nothing but soup.' According to Lieutenant Archer Cust at Graudenz:

> Everyday there was an imposing menu of about eight items put up, but except for beetroot about three times a week, jam substitute twice, gherkins twice, and a bit of sausage once, and the daily coffee and tea substitutes, everything was in the soup.

The worst day of the week at Graudenz *Offizierslager* was Wednesday, when flakes of fish were served in water with mustard, and a dash of meal. A dog could scarcely be asked to eat it, Cust believed, 'yet from hunger, I have eaten platefuls of it'.[40]

To try and stave off hunger 'the whole camp to a man' lay smoking on their beds in the afternoon. The protruding bones of Cust's malnourished legs rubbed together at night. Others, perversely, bloated out hideously; the liquid nature of the *Lager* diet caused dropsy, leaving many camp survivors with a legacy of gastric disorders.

The hunger was greatest for those sent to slave for the Wilhelmine Reich. Corporal Arthur Speight, 7/Durham Light Infantry, in a forced labour gang behind the German lines on the Aisne in summer 1918, left a description of his rations:

> We began our day's work by being walked on and walloped with sticks while it was still dark. Then we were shoved into lines of four men and issued with a drink of coffee made from burnt barley. A piece of bread was the day's ration but as most of the fellows were nearly mad for food the first one got the most – if he was strong

enough to keep it! Our work would carry on until about five in the afternoon . . . On arriving at the lager we were issued with another meal. This meal consisted of stewed something. At first this was sometimes macaroni with a very little meat mixed with it. By about June it had become dried vegetables. This mess of pottage consisted of turnip skins dried almost to resemble chips of wood, chopped up like sawdust and mixed with boiling water.[41]

There was worse. Private Reginald Morris, toiling at Douai in 1918, had a daily allotment of coffee at 4 a.m. and nothing at all until 5 p.m., when he was doled a dinner of horse beans, an inch cube of black sausage, and a teaspoonful of turnip-saccharine jam.[42] He sold his precious watch for a bag of crusts from the Italian chef. Morris' barracks were 'a cold, dry, dark, dirty dungeon of a brick-kiln'.

There was yet worse. James Farrant was dispatched in early 1917 to Reiskatte on the Russian Front. The sign hanging over the gate of their barbed-wire enclosure read 'Vergeltung Lager' – Reprisal Camp. Farrant and his fellows were victims of one of the tit-for-tats between the British and German governments over the treatment of prisoners; in revenge for Britain supposedly making German PoWs work within 7 kilometres of the Western Front, the German government made British PoWs work 0.137 kilometres from the Russian front line. The work was clearing snow out of German trenches and cutting timber for nine frostbitten hours a day. When they weren't dodging Russian machine-gun bullets, that is. The rations were two-fifths of a three-pound loaf per day (the only solid food), one cup of coffee, and bowl of soup. Farrant's accommodation was a dug-out. 'We were like skeletons; shoulder bones, hip bones, knees and elbows were horribly prominent.' Eventually the reprisal was lifted, but not before Able Seaman Young, RND, had died.

Starvation reduced British troops to savages; their treatment portended that of the Jews and other concentration camp inmates under the Nazis. Arthur Speight was watching as a fellow inmate, Corporal Costello, sorted mouldy bread from good, throwing the former into the open midden of Ramecourt camp. As Speight looked on,

Two wrecks of humanity crawled to the latrine on hands and knees

and plunged their arms into the filth to recover the bread. Costello
yelled at them that the stuff would kill them, but still they were
intent on getting it, whereupon Costello ran forward and flung them
bodily from the hole. He then turned away and said: 'Well, I don't
know, the poor —s will die anyway.'[43]

That terrible scene was repeated elsewhere. Corporal R. Burrows,
Royal Scots Fusiliers, when imprisoned at Güstrow recorded that:

Many men died from eating dirty rubbish, such as potato peelings,
mouldy bread thrown away from the stores etc. I remember the
following names of the men who died so:-
    Private Worsfold, the Queen's
    Private Robinson, the Lincolns
    Private Poulton, Royal Scots Fusiliers
    Private Wilson, Royal Scots Fusiliers

Not infrequently, the German method of dispensing bread and
other food was a 'parade' where it was handed out first come, first
served. Private Page at Munster remembered:

I was successful in gaining possession of a plate containing two or
three potatoes and a little burnt rice, after a struggle, for we were
not much better than a pack of hungry wolves, and shared it with a
corporal of Marines, McKerdle by name, who had the misfortune to
lose the sight of one of his eyes at Antwerp. Standing in the pouring
rain, holding the plate between us, we ate the contents ravenously,
listening to the howls and shouts of our less fortunate comrades,
who not being successful in securing a plateful at the general issue
– there was not sufficient to go all round – were fighting amongst
themselves over the burnt remains on the bottom of the copper.[44]

It did not pay to investigate the contents of meals too closely, as
Frank MacDonald discovered:

One day Wallie and I, who had managed to stick together, picked
all the bones out of a potful of soup and, sorting them out carefully,
managed to piece together the skeleton of a German dachshund.[45]

Corporal Speight recorded seal, horses' lights (lungs) and pickled spinach on his menu list. Thomas Higgins lived – if it could be called living – for weeks on thin skilly made from either boiled turnips or mangelwurzels. 'Another fearful meal was white cabbage kept until it was sour, then boiled.'[46] Sauerkraut. Much of the food given prisoners was preserved in salt, leading to desperate thirst at night. Watery food, on the other hand, led to a need to urinate and sleeplessness. Visits to the latrine were accompanied by a guard, who always seemed too free with the butt-end of a rifle.

In the absence of food, men dreamed or thought of little else. Or pathetically tried to make the German diet more interesting. In Rastatt, Archer Cust gave over hours to 'making pies':

> I used to line a small mug with thin slices of bread, pour in a few spoonfuls of vegetable or barley soup, and let it set, the result being a poor but very acceptable substitute for bacon and eggs in the morning.[47]

Officers were charged for their food. Gilbert Nobbs was billed forty-five Marks per month at Osnabrück in 1915 for repasts 'only fit for pigs'. By the end of the war many officers were paying up sixty Marks a month for 'swill.' It is no coincidence that these sums matched exactly the pay sent to subalterns in prison in Germany by HM Government.

German rations *could* be supplemented. When Arthur Speight was working on the railway near Amifontaine in 1918 German troops used to lob him bread and cigarettes from their trains as they passed to and fro the front. An old *Landsturmer* allowed him to gather snails from the hedgerows of Arras. He probably collected nettles too, for most prisoners did, the snatched haul of plants being carried desperately back to camp to make a soup.

Sapper George Waymark enjoyed a different sort of foraging at Fromelles, where he was put to work repairing roads; he found a tin of Fray Bentos in a trench, recording in his diary: 'First meat I've tasted since I have been a prisoner. I never realized until now how good bully beef is.'[48]

Officers' camps and some main *Mannschaftslager* had a so-called *Kantine*, which sold just about everything save food. The paucity of edible goods was not just the result of 'frightfulness'; the Allied blockade of Germany had real effect. All Archer Cust could purchase from the canteen at Graudenz were: Salem Aleikum cigarettes from Dresden (1.15 pfennig each) and 'Russian salad', a vinegar salad containing mussels: 'we ate this relish, disgusting as it was'.

One commodity the *Kantinen* provided in abundance was water, and anyone with spare cash and opportunity availed themselves of it; Schwarmstedt was hardly unique in having latrines that leaked into the drinking water supply. The manager at Osnabrück charged Gilbert Nobbs five pfennigs for a kettle of boiling water. Like many a German behind the counter, he was an arch wheeler-dealer. The *Kantine* manager at Cassel 'fleeced us of our money', declared Sergeant George Wells after paying 2 Marks for a small packet of tobacco that turned out to be 'rank stuff composed of rose and violet leaves'. This was modest extortion compared to the 20 Marks for a tin of sardines at Friedrichsfeld *Kantine*, which 'Englishmen could not afford', lamented a hungry Private George Agnew of the Light Black Watch. At Holzminden the *Kantine* was run by the commandant, 'Charlie' Niemeyer, who profiteered with abandon; according to one estimate he made 55,000 Marks from selling fuel to his captive British customers over a six-month period, from September 1917 (when the camp, another former cavalry barracks, opened) to March 1918. In searching for a cheaper fuel alternative, the British prisoners discovered that German war-issue black bread burned pleasingly well.

From the beginning of the war, there was one obvious lifeline for starving prisoners: a food parcel. Despite the war, packets and letters still travelled between Britain and Germany via the neutral countries of Denmark, Switzerland, and Holland. The first parcels were sent informally by friends and relatives, often more in anxiety than sense; one prisoner recalled being sent a packet of sandwiches. Unwilling to miss a commercial opportunity, London emporia such as Fortnum & Mason, Harrods, the Army & Navy Stores, and Selfridges all advertised parcels for prisoners ('What to send to Germany') by the end of 1914, with prices ranging from 5 shillings to £1. Since the first prisoners were Regulars, their depots naturally became the place for prisoners' friends and relatives to meet. Under the auspices of the Church Army, an Anglican charity, these associations of family and friends became 'Regimental Care Committees'; by June 1915 there were ninety-three Regimental Care Committees across the land, an extraordinary voluntary effort. Inevitably, some Mister Pooter in government decided that the Regimental Care Committees required coordination and set the Prisoners of War Help Committee (PWHC) above them. The Savoy Hotel was deemed the suitable seat for this bureaucracy. The PWHC found supervision of the massive traffic in parcels wholly beyond its ken, with a large percentage of the prisoners getting too little food; and a small percentage too much. One report into the PWHC's doings calculated that the excess food trundling to certain prisoners in Germany was 'enough to feed an entire German division'. The Army, meanwhile, was concerned that outbound parcels might contain articles and information likely to be of use to the enemy. An exasperated War Office handed responsibility for food and clothing supply to prisoners to a Red Cross-run Central Prisoners of War Committee which moved into premises at Numbers 3 and 4 Thurloe Place, South Kensington, London. By the end of the war 750 people were employed at the Thurloe Place depot. The goal was to provide each prisoner with three 10 lb parcels and 13 lb of bread once a fortnight. A typical Red Cross parcel contained:

1 lb Beef
½ lb Vegetables
1 lb Sausages
½ lb Cheese (Tin)
¼ lb Tea
½ lb Nestlé's Milk
½ lb Sugar
½ lb Margarine (or Dripping)
1 lb Jam
1 lb Biscuits

50 Cigarette (or 2 oz Tobacco and Papers)
1 Tin Sardines
Quaker Oats
1 Tablet Soap.[49]

The meat and the vegetables were not fresh but tinned, leading to the lament (when the lovely novelty of parcels had worn off) that 'everything tasted of tins'. The blessedly white bread in the Red Cross ration was mainly courtesy of the redoubtable Lady Evelyn Grant Duff, who arranged shipments of flour from Marseilles to Switzerland, where it was baked into loaves. Known to all PoWs as 'Swiss Dodgers', Lady Evelyn's moist, white loaves were delivered into Germany by road and rail. By 1917 her 'Berne Bread Bureau' was packing 15,000 loaves a day, and had been supplemented by a Copenhagen Bureau to supply camps in the north of Germany. In summer, when bread tended to go mouldy quickly, the bakeries substituted hard biscuits or rusks for Lady Evelyn's baps.

With admirable foresight and initiative, the Red Cross also distributed 'emergency parcels' of iron rations and hard biscuits, enough to keep a prisoner alive for two weeks, while he awaited his own individually addressed parcel. About 20,000 of these were in the hands of 'Camp Help Committees' in the *Lager*.

Thomas Higgins was only one of many to gorge himself on his first Red Cross parcel; 'I nearly killed myself with eating.' He suffered fearful pains for a day or two after eating most of the contents, including a whole tin of dripping. The cold made men yearn for fat.

One Australian officer spoke for all PoWs when he declared to an Antipodean inquiry on prisoner maltreatment: 'We feel that we all owe a debt of gratitude to the Red Cross that can never be repaid. Most assuredly the Red Cross food parcels enabled us "to live and tell the tale".'[50]

With opportunities for exercise limited, prisoners not slave-labouring for the Hun sometimes went from bone-thin to obese on receiving parcels. Which was hardly surprising since the standard parcel plus Lady Evelyn's Dodgers was intended to provide 3,345 calories a day. Some of Archer Cust's fellows in Graudenz acquired 'vast aldermanlike' proportions.[51] Still, 'It was a change from misery to a decent life, and one felt able to do things again.'

Generally, officers and men alike shared parcels and messed for at least some of their meals in their rooms, cooking either on the room stove or 'Tommy cookers' (small camping stoves run on paraffin or oil). At Karlsruhe, Joseph Lee described life after parcels as a 'ceaseless culinary operation'. He thought he might write a cookbook entitled 'Mrs Beeton Beaten'.[52]

Imprisoned alongside Cust in Graudenz on the Vistula River, Captain G.D.J. McMurtrie, 6/Somerset Light Infantry, detailed the 'procedure for parcels' in the camps:

One English officer and three English privates [Orderlies] went down to the post office each day with a guard. There they picked up the parcels and the officer checked the numbers. When the parcels got to the camp, they were immediately taken to the 'parcel house', a small building with about six small rooms in it. Here they were unloaded and parcels for half the officers in the camp went to the 'right' rooms and the other half to the 'left'. They were all set out in order, numbered, and then the number was put against the officer's name on a printed list which was posted on the notice boards.

The next day those officers for whom parcels had come would queue up in the required 'margarine style' queue and would get their parcels in alphabetical order. There was always a German officer, one or two sergeant majors and four German privates watching. The parcel was opened and all tinned goods were put in the officer's tin locker (every officer had a tin locker in the parcel house). The number of tins would be entered in a book. The rest of the parcel the officer would take away unless there was some forbidden article, which would be confiscated. In the case of clothes, all civilian clothes were either kept by the Huns until the Armistice was signed or, if the officer wished, broad stripes were sewn into the clothes. All clothes parcels were carefully searched by the Boche before being passed.

Candles, compasses and books were kept by the Boche. Books

were censored and then returned. There were about eight English officers in each room doing the work and running everything to do with parcels. The Boche simply cleared away the rubbish and saw ... that tins were taken out unopened; I suppose for fear of compasses etc being hidden in them. Once or twice a day, officers could draw their tins. They came with plates and stated their locker number and the tins would be opened and deposited on their plates. Needless to say, all these queues were a constant source of annoyance.[53]

Comprehensive records were kept by the Red Cross to ensure that parcels reached their intended destination, with addressees expected to return a card acknowledging safe receipt. In the event of Thurloe Place not receiving a response within three months, the German government was asked for an explanation. Remarkably few Red Cross parcels went missing, about one in five. A prisoner's pleasure at safe-receipt of a parcel, however, could be spoiled by a bloody-minded or careless camp censor. The censor at Munster, Frank MacDonald recalled, liked to 'jam that dirty old knife of his down a can of herring one minute and then into jam the next'. Everything tasted of salty fish.

The British War Office was capable of its own insensitivities: on 1 February 1917 it banned all private parcels to prisoners. Uproar ensued, with irate mothers (especially) complaining that they were being prevented from looking after their sons. Eventually the War Office softened its stance and sanctioned a 'Personal Parcel' scheme which allowed each PoW to receive a quarterly parcel weighing between 3 lb and 11 lb. In this could be packed toiletries such as soap, toothpaste and insecticide, together with clothes, brushes, hobnails (to repair boots), and brass polish. Overcome by giddy joie de vivre, the War Office also permitted the inclusion of such luxuries as pencils, a chess game and sweets ('8 oz only'). Prisoners' dismay at the austerity of Personal Parcels vanished when they realized that soap – an almost extinct luxury in Germany by 1917 – could be bartered for anything, up to and including, so Tommy wits had it, 'the Kaiser's daughter'.

By November 1918 over 9,000,000 food parcels and 800,000 clothing parcels had been dispatched from Britain to prisoners abroad, at a cost of £6.5 million, of which two-thirds was contributed by the public, with the remainder coming from the General Fund of the Red Cross. Britannia had taken the prisoners to her heart.

Yet nothing is simple in the love of a people for their warriors. So phenomenal was the parcel-provision of the Red Cross that it left the indelible impression all PoWs lived out their captivity in comfort. Some did; but many thousands of prisoners working behind German lines never received parcels, while those attached to an *Arbeitskommando* may only have received them on an intermittent basis, if at all. And withholding parcels was a routine German punishment. Prisoners transferring camps or worksites invariably found that their parcels were slow to catch up with them.

Sapper George Waymark offers a stark, skin-and-bones example of existence without parcels. When imprisoned in the penal fortress at Fort Flines on hard labour Waymark weighed 12 stone 6 pounds; at the Armistice he weighed 8 stone. Prisoners on penal hard labour or twelve-hour shifts of manual labour were given less than 750 calories a day due to the deficiency of the German diet. All became white wraiths with hollowed eyes, or hideous shapeless oedemic approximations of the human form. Unless they died from starvation, as 3,000 or so British prisoners did.[54]

*

. . . if I got another chance to go to the front, I would willingly, but I should never be taken prisoner again.

Sergeant A.J. Parsons, 11/Rifle Brigade

On their transfer from the quarantine block into the camp proper, prisoners began a life of strict Prussian conformity. As demonstrated by a typical day in the life of Private Caine at Güstrow:

We paraded every morning at 7 a.m. for roll call and telling off working parties, and were dismissed at between 10 and 11 a.m. At 1 p.m. we were paraded again and not dismissed till 3 or 4 p.m. Parades were always in the open regardless of weather; consequently many men suffered from frostbite, and one, Drummer Eaglefield, Grenadier Guards, lost both his feet as a result of this. All had to be in the tents at 8 p.m. and to quit the tent after that time was to risk one's life, as sentries made free use of their bayonets and police dogs were let loose. Men who were able were made to work about six hours a day.[55]

The life of officers was hardly less regimented. At Mainz there were five roll calls (*Appell*) per day; at 9 a.m. (outside), 12 noon (dining room), 5 p.m. (outside), 6.30 p.m. (dining room) and 9 p.m. in prisoners' rooms. Between *Appells* prisoners were expected to queue for the *Kantine*, the paymaster's office, the library, the parcel office. Alec Waugh thought queues the 'distinguishing feature' of his day. Douglas Lyall Grant found Gütersloh suspiciously 'like being back at school again', what with the relays in the dining room for breakfast and dinner, and the room lights being turned off at 10.30 p.m. Sharp![56]

Rules. There were so many rules.

A 'long rigmarole' about the German military law under which prisoners lived was read out once or twice a month. Additionally, prisoners were informed by the commandant (via his interpreters) and by written notices pinned to barrack walls of camp regulations. These were 'so long', observed Private George Agnew, 'that I could not remember what they were.' Typically, Number I regulation warned that guards had orders to shoot any prisoner trying to escape. The commandant at Crefeld added for emphasis that his guards were 'all earnest men, knowing their duty'; henceforth the camp's sentries were always nicknamed 'the earnest men'. All German officers and NCOs were to be saluted, even if of lower rank, since, as the commandant at Crefeld informed the bewildered British, any German was superior to every 'English'. Individual *Lager* commandants added idiosyncratic yet trying and pettifogging orders. Private R.S. Baillie, 1/London Scottish, a twenty-five-year-old bank clerk from Thornton Heath, found that his camp's rules included not lying on one's bed in the daytime;[57] the rules at Merseburg, to the ire of the sociable Corporal Alexander Fyfe, Cameron Highlanders, forbade men from talking in groups of more than three. Smoking was permitted at specified times only.

Transgressors, particularly escapers, could expect draconian Prussian-style punishment. The penalty for smoking inside the hut rather than *outside* it at Friedrichsfeld was solitary confinement for fourteen days on a bread and water diet.[58] What inmates could also expect was Prussian-type brutality, from casual everyday beatings through rank sadism to pure murder. Even prisoners who after the peace tried to make the best of their camp experiences and be friendly towards the Boche could not expunge Wilhelmine brutalism. Concerned that Thierry Sandre's famous autobiography, *Le Purgatoire* (*Purgatory*) painted too harsh a picture of life in a German *Lager*, the French officer and *prisonnier de guerre* Georges Connes penned an apologistic 'Counter-Memoir'. But: 'All the same, one has to admit that brutality . . . among the Germans, is more general, almost systematic.'[59]

The ingrained, pervasive violence of the German military was no surprise to Imperial soldiers, or to the German Left, which had long highlighted the '*Dramen*' (tragedies) it caused. In July 1914, as the fuse of war was burning, the Socialist leader Rosa Luxemburg was tried for supposedly calumnying the Prussian military establishment by bringing to public attention cruelties committed by officers and NCOs in training camps. Her lawyers defended her with 'innumerable' examples.[60]

Added to the 'natural' brutality of the Prussian military system was febrile wartime hatred of the '*Englische Schweine*'. Not content with having '*Gott strafe England*' painted on barracks, commandants did everything they could to help the Lord in punishing the English. Commonplace cruelties towards British troops were legion. At Güstrow, Corporal Walker, 1/Cameron Highlanders, noted: 'It was an everyday occurrence for men to be butted with the rifle and hit with sticks etc.' There were wild charges by the guards through the camp at night in which inmates were bayoneted. A soldier in the Coldstream Guards, Private William McGraa, died through the effects of being tied to a pole.[61] Again at Güstrow: Private W. Elvin, 4/Royal Fusiliers, recorded: 'Under-officer Deutschmann was particularly harsh and cruel in his treatment of Englishmen; he went about armed with a truncheon, with which he used to hit our men promiscuously for no reason.'[62]

Imprisoned at Süderzollhaus, Corporal Robert Burrows recalled:

The officers and unter-offiziers were terrors, especially the adjutant and the unteroffizier of the 3rd and 4th huts, whom, I believe, was called 'Funk'. He and the adjutant came round nightly . . . and woke us by beating us with swords. They were generally drunk.

Some of the brutality bordered on voyeuristic love of pain. According to Güstrow prisoner Private G. Cox, Duke of Wellington's Regiment:

A favourite afternoon's sport for the Germans was to make the English go through a lane, flogging them on the back with a sjambok as they passed them. The General in charge of the camp with his friends (some female, whom we thought must represent German ladies) watched this.[63]

Cox's statement was supported by five others.

Prisoner diaries reveal a steady black line of murder. Rifleman Alfred Hall recorded in June 1916 that two Englishmen and two Frenchmen were shot for refusing to work in a munitions factory. Later, in November 1916, Private Logan of the King's Own was killed at Giessen by one of the guards 'for some petty offence' chronicled Hall; not long after, Private Moreton of the London Regiment, an invalid, died of hypothermia after being left in a cold bath for one and a half hours. 'KULTURED COUNTRY THIS,' wrote Hall. He fantasized, like so many others, about 'What a beautiful massacre there'll be, when English PoWs meet Germans on level ground'.[64]

More than five hundred British prisoners died directly at the hands of their guards, through beatings and shootings. No murder was more cold-blooded than that of Private J. Barry, 2/Scots Guards, shot in his barracks at Sennelager on 17 January 1918. To ensure comfortable and certain aim, the guard unbuttoned his greatcoat and pulled it off the right shoulder so the stock fitted more securely.

It was a busy, bloody month for murder in the Kaiser's camps; only ten days before Rifleman John Russell had been taken to the closed guardhouse at Chemnitz, after some 'trouble at work', and shot twice.

Alarmed by reports of maltreatment of the prisoners, the British government protested to Berlin. After several months of negotiations the German government agreed in early 1915 to a system of inspection by members of the American Embassy in Berlin. (The Swiss took over when the US entered the war; other neutral powers also made inspections.) Naturally, the system of inspection had to be reciprocal; the American Embassy in London visited German PoWs in Britain.

So far as British PoWs in Germany were concerned, the weakness of the inspection system was that it was so easily evaded. Frequently, prisoners were not allowed to speak with the visiting diplomat privately, and in some cases were prevented from seeing him altogether. At Wittenberg in 1917 the civilian contractor in charge of PoW labourers – of whom there were hundreds – point-blank refused to allow the ambassador anywhere near them.

There were *Kommandanten* who set up reigns of pure terror, turning their personal fiefdoms into mad-houses of pain and punishment. British prisoners at Holzminden mocked Karl Niemeyer for his 'bartender Yank' way of speaking (he'd been a waiter in Milwaukee) and his caricature Prussian-appearance, but his strange cruelties were far from humorous. Niemeyer conceived a special animus for Lieutenant Leefe Robinson VC, and swore to avenge the death of Wilhelm Schramm, the Zeppelin commander shot down by the RFC hero. Robinson was duly persecuted by Niemeyer, with incessant sentences of solitary confinement. Once, Niemeyer gave Robinson a whipping which left him on the point of collapse. In the end Niemeyer broke Robinson's health, and broke it so much that he died.[65]

To British PoWs Germans were the 'Hun' or the 'Boche'; unsurprisingly the fraternal 'Fritz' was less employed in the camps than the trenches. Hating the Hun, though, had its price in a little internal diminishing of the soul. Captain Geoffrey Phillimore for one was aware of the corrosive effects of Hun-loathing:

> One of the worst parts of being in prison was the hatred one felt for
> the Huns. It is frightful to live for years with that emotion as a pre-
> dominant one. Every day it grew and grew, fed constantly by cruelty,
> or daily slights, or offensivenesses, either to oneself or to someone
> else.[66]

Private Edward Page was careful to distinguish between the
German 'military caste' – the Niemeyers – and the German people,
who 'were completely overwhelmed and crushed beneath' them. A
distinction as useful to the historian as it was to the imprisoned
Tommy. And everybody met at least one German whose absolute decency militated against quick and easy racial stereotyping.
Sapper Waymark, repairing roads at Fromelles, was guarded by a
Landsturmer of about sixty 'and quite a decent sort'. His son was
a PoW in the Isle of Man. (A photo showed the son to be 'quite
fat'.) Prisoners at Parchim, meanwhile, were unfailingly helped by a
guard known to all Brits as 'Good Paul'. Benjamin Muse was moved
to implore:

> Whatever else may be done at the Peace Conference, I want the
> Allies to make a search of Germany and Alsace-Lorraine until they
> find one Paul Sanchez formerly attached to X Kompanie Ersatz Bat-
> talion of the German Army – a little man with a blonde moustache,
> and a kindly face – and give him a Victoria Cross.

Good Paul's help and kindness was offered at great risk to himself
and despite the curses of his comrades.[67]

Private W. Chambers, 14th Battalion Canadian Infantry, encountered that *rara avis*, an easy-going commandant. Lichtenhorst
was a camp on the edge of Lüneburg Heath, where the work assigned to prisoners involved digging ditches and cutting heather.
What should have been a hell on earth Chambers found to be
the best *Lager* of his three-year captivity. After prisoners had dug
their three metres a day, they were free to amuse themselves with
games and recreation. When an Irish sergeant secured a St Pat-
rick's Day celebration and the rest of the camp suddenly developed

Irish nationality overnight, the commandant saw the joke and gave everybody a day's holiday. Almost uniquely, the commandant ('a real sport') did not believe that physical chastisement and verbal abuse was the way to make prisoners work.

> If only we had had the same treatment at other camps, there would not have been half the trouble ... It was the continual 'Schwein-hund' business which put our back up.[68]

Joseph Lee even counted the commandant at Karlsruhe worthy of poetic praise:

> A stately walk, a kindly face,
> Always ready to examine your case,
> Never attempting to hustle about,
> Though he's our Foe, he's never a lout,
> That's the Kommandant.[69]

The guard at Fromelles, Good Paul, the *Kommandanten* of Lichten-horst and Karlsruhe were all definitely Fritzes.

Prisoners released into the main *Lager* were fresh faces, sources of news, even gossip. Frequently too they were objects of pity to be fed and clothed. Sometimes newcomers were resented as Johnny-come-latelies who might stretch and stress meagre resources. And a few British officers entering camp complained that Regulars kept up the regimental mess tradition of not acknowledging newcomers for a month. Geoffrey Phillimore was on the wrong end of such inappropriate and outmoded custom at Gütersloh: 'The old established prisoners treated the wretched last comers as if they were an impertinence on their part to exist, let alone to draw the attention of the select tenants of Block D to their deplorable existence.'[70]

Later arrivals took humorous revenge on such fossilized 'Four-teeners' and 'Fifteeners' by calling them 'Bow and Arrow Men' because they had never sat under a Somme barrage.

As a result of mess snobbery, Phillimore's 'first friends were for-eigners'. To the disappointment of the Germans, mixing Allied nationalities in the huts and camps caused nowhere near as much friction as anticipated. Generally, the British harboured a conviction that the Germans were soft on the French and assigned them the most favourable jobs; aside from sabot-making these included tailoring and, especially, cooking. The parcel-less Russians roused widespread sympathy, although Lance-Corporal Higgins recalled 'many a fight' with them in the starving time over who should get the cook-house leavings.[71] When Red Cross parcels flowed, it was common for Tommies to pass their German rations over to the Russians. But goodwill among Allied men never extended to sleeping arrangements. In mixed huts the argument over whether the window should be open at night lasted the duration. All Britons favoured opening the apertures to let in fresh air; but the French suffered a paranoia about draughts. John Caunter lamented: 'We English wanted a fair proportion of the windows open; the French on the other hand wanted them shut, complaining of "les courants d'air mortels".'[72] The Russians, who liked thick, warm fug, sided with their older ally.

Questions of fenestration aside, Lieutenant Joseph Lee concluded overall that the presence of Allies made for 'a gaiety of Nations':

> Splashes of blue and red and grey,
> Some of 'em sad, but most are gay,
> Joking around like so many boys,
> Always making a deuce of a noise,
>   That's our Allies.[73]

One nation the Germans did incontestably favour were the Irish. Over the winter of 1914 Irish prisoners were siphoned off to a special deluxe camp at Limburg, with the intention of recruiting them into an 'Irish Brigade' commanded by the nationalist politician Sir Roger Casement. In return for service under the Imperial Eagle the Irishmen were promised a ticket to the USA at the war's end and a thousand dollars in their pocket. Their uniform was to have a catchy harp and shamrock insignia.

Only 54 out of 2,500 volunteered to join Sir Roger Casement – who, far from being lauded as the commander of the Free Irish, needed an armed escort to protect him from his 'countrymen'.

Incensed at the reluctance of the Irish to switch sides, the Germans switched to their default understanding of 'special' treatment. Rations were reduced to basics, two men were reportedly shot, and others of the '*Nein*' men sent to coal and salt mines.[74] Irish refuser Corporal R. Dempsey, 2/Royal Scots Fusiliers, was tied to a post in the snow for an hour and a half, and used for spitting practice by the sentries. 'I fell into a very bad state of health and passed blood with my urine.'[75] Other refusers were sent to the salt mines.

After the Irish fiasco, the *Kriegsministerium* tried seducing Muslim, Indian and African soldiers, who were sent to Zossen (Wunsdforf) near Berlin, where a large mosque was constructed 'at the Kaiser's command'. According to the Germans, they enjoyed moderate success in enticing prisoners to fight for their ally Turkey.

Incarceration turned up one or two dodgy British sergeants more prepared to do the Germans' bidding than anyone was comfortable with. Corporal Edward Edwards met one Regimental Sergeant Major for whom:

> The pleasure of the guards was his delight, their displeasure his poignant grief. He assumed the authority of his rank with us, he reported the slightest of misdemeanours amongst us to the guards and was instrumental in having many punished.[76]

He also stole prisoners' boots and sold them on.

Frank MacDonald likewise came across a 'galling' senior NCO who used his 'authority to force us to obey [German] orders'.[77] MacDonald got his revenge; when he escaped to London he reported the turncoat to the War Office.

Although there were occasions, especially when starvation was roaming the camps, that the historic comradeship of the British Army became threadbare, it never broke. If anything, adversity under 'Hun' attack eventually bonded men together. Horace Gilliland considered the esprit de corps in Ingolstadt punishment *Lager* – a black hole by any standard of incarceration – exemplary: 'Everyone helped his fellow prisoners.'[78] There was no space or time for cliques and personal animosities. Lieutenant T.J. Dobson, in a room so overcrowded at Mainz that the beds were put on top of each other like bunks in a ship, believed: 'The cheerful and unselfish behaviour of one's companions was the only thing that made life in any way possible in these horrible quarters.'[79] Looking back on his imprisonment, Will Harvey concluded that the remembrance of 'men united in comradeship with a fine gift of courageous laughter' was more worthy of record than the *strafes* and miseries.

In the claustrophobic confines of a dormitory or barrack-room, as in a dug-out in the trench, men had no choice other than to extend the hand of amity and get along as well as possible. 'By now I had made many friends,' wrote Archer Cust after a month or so of captivity, ' for adversity is the mother of friendships.'[80] Nowhere was the fine fraternal feeling of British prisoners in the Wilhelmine Reich more glaringly evidenced than in the relationship, surprising as it may seem, between officers and their British orderlies.

As a rule, British officers in captivity were supplied with servants. In that long-gone era of 'Upstairs, Downstairs' class distinctions, few other ranks saw anything demeaning in being a Jeeves. On the contrary, when volunteers for valeting were asked for in the enlisted men's camps, whole rows stepped forward. The relationship between manservant and officer had been cordial and respectful in the trenches; in the camps it was nothing less, and may have been considerably more. In the words of Private Norman Dykes, who was an orderly at Gütersloh and Schwarmstedt:

> As a rule a strong bond of friendship developed between the officers and the orderlies, and a genuine interest was taken in our welfare. An orderly need never be short of food or clothing (officers seemed to get unlimited supplies out from Britain). We were frequently asked about the condition of our wardrobe.[81]

Respect and affection flowed in the other direction too, from officer to orderly. Gilbert Nobbs' valet, Private Cotton, was from his own London Regiment and 'we became very much attached to each other'.[82]

An orderly looked after about half a dozen officers, making tea, meals, beds, and performing general tidying. Beyond this, orderlies were also indispensable helpmates in escaping. The success of British officers in escaping the Kaiser's camps was due in great part to British orderlies. When Private Dykes (who also made his own valorous breakout) and other orderlies were moved on from Schwarmstedt for succouring the escape of Fox and Groves[83] in 1917:

> The officers en bloc had wished us the very best of luck, and individually would have loaded us with any and every type of tinned goods, articles of clothing, books, or anything else either useful or merely ornamental which we might have desired, but which we could not possibly hope to take with us because of the insurmountable difficulties of transport.[84]

The arrival of orderlies at an officers' *Lager* was likely to be an eye-opener. On 15 August 1918 Archer Cust watched forty-one British detailed to become orderlies enter Graudenz.

> I have never seen such a sight, and may I never again. They were simply skin and bone, in rags, altogether the most pitiable, sepulchral figures conceivable ... Their clothes hung on them like a scarecrow, and you could see the vermin crawling over them. Poor fellows, most of them young lads of nineteen to twenty-four, broken by sheer deliberate cruelty.[85]

These orderlies had been among men captured on the Somme in March, and put to toil behind the lines. They had to be rested for a fortnight before they could undertake any valeting; their sores took weeks to heal. Many had died en route to Germany, to which they had been forced to walk.

> Such things will not be forgotten. No.

So wrote Archer Cust in his journal. Perhaps it was small wonder that enlisted men volunteered for valeting when the other work offered by the German authorities was deadly.

*

Putting prisoners to work was unambiguously legal. The Hague Convention Article VI after all decreed:

The State may employ the labour of prisoners of war, other than officers, according to their rank and capacity. The work shall not be excessive, and shall have no connection with the operations of the war.

Prisoners were to be paid the going rate.

Only in a bare minority of cases did German authorities defer to the fine impulses of Hague statesmen, or even the *Kriegsministe-rium*'s own *War Book* of 1915 with its noble prescription that tasks given to prisoner-labourers 'should not be prejudicial to health nor in any way dishonourable'. The German war machine needed a mass of cheap labour, and it found it in the million and a half Allied soldiers sitting in the Fatherland's *Lager*. Mars trumped Eir. By 1916 over 80 per cent of British other ranks prisoners were at work. For the most part they were not labourers, they were the Kaiser's unwilling slaves.

Camps for other rank prisoners became *Stammlager* (depot or parent prisons) for tens if not hundreds of *Arbeitskommandos* (working parties) over the surrounding region. One of these depot prisons, Soltau, had a capacity of 30,000 but, swollen by the men in the *Arbeitskommandos*, it had 50,000 on its books. A number of permanent working camps were also founded. Prisoners were hired out to local employers, who ranged from the chemical conglomerate BASF to peasants needing a single hand. The employer undertook to pay, feed and accommodate the prisoners and their attending elderly *Landsturmer* guards.

And there lay the problem. The *Kommando-Führer* of the guards had every incentive to ensure the exploitation of prisoners, since if the prisoners failed to work satisfactorily the guard himself was liable to be punished by being sent to the Western Front. Out of sight of the neutral inspectors, countless *Landsturmer* NCOs set themselves up as small-scale Teutonic tyrants. Employers, of course, had a direct financial interest in working their prisoner labourers like dogs; one German banker was unwise enough to inform the American ambassador, Mr Gerard, that his (the banker's) Prussian landowner clients were 'in favour of continuing the war, because of the fact that they were getting four or five times the money for their products while their work was being done by prisoners'.[86] *Kommando-Führer* and employer joined together in an unholy alliance of forced profiteering.

Prisoners' accounts record endemic brutality in most *Arbeitskommandos*, with sentries kicking, punching and clubbing their charges to make them work harder, faster. 'It made me think', wrote Lance-Corporal Higgins

> of the slaves I had read about in Uncle Tom's Cabin. Still I think the slaves were better fed than us, as a slave cost money, and it did not matter whether we lived or died, there were plenty of prisoners and they cost nothing.[87]

Higgins could be forgiven for believing himself an expendable item. During the winter of 1917 he was sent to a stone quarry at Elbingerode in the Harz mountains. He was still wearing the clothes he was captured in almost two years before and the cold was intense:

> The men began to give in one by one. They were dropping at work like dead men. When a man fell, the sentries put them to lie in the snow until they were driven back to work again . . . I could hardly crawl, but I was made to work as well as I could. When I awakened in the morning, I could hardly see out of my eyes, my face was that swollen up.[88]

Given a choice (and they rarely were), most prisoners opted for farm work, which seemed healthier, war-neutral, and likely to offer extra grub. Benjamin Muse, sent to a farm in Mecklenburg, was astonished – and delighted – to be provided with five meals a day. What neither Muse nor most volunteers for agricultural work understood, though, was the grinding length of a German peasant farmer's day.

A typical working day down on the farm in Mensfelden, in the picturesque Lahn valley, for Rifleman Alfred Hall:

> I have been working from 6.30 a.m. to 9 p.m., and on the go from early morning to late evening with a few short lapses for meals. 15–20

minutes breakfast 20–30 minutes dinner and 15–20 minutes afternoon coffee. Of course I must remember I am a prisoner of war and these people can do with me as they like . . . We have been having very hot weather recently and one feels it especially in the fields ploughing harrowing rolling sowing. Continually walking, walking. Thistle snatching is a tedious job. I must say I am in very good health but Heaven knows what we PoWs would look like if it was not for our parcels from England. Yet I think we should consider ourselves lucky in working on a farm. A man could not possibly live in a lager 6 months without parcels from home, and I *absolutely refuse* to work elsewhere than at those occupations agreed upon at the Hague Convention.[89]

Rifleman Hall had a fisticuffs falling-out with his employer, Herr Lieber, and was sent by way of punishment to a *Strafekommando* at Welzar ironwork. As Hall's diary makes clear, the work almost killed him, as it did kill others:

August 19th 1917
My mind is wandering a bit back to the green fields of old England and Suffolk. Oh, my darling please forgive me. The end doesn't seem so far off so perhaps it is all for the best. I see our meadow and those happy days. It is time for the guards to come. There is no rest.

August 20th 1917
Still holding on but very weak. Perkins and 5 Russians were buried yesterday. Rogers and I are the only Englishmen left. Do you remember the race to the farm and the glass of milk. Rogers is lying on some clinker. He seems bad I must go to him.

August 21st 1917
Feel a bit better today. They put fat in the soup yesterday. Rogers is still weak but sticking it. 2 Frenchmen carted away. What cattle we are.
Thank you darling for your great love. I have proved so unworthy of it. Can I hold on. I must.[90]

Somehow, despite the odds, he did.

Cushy jobs did sometimes happen. Rifleman H. Jeffrey, King's Royal Rifle Corps, a tanner by trade was, with unusually happy logic, put to work in a tannery near his parent camp at Parchim. Although he started at 6 a.m. and finished at 8 p.m. he had two and a half hours off for meals. He and his mates were 'as happy as sandboys'. James Farrant was once deputed to assist as artist in the decoration of a new Roman Catholic church in Berlin; later in the war he had 'a very good number' sorting PoW letters. Even unloading cargo on the docks at Libau turned out to have its brighter side, thanks to the two thousand Lettish girls working there. Plus, of course, a golden opportunity to pilfer.

And Thomas Higgins, to his delight, ended up working in a forest *Kommando* attached to Munster camp, planting young trees: 'I have often wondered since, if they have grown.'[91] The weather was splendid, the guards unusually were chaps who had been to the front, so 'we had many a friendly chat with them'. And Higgins liked the sound of the birds singing.

But good jobs seldom lasted because prisoners were shoved and shuffled around by the diktats of the German economy and the whims of punitive commandants. During three years working for the German Reich, Higgins laid railroads, unloaded barges, worked in a stone quarry, worked in a forest, made hay at Otterberg (where his accommodation was unbelievably palatial: the village hotel, complete with eiderdowns), worked in a sawmill, and in a salt mine.

By common consent, the worst working fate for prisoners was to be sent to the coal and salt mines. A British wartime report described coal and salt mining as 'a singularly cruel and dangerous form of slavery';[92] a general order issued by the German government, meanwhile, specifically mentioned the British as suitable for this line of employment. Mining in any setting is dangerous, it was especially so for famished men who did not understand the orders barked at them. Some flavour of the hazards is caught in a laconic entry in the diary of Corporal C.E. Green toiling in Preussengrube coal mine dated 23 October 1917: 'Buried the Englishman Wheatley today, near to Frank Johnson's grave.' Both men had died in accidents. No less than 62 other British PoWs perished in mining incidents. While German civilian miners hewed the coal or salt, prisoners were put to work loading trucks and dragging them along the underground galleries. Since the war-exemption of the miners depended on their private employer being satisfied with their output, they and the civilian foreman (the *Steiger*, armed with a revolver) kept the PoW slaves hard at it. Output was easily judged by the number of loaded carts. Any prisoner not meeting his quota was beaten with shovels and pickaxe handles. After a long shift at the infamous Auguste Victoria or K-47 coal mine, Europe's largest pit, Private Jack O'Brien was forced to run a gauntlet of miners every time his target was not met.[93] In the darkness underground at K-47 there was uncontrolled tyranny.

Men would do almost anything to get out of the 'Black Hole' that was Auguste Victoria. Self-inflicted injuries were common. Frank MacDonald got a mate to push a loaded coal cart over his toes; this secured MacDonald a stint in hospital, but he soon ended up back at Auguste Victoria as punishment for an escape attempt. This time he was put to labour in the coke plant. Some considered the *Kokerie* more terrible even than the pit proper. One British PoW wrote:

> The men had to do shifts of from half-an-hour to an hour unless they dropped out before, which they frequently did. The heat was intense and I have seen men with their feet and faces scorched and blistered . . . The work was shifting 32 tons of coke in twelve hours; sometimes it was quite impossible to do this in the time, and the men simply had to work until it was done.[94]

And they themselves were done in.

Shirking in the *Kokerie* was punished by having the offender stand next to the furnaces so that the heat blistered their skin. To get out of *Kokerie* work Frank MacDonald devised a truly dire self-inflicted injury: he poured boiling water over his left hand. Later, 'when the doctor ripped off the dressing he took all the skin and most of the flesh from the hand, so that the cords and bones were almost bare'.[95] Working at Auguste Victoria was, it hardly needs saying, a causal motivation in MacDonald's eventual successful escape from the German Babylon.

Wretched accommodation added to the strain of long hours underground or in the *Kokerie*. Rifleman Tich Evanson at Westerholt coal mine in the Ruhr slept on 'beds of coconut matting' stretched between wooden uprights.[96] There were 221 other men in the barracks; the adjoining latrine overflowed; the guards deliberately prevented the men from sleeping by calling an *Appell* at midnight. Floggings with a length of tubing by an under-NCO were 'frequent and severe'. [97]

A British soldier wrote of his quarters at Neuhof salt mine:

> We were very overcrowded and slept in triple-deck beds, with two men in each bed; except for a narrow passage about two feet wide between the beds, there was no room to move about. The beds were full of vermin, and there were a large number of black beetles and other insects on the walls and floor. Owing to the crowded conditions it was impossible to keep the place clean. The blankets were very dirty. There were no windows and no means of ventilation of any sort except the door.[98]

Slaving in the white pit of a Reich salt mine was more dreadful even than working in the 'Black Hole'. The salt was blasted into large heaps of crystalline shards, which the prisoners loaded into carts with their bare hands. There was blood on the salt, every load of it speckled and sprinkled with the blood of British servicemen.

Life in a salt mine: Lance Corporal Andrew Jones, 15th Battalion Canadian Infantry, worked at Beienrode 6 a.m. to 9 p.m. seven days a week. If the ten-man working party failed to load fifteen trucks during their shift, they stayed down until the work was done; in November 1917 the rate was upped to thirty trucks per shift. No protective clothing was issued so the men were soon covered in salt sores. When a camp medical officer was *finally* summoned, he lanced the boils. And left them to bleed and to absorb more salt. Some guards generously did the lancing themselves, breaking the boils with clubs – a sport which they seemed to find amusing.[99]

Toiling for Kaiser Wilhelm's regime truly was slave labour. Pay was token. One miner recorded that he received five Marks per week for his work; of this, four was taken off him for food.[100] At Preussen-grube coal mine Corporal C.E. Green was docked 1½ Marks of this three Marks pay as a 'voluntary' contribution to the German war effort. This was at least a greater rate of remuneration than enjoyed by those sent to *Kommandos* behind the front in 1918. Here Private Tucker received ten pfennigs for his week's work in a motor depot. In English currency that amounted to one penny.

Of course, if the work and starvation did not kill you, there was always the distinct chance, if you were in an *Arbeitskommando* behind the front, that your own side's 'friendly' fire might. 'We were under shell fire the whole time,' one prisoner held in the cage at Ecoust told the British Government's *Prisoners of Prussia* investiga-tion; a corporal in the West Yorks was killed by the blasts. As were four men at Villers. And so on, and on, and on.

To live as a British prisoner in the wire world of the Wilhelmine Reich was to court death. When the mortality rate of Allied PoWs is calculated with due adjustment for length of incarceration and with the exclusion of death from battlefield wounds, British pris-oners were five times more likely to die than French ones. During the period from October 1917 to September 1918 the death rate of British other ranks on the battlefield was 4 per cent; the death rate of British PoWs, *excluding* deaths from wounds, meanwhile was 5.2 per cent.[101] Better to be a Tommy in a trench, then, than a Tommy in a German camp. Overall, about 10.3 per cent of British PoWs taken captive died whilst captive in Germany.

*

Men lived for letters and postcards from home. 'The coming of one's first letter was a memorable event in camp life,' recalled Lieutenant Joseph Lee. Only the first parcel with its life-saving contents was of greater importance.[102] A letter was tangible evidence that a prisoner was not forgotten, as well as a window into life beyond exile. '*Never* shall I forget the thrill of excitement that ran through me,' wrote Archer Cust about receipt of his first letter in captivity. Working in that stone mine in the Harz Mountains in intense cold, Thomas Higgins thought of suicide. Then, in November 1917, a postcard from his wife arrived:

How I read, and reread that postcard. I kissed it many a time, thinking of the one who wrote it and still cared for me. It was good to
know that someone thought of me still among the brutal conditions
I was living under. I knew that postcard off by heart.[103]

Registered prisoners were allowed to write two letters – of four
pages and no more – and four postcards a month home. These
were strictly censored and any unflattering comments resulted in
the missive being binned and the author *strafed*. Letters were to
be written in pencil and in 'large and plain characters'.[104] Usually,
letters and postcards were not dispatched immediately but kept in
the camp for ten days in the hope that any secret ink would reveal
itself, or any military secrets become too stale to be of use.[105] This
was a reasonable supposition, because escape-minded PoWs used
inks and ciphers to request useful articles from home, while other
captives sent hidden messages to alert all and sundry to conditions
in the camps.

It was not only German censors who delayed home-bound letters, all of which were routed through neutral countries; the War
Office opened and scanned epistles too, seeking possible military
intelligence. Many a letter took months to arrive at its destination.
Assuming it arrived at all. Lieutenant Peter Anderson reckoned
that while 80 per cent of letters sent to him from Canada arrived
at Bischofswerda *Lager*, the success rate for traffic in the opposite
direction was considerably lower.

Whether they were slow to arrive, or whether they necessitated
standing in line at the prison letter office for hours to collect them,
letters were always welcome. In a diary entry dated 7 July 1918,
Second Lieutenant H. Ringham, 16/Manchester Regiment, incarcerated in Mainz, expressed the sentiment of all prisoners: 'I hope I
get some letters next week.'[106]

*

In the wire world, there were few atheists. Private William Tucker
was adamant: 'I never heard a single soldier declare himself an
unbeliever.' No sooner did the first officers arrive at Torgau than
they erected a church in the top of the wagon shed. 'The altar was

draped with dark hangings,' recalled L.J. Austin, 'and lighted with two candles, and made a simple but very effective picture. We used to have services twice a day on Sunday and choir practices nearly every day.'[107]

Everywhere the British went they made 'churches' out of huts, the corners of stone barracks, and tents. The simplicity of these places of worship gave them a touching poignancy. The church at Friedrichsfeld was a little ramshackle hut yet Fred McMullen recalled: 'We used to enjoy these services too. In some way they seemed to mean a good deal more to us than such things had done at home.'[108]

Services at Friedrichsfeld were on Wednesday night and twice on Sunday, conducted by Corporal Oliver, who had been a preacher in England. Almost every camp turned up a lay preacher, while the thirty-seven army chaplains taken captive in the war found there was no rest for the righteous. The pastor at Rastatt was a one-armed South African missionary named Hill, 'a Community of Resurrection man', who Archer Cust was pleased to note 'had the spirit of God in him'. Pastor Hill gave daily evening classes on the Acts, a service in the dining hall every night, and on Sundays in the wooden church built by the Russians. In those rare *Lager* bereft of a practising minister of some denomination or another, the senior British officer or senior NCO would conduct services.

Drummer V.G.S. Champion at Munster (Rennbahn) was an almost legendary character, a one-man Christian mission. In the words of Private Edward Page:

> His heart and soul were in the little wooden room placed at his disposal for the holding of church services, and, although faced at the commencement with many difficulties, he gradually converted that bare room into a nice little church with altar, organ, forms, and pictures complete.[109]

Sitting in Champion's chapel, Page always found arising in his mind 'a picture of a quiet village church; you could almost imagine you heard again the old familiar sound of the bells'.[110] There were reasons to attend church in camp other than religious ones. Nostalgia, an antidote to boredom, and patriotism were among the lures; the services attended by Lieutenant Joseph Lee at Karlsruhe – where the chapel was 'used alternately and harmoniously by English Churchmen, Roman Catholics, and Non-Conformists' – concluded seditiously 'with the lusty singing of a verse of "God Save The King".'[111] In some camps a church service was the only place where Britons could congregate without being dispersed by guards, bayonets and dogs.

In the Christian hearts of British PoWs in Germany, only the Reverend Henry Williams rivalled Drummer Champion for respect. Williams was the minister at the English church in Berlin, given special dispensation from the *Kriegsministerium* to remain in Germany after the start of hostilities to tend to a growing PoW flock. He was the *Lager* and lazaret equivalent of 'Woodbine Willie' – the nickname bestowed on Reverend George Studdert Kennedy, who famously dispensed good will (and cigarettes) in the trenches. Williams was eagerly awaited in the camps. Lieutenant Horace Gilliland explained:

> Mr Williams was always so bright and hopeful one could not help catching a little of his cheerfulness, and I think I can speak for all of us in saying that we looked forward to his visits very much and felt the better for his coming.[112]

For Lieutenant J. Harvey Douglas, a patient in Cologne lazaret, Williams' visit was 'the big event' of his entire convalescence. Douglas found himself laughing at Williams' jokes; the cleric told the small congregation of British prisoner patients who assembled in the chapel that perhaps they wouldn't sing the hymn 'There is a Happy Land'. Blessed with an obvious and genuine spirituality, Williams had yet another gift as far as camp inmates were concerned: he was a fount of war news. When Williams attended Bischofswerda, Lieutenant John Thorn was all ears because Williams worded 'his services so cleverly that we were able to gather the exact state of the war'.[113] Pastor Williams visited camps once or twice a year until the Germans tired of him and interned him. In his memoir of life as prisoner of war in Germany, John Thorn addressed an acknowledgement to Williams directly: 'Pastor Williams, your good works among the soldier and civilian camps will not be forgotten'.[114]

But who today remembers the Reverend Henry Williams?

*

Walking round our cages like the lions at the Zoo,
We think of things that we have done, and things we mean to do.
Of girls we left behind us, of letters that are due,
Of boating on the river beneath a sky of blue,
Of hills we climbed together – not always for the view.

Walking round our cages like the lions at the Zoo,
We see the phantom faces of you, and you, and you,
Faces of those we loved or loathed – oh every one we knew!
And deeds we wrought in carelessness for happiness or rue,
And dreams we broke in folly, and seek to build anew,
Walking round our cages like the lions at the Zoo.

'What We Think Of', Lieutenant Will Harvey
Written at Gütersloh *Offizierslager*

There *was* something uncannily zoo-like about a prisoner-of-war camp. For some men, imprisonment was all too much from the outset. Having survived capture they, like animals taken from the wild for confinement, started to die inside, all hope having fled them. Will Harvey wondered whether the 'highly strung' suffered most, whereas Alec Waugh considered confinement hardest on men of action.[115] Whatever, a small but worrying number of prisoners strickened as soon as the rough wood-and-wire gates of the cage creaked shut. Stretcher-bearer Reginald Morris noted the phenomenon in his *Arbeitskommando* at Douai: 'Some fellows lost heart from the first. Their spirits gradually sank, their bodies with them until to live became too great a burden. They just passed away.'[116]

Every hut or dormitory had someone who had given up, someone who turned to the wall. Sometimes inertia overtook whole groups of men, who would shuffle or sit like a collection of aged ghosts. Private Gibbons found: 'It was a common sight in the camp to see a group sitting around not saying a word or uttering a sound – just sitting there, brooding silently.'

Sometimes men passed beyond depression and went mad, and the guards would lead them to the asylum. All the big camps, such as Munster, had an asylum attached. Said Will Harvey: '"God give me forgetfulness!" has been the prayer of many a man driven morbid and mad . . . and in some cases the prayer has been answered.'[117]

Suicide was not unknown. French sociologist Emile Durkheim was the first to notice the close correlation between suicide and military service, suggestively proposing that the men whose sense of military honour was most acute were the likeliest to take their own lives.[118] When honour was tainted by surrender and the life of service thwarted by captivity, the conditions for suicide were rich.

Depression was generally delayed in its onset. Durkheim's fellow countryman Georges Connes fashioned a rough psychological profile of imprisonment his British PoW comrades would recognize. In the first stage of captivity a prisoner's mind was occupied with hunger; there then came six to twelve months of maximum health and wellbeing before, finally, 'collapse sets in for the soul because of the confinement and the feeling of being stifled'.[119]

Eventually, the medical profession categorized this collapse of the soul as 'barbed-wire disease', a form of neurasthenia. According to Carl Dennett, an American Red Cross deputy commissioner dealing with Allied prisoners, barbed-wire disease was one of the commonest complaints in the cages. In severe cases men were repatriated as being unfit for further military duty as surely as if they had lost a limb.[120]

Depression could have causes beyond feelings of being stifled or confined. In the madding crowd of a barracks, a man might be ever so lonely and not know until the very last, until November 1918, when he might see his loved ones again. If ever. Poor Second Lieutenant W.G. Allen, Lincolnshire Regiment, was captured at Bullecort on 21 March 1918, just days after his marriage. 'I long for h[er],' he wrote in his diary at Graudenz about his bride. He counted the days until a letter from Nancy finally reached him.[121] The loneliness of

the prisoner was a favoured theme of the wire-world poets, led by
the *Lager* laureate Will Harvey:

> Oh where's the use to write?
> What can I tell you, dear?
> Just that I want you so
> Who are not near.
>
> Just that I miss the lamp whose blessed light
> Was God's own moon to shine upon my night,
> And newly mourn each new day's lost delight
> Just – oh, it will not ease my pain –
> That I am lonely
> Until I see you once again,
> You – you only. [122]

Will Harvey was one of those officers who constantly tormented
himself for surrendering, spending hours a day picking over the
rotten bones of capitulation:

Again and again I asked myself if I could in any way have avoided
being taken. Again and again, wise after the event, I discovered ways
in which I might have done so. Oh, why did I risk getting into that
trench at all? Why, why did I never guess that there were Germans
inside that damned shelter which had been my hope of cover when
I heard footsteps behind me? and so on and so on – the whole tor-
turing cycle of vain questions which come tormenting prisoners at
such a time, and even long after, as they prowl round and round
their wire cages, and long after that too, when they have arrived, by
various roads, at the truth of the whole matter, which is, 'I being I,
and the circumstances being what they were at the time, it was quite
unavoidable.' [123]

Alec Waugh was another who found his surrender a constant
dishonourable shadow. But then there were so many grey clouds in
the prisoner's life:

The wearisome sameness of the days, the monotony of the faces, the
unchanged landscape, the intolerable talk about the war, all these

tended to produce an effect of complete and utter depression. This was far and away our worst enemy: whole days were drenched in an incurable melancholia.[124]

Officers, who were debarred from work, found the monotony a particular cross to bear. In his diary for 14 February 1915, Malcolm Hay, incarcerated at Festung Marienberg in Würzburg wrote: 'Nothing to record.' He suffered much mentally:

> But the misery and inactivity when so much is needed to be done, the monotony, the aimless futility of existence that is no longer useful, this is the real trial which makes imprisonment intolerable.[125]

He yearned for news of England, for liberation, and recognized 'an intense desire to witness some day the defeat and humiliation of our insolent enemy'.

On reflection, why not bring that day forward?

After settling into camp, it really was time to fight back.

IV

SMILE BOYS, THAT'S THE STYLE:
THE WAR OF RESISTANCE BEHIND THE WIRE

WILHELM
FUCK HIM

Graffito, complete with portrait of the Kaiser, scrawled on the wall of
British PoW urinal at Roubaix labour camp

They sang. What songs they sang.

Watching three hundred British prisoners hobble away in rags and sabots in the middle of winter for forced labour behind the front line, Benjamin Muse, the American volunteer in the King's Royal Rifle Company, could hardly believe it when they burst into the ironic song: 'Here We Are, Here We Are, Here We Are Again'.

And they sang it 'right lustily', added Ben Muse.[1]

The story of British PoWs in the Kaiser's camps has been called the 'silent battle'. This is a demi-truth. The British, unless they were dead and buried in that dismal cemetery tacked as an afterthought to the outside of the *Lager,* never stopped singing. When there was nothing else left, nothing else to scrap with against the Germans, the British would wield hymns, arias, Tommy marching songs (rarely trench songs), music hall ditties (with the words topically changed, a British soldier's speciality), and anthems.

But there was a *battle*, in the conventionally understood sense of seeking to destroy enemy morale and *matériel*. British soldiers were wholly conscious of this. In the unambiguous words of one private soldier:

. . . when we realised fully that we were prisoners we determined that the fight should be carried on behind the lines as well as in front

> of it . . . We were fighting a war against the Germans, in their own
> territory.[2]

Only the weapons were unorthodox. Songs were one (trifling
weapon in the armoury of the ragged resisters, along with 'Boche-
baiting', arson and propaganda. And then there were the big guns
strike action, sabotage, and, most spectacular of all, 'jug-cracking'
or escape. This is treated of elsewhere.[3]

Few were the prisoners who did not take up some form of 'arms'
against their captors. So pervasive was resistance that it cannot be
explained by the natural inclinations of a few troublemakers suffering from anti-authority syndrome. The great motivation of the
majority of the ragged resisters was not chemical imbalance in the
brain or psychic remnants of Freudian struggles with Father; it was
the greater war itself.

British soldiers taken prisoner up to the end of 1916 were either
shilling-a-day men, part-time professionals ('Saturday Night' soldiers) or volunteers. Every reason that had got them into khaki
in the first place was a reason to continue the war now that they
were behind barbed wire, be it professional pride in arms, the
wish to defend Blighty, or to fight an ideological struggle against
German tyranny. If anything, the act of surrender made some British soldiers more warlike than ever. Defying the Germans in the
camps was a chance to erase shame, a way of restoring the sense
of self and repairing emasculated manhood. A further fillip to resistance came when PoWs at Döberitz asked the British Foreign
Office whether they should volunteer for work as their captors
wished; the reply from Sir Edward Grey was that: 'His Majesty's
Government did not wish them to work in the manner referred
to.'[4] What Grey intended by this piece of diplomaticese is open
to endless analysis; the men in Döberitz interpreted it to mean
'No'.

Conscripted soldiers when taken captive proved to be composed
of similar stuff to the professionals and the volunteers. Maybe this is
not so surprising. All British soldiers, no matter how they ended up
in khaki, hailed from a society that inculcated the virtues of pluck

and patriotism, whether it was in the pages of *Boy's Own*, the classroom, the public house, or in sermons from the pulpit. The bulk of British soldiers were also from the industrial working class – the most assertive, bloody-minded, proud working class in the world, one which carried high a banner of rights and freedoms won. It did not doff its cap easily.

British soldiers, no matter their social or military rank, expected to be treated with respect. And there was the rub: the Prussian military system was based on coercion and bullying. 'Our men were not used to being shouted at,' observed one British officer in what will serve as metaphor, 'and when they were, they usually responded with spirit'.[5] What went for the men went for the officers. Old Etonian Archer Cust was in Graudenz camp when the commandant sought to impose on officers an unfair collective punishment; Cust's response: 'This was not going to be taken lying down.'[6]

Where resistance did not exist, the Germans brought it upon themselves. Men who wanted a quiet life in the camps rarely found it. The British government's report on British forced labour in the coal and salt mines put the matter succinctly:

The German system has been to enforce discipline first by abuse, and where that has failed, by unrestrained violence, thus provoking opposition from the start and continually hardening the men's determination to resist.[7]

Another culture clash in the camps boded ill. The Germans inexplicably failed to realize that the *British* were the greatest people in the world, not themselves. Mightily zealous and prickly too were the British about this honour, as Private Elvin, 4/Royal Fusiliers, showed at Güstrow in the war's early days:

On November 30th, 1914, while standing in the queue for bread issue, a German sentry standing near me talking to some Russians said that when Englishmen were captured they went down on their knees and cried for mercy. I told him that it was not Englishmen but Germans who did that. Whereupon the sentry rushed at me with his bayonet and made a deliberate thrust at my heart; I warded off the blow and the bayonet pierced my left arm. The sentry kicked and clouted me all over.[8]

One repercussion of this sense of British entitlement was British other ranks' refusal to salute in the required Prussian manner and refusal to salute German *Unteroffiziers* (which they considered humiliating) in any manner whatsoever. That faultline ran through the camps from the first day of the war to the last.[9]

British officers were no less ardent in upholding the national superiority. At Holzminden one officer, when bawled at by 'Milwaukee Bill' Niemeyer, the commandant, was unable to refrain from answering back, 'All right, don't shout at me, you bloody foreigner!' Even Prussians were no match for British conceit. When officers of the Royal Navy, picked up from the grey sinking sea of Jutland, arrived at Mainz they coolly refused the salute of the Prussian commandant at *Appell*. To Frenchman Georges Connes, who was watching:

> the patriot in us approves the insult to the enemy; the soldier disapproves the offence to the man who, according to military conventions, is undeniably our chief . . . [But] What is a Prussian colonel next to a lieutenant in His Majesty's navy![10]

For Connes it was a scene of silent high drama amid the towering walls of the Citadel he would 'never forget'.

In one camp inhabited by Brian Horrocks the commandant put up a sign which read:

> German sentries will refrain from striking British prisoners of war, because they are mad.[11]

They were. They were mad enough to strike back. As Horrocks noted, 'British, mind you' – not French, Russians or Italians. Horrocks was always known to his friends as 'Pup', on account of his youth. When he reached the grand age of twenty-one in 1916 they marked his passage to adulthood by changing his nickname – to 'Dog'.

Humour. Humour was a good weapon. Parodying the Germans, or 'Hun-baiting', was an endlessly fruitful pastime in the camps.

There seemed something insufferably pompous about German military culture, which made it an easy target for that aged strain of British humour which is fiercely democratic and delights in pricking pretension. German drill was simply made to be mocked. Douglas Lyall Grant was only one of numerous officers sentenced to 'cells' for imitating the goose step to comic effect. While detained at the Kaiser's displeasure in Holzminden Lyall Grant recorded in his secret diary:

5/11/17: I am writing this in jug, where I have retired for three days' rest for doing the goose step on appell. My cell is simply a cellar, about 8' high, 6' broad and 15' long, with one small window up at the ground level. It is very cold but I get a stove lit in the afternoon so am really better off here than outside.

By shouting I can talk to the two fellows next door on either side. As I brought my own mattress I am quite comfortable in bed and stop there most of the day. The other furniture is a table, stool, tin basin and jug.

9/11/17: Had an interview with the Commandant on the subject of my imprisonment for doing what he called a 'comic walk'. I pointed out that some people were born with a stammer and some with peculiar walks and I was one of the latter. He said that, that being so, he would tell his officers that I could walk as I liked on appell. Truly the Hun has no sense of humour.[12]

In the wire world anything Prussian and overstated was fair comic game, not excluding discipline and punishment. After one attempted escape at Holzminden, Niemeyer ordered his guards to shoot any prisoner who so much as looked out of the windows of the stone barracks blocks. Such a disproportionate consequence got its inevitable ridiculing. A British officer made a human dummy and worked it up and down in front of a window with a string. There was much 'splintering and smashing of glass', remembered Will Harvey, as the guards shot frantically at the model human. The British officers, meanwhile, were 'crawling about on our hands and knees . . . laughing until we could hardly move'.[13]

Harvey would have appreciated the 'ragging' his fellow officers at Schwarmstedt daily gave the staff. Every time a guard in the tin-office, where spare PoW food was kept, punctured a can with his tin-opener as he began his search for contraband, someone in the waiting queue screamed 'Handgranaten!' or 'Bomben!' And the staff jumped. Every time.[14]

One prejudice held by the British was not quite true: there were Germans who shared their sense of humour. Brian Horrocks was delighted when Custrin's commandant hung a sign saying 'Useless' by a window bar some would-be escaper had sawn through and replaced with a putty version. Naturally, the British had to have the last laugh. The following night, using a set of duplicate keys, a group of officer prisoners entered the commandant's office and hung the sign up over his desk.[15]

In photographs of British officers of the Great War the subjects, with their oiled-down hair, their moustaches, their faces creased by the cares of combat, always look far older than their real age. By and large British officer PoWs were very young, the vast majority of them under twenty-five. They had not yet grown out of pranking, or youthful japes. And why would they now? Ragging the Hun passed the time of endless day, it scored small subversive victories against the enemy's morale, and it helped maintain, even increase, the spirits of the tribe in khaki. Ragging helped daily endurance, helped men find the courage to carry on. Ragging cut the German captors down to a size where they no longer seemed invincible, or worthy of fear. To dismiss 'Hun-baiting' as some facile public school arrested development is to marvellously miss the point.[16] Ridiculing the Germans was a weapon in the battle of minds.

Besides, all ranks of the British Army in captivity parodied the Germans. It was irresistible. Private Tommy Gay, walking back to camp with his Arbeitskommando, was ordered by the guard 'Augen links!' ('Eyes left') as a German officer strode into sight. Somebody blew a raspberry.[17]

Taking the piss became literal at Roubaix motor depot in Northern France, where British PoWs chalked a portrait of the Kaiser on the wall of the urinal, with the inscription:

WILHELM
FUCK HIM

The drawing was used for 'target practice'. To soothe the ruffled feathers of the Germans, 'ferocious and scandalized' by the artist's conception of His Imperial Majesty, took all the wiles of the PoWs' representative, William Tucker.[18]

Had the Germans but known it, PoWs urinating on an image of the Kaiser's head was the very least of their troubles at the Roubaix depot, where Tucker and his comrades were commanded to repair the grey wheezing lorries of the Imperial Army. 'In this,' considered Tucker, 'the Germans simply asked for trouble – and got it.' Sabotage was easily and efficiently committed. One favourite trick was to put old screws and bits of metal off the workshop floor into the engine cylinders. Also:

> Those of us on our backs underneath lorries would never dream of replacing one split pin without removing two others – and loosening operational nuts elsewhere in the bargain.[19]

The resistance campaign of the PoWs at Roubaix was highly organized. Every night after the day's sweat and toil the PoWs held a surreptitious meeting to give an account of damage they had done, compare ideas, and discuss 'ways and means of inflicting the maximum sabotage with the minimum fuss'.[20] There was one fly in the grease:

> It did happen several times that German mechanics were unjustly removed from the garages as a result of our sabotages and I must record that it weighed very heavily on our consciences. So much so that prisoners who had caused the particular damage would sometimes be on the point of confessing involvement and so save a German mechanic, whom they had grown to like, from being unfairly accused and sent to the trenches. In the final, rather painful, analysis, however, there was always the consolation that we might be saving the lives of our compatriots on the other side.[21]

The curious inability of the guards to detect the sabotage going on around them was not exclusive to Roubaix; the phenomenon was widespread. It was almost as though the Germans could not conceive of anything so irregular, therefore it did not exist. But it did. Sabotage by PoWs in workplaces was carried out on an industrial scale, and if done slyly brought results for little risk. Sent to work on the lock at Dieteheim, Private Don Corker dropped tools in the river or buried them; the guards blamed civilian employees for carelessness. Corporal Edward Edwards, working at a brickyard near Giessen, recalled:

> There were twelve of us all told on that brick-yard job. Three or four shovelled clay into the mixing machine, two more filled the little car which two others pushed along the track of the narrow-gauge railroad ... Sometimes we forgot to brake the car so that it would ricochet on in a flying leap off the end of the track, and so on over the dump. The guards would rage and swear but could prove nothing so long as our fellows did not get too raw and do this too frequently.[22]

Then there was Private Frank MacDonald of the Canadian Mounted Rifles, a fire-eater of a resister; at Auguste Victoria coal mine he skived by hiding in the workings during the day, and joining the tail of the detail as it made its way back up at the end of the shift. When this wheeze was rumbled, he went on go-slows and broke tools. Put to work planting cabbages, MacDonald pinched them at the junction of root and stalk before interment so they would die. Because of the geographical spread of farms, agriculture tended to be difficult to supervise; it therefore offered almost unlimited opportunities for injury to the German economy. On many peasant smallholdings there were no guards for PoWs, just a tired, distracted farmer as overseer. So, singing while he worked, Edward Page, RMLI, buried more potatoes than he picked. To the words of 'One for the Kaiser' he put one small potato in his basket, and on the refrain of 'and six for King George' covered over half a dozen as deeply as possible to rot in the black German earth.[23]

Woe to those caught indulging in sabotage. A prisoner who put sand instead of grease in the wheels of carts in a munitions factory received a punishment of ten years detention in a German civilian prison.

Regulars and reservists like Edward Page tended to make particularly poor slaves. Having spent years in Her or His Majesty's armed forces dodging manual labour – something British servicemen had an almost pathological loathing of – they knew all the tricks of the work-shy. Behind Boche barbed wire the British serviceman's innate desire to avoid labour received an ideological justification. In the words of one old hand, Leading Seaman Eric Surrey Dane:

> A dislike of work is inborn in every average servicemen and it is just as much part of his kit as his tunic. But with prisoners of war this dislike, backed by the very acceptable theory that all work done for the Boche was an unpatriotic act as it released labour to be used against our Forces, developed into a highly specialized act.[24]

The commonest way of dodging work or 'swinging the lead' was to go '*krank*', i.e. report sick. This usually failed, since the German stock response to illness was to offer a cure of aspirin and *Arbeit*. Or a prick of the stomach with a bayonet. Or a gun to the head. Or a kicking. When the interpreter asked Sapper George Waymark's little group of prisoners parading for work at 5 a.m. at Illies, near the front line, whether anyone wanted to go sick, one man unwisely said he did: 'The officer came and looked at him, and then gave him a punch in the face which knocked him down. He had to march with the rest of us.'[25]

Yes, a punch to the face was a typical response too. However, a practised dodger such as Surrey Dane or a man with imagination might just achieve a skive by going *krank*. Suffering from an unusual or difficult to diagnose condition stood the best chance of success. Having invented an excruciating ear pain, Surrey Dane had 'two glorious weeks in hospital' while everyone else on his sick parade, with their familiar flu, stomach ache and painful feet, was sent off to toil.[26] The irrepressible Frank MacDonald once avoided work at the satanic Auguste Victoria coal pit by plastering mustard, soap and salt from his Red Cross parcel on his skin. The camp doctor was convinced the resultant spots signified plague and sent MacDonald to Munster Hospital.

Madness was the best illness for securing a skive. A bugler from the King's Own Yorkshire Light Infantry imprisoned along with Surrey Dane filled his mouth with Koynus toothpaste to make foam in a mock epileptic fit. He was given permanent light duties around camp. Even in a godforsaken reprisal camp in Russia, where pretence at physical illness stood next to no chance of success because the near-dead were made to work, insanity could be a let-out from labour. In the chimney of the piggery serving as the prisoners' quarters at Reiskatte, Sergeant 'Paddy' Oliver of the East Surreys abased himself with earth and chanted gibberish. The guards thought him quite mad and left him alone.[27] The problem with feigning madness, as everyone recognized, was that eventually the imitation of the condition might bring its reality.

Sergeant Oliver was unlucky in being required to work. Generally the Germans observed the tacit international convention that NCOs of the rank of corporal and above were absolved labour.[28] In the first year of the war, before the camp authorities became wise, this dispensation was roundly taken advantage of by any Tommy with V stripes near the cuff denoting long service. Removed, sewn upside down and higher on the arm, they gave the wearer the appearance of holding the rank of corporal or sergeant. Such fake NCOs were known as 'buckshee' corporals, as opposed to 'pukka' ones. A few buckshee NCOs avoided work throughout their captivity, although self-promotion tightened after yards of stripes were optimistically but incautiously ordered from Britain.[29] The ruse also lost its allure because German camp authorities, increasingly irritated by British NCOs' insistence on an absolute right not to work, sent uppity NCOs to Minden or Grossenweidenmoor – infamous *strafe* camps – as punishment.

Duty-bound to provide men for labour, some commandants anyway ignored the exemption for NCOs and 'harshed', drilled or exercised them until they did work. Or the NCOs accepted that their days would be punishingly filled with running up and down or Prussian-style parading for ten hours at a time.

*

Their spirit of resistance in the face of oppression and injustice has been unconquerable; but these small parties, cut off from the outside world and without means of effective appeal, have, of course, been powerless against systematic violence.

> *Government Committee on the Treatment by the Enemy of*
> *British Prisoners of War regarding British prisoners'*
> *refusal to work on behalf of Germany*

Let us now praise famous men. There was no corner of Germany and the occupied lands, from Belgium to the Russian front, from Schleswig-Holstein to the Swiss border, that did not see strikes by British PoWs. These refusals to work are the unheralded heroics of British military history, 1914–18. They run to thousands of instances, and are as rousing in their dignity as they are pitiful in their frequently tragic outcomes. Sometimes the strikes were patriotically motivated – such as the refusal to *Arbeit* by five British prisoners at Celle's Zeppelin works[30] – and sometimes prompted by the dire conditions of employment. Up to 250 prisoners took part in a strike at Westerholt coal mine in the Ruhr, a reminder that resistance was not a minority activity. Typically, strikes were undertaken by 10–20 men in some backwater of Germany. On occasion, a single man would make a stand.

A man such as Corporal John Brady, King's Own Yorkshire Light Infantry.

Brady was an Old Contemptible, captured at Le Cateau. By December 1915 he had had enough of conditions in the stone quarry near Sennelager to which he had been sent, and informed the German guard that he and the other British prisoners were going on strike. Brady later wrote:

> I thought he was going mad . . . you must get your men to work you swine out came his revolver and call for the sentrys to fix bayonets . . . we still refused so he cooled down . . . then we had bit of a rough time till 12 a.m. when a Captain and Corporal and fifteen Germans came to the place the very first thing I saw the sentrys changing

> Magazines and fixing bayonets then I thought our time had come then we were fell in parade.[31]

The men were put in prison, then placed on trial, with the strong likelihood they would be shot. In fact, the court martial was fair:

> An officer came from Berlin and told me that he was our solicitor so I told him all I knew and what he did he said he would do his very best for us but we stood on a charge of mutiny and rebellion I don't mind telling you I did not sleep that night the next morning at 10 a.m. we were in court the case lasted four hours. Our solicitor spoke very well for us so [while] we were found guilty of Mutiny and sentenced to six months with hard labour, we were all smiles after that some said they could do that on their head.

This was heart-breakingly misplaced optimism. Although the Kaiser's regime would boast to the international press that its courts martial never ever sentenced any British PoWs to death, in reality the conditions endured by PoWs in military or civilian prisons – the hard labour, the beatings, the lack of food, the cold, the isolation from friendly faces and voices – amounted to execution for some. Sure enough, out of Brady's party one died in prison and another was taken to hospital, where he was presumed to have perished.

Weak, barely able to walk, Brady returned to Sennelager stem camp to finish his sentence. He was put to work sweeping the streets of Paderborn, during which time he was frequently abused and hit. A refusal to work in a mine resulted in fourteen days *Dunkelarrest* – incarceration in a dark cell on a diet of bread and water for three days, camp rations fourth day, the cycle repeated until the sentence was finished – before transfer to Minden, where he did not receive a food parcel for two months, 'so I had to live like a pig again'.

Brady and fellow Britons, plus sixty Frenchmen, were then ordered to work in a nearby factory, making barbed-wire. But the factory produced barbed-wire for the front, so they refused the work on the principle that it contravened the Hague Convention by which prisoners were excused war work, at which

> the Corporal lost his temper and struck us with his bayonet and

kicked us around the room then I said to my pal stick it Harry we
will get over it so at 4 p.m. we were marched to prison I thought my
pal were going to break down his first time in prison we stayed seven
days and returned back to that place [the barbed-wire factory].

Again Brady and his pal refused to participate in war work, so they
were forced to stand at attention (*Stillgestanden*) from 5 a.m. to 9
p.m. on a slice of bread daily till they consented to work. They 'stuck
it' for several days, after which they were offered work on the land.
To this they consented. Unfortunately the new job, which was not
too onerous and included decent food, lasted only a month. Brady
was then transferred to Munster:

> ... my pal had to go in the pit so I told him to refuse but he was
> broken hearted and went to work so I went to have a look at this shop
> I thought it was not too bad I would give it a trial it were nothing
> concerning the war.

Alas, the Yorkshireman was soon in trouble for striking a civilian
worker. The camp guards beat him 'black and blue' and threw him
in a cell. Undaunted, he continued his one-man resistance struggle:

> When my time were up I once more refused to go out to work well
> I were just about killed and kicked into a cell 28 days before I seed
> anyone I suffered very much in the 28 days ... then I started plan-
> ning my escape.

Brady made repeated escape attempts, and took all the consequent
punishments. His travails and troubles were ended in April 1918
when he received, to his great surprise, a telegram informing him
he was being exchanged for a German corporal and was going to
Holland. Only his health was broken. He had not yielded. The Germans were doubtless glad to see him go.

Corporal John Brady, King's Own Yorkshire Light Infantry, received no medals for his unvanquished valour behind the German
line.

The men of the 'Iron Twenty' would have understood what motivated Corporal Brady. At Geisweid Iron Works in Westphalia,

twenty Canadian PoWs banded together in a point-blank refusal
to work. Whenever. Whatever. They also determined to show the
Germans that they could take any punishment inflicted without
giving in.[32] For their mutinies the Iron Twenty received beatings
that another prisoner claimed he could not imagine anyone surviving.[33] The beatings sustained were beyond belief; James Martin,
a twenty-six-year-old timber worker from British Columbia captured at Ypres with the 7th Battalion, had his head slashed by an
officer's sword, two ribs broken by rifle butts, and was then thrown
into solitary confinement. His cell was a coal bin. Another of the
Iron Twenty, Lawrence Kane, was kept in Geisweid's steam room
for five consecutive days, when most collapsed after only an hour
or so. To add to his torment, two of his ribs were smashed in. Still,
he refused to recant his vow not to work. On top of the unofficial,
off-the-record beatings and torture, the alleged ringleaders of the
Iron Twenty were officially sentenced to two years each in prison.
The sentences were served in the military jails of Buzbach and Cologne. Despite all this, the men of the Iron Twenty refused to crack.
On his release from prison Charles Riley, a sometime acrobat from
Montreal, almost immediately received another sentence, this time
of three months. For again refusing to work.

The members of the Iron Twenty chose their name well. They
were hard men.

Punishments for striking were promiscuous, random, and only
consistent in their harshness. Corporal Robert Burrows, Royal
Scots Fusiliers, was imprisoned at Süderzollhaus, where the men
were required to work in a peat bog in water up to their knees, their
only clothing a blanket, on pitiful rations. One day in early 1915:

> I myself was tied up for four hours on the charge of refusing to turn
> the men out for work. No man was fit for work as they were suffer-
> ing from dysentery, and I was myself. We were obliged to put paper
> inside our trousers to prevent the dysentery staining them as we
> were too weak to get to the latrines.[34]

By 'tied up', Burrows meant he was given the German Army field
punishment of being tied to a post, no coat, with his arms over his

head, and his feet barely touching the ground, which caused agony as the blood drained from his extremities.

Despite being put in front of an Uhlan firing squad, thirty-four British strikers at Kilizeem on the Gulf of Riga refused to work. Their punishment? The Uhlans tied them to trees, so they hung by their hands 'being bitten by mosquitoes and the sentries butting them with rifles'. When the prisoners fainted their faces were beaten to a pulp with fists. The refusers stuck this for three days on no food, until their mates advised them they had done their 'bit and it was useless going through unnecessary torture'.[35]

Putting 'nix Arbeiter' before mock firing squads was a commonplace, as were beatings with swords, fists, rifle butts, not forgetting thrashings with sjamboks and 'pieces of rubber about 18 inches long, the thickness of solid bicycle tyres'.[36] Then there was *Stillgestanden* and *Dunkelarrest*.

The torture of *Stillgestanden* was well described by Private Cleeton. After refusing on principle to toil in a Dortmund shell factory, Cleeton, along with others, was beaten with rifle butts then put on *Stillgestanden*:

> . . . you were stood there and they told you in German to stand erect, toes at an angle of forty-five degrees, thumbs in line with the seams of your pants . . . They stood us up there from five o'clock in the morning until ten o'clock at night, fifteen of us . . . On one occasion one of our number, MacArthur, who was wearing a British Warm, felt his nose running. Of course, you couldn't do anything about it. Even if you wanted to go to the bathroom there was no moving, you performed your business right there and that was that. So he hinted; he just turned his head, that was all. A German struck him across the back of the neck. MacArthur jumped and of course theres a dozen [guards] there, but he did have time to open his British Warm and say 'Here, you bastards, stick it there'. That was the last I heard of Jack MacArthur, the last I saw. We all went down eventually. Finally I collapsed too.[37]

Cleeton developed double pneumonia. He survived, yet his health was so wrecked he was unable to work thereafter. (No one would accuse the Kaiser's overseers of being sensible managers of human resources.)

As one British wag noted, the only days when *Stillgestanden* did not occur were when the weather was pleasant. Working from 6 a.m. to 6 p.m. in a stone quarry at Elbingerode in the Harz mountains, in winter Lance-Corporal Thomas Higgins' starving body became so bloated by oedema 'my legs were all one thickness'. One rainy day he too rebelled:

> We threw our tools down and refused to do any more. The sentries kicked punched and threatened to shoot, but we stuck it out and they took us back to billet. That devil of a Sergeant Major met us at the doors, and he said 'The Englanders want a holiday, do they?' – for by now most of us understood German. He said get inside and dry yourselves. We got in and got our tunics and shirts off and were in our bare feet getting dry as well as we could, when that devil, and the sentries rushed in the room with revolvers and rifles pointed at us. 'Fall in line,' he roared, 'Just as you are', at the same time helping us along with kicks. 'Now march', he yelled. The doors were opened, it was still pouring with rain, but we were driven out in it, as we were, and had to stand in line for about an hour. I had bare feet, but I had my shirt on. Some had their shirts off. The sentry stood under cover with loaded rifles pointed at us, and the major stood grinning and asking us how we liked our holiday. The cold was terrible. After this we got no bread that day.[38]

Higgins once again contemplated suicide, but 'self-murder takes a bit of doing'. *Stillgestanden* was an ordeal for a healthy soldier; for a man like Higgins, weakened by disease, in bad weather it made for unbearable pain.

The punishment for Private Edward Page after going on strike when he was transferred to Duisberg electrical works was a particularly austere form of *Dunkelarrest*:

> Our overcoats and the daily ration of bread were also taken from us. The place in which we were confined was an old, disused storehouse, a most filthy, rat-infested den, with a large hole in the roof.

Prisoners had been previously confined there, and, as they had not been permitted to leave the place under any circumstances, the corners and floors were filthy, with a most horrible stench. To make matters worse, iron bars about four feet from the ground traversed the building every three or four yards, making it almost impossible to walk upright.

Our countrymen employed on the night-shift soon joined us, as they refused to work while we were suffering confinement. We were kept surrounded by rats and filth in a state of starvation, with no blankets or covering of any kind during the bitter cold nights, until, thoroughly exhausted, we were forced to submit. Had we not done so, in our enfeebled condition, many would have succumbed as the result of this inhuman treatment. On our arrival at the works the following day we were subjected to the jeers and taunts of the Hun officials and workmen at the failure of our effort.[39]

The stock of punishments was not yet exhausted. Many camps had a *Strafbaracke* in which men were made to sit on low benches in perfect silence. If they moved or spoke, they were hit. At Giessen, PoWs who refused to work in munitions were made to carry a sack of bricks on their backs up a steep hill at the point of a bayonet. Or, in two cases shot dead.[40] On occasion the 'butcher's knife' went into flesh, all the way in: at Bokelah 3 in May 1916 a group of British and Canadian prisoners refused to work laying railway sleepers; the elderly and usually lackadaisical commandant, 'Farmer Bill', reverted to the ferocious Prussian warrant officer he had been before the war and summoned his guards; Private Alexander Logan, 2/King's Own (Royal Lancaster Regiment), a father of six, was bayoneted to death. His remains are now in Hamburg cemetery.

Since '*nix Arbeit*' could be construed as mutiny under the German *War Book*, hundreds of striker PoWs joined Corporal John Brady in being tried on this severest of charges. By the end of 1916 there were at least eighty British PoWs in Cologne military prison serving sentences for 'mutiny' or hitting German guards in retaliation. They included Sergeant A.J. Parsons, 11/Rifle Brigade, and thirteen other NCOs who had refused to act as 'sentries over the men' on an *Arbeitskommando* in East Prussia. It was a matter of pride to Sergeant Parsons that the good fight was carried on behind bars, by slyly wrecking the compulsory prison work of shirt-making; he put wristbands where collars were meant to go.

Overall, 760 British PoWs served time in a German prison, usually Cologne, for 'crimes' that clearly constitute action against the enemy (mutiny, sabotage, riot, arson, disobedience, 'lack of respect', assaulting guards, sedition, with one brave heart banged up for 'insulting the Emperor').[41] On a dark note, conditions in Cologne continued to take the lives of British forces. Private Brook, one of the Brokelah 3 'mutineers', died of pneumonia contracted in his damp cell. On a lighter note the survivors included Corporal Cullen, Queens' (West Surrey) Regiment, whose courtroom attempt to avoid imprisonment for mutiny deserves to be noted in history for its sheer chutzpah. Cullen appeared in court with his head shaved except for a top lock, which was greased and 'standing up like an attenuated spike', and proceeded to explain to the august judges that he was a Hottentot, his hair was part of his religion, and he had gone on strike because he was forbidden to work on a Thursday by the credos of his creed. He got five years servitude.

Cullen had the last laugh. When a British-German exchange of officers and NCOs was arranged in early 1915 a special clause allowed that prisoners undergoing terms of imprisonment in fortresses should be given priority. Cullen was among the first to go to Holland.

What was *really* funny was that Cullen wasn't a real corporal. He was a 'buckshee' one.

As so often in war, leadership was crucial in determining whether men struck or not, whether they stood tall or bowed down. Someone, either because of rank, experience, training, or personality needed to be the first to say 'No'. Private Walter Humphreys had worked loading ammunition onto trucks – a clear-cut case of illegal war work – several times, but one day his labour gang was joined by an older prisoner, who said they should reject such aid to the enemy because: 'It's against international law.' After a group discussion they agreed to boycott the work. An officer blusteringly threatened to shoot them, yet eventually did nothing and marched them back to their compound. He then got the French to do the work instead.[42]

Strike action in 1915–16, when German authorities were unprepared, had a better chance of a happy outcome than later in the war.[43] Overall, about 10 per cent of strikes were successful – either because the Kaiser's overseers had an outbreak of sanity and compassion, or (more usually) because a few elderly *Landsturmers*, armed with equally venerable Mauser rifles, did not fancy their chances in the melees that would ensue if they kept pushing prisoners too far. Which is what happened at Munster II when prisoners refused to work at a horse depot preparing remounts for the front. The guards rounded up the prisoners at bayonet point; an affray started in which one soldier in the Cheshires was bayoneted in the arm; he, in turn, near throttled a guard. The Germans subdued the immediate protest by force of arms. However, they halted their attempts to use British prisoners at the depot.[44]

Strikes could bring positive outcomes in unlikely ways. At Roubaix motor depot William Tucker and his fellow prisoners decided 'whatever the risk' to protest over the refusal of Germans to allow them to communicate with home. At parade next morning the prisoners declined to move off, and Tucker explained to the German officer commanding that they were protesting about the German unwillingness to provide facilities for the prisoners to write to their parents. The response of the officer was predictable:

> He strutted to the extreme right-hand man of the line of prisoners, fixed him with a grim stare for a second or two, positioned his revolver about an inch from his throat, and simply growled, 'Rechts um', his finger ominously on the trigger.
>
> After about ten seconds, but what seemed to me a good ten minutes, our involved prisoner sullenly but obediently turned right. The German then subjected the next prisoner in line to the same operation. He turned in five seconds. The next turned immediately and the remainder turned without further command.[45]

But the protest wasn't a humiliating fizzle. Tucker was required to make a written report to the *Lager*'s commandant, who ('to his credit') passed it to his headquarters. As a result, a postal address for the prisoners was set up, and the PoWs were given two postcards to write home.

*

They sang. What songs they sang. Verses three and four of 'Rule Britannia' were always good to belt out in adversity:

> Still more majestic shalt thou rise,
> More dreadful, from each foreign stroke;
> As the loud blast that tears the skies,
> Serves but to root thy native oak.
> 'Rule, Britannia! Britannia rule the waves:
> Britons never will be slaves.'
>
> Thee haughty tyrants ne'er shall tame:
> All their attempts to bend thee down,
> Will but arouse thy generous flame;
> But work their woe, and thy renown.
> 'Rule, Britannia! Britannia rule the waves:
> Britons never will be slaves.'

When officers at Graudenz sang 'Glory, Alleluia' on parade in protest at the stopping of parcels as punishment for a tunnel escape, the camp's guards weighed in with the butts of their rifles. 'Quite an ugly scene followed,' recalled Archer Cust, 'when twenty or thirty of us were clubbed through the doors.' The matter, though, ended with a musical finale. When the most offensive German officer, 'the Green lizard', stalked away from the apparently put-down revolt he was treated to a mass serenade of 'Good-bye-eee' from the windows.[46] Tired of the British constantly singing their national anthem, the commandant at Döberitz lost patience and banned singing altogether.

*

Officers, being purportedly privileged beings, were exempted from work by the Geneva Convention, so could hardly go on strike or sabotage industry. Yet they too had their methods of resistance, beyond the tried-and-tested escaping business. Theirs was a war of resistance by any imaginative means possible. Archer Cust, when starving children gathered outside Graudenz camp in autumn 1918 calling for 'englische Kuchen' threw them absolutely heaps of biscuits, 'as it is excellent propaganda'.[47] Conversely, an officer at Crefeld, annoyed by a crowd of schoolchildren gathered at the perimeter wire singing 'Deutshcland über Alles' – the habit of German civilians gawping and chanting at prisoners really galled – dressed up like a pierrot and suddenly appeared at a window: the group of children 'exploded' and ran off. At Fort 9, Ingolstadt, officers plumped for the decidedly less sophisticated burning of paper and cardboard from their Red Cross parcels, the materials being scarce and valuable in Germany. Horace Gilliland and friends (all full of 'offensive spirit') systematically vandalized their camps in order to bleed Germany of resources. Boycotting camp *Kantinen* – thus hitting the Germans in the pocket – was always a peculiarly successful tactic in righting wrongs. And in Neusse, John Poole was among the happy miscreants who, 'not unintentionally', kicked their recreational football over the fence to land amidst drilling soldiers at the training camp next door. Pickelhaubes went flying in every direction.[48] Claude Templer could not resist a battle of words with the enemy; on being escorted through Berlin on a change of camp, he replied to the jeering crowd in the street after they shouted '*Gott strafe England*', 'You do well to leave that to God for you yourselves can never do it.'[49]

Almost inevitably, the bad boys' camp of Hellminden saw the best of officer resistance. When a captured escaper from Holzminden, Lieutenant Mortimer-Phelan, RFC, was brutally kicked by a camp sentry, the Senior British Officer, Colonel Stokes Roberts, threatened to abdicate responsibility for the future conduct of British officers – an apparently small gesture which actually hid the extreme and momentous message that he regarded the camp as so monstrous as to be a common gaol, not a PoW camp covered by the Hague Convention.[50] The ultimatum was ignored by Niemeyer, so the British began passive resistance, shuffling onto 9 a.m. *Appell* the following morning wearing, for the most part, cardigans instead of their tunics, and innocent of all headgear. When the German officers appeared, no one saluted. Matters quickly escalated. Niemeyer punished the prisoners for not appearing on *Appell* correctly dressed; Colonel Stokes Roberts countered by ordering another mis-parade. One overly combative officer dropped a large faggot of wood from an upper window of *Kaserne B*, missing Niemeyer by inches. Niemeyer ordered sentries to open fire. Only the poor marksmanship of the *Landsturm* guards averted deaths.

An official British complaint to the *Kriegsministerium* brought forth a government representative to investigate the happenings at Holzminden. Laughably, Niemeyer acted as translator. To no one's amazement, the representative went away convinced that the British were exaggerating. On the plus side for the British, Niemeyer's accusation of mutiny was quietly dropped.

Disorderly conduct on *Appell* became a standard protest method by officers, not just at Hellminden but elsewhere. At Strohen, fed up with petty tyrannies – confiscation of cigarettes from England, lack of exercise facilities, failure to pass on letters of complaint to the Dutch Embassy and *Kriegsministerium* – prisoners subverted *Appell* held under a particularly Prussian major by performing synchronized bowing, being late, slouching exaggeratedly, all to 'screams of laughter'. Lots received days 'in the jug'.[51]

Prisoners at Fort 9, Ingolstadt, annoyed at an extra *Appell* being added to the day (at 11.30 a.m.) constantly turned the parade into a shambles by arriving late, refusing to keep still to be counted, and not being properly attired. According to Fort 9 inmate, Lieutenant A.J. Evans, RFC,

> Very often the riot [at *Appell*] got so bad that the C.O., after glancing anxiously over his shoulder, beckoned the guard to come in to overawe us. The old Landsturm, as they came pouring through the gate over the moat, were greeted with hoots and yells. At the order of an N.C.O. they loaded – this had no effect on the Frenchmen, who laughed and ragged the C.O. and sentries in French and bad German. But why did the Germans never shoot? It is not difficult to understand. We had no reason to suppose that the Commandant

was tired of life, and we knew that his Feldwebel was an arrant coward; and the one thing quite certain was, that if the order to fire on us was given, the first thing we should do would be to kill the Commandant and the Feldwebel, and they knew it very well – and that was our safeguard . . . We should have won easily – and the Germans knew it. At any time we wished, we could have taken that fort and escaped, though if we had, none of us would have got out of the country alive. You must understand then that the Germans did not tolerate this insubordination because they liked it or because they were too kind-hearted to fire, but because for the sake of their own skins they dared not give the order to fire. The prisoners, on the other hand, were prepared to risk a good deal for the sake of demonstrating how little they cared for German discipline, and for the sake of keeping up their own spirits, but most especially just for the fun of ragging the hated Bosche.[52]

The Germans eventually dropped the 11.30 *Appell*, excepting the announcement of important notices.

To prevent mis-parades becoming riots, camp commandants would concede prisoner requests – after a decent face-saving interval. Restrictions on British officers at Graudenz were lifted two days after the mis-parade in which Archer Cust was clubbed; but, as he remarked, 'anything might have happened if they hadn't been'.[53]

If the inconvenience of an extra *Appell* at 11.30 a.m. seems a trivial reason for constant mis-parades it was not; British officers, especially in *strafe* camps like Fort 9 and Holzminden, lived by the rule that, in Hugh Durnford's words, if 'you conceded the German an inch, he was pretty certain shortly to make overture for a mile'.[54] Acceptance of the 11.30 *Appell* would have ended where? With *Appells* at 2.30, and 4.30 too? Besides, *Appells* were a form of control, of demonstrating dominance. Consequently, as far as PoWs were concerned, the fewer the *Appells* the better. They also, as far as escape-minded men were concerned, got in the way of the day's work: endeavouring to break out.

What constituted the proper treatment of incarcerated British officers made for an endless, fractious tussle between captives and captors. Aside from the period belief that a British officer was deserving of certain standards because he was a gentleman, every man holding a commission from His Majesty was highly conscious that he represented his country. The officer was a British emblem in khaki, pips and crowns. Personal dignity, class convention, and national honour all demanded that British officers be treated with the respect they believed they deserved.

By and large, the Germans played the game. Where and when they did not, they had to be forced into so doing. Or at least just fought. On the first ever *Appell* at godforsaken Stohen, with the wind blowing off the moor, a German sergeant major bawled at the newly arrived British officers to dress right, as if they were his recruits. The British officers, acting as one, acting as though conducted by an invisible hand, refused to move, refused to answer to surname without rank. Only when the German staff addressed them properly did they cooperate. This, considered inmate Lieutenant Gerald Knight, RFC, was victory 'No. 1'[55] for the prisoners. In a camp like Strohen, considered Knight, 'it is very necessary to stand up for one's rights when treated unfairly, otherwise the Germans soon forget that you have any rights'.

Gerald Featherstone Knight, from the Cambridgeshire village of Bow Brickhill, where his grandfather was parson, practised his own principles. And was infamously bayoneted as a result. When a *Landsturmer* ordered him to move in an offensive tone:

> I replied that if he addressed me as a British officer and not as a dog I should obey him at once, otherwise I should remain where I was. After a few more unintelligible threats he advanced, brandishing his weapon, at which I turned sideways to call to a German NCO and protest against such treatment. The kindly sentry aimed a smashing blow at my left foot, which I was luckily able to partially deflect by a slight movement of my knee. Things were certainly quite disturbing, for the next instant he stuck the bayonet almost through my right thigh . . . Not being particularly partial to bayonet thrusts, I decided that I could now abandon my argument without loss of prestige.[56]

Knight was sent to Hannover hospital. On his return to Strohen he happened to be watching, on 15 July 1917, as a small crowd gathered at the wire to welcome Britishers arriving from another camp. The gathering, though small and orderly, was not to the liking of the commandant, who rushed out screaming at the men to move. Two guards came through the gate with fixed bayonets to make the men disperse faster, bayoneting Captain Downes, South Staffordshire Regiment, and Lieutenant Woodhouse, RFC. Woodhouse was only superficially hurt, but Downes had his lung punctured and was conveyed to Hannover hospital, where he later recovered.

Of the bayoneting, Knight wrote:

> It is the worst feeling I know to watch a cowardly display of this sort and yet be able to do absolutely nothing ... Meanwhile, the news reached some Britishers who were half-way through a concert. By mutual consent it was at once broken up by the singing of the National Anthem. Everyone outside at once stood to attention and heartily joined in the last few bars. It was the most impressive scene one could possibly imagine.[57]

What songs they sang.

Some would disagree with Gerald Knight that the singing of the National Anthem at Strohen was the most impressive imaginable scene. They would say his own escape from Strohen had that honour.

Singers, strikers, Boche-baiters, shirkers, piss-takers, saboteurs: Resisters all.

V

THE BARBED-WIRE SCHOOL:
PASSING THE TIME OF DAY UPON DAY

Visited the Art Exhibition now being held here. Everything on exhibit is made or painted in the camp and one would never believe that the hand of man could turn such extraordinary things out of nothing. A grandfather clock, made entirely out of odd pieces of wood and scraps of wire, which keeps perfect time, is only a small example of what is on view.

Captain Douglas Lyall Grant MC, 14/London Regiment
at Gütersloh *Offizierslager*, 25 July 1916

In the wire world, there were days without beginning, days without end. Time was a grey sea stretching featureless towards an horizon that was for ever. The life of a British PoW in the Kaiser's cages was the perverted proof of the maxim that a soldier's lot is 90 per cent boredom, 10 per cent action. Boredom was another enemy to be battled. The stakes were high: a man overcome by *ennui* was likely to lapse into the melancholic apathy that was 'barbed-wire disease'. Will Harvey, being a poet as well as a soldier, gave a telling, memorable description of neurasthenia, portraying it as a 'mould so thick, so gaudily green' which took over and destroyed the minds of men.

The boredom which bred the mould was, Harvey averred, worse for officers as they had nothing but time on their hands whereas

at least soldiers, brutally forced to work in factories or salt-mines, or more pleasantly on farms, score over their officers compelled to idleness, except they make employment for themselves and for another.[1]

True enough, except that NCOs were often idle, and not all prisoners worked all the time. Boredom was not wholly the burden of the commissioned. Besides, all men wanted entertainment, excitement, intellectual stimulation, pleasure, escapism, freedom in the head. Working at a sawmill at Drentwede, Lance-Corporal Thomas Higgins was, despite exhaustion, so desperate for a life of the mind he sat up in his bunk 'reading anything I could get hold of for half the night'.[2] Men in the camps, whatever their rank or station, wanted and needed things to do.

In this the Kaiser's regime was not accommodating, despite Hague Convention clauses requiring captors to provide basic facilities for exercise and recreation. On exchange back to Britain, Corporal Alexander Fyfe, 1/Cameron Highlanders, who had been captured in September 1914, was debriefed about the facilities in the two camps he attended:

At Giessen

Q: Exercise. Facilities for. Games allowed.

A: *None except drilling. No games allowed.*

Recreation. Indoors. Smoking: when, where; ever stopped? Why?

A: *None. No books or even papers. About two days before I left smoking was permitted for about an hour, 10–11 a.m. At no other times.*

At Merseburg

Q: Exercise. Facilities for. Games allowed.

A: *Only football* [not much good to Fyfe, whose leg had been amputated due to the severity of shrapnel wounds].

Q: Recreation. Indoors. Smoking: when, where; ever stopped? Why?

A: *None provided. Smoking allowed at stated times only.*[3]

For four whole years almost all recreations enjoyed by British PoWs were set up by themselves. When the Germans did provide entertainments they tended to be propaganda exercises. To his ire William Tucker, slaving away in motor depots in the occupied territories, was charged 10 pfennigs for a compulsory viewing of German news films.[4] Disgusted, Tucker and the rest of the PoW audience provided their own soundtrack, singing

We are Fred Karno's Army, the Kaiser's Infantry
We cannot shoot, we cannot fight, what bloody good are we . . .

The screening was brought to a rapid close. 'We were not invited to any more film shows,' remembered Private Tucker. Nor were PoWs in countless other camps. Such 'entertainments' invariably ended badly, if not in riot, in uproar.

In the twilight half-world of the camps, men took up many of the pastimes with which they had filled the voids in the trenches and in billets. Beginning with sport and physical exercise.

Wheresoever two or more British troops gathered they kicked, batted, or threw a ball about. As long as they could find a ball. Or space. In most camps any potential '*Spielplatz*' doubled as the *Appell* ground. What was good for standing on *Appell* was by definition bad for sports. Will Harvey was laid up for eight weeks with a poisoned knee after falling over in the square at Crefeld; the camp had previously been a cavalry barracks and the stones on the parade ground were septic from horse faeces. That keen gamesman Douglas Lyall Grant lamented in his secret diary, 'It's rotten, I'm off games for a bit.' He'd broken a rib playing rugger on the cinder surface at Gütersloh. When at Schwarmstedt, Lyall Grant found an even more perilous pitch:

> The ground can hardly be called suitable, being only 50 yards long and 25 yards wide, while a pump and an electric light pole are obstacles to be avoided. However, we had a good enough game with eleven a side and got hot, dirty and scraped.[5]

At Schwarmstedt, the usual division into teams was '[British] Infantry v The World'. This was wishful thinking; not many Allies fancied rugby on a hard surface dodging unyielding obstructions, let alone tackling British hearties. Even Lyall Grant, nobody's idea of a sensitive flower, was dubious about cricket at Holzminden, where 'it was quite impossible to make anything like a true pitch so the game is more dangerous than amusing'.[6] Cramped space for sport meant team sizes unfamiliar to the MCC, FA and RFU. Nine aside was a standard soccer team at Holzminden.

The exercise ground at Magdeburg was notorious for injury, being a cobbled courtyard 90 by 45 yards to serve 450 officers.[7] Munden's *Spielplatz* was softer, being mud, though spoilt, complained Horace Gilliland, by an intersecting row of long wooden latrines, 'a series of holes cut in the ground, with no form of drainage'.[8] The provenance of the 'mud' was open to question. The same quad also housed the general rubbish heap of the camp, which swarmed with flies; 'On warm days the smell was so overpowering it was impossible to take exercise.'[9] Stench also spoilt play at Festung Marienberg in Würzburg, where officer PoWs were allowed to walk, at 10 a.m. on the dot, around the castle terrace. The view over the Main was spectacular, yet the noisome emanations from the large cesspit on the terrace prevented any semblance of pleasure for the convalescing Malcolm Hay.[10] Exercise in such camps consisted of shuffling convict-throngs all walking in the same direction in a confined space, what Alec Waugh termed 'a grey constitutional around the square'.[11] Walking round and round mindlessly had one advantage; it took Lieutenant Archer Cust's mind off his evening hunger pangs and encouraged the 'goddess Sopor'.

In *Lager* pinched for room or lacking kit, ingenuity was indispensable if any sporting life was to be enjoyed. Strohen sports days consisted of short races, jumping, cock-fighting, and a competition, wrote Gerald Knight, 'which necessitated each individual eating a stick bun dangling from a lightly stretched string without using his hands'.[12] With no leather oval available, officers at Magdeburg played rugby with a loaf of bread. (The Germans thought this insulting towards their *Brot* and gave everyone concerned eight days 'cells'.)[13] Stuck for a ball in a newly invented sport that mated rounders and baseball, Freiburg inmates covered a globe of old socks with leather from RFC thigh boots.[14] A shoemaker prisoner was useful at Döberitz when Able Seaman Farrant determined on playing cricket in the summer evenings; the cobbler covered a tennis ball in leather for him. Teams were raised for Army v Navy, or regiment versus regiment. 'Many keen contests took place,' wrote Farrant in his memoir, 'promoting good fellowship through the camp'.[15]

The more motivated prisoners – and especially those preparing themselves for escape – often adopted the patented exercises of the Danish physical fitness enthusiast J.P. Muller, author of 'My System'.[16] This required no kit, and no more space than a cell. Among the 'Mullerites' was A.J. Evans in Fort 9, Ingolstadt:

> Muller's exercises were introduced, and Medlicott and Gaskell, Buckley & I, and many Englishmen and Frenchmen, did them regularly for the rest of the time we were in Germany.

As a result of this strenuous regime (proper Mullerites did the keep-fit exercises in open air, with a cold bath to follow), they were 'never sick or sorry for ourselves the whole time'.[17] The Sports Committee at Bayreuth was likewise of the opinion that sport was 'vitally necessary as a preventative against disease' and organized a full range of activities to keep men happy and healthy. Where committees did not exist a man, with luck, would step forward to ginger and organize. Lieutenant Dobson was hugely admiring of Lieutenant C.M. Usher who

> did a very great deal to keep up the spirits of his fellow-prisoners. He conducted a gymnastic class every morning, encouraged games, taught Highland dancing (he is in the Gordon Highlanders), and even gave instruction on the bagpipes.

Dobson added, tongue in cheek: 'It was an open question whether this last form of sport could be considered a benefit to the community.'[18]

When funds allowed, sports kit could be purchased from canteens, local shops, or ordered in via parcels. The British government also tried to send out supplies, though one football per hundred men was unlikely to occupy many. Soccer was by far the most popular sport in the camps, classless and international. In officers' *Lager* when the commissioned tired of playing each other, they played the orderlies, although orderly Private Norman Dykes thought the servants 'didn't appear to have the stamina of the officers'.[19] Football could even achieve a ceasefire across the wire. Rifleman H. Jeffrey, King's Royal Rifle Corps, detailed to a tannery near Parchim:

On Sundays, they used to take us for a walk and we played football. The director's son at the tanyard got the ball for us. He liked football, and we used to have a kick-about at lunchtime. After the football games on Sunday the guards used to take us to the pub and we'd all have a drink. That happened every Sunday.

Yet playing football and sport had one ominous drawback, as Private R.S. Baillie of the London Scottish Regiment discovered. The commandant of Celle, a camp for other ranks, allowed the men a football ground. But: 'if the prisoners played they were picked for work'.[20]

Work was always the Germans' preferred method of providing exercise.

If football was the most popular sport in the camps, other sports had their fans. The Canadians, wherever they ended up, tried to introduce baseball (to which the Brits never truly took), hockey was easy to organize once enough sticks had been bought or fashioned, and most *Offizierslager* where space permitted built tennis courts. Often the work was done by the prisoners themselves, or they paid for the construction. At Mainz, a 'crude tennis-court was made by scraping the cinder surface into some semblance of flatness'.[21] The net was wire-netting, since the commandant considered a string net might be used for the purposes of escape. Prisoners at Clausthal paid for two squash courts to be constructed, and made a miniature golf course themselves; playing rounds on the latter, adjudged Flossie Hervey, was 'the vice that predominated'. Some officers' camps eventually stretched to pleasant and extensive facilities; Gütersloh had ten tennis courts, and the pines, so claustrophobic in winter, provided pleasant shade in summer. Of the *Offizierslager* Crefeld ended up being the best provisioned. Captain D. Baird-Douglas wrote of the camp:

The English officers keep fit by tennis and football, and have every opportunity of playing either [sic] games, there being fourteen gravel tennis-courts, which in winter are turned into the football ground, and also two fives-courts built at the expense of several officers.[22]

There was also a gym for 'single-sticks', fencing and a boxing class, which the ever eager Lyall Grant joined. At Freiburg officers were allowed a swim in the town baths once a week, 'a very welcome diversion' considered Flossie Hervey. At Torgau's Bruckenkopf, a fort constructed by Napoleon the Great,

> an attempt was made to play the Eton Field Game, but as there were not quite enough Etonians to make two complete sides others who had never ever seen the game played indulged for the first time in it. The French were highly delighted at the formation and manoeuvres of the 'ram'.[23]

Playing sport helped keep body and soul together, helped pass the time. 'Sport,' wrote Archer Cust, 'is a wonderful time-killer.'[24] Except it did not kill time stone-dead. There were only so many games of tennis one could play against the same faces in the same cage. And no one ever fully relaxed into the sporting amenities they had constructed or financed. Because what privileges the Germans gave, they were equally likely to take away. When a football accidentally broke an arc light at Holzminden, commandant Karl Niemeyer banned all sports henceforth, despite the prisoners paying for the damage. Withdrawing the right to sporting activities was always an easy punishment in the camps. In mid May 1918 Niemeyer, because the British government had complained about his and other X Corps camps, ordered a month-long reprisal in which games, music and theatricals were banned.

Winter brought the best of times, the worst of times in the camps. Men shivered in blankets and rags around inadequate stoves, and were laid low with colds and influenza. Winter also brought the snow. Rifleman Alfred Hall hated working down on Herr Lieber's farm in the village of Mensfelden; then in January 1917 the snow fell. Hall wrote in his diary:

> The snow is about 8" deep and being in a frozen state the people here have taken to tobogganing. We, being POWs, could only look upon them with envy but, the snow lasting, our envy could not. So, taking the matter into our own hands and being quite ready to answer for

the consequences, we begged and stole sledges and tobogganed to our hearts content . . . Our journey took us down a steep hill and we attained a most glorious speed. The inhabitants were astonished at our audacity but eventually came to their usual conclusion that all Englishmen were mad. We arrived at the Barrack [the *Turnhalle*, where the *Kommando* slept at night] late of course and received a sound rating but soft soap and humble pie were effectual. Here endeth the most enjoyable day I've had for nearly two years.[25]

Snow provided thousands of other PoWs with the best sporting fun of their captivity too. Even in the 'Hell-Hole' of Ingolstadt Horace Gilliland managed to make a toboggan run, which coursed down the ramparts of the interior earthworks:

About one hundred yards was the longest course obtainable. To essay this, one had to be an optimist, a fool, and a prisoner. We had to start the sled from the top of the highest gun platform. In about twenty feet, we had to get our impetus and turn a complete right angle, in order to shoot down a small path, leading down into the yard, a sheer drop of about fifty feet, to the gravel yard beneath. Some good fractures were secured in this way, but the exhilarating excitement was a wonderful nerve tonic.[26]

At Osnabrück *Offizierslager*, Captain Gerald Knight was among those who made a snow slide, the spills from which – including into the barbed-wire perimeter – 'remain with me to this day' wrote Knight in 1919.[27] So enamoured was Knight with this sport that when he transferred to Clausthal he constructed a toboggan run there too.

The great freezes of the German winter provided other sporting opportunities. When orderly Private Norman Dykes was at Gütersloh

The officers soon hit upon a splendid idea. They set to work banking up the snow and rolling it flat on the hockey ground, approximately 60 yards by 20. The prepared area was flooded with water, and then left for nature to get to work on it. Soon, as perfect a skating rink as could be desired was ready for the skaters, of which there were a goodly number in the camp. Great care was taken of the rink, and it was religiously brushed and reflooded at the end of each day of the seven weeks that the frost held.[28]

There were 'many thrilling games' of ice hockey, and Russian officers performed exhibitions of figure skating. Officers lent skates to the orderlies, some of whom had not skated before (Private Dykes among them). The highlight of Gütersloh the ice-skating season was an Ice Carnival with a hockey match, Russia v Britain & France. Afterwards, refreshments were served and the officers' orchestra played. 'The fete,' thought Private Dykes, 'bade fair to be one of the outstanding events in the annals of Gütersloh Prisoner of War Camp.'[29] Zorndorf did not require the making of a skating rink; officers skated on the nearby flooded Oder marshes. A German officer supplied the skates – at a price. He had been an ironmonger in better times but now provided 'an unlimited supply of inferior skates at superior prices'.[30] When a local girl, Anna Schutz, fell through the ice, Henry Cartwright plunged in after her and earned a column of praise in the local paper.

Writing in his diary at Gütersloh on 3 July 1916, Douglas Lyall Grant recorded a momentous event in the lives of the officer prisoners:

> This afternoon, in company with 39 others, I went for a walk. This is a new idea, a mutual arrangement between British, French and German Governments, by which officers give their parole not to escape while out walking, and in return no guard is sent with them but one man as a guide. We have parole cards which we sign and give up on our return. We go out in batches of 40 twice a week.[31]

By the mores of the time, an officer, irrespective of his nationality, was a gentleman, and thus a man of his word. If he agreed not to escape, he would not. Other ranks, not being gentlemen, could not be presumed to be men whose word was their bond. Consequently, paroled walks were not extended to them. Under the parole system officers signed an identity card, on the face of which was their photograph, and on the inside a written promise not to abscond. The wording of the parole card used at Treves (Trier) *Offizier Kriegs-gefangenenlager*, on the banks of the wine-growing Moselle, was typical:

> By this card I give my word of honour that during the walk outside the camp I will not escape, nor attempt to escape, nor will I make any preparation to do so, nor will I attempt to commit any actions during this time to prejudice the German Empire. I also give my word of honour to use this card only myself, and not to give it to any other prisoner of war.

The card was held by the camp while the officer perambulated the locality.

Captain D. Baird-Douglas noted of the walks at Crefeld:

> These walks have helped a great deal to keep the prisoners' health in the state it is . . . The prisoner suffered, naturally from depression, and in many cases if captivity continues it will affect their brains. One of the drawbacks of Crefeld Camp was that, except when you were out on parole, a prisoner was never able to see more than two hundred yards or so each way owing to the high walls around the camp.[32]

Actually, Crefeld was so oppressive and claustrophobic that prisoners would voluntarily choose to visit the dentist in the town because it enabled them 'to see new sights and get away from the horrible prison for a few hours'.[33]

For men erring towards barbed-wire disease, getting out of camp for any time at all was a godsend. Lieutenant A.J. Evans found the scenery around Fort 9, Ingolstadt, in lowland Bavaria less than intoxicating: 'However, it was certainly a relief to get out of the place every now and then.'[34] Some fortunate prisoners did find their camp situated in a stunning locale; Archer Cust at Graudenz enjoyed the views of the Vistula and it 'was certainly very delicious to be out under the trees again', although there was a downside: 'it gave one a terrible hankering after freedom and a good tea to come back to'.[35] Weakness from hunger also prevented him always taking up the opportunity to promenade. Will Harvey, the country boy from

Gloucester, liked the wild woods around Schwarmstedt, while the inmates of Pforzheim rambled for hours in the Black Forest for all the world like enchanted tourists behind their *feldgrau* guide.[36] The job of this German escort was not simply to show lovely landmarks and ensure that the *Engländer* did not get lost; it was to deal with the hostile reaction of the locals, though that declined as the war wore on and on. By 1917 the greatest threat to officers on paroled walks was to be accosted by German children begging for chocolate.

Under the usual autonomies of the Kaiser's PoW system, commandants were free to set the frequency and duration of walks. At Torgau, the prisoners went out up to three times a week, and at Strohen there were, for a considerable period, no walks at all.[37] Another Area X camp, Holzminden, saw prisoners refusing paroled walks in protest at the wording on their parole card, which contained the clause 'I know that . . . a prisoner of war who escapes in spite of the word of honour given is liable to death'. Whether calculated to or not, the extra condition impugned the honour of British officers and was hotly resisted. When the X Corps Commander General von Hanisch appeared at the camp on inspection, the SBO, Major Wyndham, protested in person. Von Hanisch curtly dismissed the complaint, accusing the British of breaking parole at Schwarmstedt. A public spat on the *Appell* ground ensued: Hanisch mentioned the *Baralong* (an RN ship whose sailors had allegedly shot U-boat crew who had taken refuge on a merchantman). Wyndham countered '*Lusitania*'. At this Hanisch snarled, 'If every Englishman in this command . . . got his deserts he would be shot.'[38]

When von Hanisch left Wyndham ordered all parole cards to be torn up. Until the Germans apologized, no British prisoner in Holzminden would take advantage of paroled walks. The apology took six months to come.

But, then, everything was a battle in the camps. When the commandant at Freiburg loftily decided one fine day to banish the weekly walk, two hundred British prisoners held a noisy demonstration on the parade ground. The camp was in a town, the commotion was undesirable and embarrassing. The commandant backed down.

*

It was on a parole walk that Flossie Hervey of the RFC saw a dachs-hund pup being dragged through the Zorndorf snow by a small boy. A few Marks and some chocolate were enough to effect a change of ownership, and Hervey joined the many PoWs who kept pets. He christened the pup, appropriately, 'Kleiner'; she slept in his room, and accompanied the prisoners on their extra-mural promenades. Once, when she disappeared in full cry after a red deer and got lost, a sentry kindly returned her.

Dachshunds, it might be said, were the PoW's dog of choice. Plentiful in supply, being a German breed, they were also small enough to tuck under a bed. Douglas Lyall Grant's room at Crefeld adopted two dachshunds, whom they named Anthony and Antoinette. He added in his diary: 'They have been trained to fraternize with the British and bark at the Boche.'[39]

Dog-keeping was not a uniquely British habit in the camps. Kleiner's arch-companion was the Russians' dog, Chort; Frenchman Georges Connes kept Nitchevo, a puppy that was petted and spoilt by everyone. But the British were dog mad. The British even befriended the Alsatians meant to guard them; in one case, so attached did an Alsatian become to his British human pal that when the latter absconded from Schwarmstedt the dog went with him.[40]

Birds and rabbits were the commonest pets in the camps. When prisoners were moved on to another camp, the transportation of these livestock provided an exercise Noah would have found taxing. On the British contingent being relocated from Crefeld to Schwarmstedt in May 1917 Lieutenant Caunter recalled:

> There was a considerable quantity of livestock of various kinds in the camp, and measures for the transportation of these furred and feathered belongings had to be undertaken. The rabbits had to have special boxes made for them so that they could be carried by hand.[41]

One officer was so careful in carrying his canary from Clausthal to Strohen that the bird never left its eggs, which hatched successfully in the moorland camp. They would have provided welcome colour;

there were few places in Germany more desolate than Strohen. It was at Strohen that Gerald Knight obtained flower seeds from England – including sunflowers, sweet peas, nasturtiums – in the hope that, planted and tended, he could create a garden that would 'enable me to believe temporarily on special occasions that I was actually amid the flowers of good old England'.[42] Officers at Gütersloh also created a garden; this attracted many wild birds, as well as the poetic Will Harvey:

> Thrushes, finches, birds that beat magical and thrilling sweet
> Little far off fairy gongs: Blackbird with your mellow surge,
> Valiant robin, thieving sparrows
> Though you wound me as with arrows
> Still with you among these flowers
> Surely I find my sweetest hours!

Around the camp were crested larks, leading Harvey's orderly to remark that 'even the blinkin' birds wore spiked hats in Germany'.[43]

Parting German children from their charges was by no means the only way of obtaining pets. Almost anything a camp *Kantine* did not have in stock could be ordered in, including, as Dobson of the RNVR discovered at Mainz, 'parrots, concertinas and other freak commodities'.[44] At Clausthal, Lieutenant A.V. Burbury of the RFC, managed to get his hands on a galah bird.

Some pets were wild animals tamed. Joseph Lee in the rambling Bishop's Castle at Beeskow was delighted to make friends with a jackdaw, Jacob, which became so utterly domesticated that it would lie on its back in Lee's hand in the morning and join in the 'rigorous joys' of a cold shower.[45] Lee had previously struck up an acquaintance with the donkey that pulled the parcel wagon into Karlsruhe; Will Harvey found companionship in the friendly ox that carted rubbish into Gütersloh and allowed him to strike matches on its great horns. When a young rabbit scampered into the camp it was much petted by Harvey and the British contingent, who let the kit go, 'to the disappointment of our Allies who would have liked it for dinner'.[46] They would have done; the French at Gütersloh trapped small birds, rooks and hooded crows for casseroles. The Russians liked cats. In the pot.

For a country man like Harvey, to touch and see animals was to connect with his pre-war self, to take his place – if only for a second – back in the natural world in which he had grown up. Not by accident is Harvey's most famous prison poem, 'Ducks', an exuberant celebration of that bird:

> From troubles of the world I turn to ducks,
> Beautiful comical things
> Sleeping or curled
> Their heads beneath white wings
> By water cool,
> Or finding curious things
> To eat in various mucks
> Beneath the pool,
> Tails uppermost, or waddling
> Sailor-like on the shores
> Of ponds, or paddling
> – Left! Right! – with fanlike feet
> Which are for steady oars
> When they (white galleys) float
> Each bird a boat
> Rippling at will the sweet
> Wide waterway . . .[47]

In the wire world, where proper relationships were impossible, pets were something to love and maybe be loved by. In the helplessness of animals PoWs saw their own suffering as surely as gazing into a looking glass. And, at the very least, as the flyer Hervey noted: 'The care and maintenance of the camp livestock provided the owners with an interest that did much towards passing the time which lay so heavy on our hands.'[48]

Not that the British were entirely sentimental. John Caunter conceded that the prolific rabbits at Crefeld were 'objects of great interest, being watched by a small crowd of the prison inhabitants every day' – and yet they 'provided many an excellent meal for their owners'.[49] In Augustabad in 1916 Canadian officer John Thorn was delighted because:

> once a week the officers usually killed one of these rabbits and invited one another to their feed. I was fortunate to be invited several times, and found the rabbit delicious after having to live most of the time on the German food.[50]

Less happily, while Thorn (a persistent escaper) was sojourning at the *strafe* camp Fort 9 pets were banned and collected up. A few days later there was an unexpectedly 'enormous supply of German sausages' on the ration. Naturally, all the prisoners concluded that their *Wurst* was composed of rabbit, dog, cat, canary and all the other fauna cherished by the British men in the Kaiser's cages.

A drink would have helped the miscellaneous meat go down. Alcohol was the privilege and curse of officer prisoners. Being gentlemen, officers expected – and were expected – to drink alcohol with lunch and dinner. At Mainz the alcohol ration was one bottle of beer or half a bottle of wine per day; in other *Offizier Kriegsgefangenenlager* prisoners could drink as much wine as they could pay for. At Vohrenbach Second Lieutenant H.T. Champion, RFC, recalled:

> There was a canteen where one could buy or order anything one wanted except eatables. Drinkables were dirt cheap, and the Hun made no objection to anyone drinking more than was good for him. In fact they encouraged it. This was the cause of a considerable amount of ill-health, and many young fellows are ruined today on account of it.[51]

Sub-Lieutenant Hugh Kingsmill's canteen also sloshed with 'awful' yet effective wine which made the question of 'how much or how little to drink one of the chief problems of captivity'.[52] Dismally, Flossie Hervey considered that drinking was 'probably the most common of all' hobbies among officers. Alcohol offered escape in the featureless void of a *strafe* camp where entertainments were few. Hervey himself obliterated existence at Zorndorf through somnambulance:

'We found the best way to pass the time was to remain asleep for as long as possible in the morning.'

Roll call at Zorndorf was not until 10.30. Thankfully, the relentless *ennui* of Zorndorf was broken when Leefe Robinson VC received a gramophone through the post, together with a box of records. All were broken, except one. 'We patched them up,' wrote Hervey, 'and through constant repetition the periodic stutter occasioned by the crack became to us part of the original refrain.'[53]

Other rank prisoners were forbidden alcohol. Inevitably, a bribe circumvented the prohibition. For Christmas 1915 James Farrant's hut at Döberitz had bottles of schnapps smuggled in with the help of a German civvy. The festive air was ruined by a German officer and two guards turning up at 9 p.m. – an hour early – to demand lights out. A Petty Officer, RN, told the Imperial Army officer to 'clear out', emphasizing his request by taking the German by the lapels. Only the level-headed intercession by the hurriedly summoned deputy commandant prevented a shooting incident. The drinking carried on.

Next day there was hardly a man in the hut who wasn't hungover and in a state of 'fixed bayonets'. According to Farrant

plenty of scrapes took place, old grievances were aired, challenges to fight any man in the place were issued by men of all sizes. In fact it was difficult to walk down the room without getting tangled up with someone. It was a gay old time.[54]

The camp was placed under punishment for a month. No sport, no recreation, every man in bed by 7 p.m.

The season of goodwill did not entirely pass the Germans by. Joseph Lee appreciated a Christmas Dinner at Karlsruhe consisting of soup, potatoes, an ounce or two of meat, one pound of eating apples and a quarter of a litre of red wine ('a red litre day'). More apples were distributed at night courtesy of the Red Cross in Geneva.[55] In the camps Christmas was a time to eat, drink (no matter how obtained) and be merry. Even the damp forbidding walls of Fort 9 echoed with happiness, where A.J. Evans and fellows sat down to a lavish dinner, with French and Russian guests, followed by a masked ball. (Who was on the guest list makes for delightful conjecture: Imprisoned in Fort 9 were one Charles de Gaulle and one Mikhail Tukhachevsky, neither of them yet famous.) At midnight they all sang 'God Save the King' and the 'Marseillaise' – which caused the guard to be turned out. To Evans' disappointment, the guard recaptured the piano Room 45 had illegally borrowed for the night's festivities.[56]

The guard was always being turned out on Christmas Night. Alcohol, high spirits, patriotism, and the desire for *once* to let rip without a care, made the prisoners exceedingly boisterous. The guards, meanwhile, were edgy at the antics and resentful at the fun. Captain Lyall Grant was at Crefeld:

Christmas in captivity and for a crowd of downtrodden mortals we made merry right well. Most people had dinner parties at night, and after appell the world at large started visiting each other in any room that took their fancy and the fun waxed fast and furious. The Germans turned out a guard of great strength and some fellows more unfortunate than the rest were removed to the jug. There was nobody actually killed.[57]

Dinner parties were not just for Christmas. For officers, dinner parties in camp, as with the dinner parties they had held in their dug-outs in the line,[58] were both celebrations and a means of passing the time, and more than this, of asserting their identity – of establishing social normalcy in the wire world. In holding little dinner parties, if only of tripe and onions, Gilbert Nobbs and his comrades forgot 'we were prisoners; we forgot that rows and rows of barbed wire bound us in captivity; we ignored the footsteps of the guard and the sharp yelping of the dogs'.[59]

Although it was the *lingua franca* of the Allies in the camps, German was usually banned at dinner parties, no matter how international the guest list.[60] Rarely was the cooking for a dinner party done by an orderly. Officers did it themselves. On his spirit cooker H.F. Champion, of the RFC cooked up a birthday meal of kidney soup, *poulet rot*, vegetables, asparagus, trifle, chocolates and liqueur brandy. 'An excellent meal,' considered Champion, 'especially considering that everything was tinned.'[61] Another RFC pilot, Second Lieutenant Joseph Allen, produced a dinner on 20 June 1918 at Holzminden 'to celebrate the birthdays of D.C. Doyle and A. Clouston'. The menu card was:

  Soup
  Tomato
  Fish
  Herrings
  Poultry
  Roast Duck
  Game
  Jugged Hare
  Vegetables
  Roast Potatoes
  Boiled Potatoes
  Peas
  Onions
  Sweets
  Marmalade Pudding
  Stewed Peaches
  Cheese
  Coffee
  Holzminden Wine
  Cigarettes by Abdullah[62]

Cigarettes by Anyone were welcome in the camps. Used to puffing away like Lancashire factory chimneys, the soldiers of the BEF, officers and men both, found the nicotine withdrawal caused by cigarette-less captivity near unendurable. Private Tanner Milburn at Dulmen 'used to get up at 6 o'clock and go about the camp on my hands and knees looking for cigarette tab ends. We used to smoke tea-leaves: that was luxury.'[63]

Other desperate men smoked fallen leaves in skins rolled from newspapers. James Farrant was reduced to smoking tea leaves and oak apple leaves in his pipe 'till my tongue was like a piece of leather'.[64]

It was quite a come-down for a twenty-nine-year-old middle-class mining engineer used to the better things in life. Luckily for Farrant on 8 December 1914, after two months captivity, 'Holtham of the RND received a packet of Smith's Glasgow Mixture and gave me a pipeful. Of all the pleasures I have had in my life, this was the greatest.'[65] Farrant was not allowed to smoke his pipeful of Smith's Glasgow Mixture in his hut. It was *verboten*: 'How that word riled us. Everything was verboten at one time or another, except work, and there was always plenty of that.'[66]

Needless to say, Farrant and his pals did smoke in the huts.

The first parcel containing tobacco was an unforgettable event in the PoW's life. 'Another treat to me', remembered Lance-Corporal Higgins about Elbingerode *Arbeitskommando*, 'was a bit of good tobacco. How I enjoyed the first smoke. It made life worth living once more.'[67] It was up there with the first postcard from his wife.

A parcel from home or the Red Cross was the usual way of obtaining tobacco in the camps, though there were prison staff willing to barter or vend. Newly arrived at Munden (where tobacco had been banned as a punishment for the Russians singing their national anthem on *Appell*) Horace Gilliland soon sourced a willing guard, who supplied him with cigarettes four pence a piece. 'I had to pay heavily for them,' lamented Gilliland.

Long wearisome years of captivity did nothing to diminish the British prisoner's addiction to the leaves of the genus *Nicotiana*. Sent in winter 1917 to Reiskatte reprisal camp in Russia, Able Seaman James Farrant had only two-fifths of a 3 lb loaf, a bowl of soup, and a cup of ersatz coffee a day. The ground in the forest, swept desolate of trees by shellfire, was as hard as cast iron. Men suffered frostbite; they seldom spoke as they battled to stay alive; the veneer of civilization wore off. Then on Sunday, 22 April 1917, they had a day of rest. The sun shone. And:

> Today each man drew tobacco or cigarettes. Men said 'Good morning' to each other. Some even whistled and sung, the first exhibition of pleasure that has ever taken place in this cursed spot. This was the happiest day I ever spent as a prisoner of war. We were men again.[68]

Will Harvey's greatest pleasure in the three camps in which he was imprisoned was not smoking or even the writing of his own poetry. For Lieutenant Harvey:

> Nothing has the power of music to lift one out of one's surroundings, and to no one more poignantly than to prisoners-of-war does Music bring her valiant reminder of things 'outside', the refreshing comfort of a world of realities transcending human chance.[69]

Even in the worst camps, in the worst times, when the groans of ill men and the shouting of guards seemed omnipresent, the sound of singing could be heard – for pleasure, as well as protest. As soon as men were freed from hunger, they entertained themselves with communal singing, be it in hut singalongs or choral concerts; they were after all the singing generation, the generation that gathered around the Old Joanna in the parlour and the pub. Ditties from London shows were always popular to sing out, bawdy barrack-room ballads had their following, no wooden barracks with a member of the Navy could escape sea shanties, no hut with an Australian a rendition of 'Waltzing Matilda'. Some hymns everyone knew. One of the reasons for the strong church attendance in the camps was the singing of familiar hymns on which one could float away to childhood, and to that earthly Heaven, Sunday morning in an English village. Will Harvey was adamant that the song most frequently performed in officers' camps was the distinctly profane 'Captain Stratton's Fancy'.[70] The song's illustrious makers aside – John Masefield wrote the lyrics, Ivor Gurney the music – 'Captain Stratton's Fancy' was a goodtime drinking tune:

> Oh some are fond of red wine, and some are fond of white,
> And some are all for dancing by the pale moon-light
> But rum alone's the tipple, and the heart's delight
> Of the old bold mate of Henry Morgan . . .

Naturally, such a song needed liquid accompaniment; for their dormitory balladeering, Harvey brewed up a home-made punch, consisting of bad German wine, tinned fruit, cloves, raisins, Worcester sauce for 'bite', the mix heated over spirit lamps.

Rarely were sung the tunes of the trenches, those compositions which lachrymosely commemorated the experience of the mud and the blood. There was misery enough in the camps without revisiting the horrors of Flanders and the Somme. One Tommy singing habit did continue from trench to camp: that of adapting ditties to take 'the Mickey out of the Germans in the most uninhibited manner'. One song by the men of William Tucker's *Arbeitskommando* in Enghien in occupied Belgium began:

> When this bloody war is over
> Oh how happy I shall be
> When I get back to dear old Blighty
> No more sauerkraut for me
> I will tell the German major
> To stick his black bread . . .

For full effect, Tucker's choral party performed the ditty standing on tables, so the local Belgian townsfolk peeking over the wall could enjoy the performance. Tucker on piano was lucky to get his hands clear when the guard slammed down the piano's lid shouting '*Los, los, es ist verboten!*'[71]

Musical relations were more harmonious at Otterberg in the Rhineland, where Lance-Corporal Thomas Higgins spent the day working on a hay-pressing machine; in the evening he gathered in the public room of the hotel with three other English PoWs from the *Arbeitskommando*. The farmer's daughter played the piano. To Higgins' astonishment the German locals knew lots of English popular songs, among them his favourite, 'Love Me, and the World is Mine'.

The desire of Britons in the camps to make music was a surprise. After two years captivity, Will Harvey concluded:

> To suppose that the British are unmusical is wrong. I have never been in a prison camp where there was not made an attempt, generally successful, to form an orchestra and perform good music.[72]

Joseph Lee would have concurred. Sojourning at Karlsruhe he enjoyed the camp orchestra's performances of Grieg, Handel, Puccini, Bach, Schumann and Mascagni.

The mandolin and balalaika bands of Russian co-prisoners exercised an exotic fascination. Numerous British prisoners took up the instruments. 'Mandolins were soon in vogue,' remembered Lieutenant Gerald Knight, 'and most rooms could boast of several. As we were mostly beginners the resulting noise is best left to the imagination.'[73] And that was always the problem with learning musical instruments in the overcrowded wire world. One man's practice was another man's aural torture. The musical beginners at Freiburg, lamented Flossie Hervey, made 'an unearthly din'.

Orchestras and bands were not only to be sat and politely listened to. They provided the soundtrack for dances, though these were sadly shorn of the romance of women. 'There was a nice brass band,' recalled Corporal L.G. Eastwood about Giessen, 'and in the evenings they [the men] used to dance out there on the parade ground.'[74]

Music hall was part of the life of the camps, as it been in the trenches with the Div's 'Follies'. The repertoire of the camp variety show mixed songs and sketches, part cribbed from London musical and part lifted from camp life. Captain Douglas Lyall Grant was an enthusiastic trouper as well as diarist and sportsman, and at Crefeld in 1916 participated in a show in which:

The first item was an orchestral selection, then a short sketch followed by a few cinematograph films, then a pipe selection played by three of us, followed by a foursome reel for which an orderly played. Then two recitations, a Dutch dance, a bottle and zylophone selection, and after the interval, our Octette.

W— at the piano dressed as a girl, and the men, bar me, in white trousers, white dress coats with black facings, black waistcoats with white buttons, white gloves and white top hats: I exactly the reverse, being black where they were white and white where they were black, while I was made up a la George Robey.

Lyall Grant, always the heart and soul of party and performance, threw himself a little too frenetically into proceedings:

As luck would have it I sprained my ankle pretty badly in the reel but managed to go through with the Octette.[75]

Variety shows were hugely popular diversions, whether small and held in a hut, or lavish and held in a 'theatre'. Hugh Durnford in Holzminden even maintained, 'There was nothing that we would have less willingly foregone than our shows.' Sunday night was the night for other ranks to stage their concerts, because Sunday was their one day off. The Sunday-night hut shows at Munster were known as 'Barrack Room Gaffes'.[76] Most concerts had 'a little dig' at the Germans and everyone 'would cheer and clap'.

A few of the biggest camps had permanent theatres, made of wood or canvas, among them Döberitz, a camp which improved remarkably from its squalid hell-hole beginning. The theatre at Dülmen could seat six hundred.[77] More usually, the theatre was the dining room with pushed-together tables making the stage. Such was 'Gaiety Theatre, Holzminden' in *Kaserne B*, where the amateur thespians of the 'British Amateur Dramatic Society' performed Galsworthy's *The Pigeon,* plus *The Just Impediment, Home John,* and *The Crimson Streak.* The lure of greasepaint at Holzminden was sufficient to prise Second Lieutenant James Whale, 7/Worcestershire Regiment, away from the bridge table, where he had been fleecing the less cerebral of their money. Whale devoted a large part of his fifteen months at Holzminden to producing plays, writing them, and painting scenery. It was time well spent. At Holzminden Whale served an apprenticeship in entertainment that enabled him to later direct on the London stage J.R. Ackerley's *The Prisoner of War* and R.C. Sheriff's *Journey's End* (the latter featuring one Laurence Olivier). Whale parlayed the plays into a Hollywood career that saw him become one of the legendary directors of the thirties, the helmsman of *Frankenstein* (1931) and *Bride of Frankenstein* (1935).

There was always someone in a camp who was either a born or trained top entertainer. Alec Waugh was convinced that the PoW theatre at Mainz was 'the absolute Alhambra of the Gefangenenlager'. He may have been right, for among Mainz's inmates was

Second Lieutenant J. Milton Hayes MC, 7/Manchester Regiment, the celebrated Edwardian actor and poet, creator of the doggerel monologue, 'The Green Eye of the Little Yellow God':

There's a one-eyed yellow idol to the north of Khatmandu . . .

Officers at Freiburg would never have allowed that any PoW theatre company was the equal of the Freiburg Amateur Dramatic Society (FADS). They too may have had a point. So successful were their shows they had to set up a booking office. Then again, Lance-Corporal Thomas Higgins on convalescing at Hameln *Mannschaftslager* recalled, 'On Sundays we did no work, and the prisoners would give theatrical performances in a hut fitted up as a theatre, and very good they were.'[78]

Props and instruments for shows and concerts were bought (from local shops or from catalogues), borrowed or made. In all cases agreement was reached with the Germans that props were not to be used for escape, and that costumes and make-up could not be used for disguise. This was one form of parole that extended to other ranks. As a price guide, Rifleman Alfred Hall in his *Arbeits-kommando* in rural Mensfelden collected one Mark from each of his fellow PoWs, French and English, thirty-seven of them in total, to buy the following theatrical props: 2 Jew's Noses, 1 Girl's Wig (Red), 1 Beard, 1 Monocle, and assorted Grease Paints.[79]

Concerts themselves were not paroled, a loophole taken admirable advantage of by Lieutenant Jack Shaw, RFC. Appearing in a concert in the guards' dining room at Freiburg, Shaw, a gifted musician, apparently hurt his foot during a comedy sketch. Left alone in the dressing room while the concert rolled along, he climbed out of the window and away. Fate was not in benevolent mood: Shaw was soon recaptured, and was transferred to the bad boys' camp of Holzminden, just in time to see a large rugby hearty attired 'in small ballet frock and tights, with a wreath on my head' star in a comedy sketch entitled 'The Artist's Model'. This was the ebullient Douglas Lyall Grant, freshly transferred to Hellminden from Crefeld.[80] As there were of course no women in the camps, men played the female parts in theatrical productions. Lyall Grant may have looked hilariously, intentionally ridiculous in drag, yet so successful were some female impersonators that they disorientated inmates willing enough or desperate enough to believe they were truly women. One cross-dressed actor told Will Harvey:

> I noticed with surprise how attentive officers were in keeping me supplied with refreshments and also that (quite unconsciously) their manners completely changed when speaking to me. They were most careful in avoiding the usual camp language and most fastidious in their choice of adjectives. They insisted on giving up their seats to me, and it was quite pathetic to see the efforts made to engage my female interest in subjects no sane prisoner of war (if any of us are sane) would consider. How pretty the room looked! And the costumes, so picturesque, weren't they? Perhaps a glass of lemonade . . . I had to pull them back into reality by swearing vigorously, and so far had they fallen under the illusion of my femininity that I fear I shocked them by doing so.[81]

In one of J. Milton Hayes' productions at Mainz the 'girls' were so persuasive that a distinguished field officer chased one 'Venus' murmuring between gasps, 'Don't call me Major, call me Jim.' Private Tucker suffered the same fate as the Mainz Venus. Fitted with a blonde wig by the entertainment committee (headed by Bombardier Leaver, 'once something in the entertainment line') a metamorphosed Tucker was 'compelled to take evading action and ward off several loving embraces' from fellow PoWs in his *Arbeits-kommando*.[82] In the pretend world of prison camp theatre, under low lights and heavy rouge, erotic tensions might be relieved by prisoners suspending their disbelief over the sex of the figure in a dress before them.

Any real women who entered the camps, usually as canteen, kitchen or administrative staff, were likely to become the objects of longing and lust. According to Lyall Grant officers used to sit and gaze at the 'two buxom damsels' in the canteen in Crefeld for hours. When the canteen passed out of private hands, the *Mädchen* left, 'to the great grief of those interned heroes who have spent two years here'.[83] The women who worked in the soup kitchens at Auguste

Victoria coal mine were, considered Private Frank MacDonald, 'really fine looking'. Although, as he acknowledged, the fact that he and his fellow PoWs had had no chance to see any women in ages made them no great judges of female flesh.

Pitifully, every camp based in a town had one or two men who spent their days trying to spy women in apartments and gain their attention, in the hope of a smile or a blown kiss. The beauteous 'Mitzi', who lived across from Freiburg officers' camp, was positively blitzed by thrown chocolates wrapped in 'billet-doux'. Against the odds, some lovelorn captives in the camps struck up reciprocated romances. Captain Robert Dolbey encountered a fellow PoW in Crefeld who flirted with the girl in the camp canteen; she offered to help him escape to Holland, and go with him. However, he had his 'own matrimonial arrangements planned' and being a 'very white and perfect knight' he could not accept her proposal.[84] The unattached might well have taken up her offer; Geoffrey Phillimore thought that:

> Most of the more youthful ones [officers] spent a large proportion of their time in concocting plans of escape in which the assistance of devoted, not to say lovelorn, enemy maidens figured largely.

He was doubtless right. When prisoner Lieutenant Jocelyn Hardy, Connaught Rangers, turned to writing fiction after the war his very first novel told of a British PoW being aided to freedom by a beautiful German girl. This was *Everything is Thunder*, published in 1935, which was eventually made into a Hollywood film.

One advantage of being on *Arbeitskommando* was access to flesh-and-blood women, up to and including sex. If Private Bill Easton, working as a carpenter in a hotel, was not having an affair with his boss, Fraulein Lenni Morrs, his mates certainly thought he was. When she walked him back to the camp each evening, ribald cries from behind the wire went up of 'Cor, I bet she's nice and warm at night'.[85] Taken to a civilian French laundry to pick up some shirts, William Tucker, attached to the motor depot at Roubaix, was smothered by kisses from the laundry girls. Some of the women were prepared to go further:

Two or three of the girls made gestures unmistakably symbolic of sexual goings on. One of them, somewhat more practical than the others, actually prostrated herself on my pile of nine shirts in willing expectation.[86]

Tucker, lousy and half-starved by his diet of sauerkraut and sandstorm, was no more physically or mentally able to fornicate than 'gallop up Everest'. But the mademoiselles of Roubaix were not yet finished with Private William Tucker. Invited for a drink by two guards (who had an illegal trade selling potatoes to the French into which Tucker was inveigled) to an estaminet on the outskirts of the town, the flame-haired waitress, on discovering Tucker was 'ein Tommy', Tucker was patriotically pulled through the bar to the bedroom. Again the hapless Tucker was unable to ascend the heights of passion. A roomful of German squaddies next door hardly provided an aphrodisiac.[87]

Captain J.R. Ackerley's play *The Prisoners of War*[88] is set among officer PoWs repatriated to neutral Switzerland, and strongly suggests that in this loosened environment the repressed homosexuality of the all-male camps burst forth. Ackerley claimed the play to be partly autobiographical; it is largely fantasy. If the intense, woman-free world of the camps did encourage some heterosexual men into homosexual infatuations they remained a minority. The bonds of male friendship in the camps were identical to those in the trenches; sometimes they amounted to love, hardly ever did they involve sex. Love among men was, above all, about care and comradeship. In any case, as many memoirists note, the lack of privacy in the camps made consummation of gay sex nigh impossible.[89] Only the most senior officers had anything approaching seclusion in their accommodation. And any man conspicuous in his homosexuality in the camps, given prevailing neo-Georgian attitudes, was likely to receive short shrift, as is suggested in a recollection by Percy Brown. A war correspondent captured in 1914, Brown was incarcerated in Ruhleben civilian PoW camp outside Berlin where: 'We had a few of those double-sexed creatures who pawed and armed the youth of the camp but on the second offence someone just put them to sleep for a few moments, a drastic but effective preventative.'[90] Regular Army officers, straight or gay, likely found the sexlessness of the camps easiest, for they were used to subduing libido.

Cards and gambling were guilty pleasures widely followed by citizen soldiers and professional warriors alike. Lieutenant J. Harvey Douglas, 4/Canadian Mounted Rifles, thought cards 'a diversion that offered great possibilities' in the camps.[91] The 'Canadoos' were especially fond of poker and became convinced that it usurped all the Old Country card games. Poker's distinct advantage was that it required no fancy setting up; PoWs played it in the barracks of the 'Black Hole', the Auguste Victoria coal mine, where no amusements were allowed and guards checked incessantly to ensure this injunction was obeyed.

Able Seaman James Farrant thought, *pace* the Canadians, that for British other ranks 'pontoon was the favourite card game; brag, nap and solo were good seconds, only a few indulging in bridge'.[92] Officers, on the other hand, played bridge in preference to any other card game, and some spent vast amounts of their captivity in its pursuit. Captain Maberly Esler, RAMC, was imprisoned at Stralsund where 'we had four keen bridge players in our room and every evening we played the same four from 8 p.m. to 11 p.m. What a wonderful game that is.'[93]

Bridge was definitely wonderful for Second Lieutenant James Whale; when he was repatriated in December 1918 he cashed in £4,000 in IOUs won playing the game at Holzminden. Sometimes gambling money was well spent. A Navy stoker in Döberitz used 350 Marks won playing Crown and Anchor – a betting game with dice, as universal in the Kaiser's camps as it was in the King's trenches and ships – to stake James Farrant's escape attempt. Sadly, that gamble did not pay off. Farrant and three other PoWs got as far as Hannover where a station official, suspicious of their shabby clothes, asked them to produce passports. They could not.

Like any other pastime in the camps, it was easy to surfeit on card-playing. 'Personally,' recalled Captain J.A. Caunter, 1/Gloucestershire Regiment, 'after the first year I spent in captivity I hated the sight of a card and played very seldom.'[94]

If one got seriously down to it, one could become highly educated in the camps in subjects more elevated than cards. All camps, when they rose above ravening hunger, put on lectures, on every conceivable subject. Captain A.J. Evans recalled that at Fort 9, Ingolstadt, he 'attended lectures which were given nearly every night on subjects varying from aviation to Victor Hugo'.[95]

More poetically, Lieutenant Archibald Bowman wrote of lectures at Rastatt and Hesepe:

> With little tasks we wile the hours away,
> Each bringing shyly forth his piteous store
> Of erudition, oft-times dubious lore,
> Since memory cupboards all we dare to say.
> One tells us how to mine, one how to lay
> A crop of good Rhodesian maize. Nay more,
> The skirts of metaphysics we explore.
> And touch the dread fringe of psychology.[96]

To the relieved joy of the evening's lecturer, there could be enthusiasm for the most arcane subjects; when Will Harvey spoke on so technical a subject as 'The Relations of Music to Poetry' at Holzminden two hundred people packed in to hear him.[97] British PoWs of the Great War were the original captive audience; any subject whatsoever that threatened to diminish boredom by an hour was given an arms-wide welcome. Serendipitously, the war thronged together in the camps British men of widely different backgrounds, nearly all of whom could be prevailed upon, with a little peer pressure, to overcome the English fear of public speaking and discourse on a subject close to their heart. At least once. Few men had no area of expertise, and some who floated in on the tide of captivity were actual masters of their topic.

Lectures provided more than an 'entrancing hour'; they offered men sundered from their careers or education a gainful way of filling the purgatorial years. Basil Willey gave numerous lectures on English Literature; after the war he became an English don at Cambridge, and eventually King Edward VII Professor of English Literature. The war caused Alex Waugh to miss out on going to

Oxford; he pursued his studies instead in Mainz Citadel:

> Every week at Mainz the head of the Educational Committee posted
> a programme allotting the rooms available for the separate classes.
> At the foot of the list was a note stating that when no classes were in
> progress the Alcove was reserved for authors, architects and other
> students. The Alcove was a small, first-floor room at the end of the
> series of rooms in which we ate. As a dining-room it could seat
> twenty at two narrow tables flanked by backless benches. It looked
> out upon the rampart, which an ancient sentry patrolled with a slow
> dragging step. This room was my equivalent for a University. It was
> here that I met for the first time adult minds upon equal terms.[98]

Waugh was in cultured company in his barbed-wire university of
Mainz Citadel: aside from J. Milton Hayes, the writer Hugh Kingsmill, Gerard Hopkins (later the distinguished translator of Sartre
and Mauriac) and the musician Maurice Besly all sat beside him.

As at Mainz, most camps organized education via a committee,
which badgered potential tutors and sought to shape a programme
of genuine benefit to prisoners on their release. In this they were
helped by the YMCA, which had an international office providing materials and support. To enhance their post-war professional
prospects after the locust years, officers at Mainz formed a Future
Careers Society. As a result, recorded Lieutenant Dobson:

> Nearly all the British officers were using their time in prison to learn
> languages or some accomplishment which would be useful to them
> afterwards. Captain Jarvis, Royal Munster Fusiliers, had a class for
> Hindustani; Lieutenant Humphries, ASC, gave a series of technical
> lectures on motor-cars and engines; others took up book-keeping,
> shorthand, etc.[99]

What was deemed a 'career' at Mainz, however, was subject to
narrow definition, as Second Lieutenant H.T. Ringham, 16/Man-
chester Regiment, discovered. Ringham, a former Stockport
draper's assistant promoted from the ranks, confided in his diary:

> I haven't a good opinion of myself at all just now. I'm not good at any

particular thing or subject. There's not much opportunity here of getting in touch with the drapery business. The Bankers, the Architects, Surveyors and Accountants – in fact most of the professions – have a kind of class each week. A sort of preparation for civilian life – but of course ones not able to do anything like that with drapery and I shall have to go back to that.[100]

Few camps were as well appointed for spare rooms as Mainz Citadel. In most *Lager* educational classes and lectures were held in overcrowded barrack rooms or recreation rooms. Horace Gilliland, incarcerated in Munden camp, struggled to concentrate on anything at all, because lessons took place in the sleeping rooms (thirty-foot square, each accommodating sixteen inmates), where perched on adjacent beds there would be, simultaneously, people learning German, Russian, and French. It was the Tower of Babel reincarnated.

Archer Cust at Graudenz took it upon himself to teach intermediate French for three hours a week. Aside from the lack of grammars, there was the lack of space:

> I shall never forget the first class I took in the lower mess-room, with a German class, conducted by McMinn, a teacher by trade, on my left, and another French class under Rogerson of the RFC on my right, and a continual banging and scraping and sluicing going on in the kitchen next door, with the result I literally had to shout the others down to be heard at all.[101]

The commandant was unhelpful on the matter of classrooms, because he didn't think it in the interests of the Fatherland that British officers should become too efficient at anything.

In reasonable weather classes were held outside, the students sitting on stools or lolling on the ground, with the capless on sunny days wearing knotted handkerchiefs on their heads. French lessons at Freiburg were peripatetic, with French and English pairs promenading round the square in earnest conversation. An air of erudition was lent by the surroundings; Freiburg *Lager* was converted from the old university buildings. Classical sculptures lined the route of the knowledge seekers, and looked over the shoulder of the speakers in the summer meetings of the Debating Society. Like all PoW debating societies, that at Freiburg tended to ethics and politics. Something of the optimism of young officers is caught in the foundation statement of the Wranglers debating club at Holzminden, which set its goal as 'the free discussion of subjects of vital interest and of problems likely to confront us after the war'.

Those with the time and the motivation could study for an external degree of the University of London during their incarceration. Almost without exception these were officers and senior NCOs, who were excused labour. But the barbed-wire universities were not just for those with pips and crowns and two or more stripes. Rifleman 'Tich' Evanson (his nickname did not lie: he was 5'4") ended up in Minden *Lager* after being captured on the Somme; the six months he spent in Minden proved 'the happiest days of my captivity'. Minden had a 'school' where men of the London Regiment taught Music, Maths, French, and German.

Lectures and classes on German were universally popular. Knowledge of German could help you escape and understand orders (and so, potentially, avoid the beatings that always seemed to come from *nichts verstehen*). Lance-Corporal Thomas Higgins, who taught himself German while working on a forestry *Kommando* at Kohlenbissen, would only learn of the Armistice in 1918 because he could read German newspapers. Despite the usefulness of German a few hoitily refused to learn the language. William Cull, AIF, and others who arrived with at Karlsruhe in 1917 were contemptuous of the language of the captor: 'We always explained our indifference to the German tongue on the ground that there would be little use for it in the outside world after the war.'[102]

Neither was German absolutely essential for escape. Second Lieutenant Jack Poole, King's Royal Rifle Corps, was simply too restless to learn any of the languages he threw his cap at. Poole suffered badly from the 'escaping bug'. He really did. He escaped three times in three months in 1916, twice with Medlicott, whom he had met at Munden. Poole was third time lucky, exiting Germany into neutral Holland at the end of October 1916.

Others threw over their studies for a sadder reason than restlessness. 'Flossie' Hervey, at least, believed that prison life had such a numbing effect on the mind that most inmates gave up 'swotting'. Although not reading. Everyone read.

Captain John Guest, 16/Manchester Regiment, captured March 1918, wrote home from Karlsruhe shortly after his arrival: 'There is a library here & so we pass the time reading.'[103]

Aside from sport, reading books was the most popular, important pastime in the camps. 'I do not know what I should have done,' recalled Sergeant George Wells of prison life at Kassel, 'but for an occasional hour with a book.'

Books were about more than passing the time of day upon day. Books prompted inner reflection, helped mediate experience. For those who had no control over their circumstances, they offered the semblance of control. Books were a means of connecting with a prisoner's pre-war self, and of building his post-war persona. Reading could be a cultural, political, patriotic injection to boost psychological resilience and self-identity. Crudest of all, in the crowded wire world a book was a shield to avoid interaction. To stick one's head in a book was sometimes the only privacy there was.

And of course, books offered escape. Literally, in some cases. During the first year of the war, itinerant book pedlars visiting the camps did a roaring trade in Baedecker's Guide to North Germany. Finally the authorities realized that their British charges were less enamoured with the jewels of Deutschland's scenery than the useful maps Baedecker's contained showing the routes out of the country.[104] The book was accordingly placed on the *verboten* list.

Arriving at Beeskow camp, a picturesque former Bishop's Palace dating to the thirteenth century, Joseph Lee's comrades thought it just the place for him, because it gave the hobbyist painter something decent to draw for once. And as Lee was a journalist by profession, thus 'bookish', he was naturally nominated librarian. (The same fate befell Norman Dykes; being the former librarian at Rochdale Public Library he was a certainty for the role in his other ranks' camps.) Unfortunately, there was only one book to be found in Beeskow. The dilemma of 'booklessness' was familiar to every arrivee in a new camp; at Munden, Horace Gilliland and his confreres could only muster twelve English novels between them, 'consequently to keep one's mind occupied, we had to read them over and over again'.[105] In such circumstances, any new arrival with a book or magazine in his baggage was warmly welcomed.

Despite Lee's inauspicious start, his library grew, as did so many of the camp libraries in Germany. At Holzminden the library eventually numbered five thousand volumes, though the library of three hundred at Karlsruhe was nearer the norm. Some camps set up small circulating libraries from parent camps for the men in the work *Kommandos*. As ever, the initiative came from the PoWs themselves.

Where did all the books come from? Lee was donated twenty volumes by some German officers. Unfortunately they were in German. Nonetheless it was a sporting gesture, a rare one too. All PoWs were allowed to order books (at their own expense, naturally) from Tauchnitz publishers in Leipzig, which produced English-language books. Lee duly did so. Until 1916 prisoners could request books from home. Indeed, along with cigarettes, clothes, food, the food for thought that was a book was the most common request for inclusion in a parcel. Private Joe Hickey, Dublin Fusiliers, wrote plaintively to his mother from Sennelager in October 1914:

> We are getting no cigarettes here, so I would be very thankful if you could send me a box of 'Woodbines' and some story books and a cake of bread . . . Tell father to send some of his books as I can't read German and they are the only thing we can get here.[106]

The biggest source of books to the camps, however, was charity. After the passing of the 1916 Defence of the Realm Act Regulation 24B (which banned the non-licensed export of 'certain . . . printed matter' to enemy and neutral countries) all books to PoWs in Germany had to be supplied by licensed publishers or approved committees. Effectively, the vast majority of books supplied to the camps henceforth came via the following charities: the Prisoner of War Help Society, the Red Cross, the YMCA (which also distributed a small monthly magazine, *The Messenger*), the Fighting

Forces Book Council and, especially, the Camps Library and the Prisoner of War Book Scheme (Educational). All were backed by the War Office, which intervened with its considerable muscle to get discounted rates on freight.

The Camps Library mainly did 'light literature'; the PWBS(E) provided improving, educational books of the sort approved by Jeeves. They were free to any prisoner who asked. Rarely was the PWBS(E) stymied; when an incarcerated cooper from the herring industry requested a tome on barrel-making he got it. Textbooks for University of London external degrees were PWBS(E) staples. The book charities themselves secured the goods gratis or cut-price from willing publishers, and from public donations. There was widespread enthusiasm for books-for-prisoners schemes, not least because of the lingering Edwardian social notion that time in prison should be devoted to self-improvement, education and reha-bilitation. Whether a man was detained at the Kaiser's pleasure or His Majesty's hardly mattered. Time in prison was preparation for life after release.

The number of books sent out by reading schemes was astonish-ing. In one week in October 1918 alone the Camps Library supplied 1,593 books to PoWs.[107] Unlike their predecessors, the khaki volun-teers and conscripts of the Great War were not by and large illiterates from the bottom of the social heap. The Tommy of 1914–18 was the man on the Clapham omnibus in uniform. He was a voracious reader. Although men in the camps were sometimes obliged to read whatever was at hand, their choice was for popular middlebrow fic-tion. The wish-list of authors and magazines compiled by a working party attached to *Engländerkommando XVII* at Fort Englos is in-structive. They wanted: Ian Hay, Conan Doyle, Baroness Orczy, E. Phillips Oppenheim, George Eliot, Sir Walter Scott, John Oxenham, Rider Haggard, Hallwell Sutcliffe, A.C. Askew, *Nash's* magazine, *London* magazine, and *Red* magazine.[108] A group of PoWs on a labour detachment near Loos asked for *Treasure Island*, *The Sign of the Four*, *The Pickwick Papers*, *Barnaby Rudge*, books by Marie Corelli and Nat Gould, but also Ernst Haeckel's *Evolution of Man*. One agricultural *Kommando* put Goethe's *Poems and Ballads* on its wanted list, a request which would have gratified the PWBS(E). Something of the pleasure a book could give a British PoW is expressed in a 'thank you' note to the book charity from Rifleman E.B. Dean, working in an agricultural *Kommando* in Bavaria: 'My three comrades and myself are out on Detachment, working on the land, living alone with the peasants . . . You can imagine how welcome a book is for the evening when work is finished.'[109]

While middlebrow fiction was the genre of prisoner choice, other reads had their followings. As with everything in neo-Georgian society, there were definite class divides in reading. By dint of their education, officers generally read more classics than other ranks. Boy prodigy Alec Waugh – who had published his first novel, *Loom of Youth*, at nineteen – read Flaubert, Maupassant, Balzac, Chekhov, Turgenev and Dostoevsky whilst incarcerated in Mainz. Archer Cust, who had been Captain of Oppidans at Eton, read and translated Voltaire of an evening at Graudenz. Literary societies in *Offizierslager* had Shakespeare for mains and pudding, though officers at Schwarmstedt singularly and heroically concentrated on the Bard's lesser plays.[110] Australians, meanwhile, loved *The Sentimental Bloke* by C.J. Dennis, a verse novel about a 'larrikin' who makes good, and settles down in the country with his wife and son. Published in 1915, with an edition for the trenches 1916, it was an unalloyed statement of the philosophy 'Life's what you make it'. And what's important in it:

> Sittin' at ev'nin' in this sunset-land,
> Wiv 'Er in all the World to 'old me 'and,
> A son, to bear me name when I am gone . . .
> Livin' an' lovin' – so life mooches on.

As a primer for helping Australian PoWs think about life after the war, it had few Antipodean rivals.

It was not always possible to escape from prison into a book. Sometimes the mere act of obtaining a book was a reminder of prison life, because it had to be queued for at the 'library', usually a hut or shelves in a common room. The incessant noise and overcrowding hardly provided a cloistered quiet for concentration and reflection. Then there was the diverting pang of hunger. In Mainz Citadel Alec Waugh tried to read Emile Zola's *La Débâcle* (1892), but on encountering the passage where Louis Napoleon Bonaparte shuts himself in his quarters, ignoring the meals brought by his servants, Waugh found

> because of perpetual hungriness, the whole effect of the incident was spoilt. I could not get into the mood necessary to appreciate the effect Zola had aimed at. All I could think was, 'Here is this appalling ass Louis Napoleon, surrounded with meats and fish, entrees and omelettes, and the fool does not eat them. If only they had given me the chance!'[111]

All books and magazines coming into the camp were censored for anti-German content. The Germans hated *Punch*. When the humorous magazine published a particularly biting cartoon, 'An average Prussian family having its morning hate', the British PoWs at Gütersloh were punished by having their deckchairs confiscated. Anything in a foreign language was unlikely to be released by the camp censor, as was any geography book with a map. There were no rules in censorship, and on a malicious or ignorant whim individual censors could, and did, ban anything that took their fancy. One censor confiscated Dickens. When Private F.C. Monk, Lincolnshire Regiment, had his educational textbooks confiscated he was haughtily informed by the camp censor that Sennelager 'was not a school'. Lieutenant Harbe, the interpreter at Bischofswerda, considered the morality of the British and French to be so dire that it was his personal duty to supervise their reading in the cause of 'Kultur'. Horace Gilliland's favourite periodical, *The Play*, with its pictures of actresses, was never going to pass such Prussian puritanism.[112]

Books that did make it past the crude hands of the censors routinely had the covers ripped off, ostensibly because they might be hiding contraband. The books, of course, then fell apart. This was a kind of violence, both against the book as artefact and against the minds of the prisoners who longed for their books to arrive. Some consolation was to be found in baiting the censor. When Alec

Waugh ordered Berta Ruck's propagandistic novel *Khaki & Kisses* followed by Ford Madox Ford's anti-German *On Heaven* he can hardly have hoped to have got them past the censor, and didn't. The author of the *Loom of Youth*, which satirized public schools, was accomplished at winding-up authority. German PoW camp censors made for an easy target.

One piece of reading matter the Germans did allow into the *Lager* uncensored was *The Continental Times*, 'A Journal for Americans in Germany', made and paid for by the Kaiser's government. It was universally loathed by prisoners. Horace Gilliland considered it 'probably the most scandalous paper ever produced',[113] Gilbert Nobbs thought it 'a rag of the worst kind, and contains lies of the worst description',[114] while Private Frank MacDonald dismissed it as the 'The Confidential Liar'. So outrageous were the lies, damned lies and statistics of *The Continental Times* that on repatriation Aussie soldier G.W. Bryce was surprised to 'know that London was still in the same place, for we had heard it was blown up'. In one month alone an amused Corporal Edward Edwards counted up 'a total of two million prisoners of war captured by the Germans on all fronts' in the paper. The publishers did themselves no favours by including articles and appeals by Sir Roger Casement, the leader of the Irish brigade traitorously fighting under the Imperial Eagle. There were also German propaganda sheets for Belgian and French prisoners, *Gazette de Lorraine* and *Gazette des Ardennes*.

English newspapers, naturally, were on the *verboten* list of goods allowed into camps. Of this Malcolm Hay, at least, was glad; he considered that the morale of PoWs would have been undone in reading about such things as labour strikes at home. Prisoners had 'an imaginary picture of Britain at war, which a knowledge of the truth would quickly dispel'. Any prisoner who did want a remotely truthful progress report on the home front or the war was reliant on two sources: new arrivals to the corps of prisoners, or the more serious German newspapers, the *Frankfurter Zeitung* (which erred to the radical and gave Allied communiqués in fullest detail) and the *Berliner Tageblatt*. Usually British prisoners were allowed these journals if they paid for them themselves. Important news items

were duly translated by German-speakers and written up for popular consumption, either as a daily bulletin or included in a camp
newspaper produced by the prisoners themselves.

Camp newspapers owed much to the self-published newspapers
of the Tommies in the trenches, such as the *Wipers' Times*, which in
turn were heavily modelled on the ubiquitous *Punch*. At least seventeen PoW camps produced a newspaper. At Bad-Colberg the prison
newspaper, the *Morning Walk*, was pinned up on the wall of the
pump-room and read by passers-by as they exercised. Treves had
The Barb (cost 50 pfennigs; it later went with its editors to Schweidnitz), Gütersloh had *The Budget*, Stralsund *The Outlook* (the editors
nervously hoped it would 'at least amuse') and Graudenz *The Vistula Bulletin*. *The Rennbahn Review* – Rennbahn was the alternative
name for Munster II *Lager* – was typical of the breed, an 18 × 23-
inch sheet double-folded, containing a mix of outside news, camp
news, poetry, fiction, jokes, drawings, cartoons, and dos and don'ts
from various committees. The camp newspapers played their part
in keeping the collective spirits up. *The Wooden City*, journal of
Göttingen *Mannschlaftslager*, asked:

'Downhearted? No!!! On the contrary!'

With rather more heart than versifying skill, Sergeant O'Shea took
to the page to implore readers to:

> Cheer up, Boys! then and stick it,
> As you would a guard or picquet,
> Though it's rough to be on duty every day,
> The new picquet will relieve you,
> And when those at Home receive you,
> You'll forget about 'the Wooden City' way.[115]

Editorial boards of camp newspapers were invariably heavy with
senior figures; on the editorial board of *The Wooden City* sat seven
sergeants, one company quartermaster sergeant, four company
sergeant majors. And one private. (Who was presumably a professional journalist or printer.) The burden of military leadership
did not die on exile to Germany; British NCOs and senior officers

continued, as far as they were able, to exercise their duties of care to those under them. Which included maintaining morale by any means possible.

The costs of paper and printing for camp newpapers were met by the staff stumping up from their pay, fund-raising concerts, and the cover price. Usually the most junior member of the board did the donkey work of production. Ostensibly Captains Pack and Thomas were the editors of the *Vistula* daily 'rag' (plus weekly digest), though young Archer Cust rather thought their main duty was collecting the 'kudos'. Cust himself

> was the intelligence bureau and printing press combined. I copied it out every day in an unusually tiresome form of cyclostyle ink, and then, after due censoring and verification of the facts, it was taken down and run off in the town.[116]

He added:

> There is no doubt that the issue circulated at 8 p.m. was eagerly looked for.

Some of the larger *Lager* had specialist publications painstakingly produced by the committed. The *Echo du Camp*, printed in English and French at Munster, was very highbrow; articles included 'the social role of the individual in a prison camp'. Drummer V.G.S. Champion, 1/East Lancashire Regiment, published the *Rennbahn Church Times* (from February 1917 *The Munster Church Times*) at Rennbahn, a lithographed two-sided journal that only contained articles of a religious nature. By every account Champion was a 'thorough good chap'.

Any prisoner who fancied settling down in the late evening with a copy of a camp newspaper was doomed to disappointment. In the camps, lights went out at 10 p.m. at the latest. Any light showing thereafter brought punishment as surely as gulls follow trawlers. Parole walks were stopped for three days for Lyall Grant and the inmates at Schwarmstedt for letting a single candle burn after the regulation hour. Like naughty children, prisoners tried to read with torches under their blanket. At Gütersloh Will Harvey's room read by shaded lights running on tapped German electricity. The 'Dear Poet' found such light useful to write by as well as read by.

Like Harvey, Lieutenant Archibald Bowman used poetry as therapy, writing in the introduction to *Sonnets from a Prison Camp*:

> It is no mere poetical exaggeration to say that in the first days of captivity at least, the writing of the sonnets was a labour that 'stood between my soul and madness' and I cannot help feeling that what, under one of the heaviest blows that can befall a soldier, has meant so much to me, may have in it something that will raise it at times above the personal to the level of general human interest.[117]

Certain themes repeat in the work of the prisoner poets and are suggestive of what went on in the minds of the men behind the wire: the crushing boredom of camp life, loneliness, love sundered by the circumstances of war, Nature, the feeling of entrapment. Home was above all the consistent looping theme. In 'Gloucestershire from Abroad', Will Harvey conjured England with a painful nostalgia to rival Brooke's 'Grantchester':

> On Dinny Hill the daffodil
> Has crowned the year's returning,
> The water cool in Placket Pool
> Is ruffled up and burning
> In little wings of fluttering fire:
> And all the heart of my desire
> Is now to be in Gloucestershire.
>
> The river flows, the blossom blows
> In orchards by the river:
> O now to stand in that, my land,
> And watch the withies shiver!
> The yearning eyes of my desire
> Are blinded by a twinkling fire
> Of turning leaves in Gloucestershire.
> The shadows fleet o'er springing wheat
> Which like green water washes
> The red old earth of Minsterworth,

And ripples in such flashes
As by their little harmless fire
Light the great stack of my desire
This day to be in Gloucestershire.[118]

The prisoner's idealization of home would turn to a heart-breaking hurt when he finally landed back on Britain's shores. Reality would rarely match the roses-round-the-door imaginings of camp time.

Officers educated at public school – meaning almost all those taken captive before 1917 – included their *alma mater* in their homewards thoughts. For the old boys of Britain's 115 public schools, School was a being as real and respected as a biological parent. Just as School had provided a sustaining relationship in the trenches, so it was in the camps. John Rose-Troup wrote 'Harrow's Honour' at Friedberg in Hessen in June 1916. The sentiments are typical of the men of Rose-Troup's class and education:

A weary time, a dreary time, a time of hopes and fears,
The weeks that pass, the months that pass and lengthen into years.
My heart goes back to Harrow, to Harrow far away,
And Harrow sends a message to cheer me on my way.
'For good come, bad come, they came the same before,
So heigh ho, follow the game, and show the way to more.'

Mourn not for those whose names are writ in gold,
They fought for England, gladly gave their all.
Kept Harrow's honour spotless as of old,
Nor feared to answer to the last great call.

They showed the way to more, their names will ring
Through all succeeding years of Harrow's fame,
Whatever changes after years may bring
Their sons will follow up and play the game.

O Mother Herga, all our thanks we give
For all your care of us, your watchful eye:
You made us men, you taught us how to live,
And in your wisdom taught us how to die.

The strongest bond of all, the bond of friends
Made in our youth, a bond that naught can break,
Binds us to you until our journey ends,
We live, we fight, we die for Harrow's sake.[119]

Rose-Troup had been captured on 31 August 1914 during First Ypres.
A Regular, he suffered paroxysms of guilt for being taken prisoner,
and yearned to do his military duty once more. He wrote 'The Listeners' at Weilburg in May 1916:

The guns!
Far, far away in the distance we hear them.
Oh, for a chance to be there, to be near them,
Borne on the wind in the stillness of night
Far-away sounds of the thunderous fight.

Guns!
Nightly ere sleeping our senses we strain,
Faintly we hear it – the muttered refrain.
Would we were free to be fighting again.
Hark to the guns!

Well do we know all the horrors of night,
Darkness made day by the calcium light,
Nothing but wreckage revealed to the sight.
Hark to the guns!

Yet would we break inactivity's spell
Just for one night in that shuddering hell,
Thunder of guns and the scream of the shell.
Hark to the guns!

The guns!
Breathless we wait for the news of the fray,
News of the guns that are nearer to-day.
Nearer they mutter, they thunder, they roll!
Nearer to victory, nearer their goal.
Guns!

Claude Templer desired war with a fervour only a Saxon or a Viking would understand. For Templer, war was 'wild strange poetry'. He never quite forgave himself – or the Germans – for the sneaky manner of his capture: being struck on the head from behind while he was reconnoitring an enemy trench. His prison verse and poems dwell constantly on heroic 'last stands', most evidently in the short story 'The Losing Fight', where he creates a sturdy British hero, Corporal Harry Thwaytes, who could have come straight from the pen of G.A. Henty or Rudyard Kipling: Thwaytes dies rather than surrender. Claude Templer wanted the romance of war, the yoke of service – and the redemptive purity of battle again. Along with Harold Medlicott, Templer was the great escaper of the First World War, making no less than twelve attempts before finally making a home run in June 1917.

Claude Frank Lethbridge Templer, at his own special request, rejoined his regiment after his escape. On the evening of 4 June 1918 he led a successful raid on the German trenches at Auchy-les-Mines. On the return across No Man's Land he was killed by a chance shell. He was twenty-two years old. He had resolved to be 'a worthy warrior. To fight to the finish, to love to the finish, to sacrifice everything but never honour. And to do all this with no hope of payment, but as a volunteer, just for the beautiful poetry of it all.'[120]

He achieved his desire.

Captain Claude Templer, 1/Gloucestershire Regiment, is listed on the Loos Memorial to the Missing. There is also a memorial to him in RMC Chapel, Sandhurst.

Of course, escaping was a form of entertainment too, a way of killing time. As Second Lieutenant Cecil Blain, RFC, explained:

After each tunnel I worked in . . . I swore stolidly that I would never work in one again, but these vows were of no use – amusement had to come from somewhere, and I enjoyed this sort of thing more than any other. It was a slow job, but in a cheery working party I found the work great fun.[121]

VI

ESCAPERS ALL:
THE ESCAPING HABIT

It was so extraordinarily pleasant to be free men once more.

Captain A.J. Evans, RFC,
having jumped off a train at 25 mph

The walls that kept men in the camps existed in the mind, as well as in physical form. There was the fear of failure, of being caught and 'harshed'. There was another obstacle too, for any prisoner contemplating escape: the sentiment of one's fellow prisoners. Escaping was not universally popular. The Senior British Officer at Torgau, Colonel W.E. Gordon, straightforwardly ordered PoWs not to escape in autumn 1914; when one officer disappeared, his absence was reported to the camp authorities. Arriving at Clausthal Flossie Hervey discovered that the camp had another disadvantage aside from being 212 miles from a friendly frontier, one which he had not encountered in other camps:

> This was the strong disfavour with which escaping was regarded by many of the prisoners themselves, chiefly due to the fact that Niemeyer had an unpleasant habit of visiting the sins of the evil-doers on the law-abiding prisoners, any attempt at escaping being immediately followed by reprisals upon the whole camp.[1]

The leader of the anti-escapers was the SBO, Brigadier-General H.S.L. Ravenshaw: '. . . a few days after our arrival at Clausthal he had us on the mat, and informed us that if we tried to escape he would have us court-martialled on his return to England.'

Those left behind by the flown birds could expect, in the wake of the commandant's wrath, additional *Appell,* room searches by raging guards, cancellation of parcels, arbitrary sentences in cells, ending of paroled walks, shutting of the recreation room and whatever whimsical punishment took his fancy. Aside from the '*strafes*' that followed escapes, some officers thought it positively *infra dig* to indulge in such activity; Lieutenant Jocelyn Hardy recalled that at Magdeburg in 1916 any potential 'jug-cracker'

> was made to feel oneself not quite a gentleman! It simply was not *done* to be breaking out of camps and travelling about Germany dressed like a tramp, and all this conspiring with foreigners [PoWs from France and Russia] was a great mistake.[2]

He must have felt very out of place; Hardy was one of the great escapers of the Great War, making ten escape attempts. He was no stranger to action, having fought a rearguard action at Le Grand Fayt, France, on 26 August 1914.

According to Canadian officer Tom Scudamore, escapees 'were looked upon with marked suspicion, for having surrendered in the first place and then acted independently in getting out of prison camp'.[3] And why escape at all after June 1917 when talks with Germans at The Hague resulted in an agreement that officers who had been in captivity for two and a half years or more could move to neutral territory for the remainder of hostilities? At Burg, Captain Henry Antrobus Cartwright encountered officers who were genuinely convinced that escape was ethically wrong, and that this was the official view at home.

They could be forgiven their opinion. Reading the smoke signals of the War Office regarding escaping was no easy matter. The Manual of Military Law 1907, page 269, stated that if the unthinkable happened a court martial would befall anyone who 'fails to rejoin His Majesty's service when able to rejoin the same'.

The devil was in the phrase 'when able'. Should one actually create the conditions of 'ableness' or wait for them to happen via diplomacy? By 1917, however, the War Office realized that escapers were valuable intelligence assets, and began to practically aid them with maps, compasses, wire-cutters and the whole get-out-of-clink shebang. Additionally, a special instruction was issued to servicemen that, if captured, no promise should be given to the enemy about not escaping.[4] Post-war, the matter of whether escaping was right or wrong was absolutely settled with the awards of medals and Mentions in Dispatches in 'recognition of gallant conduct and determination displayed in escaping or attempting to escape from captivity', the news published for public adulation in *The London Gazette*.

There were no awards for Naysayers.

All this was of magnificent unconcern to British prisoners. Whatever the ethical-political-military musings of the War Office, the majority of PoWs supported or tolerated escape and got on with it. Almost symbolically, while Colonel W.E. Gordon was decrying escaping at Torgau, Lieutenant Claude Templer, in collaboration with Lieutenant A.B.W. Allistone, 6/Middlesex Regiment, was digging a tunnel under his very feet. Nonetheless, anti-escape feeling was strong in some camps, usually the more comfortable ones, such as Friedberg. Older officers, in the view of the escape-minded Lieutenant John Thorn, were less in favour of absconding than younger ones,[5] while Jocelyn Hardy's experience at Magdeburg suggests Regulars in smart regiments were not always in the front rank of 'jug-crackers'. Overall, however, Henry Cartwright's conviction that 'they [the scoffers] were a very small minority, but they did manage to make things appreciably more difficult' is likely accurate. Tellingly, when the SBO at Mainz called a meeting in early 1916 to discuss whether it was right for a prisoner to attempt to escape and get home to fight again, the majority decision was in favour of not hindering attempts.[6]

What really rankled were stupid escapes that had no earthly chance of success.

The sheer amount of escaping activity among British PoWs indicates that many prisoners went beyond 'not hindering' to 'actively helping' or escaping themselves. There were 573 home runs (54 officers, 519 other ranks) by British and Empire prisoners from Germany in the Great War, nearly half of whom had made two or more previous efforts. Several hundred successful escapes from *Arbeitskommando* on the Western Front do not appear in the official tally. Memoirs, together with interviews taken by the Government Committee on Treatment by the Enemy of Prisoners of War, show over 3,000 escapes and attempted escapes by British PoWs in Germany and occupied France and Flanders. And this is the tip of the iceberg. No one now will ever be able to give an absolutely accurate reckoning of Great War escapes, but a fair estimate would be that between 5 per cent and 10 per cent of British PoWs held in Germany and the Western Front made one or more escape attempts during the Great War.[7] Put another way, the British made over 10,000 attempts to flee the German Babylon.

Courtesy of the Germans congregating troublemakers in punishment camps, some *Lager* became veritable factories of escapology. For officers the principal *strafe* prisons were Holzminden, Strohen, Fort 9 at Ingolstadt, and Zorndorf in East Prussia; for other ranks the *strafe* camps Fort Flines or Fort MacDonald would long be notorious. As a consequence of the Germans bringing all the 'Bad Men' together, Captain A.J. Evans calculated that 75 per cent of the prisoners of Fort 9 were scheming to escape; 'The camp was nothing less than an escaping club.'[8] Moreover, 'If you asked for help, almost any man in the fort would have helped you blindly, regardless of the consequence.'[9] Horace Gilliland concurred on the industrial scale of escaping that went on at Fort 9:

> I can safely make the statement that from the time I went to Ingolstadt until I left, there was never a moment, night or day, that the prisoners were not working their fingers to the bone in order to effect some means of escape.[10]

Captain Michael Harrison, Royal Irish Regiment, thought that most of the 430 inmates at wire-and-wind Stohen had made one or more attempts to vamoose. Not that other camps were lacking escapers; 'The principal amusement of this camp was escaping,' wrote Lieutenant Ernest Warburton of Schwarmstedt in 1917.[11] Burg, Schweidnitz, and a score of other *Lager* would see escape attempts galore.

In bringing the escape-minded together, the Germans only made difficulties for themselves. Rifleman Tich Evanson was segregated in the 'Bad Men's Party' at Westerholt coal mine in the Ruhr:

For those who wanted to escape it was about the best possible thing that could have been done. When new men joined the party . . . we all got together and shared their experiences . . . The whole topic of conversation in the 'Bad Men's Party' was the best route to the border.[12]

Too often the Great War escapers are explained away in psycho-babble as men motivated by a dislike of 'regimentation' or 'authority'. British prisoners of war in those vintage years between 1914 and 1918 were not civilian criminals, they were incarcerated soldiers. Their frustrations in captivity were those of defeated warriors. In the words of Captain A.J. Evans, a five-time escaper: 'It seems to me that we owed it to our self respect and to our position as British officers to attempt to escape, and to go on attempting to escape.'[13]

Will Harvey attributed his attempted escapes to a duty to country, a duty which required him to rejoin the war on the main front, in the mud-and-blood trenches of Flanders and the Somme:

His [the captured officer's] friends and brothers are 'out there' killing and being killed. *He* cannot help them. He is futile. He can not join any more in that dreadful and glorious fight for England and her liberty. He may be a prisoner through no fault of his own. He may have endured much hard fighting prior to capture. He may have carried himself bravely, won coveted distinctions, and so forth. He may have already 'done his bit,' to quote the foolish and vulgar phrase. The 'bit' is not enough. The 'bit' is *never* done. England is still fighting.[14]

The duty to return to the major front did not preclude other reasons to escape. Private Edward Page viewed 'jug-cracking' as a means of inflicting defeat on the Germans in their homeland, an act of war in and of itself. He was inspired by the example of another, an NCO in the Glosters, just as Page himself would inspire others, in a virtuous chain reaction of resistance:

It occurred to me that what one man could accomplish, by grit and determination, so could another, and from the day I heard the news of the success of his efforts I became fired with his gallant example, the outstanding thought always uppermost in my mind being the determination to shake the fetters of captivity from my feet . . . This determination to defeat them by escaping their clutches, and again reaching my native land, sustained me month after month, while I plotted, waited and watched.[15]

Page made his successful escape with Sergeant Billy Ward, King's Own Yorkshire Light Infantry, slipping away from a work party on the railway sidings at Friedrichsfeld in the gathering gloom of a November 1917 evening.

For Brian Horrocks even unsuccessful escapes had positive military outcomes, because to keep escaper prisoners in the jug required the Germans to divert men and resources (electricity and oil for lighting, metal for lamps and wire) from the Western Front. Thus 'failure was of service'. Imprisoned in Magdeburg gaol, Captain Michael Harrison calculated that no less than four German guards were required to contain six escapers, which gave the latter fellows 'great satisfaction'.[16]

The motivation of Captain Duncan Grinnell-Milne, RFC, in escaping came from the soul not the head. Twenty when his BE2c was shot down in 1916, Grinnell-Milne was a caged warrior. Escape for boys of his type – and there were many – represented romance and excitement, whereas in captivity he was living their antonyms: banality and boredom. Imprisonment, Duncan Grinnell-Milne considered, was 'that most awful state of things for a young man in wartime – inaction'. Digging an exit at Weilburg 'was more than a tunnel; it was a conspiracy'.[17] Certainly the confederacy of escapers contained a disproportionate number of the adventurous; some forty of the British 'home runs' were by men of the Royal Flying Corps, who were daredevils almost by definition.

Alec Waugh (who did not try to escape from Mainz) took a rather jaundiced view of escaping, opining that its

chief allurement was the love of reclame: every man is at heart a novelist; and they would picture to themselves the days of 'What did you do in the great war, Daddy?' and the proud answer, 'I escaped from Mainz,' and there was also the glory of standing in the centre of the stage. They liked to be talked about in undertones, to hear a whisper of 'Don't tell any one, but that fellow's going to try and beat it tomorrow.' They hankered after excitement, and in consequence when their schemes began to ripen to maturity, they enveloped their actions in all the theatrical paraphernalia of Arsene Lupin . . . But to the majority an escape consisted chiefly in a bid not for liberty but for fame.[18]

Undoubtedly, there were poseurs and fantasists among the escapers. But Waugh was too much the dramatist himself; as he more soberly allowed:

Of course to those who really took the business seriously every credit is due. They spent hours preparing maps, and ropes, and many Marks in bribing sentries.

One escaper who met Waugh's approval was Colonel Wright, a sort of latterday Scarlet Pimpernel, who managed to get over the outer wall of Mainz at night but alas landed right in the arms of two lovers who had chosen the spot for an amorous dalliance. As Flossie Hervey so wisely concluded, luck played an important part in escaping, since 'at times the most impossible ideas worked as if by magic, at others an entirely unforeseen circumstance proved to be one's undoing'.[19]

At the very least, escaping passed the time of day, gave men something to do. Escaping banished 'mouldiness'. A.J. Evans was convinced: 'Attempting to escape, especially by tunnelling . . . is the most effective occupation for assuring the health of prisoners of war.'

According to Dog Horrocks – another escaper whose sense of purpose Waugh would have approved of – 'my whole life became devoted to one thing – to outwit the Germans and escape'.[20] 'This business of escaping was all-absorbing; it was a battle of wits between the prisoners and the Germans.'

Horrocks, like John Thorn, thought younger officers more likely to escape than older ones. Age was no bar, however, in the escaping business; Major Vandeleur was forty-seven when he exited Crefeld, the same age as Lieutenant Peter Anderson, 9/CEF, the first and last maple-leaf officer to reach a neutral country. Captain Charles Fox, 2/Coldstream Guards, was in the prime of his military career when he escaped Germany in July 1917 aged forty, after nearly three years banged up. The average age of Great War escapers is slightly higher than young pup Brian Horrocks supposed, being around twenty-six.[21]

Surveys of the escaping habit generally miss the most pertinent cause. Other ranks escaped because of all the above reasons, plus another compelling one: their conditions were unbearable. One British other ranks escaper, George Robert Hill, told his interrogator on recapture in July 1918 that he had fled for fear of being beaten by the *Lager* sergeant. So pervasive and usual was violence against British PoWs, his explanation was accepted without question. The German interrogator noted 'the British have a strongly developed sense of honour. For this reason physical mistreatment should absolutely not happen.'[22]

Not-so-casual brutality, crippling overwork and lack of food proved strong motives to abscond; in one sample of sixteen other ranks prisoners taken between March 18 and May 18 in 1918 no less than eleven tried to escape. Such a high rate of attempted escape was not atypical of British soldiers in *Arbeitskommandos* behind the front, as Corporal Arthur Coney confirmed:

> The men in our compound all felt that they might as well risk being killed getting back to British lines, as remain in German lines and be killed by our own shells and starved by the Germans.

Private William Tucker, assigned to German motor depots in Flanders, was adamant: 'Escape was never far from our thoughts, whatever the circumstances.'[23]

Tucker himself escaped three times, once with the help of the Belgian underground. Rifleman Ernest 'Tich' Evanson recorded 120 individual attempts at escape within twelve months from Westerholt mine. Evanson reached neutral Holland, with Private Edward Gardiner, AIF, in February 1918, on his second venture out. They had joined a group of German miners underground, and simply walked out of the bath-house through the civilian door.[24]

Patriots, resistance fighters, adventurers, frustrated warriors, brutalized slaves, all escapers had one characteristic in common. They were brave men. Persistent too. Escapers tended to be serial offenders, not dissuaded from their eventual goal despite all the dire and dread punishments inflicted on the recaptured. The die-hard escapers from Britain and the Empire were:

> Second Lieutenant H.W. Medlicott, RFC – 14 escapes
> Lieutenant C.F.L. Templer, Gloucestershire Regiment – 13 escapes
> Lieutenant J.L. Hardy, Connaught Rangers – 10 escapes
> Lieutenant D. Grinnell-Milne, RFC – 10 escapes
> Private Frederick Rew, CEF – 8 escapes
> Private Don Corker, CEF – 7 escapes
> Captain A.J. Evans, RFC – 5 escapes

Captain Michael Harrison who, having made four escape attempts (two with his great friend Henry Cartwright), was something of an expert in the field, thought escape divided into three phases:

1) Getting out of the camp
2) The walk through Germany
3) Crossing the frontier

It was in the exiting of camps that the psychology of the individual truly came into play. This was the how of escape, not the why of it. Whereas some men would never bear the painstaking, patient grind of tunnel-digging, others would never place everything, life and future, on a desperate five-second run up the perimeter wire when the guard's back was turned.

Some escape attempts from *Lager* were engagingly eccentric. (Waugh would not have approved.) One Holzminden inmate – rather Britishly – contemplated using his umbrella as a parachute and launching himself off the second floor of the *Kaserne*. Either because the wind never reached the required velocity or because his courage failed (understandably) he thankfully abandoned the plan. Another Hellminden prisoner, a nineteen-year-old in the

RFC, tried vaulting the perimeter with a pole fashioned from the spars of deckchairs; it snapped; he plummeted twenty feet, narrowly avoiding the railings of the palisade.[25] Also crashing to earth at Holzminden was Second Lieutenant R.S. Capon, RFC, who shoved planks intended for shelves out of the second-storey dining-room window so that the far ends rested on the top of the wire. Down the slanting runners Capon slid, over the head of the sentry . . . whereupon the planks buckled and he, like the ill-fated pole vaulter, fell inside the perimeter. This caper led to the great joke that Capon, an astronomer at Greenwich Observatory who had recently delivered a talk on the solar system, 'now saw stars as well as lectured on them'. In honour of the incident a humorous song was composed, which contained the fabulous lines:

> The frightened guard shrilly blew his whistle,
> Then the great Niemeyer bravely waved his pistol,
> And he did resolve to extirpate the vipers
> All the men of Mons, All the boys of Wipers.

Since the planks had been abstracted from the dining room, Niemeyer soliloquizes:

> Fat is dis dey do? Dare dey cock der beavers!
> I will teach dem so,
> Fat is good behaviours.
> I a sight will have
> For mein gaze to gloat on:
> I will notice give Dining-room's verboten.[26]

The dining room was, indeed, placed out of bounds. Which led to something approaching a riot.

On arriving at Strohen, Duncan Grinnell-Milne was inveigled into a scheme almost as ambitious as Capon's wooden skyway at Holzminden. He was asked to join a battering-ram party. Using a heavy metal bar from the gym, six men charged a perimeter door lock. In the darkness they misjudged the distance, and missed the lock. There were bloodcurdling screams from the men who hit the wall with their faces. At Clausthal Brian Horrocks came across an idea that he thought *the* 'most harebrained scheme' which was to build two ladders from bed boards, rush to the perimeter, place the ladders on the fence, climb up and jump over. But the weather was never bad enough to keep the sentries in their boxes while the deed was done. Harebrained possibly, popular definitely: Grinnell-Milne and Jocelyn Hardy (with the French) actually tried the scaling method. Unfortunately, their ladder turned out to be a foot too short to get them over the top of the wire. Two Australians at Strohen were more lucky, or clever, putting their ladder against the perimeter wire one foggy night while the sentry had his back turned. With split-second timing they scaled the ladders and dropped over. The sentry saw them, but in the excitement and in the shrouding mist his shots went wide and they got away. The American mass escape from Villingen in October 1918 also used, among other methods of exit, a scaling bridge made from bed slats and the tennis court marker.[27]

The line between madcap and mad was fine. Few would have judged the effort of A.J. Evans, with Lieutenant B. Wilkin and Kicq (a Belgian) at Fort 9, Ingoldstadt, as anything but crazy. They decided to dash across the ice in the moat. In a masterpiece of understatement, Evans wrote later: 'It would have been extremely unpleasant if the ice broke for we would be wearing a lot of very heavy clothes. Still, anyone who thinks too much of what may happen will never escape from prison.'[28]

On the great day itself, the trio were equipped with rucksacks containing ample rations for ten days' marching:

We managed to get our bags and coats up into the jumping-off place without being seen by the sentry and without much difficulty. I remember walking across the courtyard about 4.30 with [Lieutenant Horace] Gilliland, picking up stones for him to throw at the ice. I think he was more nervous about it than we were: as is often the case, this sort of thing is more of a strain on the nerves for the onlookers than for those actually taking part. We were all in our places and in our kit, with our sacks on our backs, a few minutes before five. Whilst we were waiting for the bell to go, there were several prisoners walking up and down the path in front of us, along the top of the rampart. Of course they took absolutely no notice of us, except one Frenchman who spoke to us without looking round and assured us that the ice would not bear us – a cheerful thing to say under the circumstances. 'Mais oui, vous allez voir,' we answered.

It was a bad five minutes waiting there. Then the bell went, and almost immediately I heard laughter and shouting and the noise of stones falling on the ice. Then we jumped up and bolted over the path and down the slope. I was slightly ahead of the other two, and when I got to the bottom of the steep bank I gave a little jump on to the ice, hoping it would break at the edge rather than in the middle if it were going to break at all. But it bore all right, and I shuffled across at a good speed. About half-way over I heard repeated and furious yells of 'Halt!' followed soon afterwards by a fair amount of shooting, but I have no idea how many shots were fired. I was soon up the bank on the far side, through a few scattered trees, and over the frozen stream by a plank bridge. Then I looked back. The others were only just clambering up the bank from the moat and were a good 100 yards behind me. What had happened was this. I had made a small jump on to the ice, thus avoiding the rotten edge. The other two did not, but stepped carefully on to the edge, which broke under their weight and they fell flat on their faces. For the moment they were unable to extricate themselves. Wilkin says he got somehow upside down and his heavy rücksack came over his head so that he was quite unable to move. Then Kicq got himself free and pulled out Wilkin. At first he thought of beating a retreat up the bank again, believing naturally that the ice would not bear, but then he saw me three parts of the way across and heard the sentries shooting apparently at me, so he and Wilkin, keeping a bit separated so as not to offer too large a target, ran across after me. The sentry in the centre, who had been well attracted by Gaskell and the stone-throwing party, only caught sight of me when I was well on the ice, but then he started yelling 'Halt!' and loading his rifle as fast as possible. He then ran to the edge of his 'caponnière' and dropping on one knee fired and missed. Cold fingers, abuse, and perhaps a few stones too, which were hurled at him by the gang on the pathway just above his head, did not help to steady his aim. After one or two shots his rifle jammed. Yells and cheers from the spectators. He tore at the bolt, cursing and swearing, and then put up his rifle at the crowd of jeering prisoners above him. But they could see that the bolt had not gone home and only yelled the more. The other sentry had started firing by this time, but he was out of sight of the prisoners in the fort, and Unett and Milne, who had been distracting his attention (Unett said the sentry nearly shot him once), ran off to prove an alibi. I don't know how many shots were fired altogether. Not a large number, as owing to the appearance of some civilians they stopped firing when once Kicq and Wilkin had got well on to the far bank of the moat. When I was half-way across the space between the moat and the cottage, I saw on the main road on my left a large four-horse wagon with a knot of gesticulating men in civilian clothes. We learnt afterwards that they were carters from a munition factory in the neighbourhood, and were fairly strong and healthy fellows. They were only about 150 yards away, and started after us led by a fellow with a cart-whip. The going was very heavy, as there were two or three inches of snow and heavy plough under-neath, so we made slow progress, as we were carrying a lot of weight in clothes and food. They quickly overtook me, and the fellow who was leading slashed me across the shoulders with his whip. I turned and rushed at him, but he ran out of my reach. The rest of them then came round and I began to see that the game was up, especially as at that moment I saw some armed soldiers coming on bicycles along the road from the fort.[29]

He surrendered to the smallest, who held on to his coat-tails all the way back to the Fort. There was a hundred-Mark reward for the capture of an officer.

Incredibly, Evans did the same run-over-the ice stunt again, this time with Harold Medlicott, after squeezing through a bent iron window bar to get onto the moat rim. They were caught four miles from the fort by the canteen NCO, who was cursed roundly by the Fort's *Feldwebel* for bringing the pair back alive. The indefatigable Evans also joined a French tunnel effort at Fort 9, designed to get the tunnellers to the inner edge of the encircling moat, from where they would swim to freedom. A naked splash in winter did not catch Evans' fancy, so he made himself a diving suit out of mackintoshes, waterproofing the worn patches with candle grease, binding legs and arms with cloth and sewing up the front. But a thaw meant the earth above the tunnel sank and was noticed by an NCO doing his round at night. As to the diving suit, Evans commented: 'Thank heavens we never tried.'

Jocelyn Hardy observed that in 1915, when escaping got under way in earnest, prisoners knew very little of its 'science'. In the science of escapology, simplicity was often a virtue, because the more elaborate an escape, the more people involved, the more planning, the more preparation, the more likely was discovery. The first Tommy to escape from Westerholt was Private MacDonald, Gordon Highlanders, who, with spare, elegant brilliance simply ran out of the ranks as his party was marching to the mine at 6 a.m. one morning. According to Tich Evanson: 'Although there were a large number of guards with us, they were too astonished to fire.'[30]

Lieutenant J.H. Honeysett, AIF, tried the same legging-it trick at Strohen as he was being escorted from the camp to the commandant's extra-mural office. He was shot in the leg before recapture. A worse fate befell Bombardier Joe Hughes when he tried the sprint for freedom at Munster II. Breaking away from a working party, his progress was slowed by snow and he was shot. Dead. Until mid 1918 when pretty much every German guard could be bought, the *Landsturmer* shot to kill.

At the other end of the escaping spectrum from the physical sprint was the mind game. Of this genus, the escape of Second Lieutenant Marcus Kaye, RFC, was the perfect specimen. Over the course of a morning in Schweidnitz *Offizierslager* Kaye hid various bits of relevant kit in the camp latrines, timing his last visit with a change-over of the sentries. He went into the latrine as a British officer, and came out as a German workman. Kaye then proceeded to take apart the ventilation pipe and do odd handyman jobs. The sentries watched him abstractedly, and got used to his presence. Indeed, so accustomed did the sentries become to the sight of Herr *Handwerker* that, when he finished his toil, it seemed the most natural thing in the world for him to pick up his tool bag and walk off through the gate of the camp.[31]

Sergeant Arthur Gibbons also played the mind game, and quite literally so, for he pretended to be insane. He had been wounded in the head, which proved useful. He imitated a 'feeble minded boy', to success, and was repatriated as being quite, quite mad.

In essence, there were three ways out of the Kaiser's camps: through or over the perimeter, which was usually wire; underneath the perimeter, courtesy of a tunnel; or via the 'front door', the main gate using guile.

Most of Harold Medlicott's exits were through or over the perimeter wire, and he was the wire-cutter *par excellence*. With a nervelessness that left all watchers shaking their heads in wonder, Medlicott effected escapes in broad daylight. Douglas Lyall Grant watched Medlicott and his partner-in-escapology, Captain Joseph Walter, 7/Royal West Surrey Regiment (Queen's Own), break out of Holzminden:

> We had quite an exciting quarter of an hour this afternoon. Two fellows M. and W. put up an extraordinarily stout show by getting across the 'neutral zone' while the sentries' backs were turned for a moment, cutting the wire on the top of the railings, pulling themselves up and dropping over. They then started to walk up the road but, by a stroke of bad luck, they were spotted by a German looking out of a cellar window who gave the alarm and assisted in hoisting a sentry over the fence after them. He fired one shot and started in pursuit, followed by most of the rest of the garrison and numerous dogs and small boys. The fugitives displayed great staying powers and out distanced their pursuers, watched by an interested mob from all the windows, but luck was against them and the appearance of a man from a sentry box put an end to their attempt . . .

Watching the same breakout, Second Lieutenant M.R. Chidson, RFC, was awed by Medlicott's cool when, on dropping to the road, Medlicott 'took out a cigarette case and lighted a cigarette with a perfectly steady hand!' Chidson believed Medlicott 'an almost legendary figure amongst the prisoners of war' and that 'our morale [at Holzminden] was raised by the fact of his coming among us.'

Lieutenant Edward Olser Bath saw Medlicott, Second Lieutenant Jack Poole, and Lieutenant K.J.P. Oliphant, Wiltshire Regiment, leave Munden:

> on the 22nd [October 1916] Medlicott, Poole and Oliphant got away by cutting a hole in the wire in broad daylight with a sentry not 25 yards away on each side of them. Med, who did the cutting would wait till they both had their backs turned and then run up and snip a strand then come back and wait for another opportunity, it was one of the most dare-devil stunts I have ever seen.[32]

Other PoWs caused a diversion by throwing stones. Later the trio got separated at the Dutch border; Poole made it across into Holland on the 'blackest and roughest' of autumn nights. He thanked God for delivering him safely. Medlicott and Oliphant did not achieve sanctuary. 'Med' would try again, but in doing so he would be recaptured and murdered. No slouch at the escaping business himself, Poole was unhesitant in according Medlicott the accolade of being the war's 'star escaper'.

Medlicott's daylight wire-cutting was unusual; it was inherently the most dangerous of all methods of exit because even the most ancient *Landsturmer* guard could see in daylight and aim his Mauser with accuracy. Consequently, breakouts through the wire generally took place at night. When Able Seaman James Farrant departed Döberitz he sensibly included in his party of three Rumbelow, an electrician. Before their exit, Rumbelow disconnected a perimeter light, leaving a section of the wire in total friendly blackness. Escapers who lacked such electrical expertise sought to short the lights by throwing strips of metal onto the circuit which was not insulated.

Exits via the 'front door' of camps were games of bluff or concealment. Going through the main gate, explained Duncan Grinnell-Milne, was far from impossible 'providing you had sufficient effrontery'. He walked out through the front door of Strohen with two others (one of whom was his brother, another RFC pilot), dressed as two German officers and a civilian. They were out for five days before recapture.

Stralsund on the Baltic was regarded as one of the better camps for officers; there was grass for sports, and bathing in the sea under parole was possible. The delights were not enough to detain Hugh Durnford, who left via the main entrance on a forged workman's permit:

> I was Karl Stein, firm of Karl Stein & Co., Furniture Dealers, Langerstrasse, Stralsund . . . I knew the shop because I had seen it the day before when I went to the town hospital under escort with a party of officers for massage. I needed no massage, of course, but had only done this to acquaint myself with the geography.
>
> With a blank stare I passed several brother-officers walking up and down the avenue and reached the gate. My great moment had come, but the sentry simply looked at my card carefully, said *schön*, and handed it back. I walked very fast down to the ferry. There was no boat on my side and I saw I should have to wait some minutes. The sentry at the ferry examined my card and handed it back. How should I avoid the two Germans who were already there on the jetty waiting for the boat? I decided to have a violent fit of coughing.[33]

Coughing at all awkward conversational moments, Durnford and his basic German made it safely to Denmark. It was his first time 'out'.

Although theatrical props were excluded from escape attempts by the parole system, it is not hard to detect the thespian art behind the escape of one PoW at Clausthal, who imitated Niemeyer, and his blustering, spitting, and waving of cane to such perfection that the sentry on the gate saluted as he let the faux Niemeyer out. Such brio deserved better than the recapture of its creator several days later.

Neither did cross-dressing in *Lager* dramas go to waste. Another officer, 'Fluffy' Sutcliffe ('a fine little sport and the chief female impersonator in our plays and sketches'), walked out of Holzminden in 1918 dressed as a typist. Her 'boyfriend', dressed as a German soldier, was recognized.[34]

Camps were busy places, with steady streams of visiting Army officials and guards changing shifts making their way in and out.

Even so it took brass nerve to go through the gate disguised as a German soldier. Cartwright and Harrison went out of Burg in 1915, with German Army outerwear they had fashioned from a Grenadier's coat (with borassic powder beaten into the cloth to lighten it) and a Russian officer's cape. Their swords had been 'very artistically' fashioned from packing cases. Henry Cartwright takes up the story:

> We left our room and the building and walked down the yard towards the gate, accompanied by an English officer – dressed as a Russian to make the party look more commonplace – who was talking bad German to us at the top of his voice. We were very much encouraged by meeting some French and Russian officers, who, in all innocence, gave us the grudging salute on which the German always insisted. We carried in our hands the bunches of papers which seemed to be part of the dress of the German staff officer, and each smoked the customary foul cigar.
>
> While the gate was being unlocked we stopped and exchanged the customary series of salutes and bows with our imitation Russian, and that over, turned and walked out by the side of the wagon. The gate sentry jerked himself to attention, the Sergeant of the guard dropped his keys and saluted, and the worst was over. We politely returned the salutes and walked ahead of the wagon towards the gate in the outer fence. Here the sentry, whose job it was to unlock it, remained at ease, staring with open mouth at the two strange officers and apparently trying to screw himself up to draw their attention to the regulations by which no pedestrian might pass through his gate. Possibly he was expecting an order from us, but this was something we were quite unable to give him.
>
> We were brought up short by the gate, and were both of us silently wondering what on earth to do next, the situation for a moment looking desperate, when, in despair, I raised a finger as if returning the salute which he had so far forgotten himself as to commit. He must have realised that he, a private soldier, was standing at ease within a yard of two officers – which, in Prussia, it would be hard to imagine a more appalling situation. Seized with remorse he hurled himself at

the gate, threw it open, clicked his heels and froze to attention. We walked out, acknowledged some jerks from the sentry on the fence and strolled down the road towards the town. We had to walk down some hundreds of yards of main road – Harrison going dead lame and rattling like a cheap-jack, a tin of biscuits having come adrift in his trousers – before we came to the turning down which we hoped to get cover.[35]

They did. After a quick change, they emerged as heavily laden civilian workmen.

Brian Horrocks also tried his luck disguised as a German soldier:

We managed to construct a 'mock up' of the German soldier's fatigue dress, a red stripe down grey flannel trousers, a pyjama jacket died in coffee and so on. It was good enough to pass muster in the dusk.

After entering the attic at Holzminden, Horrocks cut a hole in the wooden partition to get into the staff part:

Carrying our food in a sack slung over our shoulders, which made us look like Germans who had been on some working party, we walked down through the building, across the yard and choosing the time when all eyes were on the guard-mounting ceremony, we strolled through the gate out past the sentry. No one paid any attention to us.

I can still remember the thrill of it; that wonderful moment when, from outside the wire, we could look back at the camp with its sentries, its arc lamps, its barbed wire. We were free.[36]

Nowhere was the good relationship between British officers and men better illustrated than in the help given by orderlies to escape-minded officers in the camps. If caught aiding and abetting escape attempts, orderlies faced, just for starters, a beating from camp guards. Corporal George McAllister, an orderly at Holzminden, suffered a permanently damaged wrist from trying to protect his head during a beating after officers escaped and he was implicated. At the recommendation of grateful escapers, McAllister was eventually awarded a Distinguished Conduct Medal.

After beatings and 'cells', an orderly suspected of aiding a break-out was near certain to return to a *Mannschaftslager*, and from there to a coal or salt mine. Time and time again, however, British orderlies helped officers escape. There were hundreds like George McAllister. As Will Harvey confirmed, 'A very large number of escapes . . . were only made possible by this perfect cooperation between officers and orderlies.'[37] Captain Edward Bath was the beneficiary of this stalwart sense of duty when, at Munden, he and others (including the irrepressible Medlicott) were lent orderlies' uniforms so they could escape as a party of orderlies detailed off for pig-feeding.

> We got up about five o'clock put on our civilian kit with orderlies uniform over it, succeeded in dodging the sentries in the building and got into the kitchen where we hid our rucksacks under the pig food, a German came in while we were there but didn't notice anything wrong. As soon as he had gone the six of us – Poole, Medlicott, Voelker, Hilpern, Pramberger (the little Rusky) and myself walked out with big buckets of pig food on our shoulders said 'Good morning' to the sentry, who very kindly opened the gate and we smiled a little smile of relief and walked into the pig pen. Once there we hid behind the pigs, slipped out of our uniforms and got out the back without being noticed.[38]

One stalwart orderly at Holzminden, the appropriately named Arthur Wheeler, trundled Second Lieutenant A.T. Shipwright out of the camp rolled up in an old carpet in a wheelbarrow. The ruse worked but Shipwright was captured soon after. In one month at Holzminden seventeen officers escaped dressed as orderlies, their kit being lent by said other ranks servants.

Even less comfortable than being rolled up in an old rug was hiding in the refuse cart. This was the ploy of desperate men; in the words of Hugh Durnford, 'the ordinary man blenched at the very proposition'.[39] Since the smell was a bit much, one officer at Crefeld, who went under the less than flattering soubriquet of 'Peeping Tom', took sensible measures against the aroma, as John Caunter recalled:

The refuse heaps and dust-bins were cleared out daily by an old German man and a boy, who removed the rubbish in a heavy two-wheeled cart drawn by an old ox. This rubbish-cart in these days used to leave the camp without being carefully searched and was emptied some distance from it. This fact was naturally well known to the prisoners, but the question, which most people took to be un-answerable, was how to remain hidden in the rubbish and yet be alive at the end of the unpleasant journey. It remained for 'Peeping-Tom' to think of a gas-mask in connection with this scheme. Borrowing one from an officer, who had been lately brought in from the front, and had retained possession of this article of equipment, he dressed himself in it, and choosing a moment when the German boy was looking the other way, and the old man had departed on some other business, he rushed to the cart and got inside. A well-trained batch of English soldier-servants then arrived, each armed with a bucket-ful of rubbish which they threw over the top of him, successfully hiding him from view. All would now have been well, had not fate cruelly intervened, in the shape of an old German who worked the bath-house furnace, and who occasionally came out for a breath of fresh air.

Seeing this extraordinary looking object disappear into the cart, the old Boche fetched his cap and went off to the commandant's office to report the strange event.[40]

Caunter filed the attempt under 'plucky . . . but comic'. Much could be said of Lieutenant Brine's refuse cart escape at Strohen. Another officer recorded:

Lieutenant Brine was one day carried out in the 'Dust Bin' tipped into the tippler-wagons which were then wheeled out of the Lager by British Tommies (who were in the secret) under the charge of German sentries. The Tippler-wagon was left in position to be tipped the following day, Lieut. Brine's idea being to await darkness and then make good his escape. Unfortunately a few hungry Huns from an adjacent village topped up the wagon, and out rolled poor Brine, dazed by the fall to such an extent that they had secured him before he was able to realise what had happened.[41]

Hiding in carts was hazardous for reasons other than the stink. Full carts on leaving were probed by guards with bayonets. Captain Matthews, Worcester Regiment, hid in the paper cart leaving Graudenz; the searching bayonet of the guard found his throat. Fortunately, it was only a scratch.[42]

For other ranks to exit a *Lager* via the front door was as simple as volunteering for work. Corporal Edward Edwards, his clothes painted with red and green circles to mark him as a dangerous character, volunteered for hoeing work on a farm. Unguarded, he left the farm 40 or so miles north-east of Bremen on 21 August 1916 for the Dutch border about 150 miles away, and crossed successfully two weeks later.[43]

A sub-species of the exit via the front door escape was leaving the camp on a legitimate reason, but not returning. Train-jumping while transferring camps was the major variant here. John Caunter calculated that no less than nine fellows made escapes from trains between March and May 1917. The experience of train-jumping was well described by Will Harvey, who decided to decline the invitation to attend Holzminden:

> Knowing my plan, and that I purposed carrying it out at once, several of my companions stood up in the carriage on pretext of reaching things from the rack, and so screened me from the sentry ... As I pushed off from the seat on which I was sitting I could hear someone directing his attention to the beauty of some stunted hills on the other side of the line, I dived. To withdraw my feet took only a moment, and there I was outside the carriage on the step, watching the ground whiz by underneath. It seemed to be going by very fast; but I had been lucky in the place, for we were doing a bend, and my carriage was then on the outside of the circle, so that no one looking out of the windows in front or in rear of the train could see me.
>
> Then I jumped. The ground seemed suddenly tilted up towards me, and I came down an awful bump with the pack in the middle of my back, and my throat across the opposite rails.
>
> I had jumped forward, but as a marble escapes from the bag which a boy swings, had been thrown outwards from the curving train. For

a moment we lay there, pack and man, flat in the trackway, while the train clanked past a few yards behind; then I realized where I was and why. I got up and ran quickly for cover, leaving the pack where it was. We were on an embankment. I threw myself over the edge of it and lay down while the train dragged its huge length past. I saw the German interpreter go by, leaning out of the window, a cigarette in his mouth. When the last carriage had passed, I got up and went to get my knapsack. It had split open in the fall, and many things, which included a towel, several tins of meat, and some very large hard Canadian biscuits, lay strewn over the railway-track.[44]

Unfortunately, Harvey had been observed by workers in the half-reaped fields below the embankment. They arrested him and accused him of being a spy:

This I did not like the sound of at all, for the Germans have a short way with spies; therefore I thought it well to explain quickly that I was a British officer.

Harvey was given a month at Holzminden in solitary confinement for the attempted escape, although the punishment was not very solitary because so many officers were attempting to escape they had to be put two to a cell. Nevertheless, disappointment, length of captivity, and close confinement began to tell on the 'Dear Poet'. He started to go 'mouldy', to let himself go.

A.J. Evans and Lieutenant S.E. Buckley, RFC, pulled the same trick as Harvey, getting everyone in the train carriage to stand at the given moment. They leapt from the train to Fort Zorndorf going at 25 mph up a gradient and walked two hundred miles from Nuremberg to Switzerland in eleven days. Horace Gilliland escaped from a train near Bonn with three others, walked twenty-one miles per night, and similarly reached the sanctuary of Switzerland. Later, in London, he formed the Escaper Officers' Club. By Gilliland's estimation the odds were six hundred to one against success in escape.

With some considerable style, young Archer Cust jumped the train to Graudenz, despite having been a prisoner just for a matter of weeks. Even die-hard escapers tended to find reasons to put off escapes, only 'beating it' when their nerves and convictions were steady, the omens good. Boyhood reading proved oddly useful for Cust:

> At last the train slowed down appreciably, though still going at least twenty miles per hour. I had always remembered seeing in that infantile paper *The Scout*, the way to get off a train in motion was to get yourself as near to and as nearly parallel to the ground as possible, with your feet towards the engine. This I proceeded to do, feeling my way cautiously down with my right foot. Suddenly I found myself sprawling among the stones, my nose bleeding, my hand cut, and the train rushing by.

At dawn, he listened to the birds: 'I shall never forget those songs that breathed freedom in every note as long as I live.'[45]

His joy in being free, 'to be able to walk about the cornfields as I chose – no guards, no restrictions, though an outlaw!' was short-lived. The woods were also inhabited by two hunters (dressed 'just like the sportsmen of the illustrated story-books I used to read when I was small'), who arrested him at rifle point, rather pleasantly, it must be said. One of the hunters was the burgomaster of Reichen-sachsen, and his wife fed Cust cheesecake.

Claude Templer, waiting at a quiet station in a small town in Germany for the train to Magdeburg, cut short the whole business regarding trains. He did not even bother to entrain. Instead, he kicked his guard in the back, chucked away his rifle, ran down the platform, vaulted a wall, mounted a bicycle and scorched down the road. Fifteen miles of fast and furious peddling brought him to the border zone. He went to sleep in a copse, preparatory to a night crossing, within sight of Holland.

His Sacred Majesty, Chance, decided to play foul. A company of the German Army chose the same place for a bivouac. Templer's luck would return.

The escape of Gerald Featherstone from Strohen's bath-house was marked by genius more than luck. The bath-house lay, Knight wrote in his memoir, *Brother Bosch: An Airman's Escape from Germany*, along a short, wired path, or bird-cage (as we called it), and thence into the bath-room. This room was situated about ten yards outside the wire, in the middle of a wooden barrack, running parallel to, and about fifteen yards away from, the wire. It is subdivided to form a dressing-room and a place for the shower baths, every exit being strongly barred, and a sentry stationed at the door. After a minute inspection of every nook and cranny, I found that it was just possible, by standing upright, to squeeze into an alcove, about eleven inches deep and a foot wide, in an angle formed by a wall and the brickwork of a chimney which projected into the room.

Though in full view of the door, it was partially hidden behind an empty stove. I reasoned that, should a well-made dummy wall obscure the aperture, it would take a very observant sentry to detect anything amiss. As a last resource, even should it be noticed, it might pass as something to do with the heating of the adjacent room. After weighing up the chances of success for several days, I decided that it was worth trying. When the measurements had been taken, behind the Bosch's back, I set to work to manufacture the false wall.

Most of my friends ridiculed the idea, calling my pet wall a doll's house and other insulting names, and bestowing on me much superfluous sympathy and pity. They argued that it had not been done before, and was, therefore, impossible, doing their level best to stop me embarking on such a mad enterprise. At first they almost succeeded in their object, but, knowing that most ordinary people remain in a camp indefinitely, working on more orthodox lines, I determined that I would put it to the test, if only to prove them wrong, or land myself in prison. One infantry officer, who had previously been through a course of camouflage, gave me his moral support, which counted for a good deal.

The wall was made of cardboard sewn tightly on to a light wooden frame, the whole being made in three sections, which, when fitted together, reached the height of about eight feet six inches. The top section was fitted with a leather hinge, which allowed the upper half of it to slope back at an angle of forty-five degrees, so that the hiding-place should not appear to be hollow. When at last the doll's house was finished, it defied all efforts to whiten it, and seemed to

have a rooted objection to being made to resemble the dirty whitewash of the bath-room. I tried melting old whitewash (scraped off
the walls) with gum and hot water, but it either fell off when dry
or showed the wet cardboard plainly through. Chloride of lime
proved equally useless. Only a little white paint was procurable,
but this was altogether too smooth and shiny. One day, when the
three sections were drying outside on the sand, a German *feldwebel*
(sergeant-major—commonly known as a 'fieldwobble') came along,
and inquired if I was making a model aeroplane. When I replied
that his surmise was correct, he asked me, with a slow smile, if I
intended flying away when the machine was completed. The wicked
old creature departed, highly amused at my answer, 'Yes, I hope so.'
Certainly many a true word is spoken in jest!

After a week's experimenting with useless colouring mixtures,
I was almost in despair, when the desired effect was produced by
coating the cardboard with a thick cornflour paste, finally toning it
down with a mixture of cobwebs and mud.[46]

On 16 August 1917 Knight put his false wall to the test:

A little before five o'clock I entered the bath-room, accompanied by
several assistants. Our journey thither was rather amusing, though
the slightest accident would have meant much 'stuben arrest.' It is
not easy to walk naturally when carrying a young wall out of sight
under one's coat, which is doing its best to give the show away by
shedding bits of plaster which fall to the ground and leave a trail,
reminding one strongly of a paper chase.

However, the sentries noticed nothing unusual. As soon as the
Hun's back was turned I slipped the sections together and squeezed
into the alcove, into which I was securely fastened by a friend, who
whispered that everything looked O.K., and asked me to be sure and
write to him when I got to England. Whether this was meant or not I
do not know, but at any rate it was just the encouragement I needed.
It was an anxious moment when everybody left the room with a final
'Good luck,' and I heard the sentry approaching to make sure that
nobody had been left behind. Previously I had determined not to
watch the Hun, as my gaze might render him more liable to look in

my direction. Now, under the stress of circumstances, this seemed a physical impossibility, and all good resolutions went to the winds. I glued one eye to the spy-hole and saw a German standing only a few feet away, with his back to me, puffing solemnly at a long pipe, a rifle slung over his shoulder. Almost immediately, as if in answer to my concentrated gaze, he turned and looked straight in my direction. I promptly shrivelled up to nothing, and developed acute suspended animation. I simply dared not breathe, and felt as if my thoughts were becoming audible.

My relief was indescribable when he turned away, and left in an ordinary manner. Though one crisis was over, the strain had been such that it took me several minutes to 'defossilise' and grasp the fact that, somewhere in the dim distance, the chances of success were increasing.

Knight waited in his claustrophobic recess for six hours then escaped from an outbuilding under cover of darkness. After two hours crawling through the peat bog surrounding the camp, Knight emerged onto firmer ground and set course for Holland. For over a week he spent the nights tramping across western Germany and the days in hiding. He crossed into Holland with only the stars to guide him.

Unknown to Knight – and this is where luck played its part – no less than two other parties also planned escapes from the bathhouse, both with the intention of covertly cutting a trapdoor in the wood floor which would allow them to hide underneath when the bathing session ended and, like Knight, then effect a moonlit flit. The two trapdoor parties joined forces, and five went out on 28 August 1917, covering their feet and ankles with garlic to put the dogs off the trail. Three made it to Holland, crossing over at Sustrum on 6 September. They were Michael Harrison, Second Lieutenant G.S.M. Insall VC (his third attempt) – and Claude Francis Lethbridge Templer, thirteenth time lucky.

Of the escaping community, Harrison had been the jack of all trades. Barely was there an escape method he did not try, including tunnelling. As a means of conveying officers out of the 'jug',

tunnelling ranked second (after going over or through the perimeter wire) in efficacy; for other ranks tunnelling was a minor
method, since after a day's forced labour a night spent tunnelling
did not appeal. Not that tunnelling in *Mannschaftslager* was entirely unknown. Edward Page worked in a tunnel at Dulmen from
which eleven escaped; his enduring memory of the dig was shared
by many. Fear of entombment:

> The thought often occurred to me whilst taking my turn inside the
> tunnel, what if it caved in behind me, and at every slight fall of sand
> from the roof in my rear my flesh used to creep. I always breathed a
> sigh of relief when our four hours' shift was finished.[47]

Will Harvey gave the line-up of the classic tunnel-digging system.
The underground shift consisted of five men:

No 1: The digger
No 2: Man behind digger – raked back and put spoil on wooden
   sledge
No 3: Pitman – dragged sledge on hands and knees to shaft
No 4: Sandbagger – at shaft, packed sand in bags
No 5: Fan Man – kept air fresh[48]

Aside from revetting the tunnel sides and roof (bed boards being
the usual material employed), the biggest problem in mining was
where to put the spoil. Over time, the most efficient system evolved
by prisoners was to make sandbags of curtains and any material that
could be bought or stolen; two of these would be tied together and
passed over the shoulders like a yoke inside a Burberry. The carrier
only had to pull a string and then the spoil shot out onto the floor or
the *Appell* ground or wherever. Tunnellers at Gütersloh moved out
thirty-three bags per day in December 1917. The rate at Crefeld when
Mulcahy was digging was presumably higher; to the unbridled joy
of Crefeld officer tunnellers, Mulcahy, an orderly, turned out to have
been a miner in civil life. He worked Herculean wonders. Despite
Mulcahy, the Crefeld tunnel was only half-finished when officers
received a sudden order to move to another camp.

Tools for tunnelling presented another problem. Sharpened

pieces of iron bedsteads were makeshift picks, as were stanchions from the walls of older fortresses. To cover up the noise of digging, miners at Neunkirchen made a Wimshurst machine – a large Frankenstein device for generating static electricity. The Germans thought it an eccentric British hobby, and never realized its true and illicit purpose. The Neunkirchen tunnel was the acme of tunnels; it had a telephone and electric lights. (Candles, torches or lights made by piercing holes in the tops of tins of shaving soda and putting in a blanket wick made for more usual tunnel lighting.) Tunnellers at Clausthal, meanwhile, dug from under the music room floor and lacking a Wimshurst machine could only find Lieutenant Capon (of Holzminden skyway fame) to provide disguising noise. The 'unfortunate Capon' had a permanent appointment at the piano, drowning the noise of tunnelling by constant piano playing if any Germans were in the vicinity. If the Germans hoved too close, he switched from ragtime to 'The Campbells are Coming'; when it was safe again to dig he started up 'Onward, Christian Soldiers'.

Since the air in a long tunnel went 'bad', fresh air needed to be pumped to the face. At Custrin, John Thorn's tunnelling party made a lengthy pipe by joining together condensed milk tins with paper, linen and mucilage. A propeller constructed from a biscuit tin and wood drove air down the pipe. After four and a half months the tunnel was 125 yards long, with fifty men ready to go, when the project was snitched on by a German plant posing as a Russian officer. The tunnellers at Clausthal, having excavated a tube 22 yards long, some of it through solid Hannoverian rock, were betrayed the very day before the planned breakout in November 1917. 'We know how it was given away,' wrote one officer, 'and there will be trouble for a certain Sinn Feiner [an orderly] after the war.'[49] There were penalties for informers before the end of the war: Captain Allouche at Osnabrück turned in a Franco-British escape attempt, and suffered rough justice. He was covered in treacle, excrement and ice-cold water.

Stoolies were only one hazard among many for tunnellers. Duncan Grinnell-Milne's tunnel at Neunkirchen (which he rated one of the truly tricky camps to break out from) flooded, as did one at Clausthal, which proved so off-putting an occurrence that another tunnel ground to a halt for want of workers. A tunnel at Sturm in the Hannoverian marches was dug so close to the surface that when it reached the entrance gate one of the sentry boxes toppled over due to subsidence. The German habit of moving prisoners about did for a nearly completed tunnel at Gütersloh; after 'a stormy meeting' the tunnellers decided to hand over the tunnel to the Russians rather than making a limited breakout of two Britons. The Russians were betrayed and the tunnel came to nought.

Tunnelling provided one of the war's minor tragedies; Captain William Morritt, 1/East Surrey Regiment, was shot dead by a guard at seven yards range when emerging from a shallow tunnel in the peat at Schwarmstedt on 27 June 1917. The incident was widely regarded by British PoWs as outright murder. Morritt was twenty-four. A fellow tunneller, Moss, was shot in the arm. Will Harvey recorded that: 'Nobody whined about it (it would have been the last thing they would have wished; they had taken their risk and paid for it), but I cannot bring myself to imagine any British soldier deliberately killing a defenceless man in such circumstances.'[50]

The commandant allowed Morritt a military funeral, which took place in a churchyard about six miles away. Among those attending was Harvey:

> His particular friends, the members of his room, and a percentage of other prisoners, were allowed to attend, and stood by the graveside when the German soldiers fired a salute of three rounds which echoed back from the overshadowing woods. There, with sunlight, branch-filtered, falling across the brown earth which covered him, we left poor M. When the echoes had fallen to silence only the sough of the trees could be heard. He was one of the gentlest and bravest souls I ever knew.

Captain Morritt's grave is now located in Hamburg cemetery.

When tunnels went well they delivered spectacularly. On 7 September 1918 sixteen PoWs escaped from Graudenz; in May 1918 nineteen went out from Schweidnitz; on 18 August 1916 nineteen went out from Torgau; and on 23 July 1918 twenty-nine departed from Holzminden.

*

I am Niemeyer. I have constructed the camp so that you cannot
escape; it is a waste of time trying.

The standard greeting of Kommandant Karl Niemeyer to
newly arrived PoWs at Holzminden *Offizierslager*

The Holzminden tunnel was the great escape of the Great War.

The brainchild of Lieutenant W.G. Colquhoun, PPCLI, the
tunnel began under the orderlies' staircase in the cellar of *Kaserne
B*. Due to the inadequacy of a compass underground and to the
rocks of an ancient stream bed, the 'rat-hole', as the tunnellers knew
their creation, rose and twisted painfully. Although air was forced
down the tunnel with bellows made from an RFC flying jacket,
it was always foul. As digging implements the tunnellers used
kitchen knives, penknives, spoons, sticks, pokers and a cold chisel
stolen from the carpenter. Then there were the rats. Cecil Blain
recalled:

> There were many rats living in the tunnel, and meeting one of them
> and seeing the glitter of beady eyes in the semi-darkness was a
> feeling of revulsion only surpassed when one of the vile and foul
> creatures scurried over you.[51]

Despite all adversities, within nine months the tunnel, 16 inches
wide by 18 inches high, ran to 55 yards in length. Long enough to
reach outside the camp perimeter.

'*Der Tag*' was the night of 23–24 July 1918. The thirteen principal
diggers were to go first, having drawn lots for the order; then, after
an hour's hiatus to allow the lucky thirteen to get clear, there followed a group of six sterling supporters of the tunnel project, led by
the SBO, Colonel Charles Rathbone. Of somewhat portly morphol-
ogy, Rathbone had been taken for a trial crawl of the claustrophobic
tunnel to see if he fitted through. (Rathbone was sprightlier than
he looked; he'd already escaped from Schweidnitz.) When the initial two groups had flown Holzminden, another sixty-six men were
waiting to flit.

Lieutenant Walter Butler was the first man through the tunnel
that night:

I left my room at about 10.15 p.m., and in ten minutes I was worming my way along the hole for the last time, noting all the old familiar ups and downs and bends, bumping my head against the same old stones, and feeling the weight of responsibility rather much. I am not ashamed to say that I did a bit of praying on the way along. When I got to the end, into the small pit which we had dug to drop the earth of the roof into, I put my kit on one side and got to work with a large bread knife. It was of course pitch dark. I was kneeling in the pit, digging vertically up. The earth fell into my hair, eyes, and ears, and down my neck. I didn't notice it much then, but found afterwards that my shirt and vest were completely brown. By about 11 p.m. I had a hole through to the air about 6 inches in diameter. It was raining, but the arc lamps made it look very light outside. I found, to my delight, that we had estimated right and that I had come up just beyond a row of beans which would thus hide my exit, with any luck, from the sentry. By 11.40 the way was open, and I pushed my kit through and crawled out. The sentry nearest us had a cough, which enabled me to locate him, but as he was in the shadow of the wall and not in the light of the electric lamps I could not see him. This made it a bit more uncomfortable, as I didn't know but that he was staring straight at me. I crawled to the edge of the rye-field and looked at my watch. It was 11.45 p.m. Just at that moment the rain stopped, a bright full moon shone out and an absolute stillness reigned. The rye was very ripe and crackled badly, and so, after a whispered consultation with L., I decided to crawl in a southerly direction down the edge of the rye-field, keeping under cover of the gardens.[52]

With orderlies in charge of 'traffic control', the escapers kept going through as per schedule until there was a roof-fall on the thirtieth man, burying his and the chances of more than fifty other men who were stood down. Somehow the thirtieth man was dragged out backwards to safety.

Next morning, at around 6 a.m., angry farmers came to the *Lager* to complain about their crops being trampled. Niemeyer himself went to investigate and found the tunnel mouth. A tally of the prisoners was ordered. When a *Feldwebel* reported that twenty-six prisoners were missing (he'd forgotten to count one room):

> [Niemeyer's] jaw dropped, his moustachios for a brief moment lost
> their twirl, his solid stomach swelled less impressively against his
> overcoat. Just for a moment he became grey and very old.[53]

There was much *straf*ing of those left. But who cared? As Second
Lieutenant Vernon Coombs remarked, Niemeyer's 'Prussian arro-
gance had been punctured'.

Ten of the twenty-nine who broke out of Holzminden on that
summer's night made it to Holland. They were: Captain David Gray,
RFC; Second Lieutenant Cecil Blain, RFC; Second Lieutenant Caspar
Kennard, RFC; Lieutenant J.K. Bousfield, RFC; Colonel Charles
Rathbone, RFC; Second Lieutenant J.N. Tullis, RFC; Captain E.W.
Leggatt, RFC; Second Lieutenant James Bennett; Second Lieutenant
Stanley Purves, RFC; and a Lieutenant Campbell-Martin.[54]

*

Some escapers made their way across Germany with next to no kit
or provisions. These were largely Canadians, used to the outdoors,
and to foraging. Indeed, the Canadian Frank MacDonald attributed
the high rate of successful escapes of Canadian British compared to
'British' British (one in a hundred Canadian PoWs achieved a 'home'
run) to the Canadian love of the wilds. In MacDonald's view, 'while
the British prisoners were ready to fight the guards they did not display the same eagerness to get away as did our Canadian lads'.[55]

Lieutenant Peter Anderson, the sole Canadian commissioned officer to make a successful escape, believed: 'The main factor was that
I had been an outdoor sportsman all my life . . . when one can fool
all the wild game animals, a sentry is easy.' He added that escape
was as natural to him as it was 'unnatural to others', and that he
would have been a traitor not to escape because he had the ability
to do so.

With the exception of backwoods Canadians, Lieutenant Capon,
and Royal Navy personnel, most PoWs were unable to steer by the
stars and required compasses and maps. The standard method of
DIY compass manufacture in the camps was detailed by Major
John Thorn:

We collected together used Gillette razor blades, and made them into compass needles by holding the blade over a flame until the temper was taken out, after which we cut out the steel to a diamond shape, leaving the centre hole, through which we attached a dress fastener, which we were able to buy from the canteen. Before attaching this fastener we again heated the steel, and by placing it immediately in cold water, tempered it again; after which, by using a small magnet, we were able to magnetize it, and by placing it on the end of a needle, it always swung to the north pole. For a case we carved out pieces of wood to the shape of a large pill box (if our people at home had only sent us a few boxes of Beecham's Pills, it would have saved us this trouble), and driving through the bottom of the box a gramophone needle, we made an excellent compass; we finished off the work by pasting in the bottom of the compass some white paper, and taking one of the luminous figures from our watches we placed it on the point of the needle, so that it could be seen in the dark. A piece of glass was then fixed in, and our compass was complete.

It took us some time to find the way to cut out a circular piece of glass without a diamond, but after a time we discovered that by cutting the glass under water with a pair of scissors, we could get any shape we liked without cracking the glass.[56]

To obtain his compass, Lieutenant Robert Paddison sent a letter home asking for an illuminated photograph of his family behind a donkey and a picture of Granny. Finally Paddison's mother twigged that the first letters of the Christian names of the family made 'COMP' and a donkey was an 'ASS'. The grandmother's initial's were 'MAP'. The 'illuminated' (luminous) compass was sent to Paddison in Holzminden in the lining of a waistcoat, and the map was put inside a hollowed-out walnut shell, the two halves glued together again, and dispatched in a box of mixed nuts.[57]

Lieutenant Cecil Blain, RFC, also obtained his compass by sending a coded letter home, which read:

My dearest Mother,

I am so sorry I am unable to account for the los of my letter home to

you, but hop this one will rive soon telling you that I am very fit and
well. I ccannot tell you how I long to be ome again – etc. etc.[58]

The missing and duplicate letters spelled 'search'. She did so, and
found a message written in milk on the inner flap of the envelope
requesting a compass. She duly sent Blain the instrument in a tin of
Pascall's Crème de Menthe. As important to Blain as the receipt of
his compass was the knowledge that he was in successful communication with his family. He no longer felt cut off. He sobbed with
relief.

Milk was a common invisible ink. In his covert requests for escaping materials Lieutenant Lawrence Wingfield, RFC, used 'Lemon
juice, spittle or, on a certain kind of paper even plain water . . . or
certain letters could be written above the line and those letters used
as code'.[59] He thought pricking the key letters with a pin a cliché
well known to the Germans. An equally crude method nonetheless
brought Flossie Hervey results in November 1917; he put small dots
under the requisite letters in his missive to his fiancée. She got in
touch with the War Office who henceforth sent Hervey's escaping
kit out to him ('the stuff being packed by experts at the job') in
his parcels, including the requested 'luminous compass in jam'. The
War Office when converted to actively helping escapers was indeed
expert at packing;[60] Flossie Hervey once spent the best part of an
evening eating prunes 'until the all important one came to light'.[61]
It held a 'small, tightly rolled document', a reply to an intelligence
message sent home by Henry Cartwright. Maps and railway time-
tables on silk also found their way into Germany inside jars of
prunes packed inside prisoners' parcels, always their personal ones.
Red Cross parcels were never tampered with, because misuse of the
Red Cross system would have jeopardized the lives of tens of thousands of prisoners.

Flossie Hervey's family had been 'not too keen on this escaping
business', hence his requests being addressed to his fiancée. How
crucial support from home could be for escapers may be judged by
the dedications in Within Four Walls, the escape memoir of Michael
Harrison and Henry Cartwright. Harrison's dedication was to

My Mother, whose untiring effort to get my invisible ink developed and send out all requirements according to instructions never failed

While Cartwright's was:

To my wife, who did all that for me

A.J. Evans dedicated *The Escaping Club* to:

My Mother, who, by encouragement and direct assistance, was largely responsible for my escape from Germany, I dedicate this book, which was written at her request.

By the end of the war German sentries were sordidly easy to bribe. In return for edibles or soap guards would supply the most blatant of escaping kit, recalled Geoffrey Phillimore at Schweidnitz, such as compasses and maps 'without any necessity for prolonged negotiation or elaborate diplomacy on either side'.[62]

Before that good time maps were mostly obtained by tracing from an original source on paper (that from Huntley & Palmers biscuit tins was especially good), although Henry Cartwright managed to have a complete set of motoring maps of the Dutch–German border sent in by his fiancée after requesting 'pictures of the edge of the dear old cheese country'. The contraband map arrived hidden in a tin.

Although the Germans assiduously checked parcels and packages coming into the camps a little criminal ingenuity got round the inspection system. Most PoW communities developed a lock-picking culture that would have impressed a Dickensian rookery. Will Harvey judged that after a month or two at Schwarmstedt 'we were pretty well able to unlock any room in the whole camp'.[63]

Captain Harrison concurred, and post-war unveiled a trick of the trade:

The art of picking locks is a trade rapidly acquired by prisoners. Two bits of stiff wire, each bent into the shape of an L, is all that is required. With one you lift the spring of the lock and with the other you feel for the notch in the bolt and slide it along. I generally used two sardine tin openers.[64]

At Clausthal Second Lieutenant Cecil Blain and Second Lieutenant Caspar Kennard were taught by a guard (of all people) how to
unlock doors with a bootlace, and actually succeeded in escaping
from the cell where they had been incarcerated for escaping. They
were captured separately, with Blain getting to within 200 yards
of the border at Venlo. On their return to Clausthal they were
treated like heroes. Where lock-picking was impossible, prisoners
made skeleton keys from melted-down camp money, with the im-
pressions taken on shaving soap, German bread (at last a good use
for the stuff!) and in extremis, when Harrison was banged up in
Magdeburg civilian gaol, Oxo cubes.

One upshot of PoW lock-picking was that crucial parcels could be
liberated from the parcel room before they were opened and examined by German staff. Brian Horrocks' contraband kit from Aunt
Maud was put in the tin-room, which he accessed using skeleton
keys. To cover the abstraction – all incoming goods were itemized
to punctilious degree – he accused the Clausthal tin-room staff of
theft. Officers at Torgau did not require chicanery to obtain contraband goods, since they had Lieutenant Hammond, a Quartermaster
in the RMLI. Lieutenant Hammond took personal responsibility
for checking off British parcels with the German staff. His 'mas-
terful manner' made them afraid of anything but the most cursory
glance at a British tin, thus none were ever properly checked. As
a result, Michael Harrison was able to assemble the 'finest mobi-
lisation kit that any prisoner ever possessed', including electric
torches, and automobile maps showing the routes to the Baltic and
Holland.[65]

Smuggling did not always bring such sweet success. Captain Jack
Shaw, RFC, in Holzminden had to watch as

> one of my tins, opened in my presence, was found to contain my
> Mark IV Prismatic compass, value £4 10s., on which my name was
> engraved . . . I endeavoured to persuade 'Milwaukee Bill' that I must
> have been the victim of a cruel hoax on the part of someone who
> did not like me in England, but he was not having any. At the same
> time, the German who was opening my packages mixed tea, coffee,

pepper, sugar, salt and ground rice all together in one heap on a piece of paper, which he pushed to me with a grin. I threw the whole lot in to his face, to his discomfiture, and was immediately placed under arrest and, for the day's work, the commandant awarded me three weeks in solitary confinement.[66]

It was truly amazing what camp *Kantinen* inadvertently supplied in the way of escaping kit. The one at Osnabrück sold a splendid manicure set, the nail clippers of which were sufficiently strong to cut the perimeter wire of the camp. Canteens also sold safety matches and oil cloth, both highly valued by would-be escapers. Some, like the one at Holzminden, sold children's printing kits which were ideal for forging identity cards, birth certificates and travel permits.

In another kind of commerce, prisoners at Fort Zorndorf were positively spoiled for choice when it came to escaping kit because a secret market was held every week by the PoWs at which civilian clothing, maps, compasses, and rubber dies cut to resemble German official stamps were sold. One keen vendor was Second Lieutenant F.J. Ortweiler, RFC, whose forged identity cards (which all Germans were required to carry) boasted an 'official stamp' complete with a German eagle good enough to fool the keenest-eyed Hun.[67] The stamp was made from India rubber and a two-Mark silver piece. To the delight of Flossie Hervey and the British contingent, a Russian colonel imprisoned alongside them, who had escaped from the Japanese in the Russo-Japanese War, was an expert at lock-picking; 'he ran evening classes for our benefit'.[68]

For men who would never have dreamed of theft in civilian life, stealing now became second nature: On his maiden escape attempt (through the wire at Clausthal) A.J. Evans used pincers stolen from the German camp electrician; at Stralsund by the sea Durnford and his two escaping partners removed, with the light fingers of a pickpocket, a workman's permit from his jacket; Flossie Hervey, with a sense of irony, stole a Homburg hat from the room at Clausthal used to hold confiscated goods.

A Homburg hat was a valued escape item, since it was worn by many male German civilians. Every escapee needed a rucksack because every man, woman and child in Germany carried one. What could not be stolen, forwarded covertly in parcels, bought or bartered had to be made. Many an escaper became proficient at running up civilian clothes. Lieutenant John Thorn took three months to make a widow's weeds, including a coat fashioned from a French officer's cape; he was arrested on Augustabad station because his accomplice, a French officer dressed as a boy, raised suspicion. So convincing, however, was Thorn's widow's outfit that the station master brought in two women to search him. At this Thorn threw up his hands and said in his best German, '*Ich bin ein Englander offizier, nicht ein Frau.* For God's sake don't let those women search me.'[69] That caused quite a sensation.

The black 'KG' suits issued to other ranks were more easily adapted into civilian garb than the Germans supposed. The tailors assigned to sew in the coloured stripes on the sleeves and legs usually sewed them on top of the material, so they were easily ripped off. When properly sewn in, they could be coloured over with ersatz coffee. Tich Evanson took no chances and had the job done properly; he bribed a Serbian tailor to remove the yellow stripes from his prison suit and to replace the military buttons with some civilian buttons Evanson had bought from an Austrian miner he befriended at Westerholt. The same miner gave Evanson and his chum, Aussie Private Edward Gardiner, civilian hats, collars and ties. And, as he'd done some smuggling over the Dutch border before the war, told them the safest place to make a crossing. Which they duly did.

Stuck alone on a farm in Mecklenburg, Benjamin Muse was unable to call on the services of a tailor, so sewed black patches himself over the stripes on his hat and trousers. To complete his outfit he swapped (without permission) his English underclothes for a German civilian coat hanging in the farmhouse hall. Out for three days, he was spotted as a PoW on the lam by a mounted Landpolizist; what gave Muse away were his English boots, 'better than any to be had in Germany'. The civilian jailer in Gadebusch looked after him, giving him bread and bacon because his son had worked in England. But then charged Muse for it when he was taken back to camp.

Prison life: it turned honest men into Fagins and forgers, Regular Army officers into tailors and craftsmen, and future US senators into thieves.

Of course, anyone confident of travelling wholly by night did not need to amend their KG or uniform. Darkness was their disguise.

The majority of those journeying across Germany needed more than a disguise. They needed kit supplies. Hugh Durnford's 'kit list' to sustain him after his escape from Stralsund consisted of:

In my pockets I carried 3 large sandwiches of German bread with English potted meat inside, 20 slabs Caley's Marching chocolate, a box of Horlicks' milk tablets, a spare pair of socks, some rags and Vaseline, my pipe and tobacco, English and German cigarettes, my compass, money and papers. I had an old German novel in my hands which I pretended to read with great assiduity.[70]

Cartwright and Harrison took the following:

Our food, which consisted of chocolate, biscuits, potted meat, 'Bivouac' cocoa, beef tabloids, malted milk, oxo, etc, with a 'Tommy cooker' and supply of solid spirit (all from home parcels) was packed all over our bodies. Some was in pockets and some down trouser legs, some in rucksacks hung over our stomachs and some in sacks hung on our backsides. The latter two loads gave the correct Prussian figure.[71]

To carry water they used a rubber air cushion. On his escape with Insall and Templer, Michael Harrison used a football bladder for water porting.

Lieutenant Peter Anderson took five months to get his kit together and it comprised: boots, a pair of home-made long trousers, extra socks, needles, air cushion for swimming rivers, rubber bag for matches, map, paper money, food (principally chocolate, biscuits, bread and meat lozenges), a rucksack, a rubber raincoat, sou'wester, medicine, bandages and maps, and a small compass, wool scarf and water bottle. He bought a small enamelled pot, Oxo cubes and cocoa from the canteen.

The anatomy of Anderson's preparation is revealing, for it reminds us that the escaper himself was the tip of an arrow. In the same way that a front-line soldier is supported by a vast enterprise in the rear, the escaper was aided by a forgotten network of helpers.

Much of Anderson's kit was provided by Lieutenant Frank Smith, Captain Streight, Captain Johnson, Major George, plus various other officers who donated or 'borrowed' on Anderson's behalf; Captain R.W. Gaskell helped make the escape rope from white tape used to lay out the tennis court, Captain Lord James Murray lent his room as a workshop; Captain Bellew and Lieutenant Vic McLean helped hide the kit. The 'assistants' also smuggled the kit, crucially the grappling hook (made out of a poker), into the right room for the off. In all about a dozen officers played a part in Anderson's September 1915 escape from Bischofswerda over the stables and over the perimeter fence to Denmark. As a last aid to Anderson, Lieutenant Streight put a pair of slippers from a Russian officer under Anderson's bed. For the bloodhounds to follow.

Why did all these men help Anderson? Why did so many orderlies help officers escape? Ties of friendship and affection, certainly, but bonds of duty and patriotism too. Fellow prisoners did not see escapers as free spirits seeking to express their dislike of authority and confinement. They saw them as soldiers going into battle against the enemy. It was *war* in the camps.

As Anderson understood all too well, a comprehensive kit was both blessing and curse. A curse because it needed to be concealed from 'snitches', plus the amiable but loose-tongued. In the wire world, where boredom was a continuous curse, any fragment of interesting news was gold dust. Any bit of gossip spread, wrote Flossie Hervey, 'like wildfire in a prison camp, and with English-speaking Germans wandering around eager to pick up information, it was always as well to keep one's ideas to oneself'.[72]

Above all, kit had to be hidden from German searches. In all camps these were fortnightly; in *strafe* camps they were frequent and random, with the guards rushing in shouting '*Los! Los!*' and tumbling bleary occupants from their beds. Sometimes the prisoners themselves were stripped naked. Contraband was hidden under floors, behind false partitions, in 'priest holes'. Michael Harrison managed to keep a metal saw concealed in his thermos flask between the vacuum and outer case in spite of many searches; it was this saw he used to cut the trapdoor in Strohen bathhouse. His friend Cartwright had a case with a hidden chamber at the side; the guards checked it for a false bottom, but never a false side. 'I used the box,' wrote Cartwright, 'for two years with complete success.' During searches some guards could be *bribed* to hold *verboten* items – a stick of chocolate usually sufficed. Cecil Blain hid his escaping kit at Clausthal in the best place of all – a German storeroom, accessed by picking the lock. During visits to the storeroom he also purloined a bottle of 1811 brandy, liqueurs, chocolates, bacon and sausages to boost rations. Sensible escapers left titbits of no real use to be discovered by searchers in the expectation this would sate their security mania, and they would not press on and uncover the important stuff. What the Germans made of a 'wonderful map' Cartwright produced to this end is not recorded; all roads on the map led to a German lunatic asylum.

Zealous commandants called in civilian detectives to undertake searches. Despite the professionalism and vigour of police detectives they were not universally successful. When plainclothes Berlin detectives paid a visit to Strohen, they left

> surrounded by a band of cheering British officers, and several of them [the detectives] complained that their pockets had been picked; their identity cards and police papers stolen. And one wretched man walked out with a notice pinned to his coat-tail: 'You know my methods, Watson!'[73]

In making their great escapes, prisoners likened the experience to going over the top in battle. Before the big moment, they experienced the same attack of nerves; then, as the escape began, an enormous sense of exultation. Before 'beating it' from Magdeburg through the perimeter wire, Jocelyn Hardy recalled that 'Breakfast was a ghastly meal for me'. A.J. Evans in Fort 9, with the hours of

escape looming, owned up to 'a bad fit of nerves, and for half an
hour or more lay on my bed shaking with funk and the thought
of it'.[74] The soldiers of the 1914–18 generation were cultured in the
non-exhibition of emotion; it did not follow they were without feelings. Even Medlicott, presumably, was more nervous than his cool
exterior betrayed.

No matter how stiff the upper lip, escapers on breaking out of
camp felt an overwhelming sense of freedom. After digging through
the second-storey wall at Freiburg (four feet thick, excavated in a
day) into the building next door, Lieutenant Geoffrey Phillimore,
who was accompanied by Lieutenant Morris, declared,

> 'Triumph and exultation filled us; we were half wild with
> delight.'[75]

Flossie Hervey also absconded from Freiburg, despite a last-
minute hitch with an orderly, a locksmith in civilian life, who,
having picked one set of locks would not pick the next as it was
outside a permitted place – and might lead him to a salt mine. (No,
not all orderlies were as resolute as McAllister; an orderly at Clausthal snitched on Second Lieutenant Robert Macintosh, RFC,[76] and
Second Lieutenant A.A. Baerlein, who were hiding themselves in
the orderlies hut.) When Hervey did eventually get through the
Freiburg attic into the adjoining church, thence onto the street, he
found that: 'Once out of range of the sentry these first few seconds
of freedom compensated for all our worries and failures during
the past months, and I wanted to skip like the proverbial young
ram.'[77] On exiting Halle via a skylight, Jocelyn Hardy felt 'absolute
elation'.[78]

Understandably, at this crucial moment of the exit, the nerve of
some men failed. Corporal Edward Edwards and an unnamed accomplice intended to abscond from a forestry working party:

> At noon we knocked off for soup and a rest. We were on the edge of
> a large wood. Some of the men flung themselves on the bank; others
> went to see if the soup was ready. A few went into the wood. The sol-
> itary guard was elsewhere. We said good-bye to the few who knew of

our plans. They bade us God-speed and then we, too, faded into the recesses of the wood.

We had no sooner set foot in it than I noticed a curious change come over my companion. He said that it was a bad time, a bad place, found fault with everything and said that we should not go that day. However, we continued, half-heartedly on his part, to shove our way on into the wood. Occasionally he glanced fearfully over his shoulder and voiced querulous protests. I did not answer him. A little further on and he stopped. A dog was barking. 'There's too many dogs about, Edwards.'[79]

They both returned to their working party before their absence was noticed. Edwards thought solo escapes were not good because of the need for daytime guard when lying up.

As Michael Harrison indicated in his breakdown of escaping, getting out of the *Lager* was only Part I of the escaper's challenge. Next came Part II, the trek across Germany. Despite all the 'Mullering' and Red Cross parcels, few PoWs were in anything like prime fitness, including officers. In the words of Flossie Hervey, 'prison life, and a diet consisting almost entirely of tinned foods were not conducive to physical fitness.'[80]

Crefeld was one of the camps closest to Holland, yet the twenty-five-mile stretch to the frontier was agony for prisoners walking in winter at night. As, indeed, was the two- or three-mile trek to the Allied line for ragged prisoners in the *Arbeitskommandos* behind the German line. The longest walk to sanctuary was made by Private Harry Drope, Princess Patricia's Canadian Light Infantry, a twenty-nine-year-old insurance agent from Ontario. Drope broke out of his camp in Heilsberg, East Prussia, on 13 June 1918 with two Russians, and walked for five weeks until he crossed the Dnieper to freedom in Russia – a five-hundred-mile trip. An outstanding solo effort was made by Captain Walter Clinton, King's Royal Rifle Brigade; in one of the last escapes of the war, Clinton left Graudenz on 4 October 1918 in a spectacular high-wire act on the electricity cables out of the Silence Room window; Archer Cust thought Clinton looked 'like a pheasant caught in telegraph wires', but that the watching guards refrained from shooting either because they were 'bought' or feared the flowerpots ready to be thrown on their heads by the prisoners. Once out of the camp, Clinton trekked to Warsaw (190 miles), where he was operated on for a septic arm. He then went on to Cracow and Belgrade. Tragically, the winter conditions and the disease were too much to bear, and Clinton died in Belgrade on 22 November 1918, eleven days after the Armistice.

If prisoners trekking across Germany had a *modus operandi* it was hiding by day, walking by night, in the hope and expectation that at night-time few Germans would be about. For lying up Lieutenant Geoffrey Phillimore thought woods were the PoW's 'natural habitat' and 'the only place where we felt at home'.[81] Bramble patches were safe but uncomfortable to hide in, hay ricks were warm, though in winter Harrison and Cartwright, on their epic 230-mile route march from Burg to Rostock (uncrowned with success, being caught in sight of freedom) chose barns instead, believing the benefit of the protection from the elements outweighed the risk of discovery. On one of his escapes, Brian Horrocks was, alas, discovered hiding in a barn in the hay. He had developed a betraying winter cough, aggravated by the hay: 'The barn was surrounded by German frontier guards, and when I emerged there was the Dutch frontier in front of my eyes – barely 500 yards away. It was a bitter moment.'

Dog Horrocks made three fully fledged escape attempts, twice getting to the Dutch border. Ironically, on every trip out 'Dog' became the bane of my life'.[82] Barking and biting dogs were the dilemma of hundreds of other escapers too.

Wherever escaping prisoners lay up during the day, it proved a tribulation. In A.J. Evans' view, it was

the worst part of the business and wore out our nerves and physical strength far more than the six or seven hours marching at night, for the day seemed intolerably long from 4.30 a.m. to 9.30 p.m. – seventeen hours – the sun was very hot, and there was little shade, and we were consumed with impatience to get on. Moreover, we could never be free from anxiety at any moment of those seventeen hours.[83]

On their route to Switzerland, Evans and Lieutenant S.E. Buckley, RFC, were pestered by insects, their faces swelling from bites. On their fifteenth day out they became incautious, and were challenged by an off-duty soldier scything grass by the side of the road. Buckley opted for the fight not flight response in this tight corner and 'demanded in a voice quivering with indignant German what the devil he meant by shouting at us'. The astonished reaper went back to work. Evans and Buckley, looking like 'villainous tramps', ran on and over the border to Switzerland.

Summer or winter, lying still for hours produced agonies of stiffness. Setting out again at night after lying up in the day, Private Edward Page recalled: 'It took us some considerable time to get any use into our stiffened limbs, and for quite an hour after the resumption of our journey we could only walk at a snail's pace.'[84]

Foraging the German countryside proved distinctly hit and miss. Most escapers foraged too, though here countrymen and Canadians had the advantage. Corporal Edward Edwards joyfully pulled up oats, turnips, peas as well as potatoes, mangels, berries, carrots, beets, and green apples on his third escape; a Tommy cooker was packed by many to make a hot stew out of such bounties. Frank MacDonald on his escape from K-47 camp (with Jack O'Brien) dug up potatoes and milked a cow: 'That was a splendid drink, the finest I ever had, and for a moment or two we had some fool notion of taking that cow along with us.'[85]

During one of his lie-ups, Michael Harrison crept down from the hayloft to milk the cow mooing below. There was mutual surprise in the gloom when the cow turned out to be a bull. Gerald Knight's upbringing in the Buckinghamshire village paid dividends on the long march since he *could* tell a cow from a bull, and could milk the former. Once, when damn near caught hiding in undergrowth, he avoided detection by coughing like a deer and crashing through the vegetation.

Gerald Knight was solo on his walk to Holland: 'The fact of having no one to talk to for so many days, combined with the uncertainty of it all, had the most depressing influence.'[86] He even imagined, in his madness, that the war might end. He spent the days killing

mosquitoes and waiting for time to pass. After ten night-marches he
reached Holland and safety.

There are few suprises in war history but the coincidence that
befell Captain John Caunter in the middle of Germany on his trek
in June 1917, having exited Schwarmstedt via a hole made in the
parcel-room office, may be counted as truly extraordinary:

> And now happened the most remarkable thing that could well have
> fallen to the experience of anyone outside a novel.
>
> I was walking along a hedge very slowly, watching a German in the
> distance, when suddenly I thought I heard my name being spoken
> very clearly and distinctly. Again I heard it and this time I was cer-
> tain, and immediately thought that I was imagining it and that I was
> really going mad. I was told afterwards that I clutched my head with
> both hands. It was an awful shock to hear this, after not having seen
> anyone or been with anyone who knew me for two and a half days,
> and having crossed two rivers and got miles from the camp in which
> my only acquaintances and friends in Germany were locked up. I
> turned round and then I heard it again coming out of the hedge, and
> not only my name this time but an exceedingly English sentence
> which told me that I was a something fool, and that I was to come
> back. I promptly did so and found Major C.V. Fox, D.S.O., and Lieut.
> Blank lying at the bottom of the hedge. I at once joined them, and
> I naturally thought that all the officers from the camp had escaped
> and were spread far and wide over Germany, and that I had found a
> couple of them without being unduly lucky. However, that was not
> the case. Fox and Blank had escaped sixteen hours after I did, but
> while I had been hung up between the ambush and the first bridge
> for four hours, they had pushed ahead and crossed both rivers and
> got to their present hiding-place at daybreak.
>
> It was a great relief to have somebody with whom to talk, and we
> set to and discussed details in low whispers.[87]

The 'blank' was Lieutenant Groves, RN, who, with Fox, had escaped
Schwarmstedt dressed as a member of a tree-felling fatigue; one of
the orderlies who helped them was Private Norman Dykes. Charles
Fox was something of a war hero, having once defended a breach

in the line and captured five German officers and two hundred men, for which he had been awarded the DSO. Groves would drop out near the border with his feet shot, but Caunter and Fox both crossed – separately, to increase the chances – into Holland, a feat for which Caunter received a Military Cross and Fox a Mention in Dispatches.[88]

Energy as well as feet gave out on the trek to the neutral countries which offered sanctuary for escapers: Holland, Switzerland and Denmark. Walking to Switzerland in winter Lieutenant Geoffrey Phillimore had to take refuge from the snow in a woodshed; his footprints gave him away. His companion Lieutenant Morris had already turned himself in to the guard at a nearby village suffering from hypothermia. On Page's second escape, the heavy rain of winter made his clothes sodden, then it snowed and the wind bit. After three days 'it was impossible to go on'. Some escapes were so gruelling they rank with Polar expeditions in endurance; as Harrison and Cartwright neared Rostock on their November 1915 escape from Burg, the temperature sank to minus 20. For moisture they had to suck snow which caused their mouths to erupt in tiny blisters.

When stamina gave out, escapers took terrible risks. As the Canadians Jack Evans and White Masters neared the Dutch border:

> Our nerves were stretched some when we had to cross a bridge to avoid two creeks. Ordinarily we would have swum or waded them but by this time simply hadn't the stamina necessary to do it.[89]

Evans and Masters had been badly enervated by blundering into a peat bog. Fortune, however, smiled on them. They crossed into Holland.

A small minority travelled across Germany by train which, for anyone who was not an expert German speaker and travelling on papers forged to the nth degree, was a constant heightened terror, above that of the trek, where the semblance of a peaceful rest might be obtained in the shadow of a remote wood. Being a fluent German speaker Colonel Charles Rathbone travelled flawlessly by train to Aachen, less than three miles from the Dutch border, then crossed on foot at night, so reaching freedom within five days of leaving

Holzminden. Having taught himself German in the camps, Jocelyn Hardy broke out of Schweidnitz in Silesia with Captain Willie Loder-Symonds, Wiltshire Regiment. Carrying forged police passes they hopped on a train and travelled across Germany via Dresden, Leipzig, Cologne to Aachen. They then took the tram to Richtericht, reaching Holland within just two days of departing Schweidnitz. Hugh Durnford also travelled by train, and suffered – not being a great speaker of German – from a never-ending anxiety that he might be drawn into conversation. He failed to read a sign on a station properly (he asked for a coffee from a stall reserved for soldiers and sailors only), which affected his confidence. Worse, he realized that in a carriage he was captive and easily caught. Everything about one, from demeanour to complexion to clothes, was open to scrutiny in those old-fashioned carriages where four faced four.

Of course, someone had to cross Germany with panache on a *Zug*. Aside from Major Vandeleur sharing his Cuban cigars with Imperial officers, Cartwright and Marshall's stopping off in Berlin for a spot of sightseeing was the stuff of legend, especially as Marshall, a French officer, spent much of the visit pissing over Germany's Imperial glories such as the Reichstag.[90]

No matter the method of conveyance to the border, it needed to be crossed on foot. Security was tight for five kilometres before the border, against escaping PoWs and German deserters. The frontier itself consisted of trenches, several rows of wires, some of which were alarmed, the whole patrolled by sentries with keen trigger fingers. Frank MacDonald's escaping partner reached the border zone – and his nerve failed him at the last. He would not cross, preferring punishment to possible death from a bullet as he ran or crawled the final stretch.

German civilians living in the border area were another hazard; duty to the Fatherland and the pecuniary benefit of catching PoWs – at up to 20 Marks a head – made them the Kaiser's willing helpers. When Corporal Edward Edwards and Private Mervyn Simmons were intercepted by a shotgun-wielding farmer and his dog on the Dutch frontier a desperate struggle ensued, in which the prisoners killed both the farmer and his dog. They managed, to the benefit of their skins, to slip into Holland. They had navigated by a tiny compass Simmons' brother had sent him hidden in cream cheese.[91]

Invariably escapers arrived at the border in the worst possible condition, exhausted, hungry and with shredded nerves. The Holland crossing involved a strength-sapping swim across cold rivers and dykes, including the formidable Ems. When the Ems flooded in winter, escapers were forced up onto the guarded bridges, often to the loss of their liberty. 'If you try to cross a frontier in a starving condition you will probably make mistakes and get caught,' wrote Harrison. The very time escapers needed to be most alert was also the time they were most senseless. Suffering agonies of cramp, almost unable to walk, Horace Gilliland and Captain Stewart, RFA, ('a more staunch fellow in a hazard of this kind could not possibly be desired') set their teeth believing:

'We must succeed, we must beat the Boches! Gad! how sick they'll be if we get over!'[92]

They got past two lines of trenches, and had mistakenly thought they were over the border when a German voice shouted out in the darkness 'Halt!' They ran for it. In the confusion Gilliland biffed Stewart, thinking he was a pursuer. They stumbled on, 'making blind progress', until they encountered the Meuse near Venlo. And then they truly were over the border.

A blind run in the right direction at night also saw the persistent Henry Cartwright – finally – to sanctuary. Having escaped via a chimney from Aachen holding camp for potential exchanges, Cartwright ran and swam the final hundred yards as fast as he could – the last dyke 'took me seven strokes' – and when he crawled out he was in Holland. It was 16 August 1918. Cartwright had been attempting to escape for nearly four years.

Luck. Escapers needed some luck at the final hurdle. Second Lieutenant Lawrence Wingfield (who went through the wire at Strohen on 4 October 1917, with cutters received in a cake) received a cat's allotment in one go. Firstly he was discovered hiding in a hayrick

– but by French PoWs, who gave him food and tobacco. Then, at the frontier, Wingfield bumped into a German sentry while casing the Ems. To Wingfield's astonishment, the guard, on realizing Wingfield was an English PoW, said, 'I can help you, I am an Alsatian.' He took Wingfield a quarter of a mile, showed him where to cross and how to sneak over the border.[93]

Captain David 'Munshi' Gray was out of luck. Gray got to the Dutch border, took the lane signed to Brecklenkamp – not realizing there were two such villages, one each side of the frontier. He took the lane into Germany and delivered himself into the arms of a German guard post. The border with Holland – the destination of the overwhelming majority of escapers from the Kaiser's camps – zig-zagged nastily in places, causing scores of escapers to come unstuck. Cartwright once crossed the frozen Ems by walking on the cracking ice, made it into Holland near Sustrum but due to a faulty compass walked back into Germany – and capture. Frank MacDonald crawled into Holland . . . and out again at Burlo, where a finger of German land pointed into the country of cheese and freedom.

Neither could the Dutch be *absolutely* relied on to provide a hearty welcome for British escapers. Of the eleven who escaped with Private Edward Page from the tunnel at Dulmen three were turned over to the Germans by a Dutch worker going into Germany whom they had approached for help. Equally cruel was the fate of Lieutenant H. Baker, Lancashire Fusiliers, and Captain Gore MC, AIF, as Baker recounts:

> In wintry weather we had a difficult and exciting time, eventually reaching the river Ems about five miles from the frontier; here we found the river in such a state of flood that we were unable to carry out our idea of swimming across; the bridges were strongly guarded at both sides; boats or rafts were nowhere to be seen and eventually, after five days we were recaptured by Dutch Gendarmes who had evidently been informed by workmen who had seen us. We were kept nine days in the civil jail at Meppen and eventually sent to Holzminden where that arch-Hun Capt. Niemeyer kept us in solitary confinement for seven weeks.[94]

Those escaping from the *Arbeitskommandos* behind the front line in France and Flanders scarcely had an easier time in reaching sanctuary. Sapper George Waymark was put to work at Fromelles, repairing roads, with the British front line tantalizingly in sight and sound. He escaped on the night of 2 June 1918, cutting through the barbed wire of the compound. After spending a night hiding in a sodden shell hole, he and two companions started for the British lines:

> When we did the excitement started too. Hiding about every ten minutes challenged 4 or 5 times, fired at from about 10 or 12 yards, 3 times. What a hell of a lot of sentries they have got.[95]

They were recaptured as it got light. Four other British PoWs almost reached No Man's Land when a German soldier stumbled upon their hiding place. In desperation they killed him, but all four were re-taken, and all four executed by firing squad. There was danger too from the British trenches, since Tommies on a firestep tended to shoot figures coming towards them across No Man's Land first, then ask questions. Private Tulloch, 7/Cameron Highlanders, escaped from a work party based at Sailly:

> I escaped on the night of 3rd May in company with Private N. Macpherson, 7th Camerons, and Private Wood.
>
> We lay all the day of 4th May in a German reserve trench, and on the morning of 5th May we reached the British lines.
>
> Being mistaken for Germans on our approach, we were fired at from the British trenches, and Private Macpherson received three bullets in the shoulder. I was lucky enough not to have been hit.[96]

Horns of a dilemma: any escapers crossing No Man's Land shouting 'Don't shoot, we're British' might not be believed by the Tommies and would certainly be fired upon by any Fritzes on their firestep.

In one way or another, failure to achieve a 'home run' entailed punishment. The legal principle regarding punishment for attempted escapes was clear: the law to be applied was the military law of the host nation. This provision had an unduly harsh effect on British and Allied prisoners because discipline in the German Army was so

rich in its penalties. (Technically, even plotting to escape was pun-
ishable by death.) Also, the Germans invariably took ages to bring
cases to trial, and added extra charges such as being in possession of
escape equipment or German Marks. Since cutting perimeter wire
or breaking a door-lock could be construed as 'damage' to Imperial
property, almost all breakouts automatically fell foul of the severest clauses of the *War Book*. Effectively, sentences for escape were
lengthened way beyond the nominal guidelines. Instead of 14–30
days in solitary confinement Captain Geoffrey Phillimore served
five months 'black cells' (*Dunkelarrest* or *strenger Arrest,* darkness
and dark bread) in Strohen for one escape attempt. 'It is a form of
punishment which, if prolonged, breaks down all but the strongest
wills.' Phillimore's cell was 8' × 6'3" × 10'2" high. A smuggled *Oxford
Book of Verse* ('just the class of book that one can go on dipping into
for weeks on end')[97] did something for the boredom; and British
orderlies did something for the diet:

> There were forty five officers in cells, and Able Seaman Grimwood
> and Private Victor Williams kept the lot of us alive. They had a busy
> time of it as a pair of old birds with a nest full of hungry fledglings,
> and like the most devoted of parent birds they were at it early and
> late; no insatiable feathered offspring were ever slaved for more
> assiduously.[98]

*

As a good escaper and soldier, Phillimore considered when put in
cells that 'my first duty to the community . . . was to smuggle out in
a hot potato a brief resume of our route and experiences'.

A jailed escaper could always rely on his comrades too. Languishing in a cell at Holzminden John Thorn

> noticed through the bars of a window an object swinging to and
> fro, and putting my hands through the bars I was delighted to find a
> packet of Players' cigarettes swinging on the end of a piece of string
> which had been let down by one of the officers from the top floor of
> the building.[99]

If there was a record for trumped-up punishment against an escaper, it was the unlucky lot of Claude Templer to be on the receiving end of it. Templer was given thirteen months imprisonment for damaging Torgau *Lager* with his tunnel and for stealing a plank.

A series of international agreements alleviated the German punishments for escaping; in 1917 Britain and Germany agreed to remission of all punishments between capture and 1 August 1917; a conference in 1918 at The Hague agreed that punishment for a single escape 'shall not exceed military confinement for a period of 14 days', or 28 days for an escape in concert with others. Where escapes gave rise to damage, the maximum period of confinement was set at two months. Collective punishment for misconduct by individuals was banned.

Not all commandants followed these rules, or the rules that had preceded them. Other ranks and NCOs who escaped and were recaptured were virtually guaranteed a 'working over'. After his failed attempt to get to Holland in October 1917 with Rifleman Sid Bidwell, Tich Evanson was returned to Westerholt mine:

> I do not wish to dwell unduly upon the punishment we received, but it was very severe. Until we were tried, we were kept in prison. Here the Commandant set the bloodhounds on us. It was quite dark and we could only kick at the brutes. They made a nasty mess of our legs. Next day the sentry from whom we had escaped visited us with some of his friends and they gave us a thrashing.[100]

Recaptured officers tended to be less thuggishly treated, though not always. Captain John Streight, a Canadian, was generously beaten up by guards and border police on being caught at the Dutch frontier. Another failed attempt resulted in a rifle butt to the face. The consequence was a split forehead, a fractured jaw, and a broken nose.

The ultimate punishment for escaping was death, albeit delivered unofficially. When Second Lieutenant Medlicott and Captain Joseph Walter escaped from Bad Colberg and were recaptured, the camp adjutant, Beetz, detailed eight guards to collect them from the railway station. Medlicott and Walter were brought into the *Lager* on stretchers on 21 May 1918 quite dead. According to the German authorities 'Med' and Walter were shot trying to escape. Unfortunately for the official version, a friendly guard had already told the British contingent that Beetz, infuriated by the pair's incessant escaping, intended the execution of the two officers; a British request to examine their bodies was refused. Medlicott had been a prisoner since November 1915, when shot down on a reconnaissance flight. (His observer on the flight was Second Lieutenant Arthur Whitten Brown, later to become world famous as half of transatlantic flyers 'Alcock and Brown'.)

The remains of Harold Medlicott and Joseph Walter are now concealed in the poor earth of Niederzwehren cemetery.

Those escapers who crossed safely to a neutral country experienced a rare elation. So overwhelming was the relief for Horace Gilliland that 'I, for one, sat down and cried like a child'.[101]

Private Edward Page and his accomplice Private Billy Ward, having stolen into Holland near Gendringen where the border scribbles back and forth, were vastly uncertain as to where they were. When a ploughman confirmed they were standing on Dutch soil, Page recalled: 'I think we danced, cried, embraced each other, and shouted aloud in our glee; it seemed as if a great burden had, as if by the stroke of some magician's wand, been suddenly removed.'[102]

Holland. For Gerald Knight: 'I should never have believed that one simple word could have meant so much.'

Corporal Edward Edwards:

> All danger was past now. We seemed to walk on air. We were once again British soldiers. And so fell to abuse of each other and grousing as all good British soldiers do when they are well off.[103]

Captain A.J. Evans, RFC, crossed into Switzerland at 12.30 a.m., 9 June 1917

> . . . feeling a happiness and a triumph such, I firmly believe, as few men even in this war have felt, though they may have deserved the feeling many times more.[104]

Hugh Durnford crossed into Demark:

I waited till it was quite dark, and then started off, taking no risks – crawling. I came to a ditch with wire on each side of it. This was the only wire I saw. When I judged I was well through the line, I got up and walked to the farmhouse. A tall figure answered my knock. I began in my best German.

He shook his head to indicate that he didn't understand. I could have kissed him.

At last we hammered it out.

'Engelsk Offizier. Fangen. Gut.'

He beckoned me in with beaming face.

I had made good in just 72 hours. Beginner's luck.[105]

Durnford had bribed a German soldier back in Stralsund camp to spectacular effect; the soldier had told him where the wire on the border with Denmark was so low they could step over it, about the slow train that went to the frontier without the complication of passport-checking, provided him with civilian clothes, tie, railway map, German money. All for sundry clothes, cigarettes, soap, chocolate and cheese.

The warmth of the welcome extended to Durnford was almost universally given to British PoWs reaching sanctuary. Horace Gilliland and his companion had their feet bathed by Dutch guards, who spoilt them by giving them the English breakfast of 'Eggs and bacons'; they then found clean clothes for them, and took them to hospital where they were 'treated like princes':

Nothing was too good for us. It was nice to be fussed over and taken care of, after being neglected so long, and we thoroughly appreciated their kindness ... O, the luxury of having a real bath once more![106]

Privates Frank MacDonald and Jack O'Brien, having slipped into Holland through the northern marshes of Germany – a popular route because it was less heavily guarded and populated – were 'deluged with good things to eat but were too sick to touch anything'.

Harrison, Insall and Templer on reaching Holland immediately went in search of a post office, from where they sent the commandant of Strohen a postcard assuring him of their safe arrival, and requesting that their mail be forwarded. Subtlety eluded Colonel Charles Rathbone; his anger is tangible down the decades. From Holland Rathbone sent the Holzminden Niemeyer a telegram which read:

HAVING LOVELY TIME STOP IF I EVER FIND YOU IN LONDON WILL BREAK YOUR NECK STOP

After food, a hot bath and medical attention, escapers were put in quarantine for a fortnight to ensure they were not carrying dread diseases. After that it was off to Blighty.

And red tape. Most escapers were debriefed by the Special Intelligence Department at the War Office, the Government Committee on Treatment by the Enemy, and any and every set of officials anyone deemed they might be of use to. Jack Poole became 'an interesting exhibit' at the War Office, having a private interview with Sir Reginald Hall, Director of Naval Intelligence. Poole was also invited to Knole by the socialite writer Vita Sackville West, where another escaper was a guest – Winston Churchill, who, nearly two decades before had absconded from Boer hands. Poole also visited his old school, Rugby, where he was 'veritably lionized'. The school sang 'For He's a Jolly Good Fellow'. His wartime exploits were more to the headmaster's liking than his school ones; he had left under a cloud after letting off a fire extinguisher at a housemaster.

Michael Harrison received a homecoming honour higher than lunch with Churchill or a rousing song from the *alma mater*. He was invited for a private interview with the King. Harrison wondered: 'could any loyal subject wish for a greater honour?' When his great partner in jug-cracking, Henry Cartwright, finally got home, he was just in time to be the best man at Harrison's wedding.

His wedding duties done, Henry Cartwright pestered for a return to action. In all such cases, the War Office dragged its feet, due to concerns about how former PoWs would be treated if captured again in action. Most escapers were diverted to training jobs. Only the truly persistent saw action again. Like Jocelyn Hardy.

Hardy, who had been promoted to captain during his captivity, transferred to the 2/Inniskilling Fusiliers and was awarded the Military Cross for leading a patrol which saw heavy action at Ypres in August 1918, with Hardy dragging his sergeant two hundred yards to safety; a few weeks later Hardy was severely wounded leading a counter-attack, and his leg was amputated. (Henceforth he was always known as 'Hoppy' Hardy.)

Willie Loder-Symonds, who had escaped with Hardy from Schweidnitz, was killed ten weeks after returning to England in an accident flying for the RAF. It must have been a heart-breaking blow for his parents, Captain and Mrs F. C. Loder-Symonds, of Hinton Manor, Berks: Willie was the fourth of their five sons to give their life for their country.

Lieutenant A.J. Evans also returned to active service with the air service, and was sent to Palestine, where his aircraft failed and he became a PoW once more. He escaped from the Turks but was recaptured and ended up in Afion-Karah-Hissar camp where 'escaping was looked upon almost as a crime'. One officer said he would go to considerable lengths to prevent any attempt to escape and many agreed with him. But Evans held true to his personal creed of escaping.

*

There were other, safer ways out of Germany aside from escape. After the papacy lent its support, the Allies and Germans agreed to the exchange of wounded and incapacitated prisoners; the first party of British exchange PoWs, 107 of them, arrived in Switzerland in February 1915. For the remainder of the war, small groups of PoWs departed Babylon, either for direct repatriation to Blighty or internment in the neutral countries of Switzerland and later Holland in the case of the less ill. Malcolm Hay was exchanged in 1916. With his head wounds and partial paralysis, Hay was a relatively straightforward case for the repatriation board to judge. Other ailments proved harder to rule on, to the frustration of those who genuinely had an illness and those hoping to cheat the system by feigning malady. Illnesses which justified exchange or repatriation included loss of a limb, paralysis, diphtheria, diabetes, emphysema, malaria, sciatica, pernicious anaemia, epilepsy, and poisoning by mercury, chlorine, or carbon monoxide. Later in the war, tuberculosis and neurasthenia ('barbed-wire disease') were placed on the list of qualifying medical conditions.

Die-hard escapers such as Dog Horrocks and Henry Cartwright turned their noses up at repatriation, because the repatriated, by the terms of the Allied-German agreement, could not take up arms again. Besides, as one PoW wrote:

> Escaping was a thing of nerve and adventure; passing for repatriation was a squalid business of medical boards and, at times, crying 'pain, pain', when there was no pain.

For other prisoners, with less fortitude or more worn down by life in the wire world, repatriation became a constant and obsessive goal. Unfortunately for those yearning, praying, pleading for repatriation whimsy sat at the head of the repatriation board, which went by the unlovely name of the 'Control Commission'. The Control Commission was dominated by German medical officers, whose decisions knew little wisdom and less constancy. One PoW in near fine fettle passed the board purely because he spoke charming German. Men with genuine ailments, meanwhile, were turned back.

Trying to pass the repatriation board was, ironically, almost as stressful as trying to escape. Colonel H.A. Picot, the commander of the repatriate colony in Switzerland, noted the effect of the repatriation process on his newly arrived charges: 'I could see that this outburst of emotion after the suppression and antagonism of the years of captivity was having a very trying effect, for all ranks looked dazed, and appeared only half conscious of what was taking place around them.'[107]

There came fresh hope for those prisoners failing the repatriation test when, in May 1917, the British and German representatives met at The Hague to extend the criteria for repatriation. By the May 1917 accord all officers and NCOs who had been prisoners for more than eighteen months were to be released to a neutral country, with priority going to those who had been held captive longest. Germany explicitly refused to release other ranks under the agreement.

Other ranks could be made to *arbeiten* for the Reich. Officers and NCOs above the rank of lance corporal could not. They were useless mouths. *Unnütze Esser*.

There is no doubting the enthusiasm of many officers and NCOs for repatriation. In June 1918 a worn-out Will Harvey, who had endured captivity for nearly two years, found that his name was on the list of officers for Holland. 'I felt,' he recalled, 'that it was not to Holland but to Heaven that we were going.' Crossing over the border to Switzerland was, judged Lieutenant J. Harvey Douglas, 'the most thrilling moment of our lives'.

Once repatriates entered Switzerland or Holland, they found conditions better than those of the camps. They could hardly be worse. British prisoners lived in villages and towns throughout Switzerland, but principally at Chateau d'Oex and Murren; in Holland, PoWs lived mainly at Scheveningen and The Hague. Wives were allowed to visit, restaurants could be enjoyed, skiing trips (in Switzerland) might be taken, and shops galore were anxious for PoW money. There were even Germans to taunt, and vast amounts of beer to drink.

Yet no one really liked it. Life in the neutral countries was life in a gilded cage. But it was a cage, and the gilding could be thin.[108] Internees who were not officers were expected to work for concerns approved by the Swiss government. Almost to a man Tommies complained that the work given was tedious (many a slipper worn on European feet was made by British PoWs in Switzerland) and low paid. The toil was not quite slave labour, yet it did not escape the notice of British PoWs that Swiss military law, under which PoWs lived, was exacting. The British government did manage to secure some beneficial changes, especially with the extension of proper training schemes to the neutral countries. Switzerland, thanks to the magazine *Autocar,* even boasted a school for motor mechanics.

But the gilt was still too thin, while the guilt was too thick. Repatriates kept looking towards Germany, to the mates and men they had left behind. Lieutenant W.G. Colquhoun, exchanged to Holland in February 1918, put the matter succinctly enough: 'I felt like a deserter, nothing more or less . . .'

The 40,000 prisoners held in the neutral countries wanted freedom and home, for themselves, for their comrades.

And freedom and home were on the horizon for all British PoWs. Thank God.

VII

GOODBYEEEEE:
LAST DAYS, ARMISTICE AND LIBERATION

'Thank God!'

Second Lieutenant Armorer Patterson, PoW

Diary entry, 11 November 1918

P eace, and rumours of peace.

The prisoners in the *Arbeitskommandos* close behind German lines were the first to realize that 'the Hun' was on the verge of defeat, and that peace must follow. The men in the *Kommandos*, from one day to the next, were accorded better conditions; units of the German 7th Army were instructed 'to pay attention to ensuring the *good treatment* of the prisoners', especially in respect of their rations. As the savvier prisoners understood, the German change of heart was not a belated outbreak of compassion; the Huns were running scared of Allied punishment for the crimes they had committed against the ragged men. For many prisoners it was all too late; they were already lying in their shallow graves.

Besides, the guns were telling their own tale of peace. Every day the boom of Allied guns came closer. The realization that the British were still a fighting force instilled in Private William Tucker an 'uplift almost beyond description'.[1] There was the evidence of the eyes too. At Trith St Leger in early September 1918 Private George Gadsby, 1/18th London Regiment, picked up a pamphlet dropped by the RAF detailing the Italian victory on the Piave and the Allied advance in the Cambrai sector. Not that Gadsby's eyes needed a missive from the air to tell him the way the war was running on the Western Front. He only had to look around him. All the roads round were clogged with retreating men in *feldgrau*, in no mood to varnish the truth. 'It became an almost daily occurrence,' recalled Gadsby, 'for some German officer to remark "The war finish Tommy", as he passed on the road with his worn column.'[2] Desperate for food, German soldiers would suddenly dash out of line, pull out their jack-knives and cut themselves a steak from a dead horse on the verge. How the mighty had fallen.

Alas, the German intention to treat PoWs better clashed with the German desire to carry on exploiting the same men as forced labour. The latter won out. On the road to Germany, alongside the retreating *feldgrau* troops, thousands upon thousands of Allied prisoners were driven in herds like decrepit cattle, carrying dismantled factories, engines – anything the Germans could transport from the occupied zone that might be useful in the twilight of their regime. Men from the labour *Kommandos*, already near-dead, dropped to lie exhausted beside the piles of horse intestines and the abandoned guns. Some never rose again. There was no salvation in Germany for those who reached there; the months and years of abuse were not easily shaken off. Captain John Findlay, RAMC, observed one batch of labour company prisoners stumble into Crossen-am-Oder in October. There were 110 Britons; six had perished on the march. Of the rest: 'They were all gaunt and haggard and ravenous for food; most of them had oedamatic legs.'[3] More died over the next days. At Aachen Private Henry Webb saw a party of 90 British arrive; they had started out 260 strong, but the rest had fallen out or fallen dead. They had been marched till they could go no further.

Skeleton. That word would occur over and over again in descriptions by eyewitnesses of the *Kommando* survivors.

Prisoners with sufficient health and nerve seized the opportunity offered by the confusion to escape. One of this number was William Tucker, who absconded from a PoW column marching towards Brussels; he set out towards Allied lines, sneaking past and through the stream of German traffic. Alarmingly, the Germans were detonating all their unused ordnance; his way was marked by incessant explosions. Perhaps two hundred other prisoners liberated themselves at this late hour, though their escapes went unnoticed and unmarked in the official War Office tally of 'home runs'. Were their escapes any less worthy because they came in the confused, anarchic last days of the war in France and Flanders? There was no *absolute* certainty even on 10 November that the war would not drag on longer. It had, after all, dragged on for four years already.

If the coming of peace was obvious to those near the Front, by October it was scarcely less obvious in the principal camps in Germany. As Alec Waugh, incarcerated in Mainz Citadel, explained:

> I was asked when I got back to England how soon I realized that the tide had turned, that an Allied victory was imminent. I fancy that I knew as early as anyone did in Britain. Censorship in Germany was strict: but the Allied communiqués were printed in the papers . . . Moreover, we could sense in the way the Germans themselves received the news that they were at the end of their resources. They no longer spoke of victory but of peace.[4]

Like Waugh, Basil Willey at Kamstigall knew from the German press that peace was on its way; moreover, the guards' 'old bluster and swagger had almost entirely vanished'. The further the Allies moved West, the more the delighted PoWs of Kamstigall upped their complaints and demands. 'If Douglas Haig advanced four miles, we demanded a piano.'[5]

Yet the triumphal progress of the Allies was bitter-sweet for young imprisoned warriors such as Archer Cust: 'It is galling beyond words to be exiled in uselessness out here with all the best of the war going on now. It is simply awful!'[6] He wondered about the fate of his war horse, a mare called Queenie, and how his RA battery was getting along without him.

It wasn't only on the Western Front that Germany was in disarray; civil order fell apart in Germany itself. By the latter days of October much of the country was convulsed by strikes and insurrections. Events then fell in a dizzying domino sequence where war front affected home front, and vice versa: on 22 October three hundred workers at the Maybach plant in Friedrichshafen went on strike; on 30 October Turkey quit the war; on 3 November Austria surrendered. The next day the German Navy mutinied. The day after that the German lines between the Schelft and Sambre on the Western Front collapsed.

The fall, when it came, came quickly. Trooper Walter Jowsey, Royal Horse Artillery was slaving in a black pit near Friedrichsfeld:

They used to shout that they were beaten and there was a lot of talk of revolution, and that the Kaiser would have to go. They were in an awful state for food, and they would offer us anything for bully beef or anything like that ... On 9 November we went to work in the mine as usual. It was our double shift. When we got there they wouldn't let us go in, as they were on strike. The Revolution was on in Germany. They said they wouldn't work until the Kaiser had cleared out and peace was declared. They broke into the place where the food was stored and looted our parcels from the truck that had just brought them up.

On the tenth about 5000 of them, including wives and families, marched with red flags flying to see the mayor of the next village about more food. The sentries of the camp then cleared off to join the revolutionaries.[7]

The collapse of the old order meant all schemes for escaping were abandoned. Well, almost all. One late escaper was returned to Beeskow, where the commandant tiredly told him, 'This is not the good time for escaping; there will be peace in two days.'

There was. On 11 November the war finished: all was quiet on the Western Front. In the strange silence Private William Tucker, starving on his escape route west, tapped cautiously on the door of a low Belgian roadside cottage in search of food. An upstairs window opened and he explained, '*Je suis un soldat Anglais qui est prisonnier.*'

There was a pause. '*Vous n'est pas un prisonnier encore,*' the old woman answered. '*La guerre est fini! L'Allemand tout parti.*'

The Armistice had been signed only hours before. The woman gave Tucker all the food she could spare, including 'what to me was a potential banquet, a real tomato'. He set off in a trance: 'The news simply dazed me. I really could not come to sudden grips with a state of affairs where I was no longer in the clutches of a wretched captivity.'[8]

In a handful of the camps in Germany there was an official announcement of the Armistice. Or at least an attempt was made to issue the news: as soon as the commandant at Munster addressed the assembled British as 'Gentlemen' instead of '*Schweinhunde*' they knew they had won the war. Up went a mighty roar. No one paid the commandant any heed after that. The days of listening to a German were gone.

The camp interpreter at Friedrichsfeld tried a no-frills approach with his announcement: 'I don't want you to make much noise, but Germany has lost the war and is finished.'[9] Not much noise? Small hope. There was wild excited shouting and singing. One bold spirit ascended the arc-light poles and nailed a Union Jack and the French flag to the tops.

In Kamstigall Lieutenant Basil Willey watched 'a revolution in miniature' as the Imperial officers were deposed by revolutionary guards led by the camp interpreter, Francke.

> Next morning [11 November] the reveille was blown two hours later than usual, but the long-suffering old *Landsturmers*, in their long fur-coats, were still plodding up and down their sentry-beat in the snow. All this seemed normal enough, but at about 8 o'clock, just as the sun rose over the Froschjes Hadd, a red flag was hoisted over the German quarters in the camp. And when we all turned out on parade for the daily 'appel', no German officer appeared to call the roll. Instead, there came none other than little Francke himself . . . now the full-blown President of the Pillau Soldatenrat, and as such the supreme authority in the camp.[10]

Except for the soldiers removing the Prussian badges from their hats, there was no revolutionary demonstration of any sort. The local railways continued working.

Aeroplanes flew over Graudenz, to the interest of Archer Cust, with red flags attached. Above the German officers' mess there appeared a large red flag instead of the Imperial Eagle. 'Many of us were no little anxious as to what might happen to us as a result of all this,' wrote Cust in his journal. Not much, was the answer, except that when the Graudenz PoWs ventured out of the camp they were allowed to walk on the pavements of the town – a privilege never usually allowed prisoners.[11] And everybody started collecting souvenirs from the guards, who were only too willing to sell anything for a price: 'cockades, eagles off helmets, swords, daggers etc.'[12] To the final victor the spoils. The commandant handed over the keys of the tin room. 'From then on,' recalled Cust, 'we were given our parcels as soon as they came in, letters were not censored and a great many of the annoyances came to an end.'

All prisoners in punishment cells in the camps were released. Almost inevitably, twenty-two-year-old Dog Horrocks was among their number, doing 'cells' for his latest escape escapade. There was a twinge of regret that he had never made it over the frontier; the award of the Military Cross later for his persistence and gallantry in jug-cracking was some consolation. So too, he decided, being the glass-half-full type, was the fact that in the 'hard school' of the camps he had learned to 'stand on my own feet and make my own decisions'.[13] He could also see matters from the enemy point of view. These were all 'lessons which served me well later on'. He was one of Britain's leading generals in the next bash against Germany.

At Schweidnitz in Silesia Captain J.B. Sterndale, MC, South Wales Borderers, captured at Lys watched

> the half comic, half pathetic spectacle of our German guards ripping the Imperial Eagles from their helmets and helping each other to cut off the epaulettes from their tunics. I am afraid that we stood and laughed at them, which made them furious.[14]

There was less to laugh at when a deputation from the local Soldiers' and Workers' Council headed by an 'unshaven, rat like little man' wearing a red armband arrived. He informed the PoWs that he was installing machine guns to protect them from the citizens. When sited, the machine guns were all pointed at the PoW dormitories. Gradually it occurred to Sterndale that the *Soldatenrat* was scared of them; German officer PoWs in Russia had sided with the Whites against the Revolution. The prisoners persuaded the

Soldatenrat that they were no threat, and gradually their freedoms were extended. They were allowed to roam the town, cash Cox's cheques ('at a ruinous rate of exchange') and spend their money in hotels and *Weinstuben*. 'We thoroughly welcomed this revolution, if only as light relief to a monotony which had paralysed us, in some cases, for years.'

Flossie Hervey in Clausthal thought news of the Armistice 'almost unbelievable'. He spent hours roaming the countryside. Alec Waugh likewise found the freedom to wander intoxicating:

> After a confinement of eight months it was a wonderful thing to be able to walk through the streets unguarded. To be free again; no longer to be fenced round by barbed wire, to be shadowed by innumerable eyes; no longer to be under the rule of the arrogant Prussia. It was almost impossible to grasp it; that we were free, free. Every moment I expected to feel a heavy hand fall on my shoulder, and to hear a gruff voice bellow in my ear, 'Es is verboten, Herr Lieutenant'.[15]

Second Lieutenant Armorer Patterson, Northumberland Hussars ('The Noodles'), wrote in his diary two bare words about the great glad day, though two words were enough: 'Thank God.' Captured at Happy Valley on the Somme, Patterson had been in captivity a mere three months. It had been enough.

Sergeant Hawtin Mundy, 5/Oxford & Bucks Light Infantry, was a PoW in an *Arbeitskommando* in East Prussia, on good terms with the mill owner, who told him that there was a telegram in the window of the post office he would want to see. It was written in German, and informed the reader that *'Der Krieg ist fertig'*. Mundy went straight back to the *Lager* 'where we was billeted, and all our boys were there. When I got back I told them, "It's finished boys . . . we're all right now. It's all over."'[16]

Across in Cologne, Captain C.M. Slack, 1/4th East Yorkshire Regiment, was annoyed to find that despite the Armistice the guards still expected them to parade for *Appell*: 'We said, "No, we've won the war. We're not going to parade anymore."'[17] They then sauntered out of the camp, ignoring the sentry's demand to 'Halt' ('half-expecting to get one in the back') and played tourist, spending half an hour at the famous cathedral. There was no hue and cry at the sight of British officers, and all in all the day proved a bit of an anti-climax. As it was for Private Fred Gied in an East Prussian lumber camp. Informed of the Armistice at noon, he was then told to carry on working, the same as before. All for the princely sum of a cent an hour, twelve hours a day.

Gied could count himself lucky to have been informed of the Armistice. Prisoners in the remoter corners of Germany were frequently left to find out about the outbreak of peace themselves. In some cases the news was deliberately withheld so that the PoWs would continue working. Able Seaman J.A. Byrne, in a mining *Arbeitskommando* on the border with Bohemia, did not learn of the Armistice until 22 November when:

> As we were settling down for the night a messenger came to our barbed wire fence and pushed a note through it, which read as follows: 'Armistice signed November 11, if you are still being forced to work act accordingly, it is up to you to take action.'[18]

They did. They downed tools and barricaded themselves in their hut. A succession of guards came, plus the officer in charge of the local prison camp, all exhorting them to work, threatening to starve them if they didn't. The strikers held out. After a week the Germans gave up and the prisoners were taken back to the stem camp at Brandenburg.

Such scenes were repeated all over Germany. Once again the British were striking for their rights. Lance-Corporal Thomas Higgins was working in a sawmill at Frentwede when on 20 November he happened to read in a yellowing discarded German paper about the Armistice; 'The Germans had kept us in ignorance and kept us working.' Higgins told the rest of the *Kommando*, who went 'almost mad with joy'. They refused to do any more work. The owner called in the Army. A roughhouse followed, and Higgins – with his one English companion sticking to his side 'like a true Briton' – fought a passage to the door and got out, only to be recaptured in the village. They had been starved too long to run. Put in the village gaol, they were sprung by Russian PoWs, who turned up armed to the teeth with iron bars and knives. Choosing discretion over valour, the German commanding officer allowed the two Englishmen and the Russians to move to Soltau camp. They left behind them the French PoWs, who had been 'too cowardly to strike'.[19]

Under the terms of the Armistice, Germany was required to immediately repatriate all Allied PoWs without reciprocity. But how to get them home? Just as Germany had been unprepared for the influx of PoWs at the war's beginning, it was unprepared for their exodus at its end. PoWs in *Kommandos* in Belgium and on the Franco-German border were simply let go – without food – to walk to meet advancing Allies. Pathetic processions of stick-figures, dressed in bizarre arrays of ill-fitting clothes, began to straggle west, often sharing the roads with the Kaiser's former soldiers drunkenly singing the Marseillaise as they headed in the opposite direction.

Tramping here, there, everywhere. That too was a definition of a British PoW's life, and sometimes his death. Private Thomas Bickerton, Essex Regiment, captured the previous April, limped along in a gang of five hundred prisoners from Freiburg towards the Allied lines under a German escort about whose intentions they were uncertain:

Most of us had only got squares of rag to take the place of socks and our boots were in bad shape. We were also very weak from starvation, and the company soon got straggled out miles down the road, our mounted guard stopping from time to time for the stragglers to catch up. After a day's march we pulled up and slept in a barn for the night, and received a reasonable amount of food. We probably marched around twenty miles that day. The stragglers came in during the night and the following morning we set out again. We could see we were getting towards the rear of what had been the German front line, and we were all terrified when we had to pass close to a large ammunition dump which the Germans set on fire. Shells were bursting in all directions; bullets seemed to be flying all over the place – it was a real inferno and we were all very much

afraid we might be injured. Fortunately we got past safely and continued on our way.

When we were within about five miles of the French front the
mounted Germans pulled up until a lot of stragglers had caught up
with us, and then waved us towards the front and said, 'Alle weg',
meaning 'Off you go', or that is what I understood it to mean.

My heart sang: I knew the hour of release had come.[20]

On reaching the French front line, the *poilus* made a great fuss of
them. Despite such fine fraternal treatment, the British prisoners
could not resist a little rivalrous national pomp in the circumstances and decided

> we would show them how British soldiers could march, and even
> after our exhausting journey we formed up into fours and marched
> proudly down the road singing, 'It's a long way to Tipperary' at the
> tops of our voices.[21]

The sheer, shocking scale of the maltreatment of prisoners on the
Western Front drove the troops who met them to cold fury, and
the British government eventually to seek justice at the Leipzig
War Crimes Trial. Annah Peck was a volunteer with the American
Mobile Canteen near the front line. She watched the ragged men
come in:

> One day we had not gone very far before we saw hundreds of men
> coming towards us on the road. They were an extraordinary sight
> for instead of the mass of blue or khaki that one expected to meet,
> we saw a straggling line of men wearing every kind of uniform that
> the Allies had used since 1914. One would see many khaki figures
> of English Tommies and American Doughboys tramping along side
> by side with French poilus in blue and Italians in their greeny-grey
> uniforms, and then to our surprise a Frenchman would appear with
> the old red cap and trousers, and sprinkled among all of these were
> men in the drab looking uniforms worn by the Allied prisoners in
> Germany. We were particularly struck with the appearance of the
> English prisoners, for on the whole they looked much worse than
> the others, Many of them were worn and thin and some looked very

ill. It would be hard to find a more dreary sight than these men presented, for they had just been turned out of the German prisons in
Belgium and had just managed to exist on the food given by the
Belgians, who doubtless had been obliged to go without food themselves in order to feed so many.[22]

The British Quartermaster General, Sir Travers Clarke, issued
instructions that PoWs returning through lines be collected at forward collecting centres in France and Belgium, and given clothing
and blankets if necessary. A Belgian relief organization, the Comité
Nationale, and the YMCA in Paris also provided humanitarian
help for the shuffling PoWs, but their numbers were so vast – there
were as many as 32,000 shadows and ghosts walking west – that the
official organizations struggled to cope. As countless PoWs would
remember all their lives, Belgian civilians stepped in to provide
welcome if not life-saving hospitality. Private Reginald Bellamy was
one of the 'adopted':

> We went out this morning and met a boy who was looking for some-
> one who wanted a billet. He took us home with him to No. 86 Rue
> de la Station [Warenne] and we are in a little palace. A room to our-
> selves – and beds! A good dinner! Clean shirts and trousers! The
> young lady looked after us very well. Had a good wash . . . Seems all
> impossible.[23]

Once collected at the forward stations, the PoWs from the front-
line *Kommandos* were quickly processed, with some reaching
Calais within four days of Armistice. Among the earliest prisoners
to arrive in Britain was Private William Albert Tucker, having had
his photograph taken for posterity by an official war correspondent:
Tucker had been the first Tommy to regain the Allied line in the
Tournai sector. The photograph now reposes in the Imperial War
Museum.

But the bigger problem of prisoner repatriation lay in Germany
itself. To sort out the PoWs there a subcommittee of the Permanent
International Armistice Commission was established on 20 November, which for the purposes of repatriation divided Germany

into four zones: the left bank of the Rhine, the north, the centre and the south. In each zone PoWs were to be gathered in collection camps. Prisoners in north and central Germany were then to be sent home via Baltic and North Sea ports; PoWs in south Germany were to be forwarded by rail to Switzerland; those on the left bank of the Rhine were to walk to meet advancing Allied soldiers. Notices were inserted in German newspapers, and wires sent to camps from the War Office, informing PoWs outside the Rhineland to stay put until officially informed otherwise.

So, the prisoners waited for repatriation. Their most cherished hope was that they would be home for Christmas; their greatest fear was that they would not.

The time between Armistice and departure was 'a time of growing impatience and irritation'. All kinds of rumours floated in Basil Willey's *Offizier Kriegsgefangenenlager* about repatriation: they were to go by train to The Hague; a tramp steamer was to be chartered from Königsberg; they were to embark on a British man-of-war . . . Anxious to be rid of his restless charges, the new commandant, Francke, tried to contact the *Kriegsministerium* in Berlin, while the SBO, a brigadier, sent a wire to local Army HQ asking for an answer to the one important question: When?

All the main camps used as assembly points became swarmingly overcrowded. Not sorry to see the back of his farming *Kommando*, US ambulance man Ralph Ellinwood returned to the parent camp at Langensalza. Fearful of being forgotten in the great repatriation, hundreds of other men from the outlying *Kommandos* had turned up too. Entering Langensalza camp, which always seemed to sit in ironic contrast to the picturesque red-tiled centre of the spa town, Ellinwood considered 'No tenement could have been worse. The men lay so close to one another that it was almost impossible not to step on them at night.'[24]

It was also bitterly, bitingly cold. If Ellinwood thought Langensalza bad he was to meet worse when he was later shuttled on to Kassel. No food was coming in, but more prisoners were by the day. 'Kassel resembled a pig pen more than a prison.'[25] Tired of obeying German commands, many prisoners now considered themselves above any orders. Even instructions by Allied camp committees and British sergeant majors seeking sane solutions to do with hygiene and the distribution of rations went unheeded.

For some the peace that came in November 1918 was the peace of the grave. The Spanish influenza epidemic – *die Grippe* in German – descended like a holocaust on malnourished, underclothed and exhausted prisoners. At Parchim, Private Jeffrey remembered 'we buried 30 in one day' from influenza.[26] Every room at Archer Cust's officers' camp at Graudenz, 'when the door was opened, resembled a hospital ward, or worse'.[27] Cust's one thought and gratitude was that they did not get *die Grippe* in June or July when they had no food. Nonetheless, five prisoners died.

In his diary, Private H.J. Clarke, Suffolk Regiment, described the death of Charles Kelly, 1/West Yorkshire Regiment, at Mensfelden. The entry expresses only too poignantly the particular tragedy of a man who had survived the camps for so long only to die days before salvation:

> Pte Kelly, West Yorks, died at Mensfelden on Nov 1st 1918 through a disease called grippe, buried on Nov 4th. How he suffered only God knows. The last 3 days or so he turned delirious. His last night was bad indeed, in his unconsciousness he gave history from Drake, Wellington, etc, then singing and finally praying. A prisoner from September 1914 how hard to die with peace so near at hand (God willed it so). With good treatment he may have pulled through, doctor too late turning up. We did our best but that was little for we did not know how to treat him. One Russian and two French have died during the last week in the next village from the same disease and several by Limburg.[28]

Private Kelly was thirty-one. A gravestone was erected at Mensfelden by his comrades. His remains were later moved and now lie in the British military cemetery at Niederzwehren, ten miles south of Kassel.

Die Grippe was only one of the killer bacilli marauding the teeming and unsanitary camps in autumn going on winter 1918; men who had worked on *Kommando* were sometimes unable to withstand even an ordinary cold. Watching one batch of 187 freed Allied slaves enter Langensalza, Ralph Ellinwood followed their fates; 75 perished within ten days. Between the announcement of the Armistice and last repatriation in February 1919, over 3,000 British PoWs died in Germany. As with Private Kelly at Mensfelden, the survivors erected gravestones in their memory and buried them with due military ceremony. Those who survived the camps considered that the comrades who perished in them were the equal of the fallen in Flanders' poppy fields. All had died for Britain. Programme notes for a concert held by British prisoners at Alten-Grabow on 13 December 1918 made explicit this understanding: 'In aid of Funds to erect a memorial to OUR BRITISH COMRADES whom we have left behind. Dulce et Decorum Est Pro Patria Mori.'

The entertainment put on was the prison camp familiar: Music hall.

1) FORTUNE & PARKER	Comedy Duo
2) KYLE	Scotch Comedian
3) PENFOLD	Character Comedian
4) PARKER	Sentimental
5) CHARLIE & CLAUD	Patter Comedians
6) FOX	Vocalist
7) WAIN	Comedian
8) BLESSINGTON	Swell Comedian
9) WILLIAM & HURST	Novelty Act
10) VANSTONE	Comedian
11) BILL & FRANK	Comedians
12) HANNAN	Dancer
13) WEBB	Comedian
14) WOODWARD	Vocalist
15) HOWARD	Serio-Comic
16) FORTUNE	Light Comedian
17) ROLLET & D'HARNOL IN A DRAMA ... 'GARDIENS DE PHARE.'[29]	in a Hut entitled

Hunger. Disease. Winter cold. The last weeks in the camps would prove some of the hardest. Germany was in a state of starving anarchy, and little minded to care for the enemy in her midst.

Unfortunately, as soon as the Armistice had been announced, the CPWC had stopped packing parcels for the camp. Not that parcels could be delivered in some parts of Germany because the railworkers were on strike, and a fire in the Kassel PoW parcel office meant that the last months of the war there were very like the first. There was no food. The starving time had come again.

Peace? There was no peace in camps where *Landsturmer* guards took private retribution for Germany's defeat, or Red Guards considered Allied officers to be the class enemy. There were shootings of prisoners at Mannheim, Sagan, Stuttgart, Stralsund (where a terrifying Robespierrean Soldiers and Workers Council took control, shooting two Allied officers in an act of 'absolute murder'),[30] and most notoriously, at Langensalza.

To accommodate the influx of PoWs into Langensalza, where numbers were reaching towards 4,000, the Germans gave permission for the 'theatre' (as the wooden and canvas barrack used for entertainment was grandiosely known) to be altered as emergency accommodation. Some PoWs 'liberated' spare wood from the theatre to burn to keep warm. On 27 November two groups of guards opened fire on prisoners in and around the theatre, killing 15 Allied PoWs – 9 French, 3 British, 1 Russian and 2 Italian. Although Germans would protest much to the subsequent Spanish and Dutch inquiry that the shootings had been necessary to prevent a riot, 30 Allied witnesses left little doubt that the shootings had been premeditated. Among the witnesses was Corporal Golding, 8/ Leicestershire Regiment:

On November 27th, at 1 p.m. we had just finished our dinner in the British Help Committee hut, and we heard an unusual bugle-call. Three of us went out. The hut was situated about 15 yards from the sentry box at the gate, which led to the tailors' and bootmakers' shops, and was about 30 yards from the theatre. The theatre contained dressing rooms, which had been put up by the prisoners, one for each nationality. At this time these dressing-rooms were being pulled down and prisoners used the woodwork for fuel. When I came out from the Help Committee hut I saw that the theatre was surrounded by a group of about 20 or 30 of different nationalities. There was no disturbance or riot of any kind, and the prisoners were only going in and out of the theatre carrying pieces of wood from their respective dressing rooms.

After the bugle call about 30 soldiers, with an under-officer in charge, named Krause, came out of the Landsturm barrack, which was situated some 40 yards from the Help Committee hut and about 40 yards from the theatre. The soldiers surrounded the British Help Committee hut and the theatre in extended order. I was standing near the gate, about 6 yards away from the under-officer. He said to me in broken English, 'What are you making trouble for?' I replied 'There is no trouble at all.' and I asked him why the soldiers were surrounding the theatre and our hut, but he made no answer. I remained where I was between the committee hut and the gate, and after an interval of three minutes I heard him give the order to fire. I am quite certain that he gave the order to fire, for I had often heard it given before when at the front. There must have been 15 to 20 prisoners standing outside the hut, and I should say about 30 others round the theatre. When the order to fire was given, I tried to get into the committee hut, but the door was so crowded by others endeavouring to do the same that I could not get in. At least 15 shots were fired in the direction of the committee hut, with the result that Private Tucker, Worcester Regiment, who was standing 8 or 9 yards from me, was killed instantly, receiving three bullets; Private Morey, East Yorks, standing 10 yards from the hut, was also killed, being shot in the head. Corporal Elrod, 6th Northumberland Fusiliers, must have been 60 yards away from the theatre, near the football ground; he was hit by a bullet in the spine, from the effects of which he died eight hours afterwards. Two of the men who were trying to get through the door of the hut were wounded – Private F. Johnson, 4th Bedfordshire Regiment, and Private Haig, West Yorks – and there were three bullet marks in the committee hut door. Private Johnson told me that when the firing commenced he threw himself flat on the ground, and that when he tried to crawl into the hut he was fired at again by the soldiers.[31]

There were camps in which the British snatched the guns of their bewildered *Landsturmer* guards and threatened to shoot any German who came close. Who could blame them?

In this great flood of history there were incidents that caught the memory, where men missed the tide, where men became stranded, or were simply left wading against the flow. At exactly 11 a.m. on 11 November that inveterate warrior and escaper Captain H.A. Cartwright was on a ship mooring in Boulogne harbour. He had achieved his wish of a return to the front line – but too late to the minute.

Corporal Speight was sitting warming his hands at the barracks stove in Friedrichsfeld *Lager* when

> a German soldier popped his head into our room and said: 'Hey! Is any o'ye b—s from Newcassel. We just said, 'Why howay in man', and in he came. His name was Nagler, I think, and he said he had been a waiter at the County Hotel for several years. His wife belonged to Jesmond [a suburb of Newcastle-upon-Tyne] and as he was going home we loaded him with tins of bully, jam, and as many biscuits as he could manage, whereupon the poor fellow cried like a child.[32]

The boys at Friedrichsfeld were among the lucky ones to have a good stash left of Red Cross parcels. Speight again:

> Our German corporal was also badly off for food so we used to stand him his grub too. In return, he used to take us down to the town of Wesel nearby, armed with a tin of cocoa or a couple of bars of Sunlight soap we used to descend on the pubs which, for this price, we would supply six men with beer for as long as they cared to stay.

The delights of domestic Germany were not lost on one British prisoner encountered by Private Preston, King's Royal Rifle Corps, at Langensalza:

> There was one objector about going home ... This chap said he didn't want to go home because, living in Manchester before the war, he had been a drop-out, very idle and of no use to his family

or society. But since he had been on the farm he had learnt all about sugar beet growing and general farming and now had the basis of a useful career. He had never been as happy in his life. He spoke quite openly of the fact that the farmer had to serve at the front and eventually he started sharing the farmer's bed with the farmer's wife. We understood his meaning and told him he could please himself, realizing that we would have our own problems to sort out after being from home for five years.[33]

Some PoWs could not or would not wait for official repatriation. Prisoners at Stralsund were becalmed, caught in the middle of a spat between the area corps commander and the head of the local revolutionaries. Tiring of the delay, the prisoners chartered their own train to take them to Denmark. Officers at Cologne also decided to travel independently, hiring a boat to ferry them down the Rhine. It did not quite turn out to be the pleasure boat cruise they anticipated; spending the night on shore at Düsseldorf's YMCA, Captain C.M. Slack of the East Yorks, was woken by a policeman who urged him to hurry back to the boat: the town was full of 'Reds' who were threatening to burn down all the places where British officers were staying. Back on their chartered ship, Slack and his friends pressed on out of the dark heart of Germany to Rotterdam, where the British authorities took over, put them on a British tub and sent them to Hull. It was Slack's hometown. He arrived within a fortnight of the Armistice.[34]

From Saarbrücken the border with France, although a hundred miles away, seemed tantalizingly walkable to Private Walter Hare, 1/West Yorkshire Regiment. And so Hare, his brother and two other prisoners decided on 'Shanks's pony' as their mode of homewards transport. The trek proved tough for men debilitated by detention, and who had to scrump for their food. One of the party died en route: 'I suppose it was just exposure and lack of nourishment,' reflected Hare. The survivors found two bottles of wine in the cellar of a deserted house. Pepped up, they set off the next day 'in good form'. Eventually they bumped into French troops on the Alsace-Lorraine border, who gave them, remembered Hare, 'the best sausages and coffee I have ever tasted in my life'. They had walked for six days.

Waiting, waiting, waiting. Joseph Lee decided to fill the yawning gap before repatriation with some sightseeing. With his friend Tim Sugrue he took the train from Beeskow (where the camp commandant had been deposed and revolutionaries, in a fit of individuality, wore white instead of red armbands) to Berlin. There the two officers wandered Unter den Linden, the Reichstag, and the Tiergarten. The Spartacist Revolt was brewing up and at the Tiergarten the two men had a chance encounter with history: they saw Karl Liebknecht, the Spartacist leader, address a mass crowd, its 'drooping red banners, like gouts of blood between the trees'. Standing on the outside of the throng, Lieutenant Lee bought an album of views of Berlin from a little girl, 'and immediately after a similar collection from an old woman poor and equally insistent'. As he left the park, Lee took a glance back:

> My last recollection of Liebknecht is of a gesticulating volcanic figure, and of a vivid face with wild eyes and the distorted mouth of a Greek tragic mask. He was killed a few weeks later, within a few hundred yards of where we heard him speak.[35]

On returning to Beeskow, they had to ring the bell and wake the camp guard . . . to be admitted. How the world had turned upside down.

Most PoWs were content to go sightseeing closer to their camp, though walks had their disadvantages. Any British prisoner strolling around was considered a fair target for 'urchins of both sexes, up to the age of twelve, all yelling for biscuits and chocolate'. Alec Waugh thought it was terrible that Germans had so far lost their self-respect to allow their children to beg from the erstwhile enemy.[36] He was pleasantly surprised, though, to find the Mainz *Völker* friendly; the proprietor of the local café generously plied Waugh and his friends with his private stock of Rhine wine on their last night. Next day the British PoWs marched down from the Citadel to the railway station to take the train to Metz. All the German officers from the camp, and a considerable number of civilians came to see them off.

Not all departures were such sweet sorrows. In areas where the revolutionaries had taken control, the PoWs were handed a leaflet, 'A Parting Word', on their leaving. The leaflet hit the wrong tone. And how.

Gentlemen: The war is over. A little while, and you will see your native land again, your homes, your loved ones, your friends. You will once more take on your accustomed work.

The fortune of war brought you as prisoners into our hands. You were freed, even against your will, from the fighting, from danger, from death. But the joys of peace could not be yours, for there was no peace. Now peace is coming, and peace means liberty. When you are already reunited with your families, thousands of our countrymen will still be pining in far off prison camps, their hearts as hungry for home as yours.

You have suffered in confinement, as who would not. It was the fate of every prisoner in every prison camp throughout the world to eat his heart out with longing, to chafe against the loss of liberty, to suffer from homesickness, brooding discouragement, blank despair. The days, the weeks, the weary years crept by and there was no end in sight. There were many discomforts, irritations, misunderstandings. Your situation has been a difficult one. Our own has been desperate, our country blockaded, our civil population and army suffering from want of proper sufficient food and materials, the enormous demands made upon our harassed land from every side. These and many other afflictions made it impossible to do all we would have liked to do. Under the circumstances we did our best to lessen the hardships of your lot, to ensure your comfort, to provide you with pastimes, enjoyment, mental and bodily recreation. It is not likely that you will ever know how difficult our circumstances have been.

We know that errors have been committed and that there have been hardships for which the former system has been to blame. There have been wrongs and evils on both sides. We hope that you will always think of that, and be just.

You entered the old empire of Germany. You leave a new Republic

– the newest and, as we hope to make it, the freest land in the world. We are sorry that you saw so little of what we were proud of in the former Germany – our art, our sciences, our model cities, our theatres, schools, industries, social institutions, as well as the beauties of our scenery and the real soul of our people, akin in so many things to your own.

But these things will remain part of the new Germany. Once the barriers of misunderstanding and artificial hatred have fallen, we hope that you will learn to know, in happier times, these grander features of a land whose unwilling guests you have been. A barbed wire enclosure is not the proper point of view from which to survey or judge a great nation.

The war has blinded all nations, but if a true and just peace will result in opening the eyes of the people to the fact that their interests are common – that no difference in flags, speech or nationality can alter the truth of the fraternity of all men – this war will not have been fought in vain. If the peoples at last realise that it is not each other who are their enemies, but the ruthless forces of imperialism and capitalism, of militarism of all sorts, of jingo-journalism that sows falsehood, hatred and suspicion, then this war will not have been fought in vain. Then peace will not be established in vain.

We hope that every one of you will go home carrying a message of goodwill, conciliation and enlightenment. Let all men in our new epoch go forth as missionaries of the evangel [sic], as interpreters between nation and nation.

The valiant dead who once fought against each other have long been sleeping as comrades side by side in the earth. May the living who once fought against each other labour as comrades side by side upon this self-same earth.

This is the message with which we bid you farewell.[37]

To blame the Allied blockade for the mistreatment they had suffered in the camps stuck in the craws of prisoners. Leaflet after leaflet was balled up and thrown away to lie as paper snowballs on the bare winter *Appell* grounds.

At last! In the third week of November the great evacuation got under way. Over the next month more than fifty thousand PoWs were moved by train and boat out of the German exile. When no transport arrived at Holzminden, where 'Milwaukee Bill' Niemeyer had long since skedaddled off in mufti camouflage, the SBO threatened to burn the place down. A train appeared next day, 11 December. Before leaving, the prisoners made a bonfire anyway, throwing on tables, chairs, old clothing, everything they could not take with them. 'The Huns, who were expecting to get all these articles as prerequisites, were furious.'[38] The fire department was called to extinguish the flames. The PoWs cut their hoses, and the fire of Hellminden raged on. On leaving the camp for the station, the prisoners marched out, four abreast, heads held high.

Repatriation *was* agonizingly slow. By the middle of December only half of British PoWs had reached Allied hands; even at the beginning of January 1919 at least 14,000 PoWs were still languishing in Germany.[39] Lack of rolling stock was the German reason for the slowness of repatriation. Bloody-mindedness was what the prisoners thought it was down to. Whatever: little final tragedies continued to occur in the exodus from captivity. Ambulance trains went west with few or no medical staff; one train arrived at Cologne with 33 of its 512 PoW passengers dead. Cologne never was good for British prisoners.

Alec Waugh, to his surprise, as he leaned out of the train window and took a glance back at Mainz Cathedral, the landmark for eight months of his young life, suffered mixed emotions:

> As I leant out of the window, to catch a last glimpse of the cathedral, it was hardly possible to realise that the war was over and that we were going home . . . I could not grasp its significance. I was almost afraid to look forward, and my mind went back to the earlier days of captivity, to the hunger and depression, to the intolerable tedium and irritation. And yet, for all that, a wave of sentimentality partially obscured the sharpness of those memories. We had had some good times there in the citadel; the grey monochrome had not been entirely unrelieved.[40]

In the best of times in the camps men had found the best of

themselves. Guts, humour, pride, comradeship. They had found the stuff of British soldiers.

To Waugh's slight annoyance, the 'glamour of the return' was dispelled by the behaviour of French trains, let alone the German ones. French trains did what they always did. Went oh-so-slowly. Waugh left Mainz on 24 November; he did not reach London until 5 December.

On being told he was to depart for Blighty, Archer Cust had the 'same feeling of rapture and childish excitement' as going on holiday as a schoolboy. Since that deceptively spring-like April day at Ploegsteert when he had been captured, Cust had trusted to luck to see him through. It held to the end. Just as Cust was leaving Graudenz on the Vistula, His Sacred Majesty Chance smiled again: a parcel containing two dozen bottles of claret and half a dozen of sherry arrived for Lieutenant L.G.A. Cust, RA.

Stuck in abeyance in Stendal, Sergeant David Gray could only dream of a drink. In his last letter home of the war, he promised a friend that on landing in Blighty they would 'paint the town RED'.

Basil Willey was getting unnervingly short of rations when the Danish Red Cross turned up at Kamstigall with a useful truckload of bread, tinned beef, pork-and-beans, dried apricots. Better still, they brought good news. The assembled prisoners were to be repatriated from Danzig as soon as they could gather their belongings. Willey's contingent entered Danzig on the morning of Monday, 9 December. In the streets placards hung demanding 'FRIEDE UND BROT':

> From this point onwards, pent-up emotion began to take command. We could see two lighted ships lying in the harbour; and as soon as it became known that they were the British light cruisers Coventry and Centaur, cheering broke out and hardly ceased till we had left the port. We walked along the quay, past the Ste Croix, which was taking the French prisoners, to our ship the SS Russ, which stood very high above the water. Somebody on board shouted down a few words of English, and received in response a loud cheer followed by renderings of 'Take me back to dear old Blighty' and other tunes.

No sooner had we embarked and found our bunks than it was breakfast time. To our jaded eyes the saloon, with its white table-cloths, clean crockery, huge piles of sliced bread, plates of Danish butter, bowlfuls of boiled eggs, jam, sardines and bins of porridge, was a vision almost too wondrous to bear. By merely crossing the gangway we had left hunger and misery behind and entered into the Promised Land, our own land, a land flowing with milk and honey.

As the day went on we had a clear, and pathetic, visible proof of the realities of the situation. The prisoners had a superfluity of bread and biscuits, and someone started throwing pieces down to the German children on the quayside. Soon the news spread that there was food to be had, and the wharf became densely crowded, mostly with children and women, stretching out their hands and shouting 'Eengleeshmaan! Eengleeshman!' The children fought for pieces of bread like animals, and almost always had to be separated by their elders. They all looked pale and starving. This was Germany after four years of war and blockade, its pride swallowed up in hunger and desperation, suing to its enemies for mercy and food.[41]

The sight of German women and children on Danzig docks crying for bread shook everyone who witnessed it. Well, almost everyone. As Sergeant Hawtin Mundy waited to embark on a Red Cross ship moored beside a crowd begging for food,

Almost all of us emptied our packages out because we knew we wouldn't want the stuff any longer. There was just one – a big lad, and I'll never forgive him – never. He just took his box of food and walked away from the lines, snapped it open and dropped it in the sea, and said, 'Let the buggers get in and fight for that.'[42]

No, not everyone was in a forgiving mood. Cecil Blain, RFC, formerly of Holzminden, took steps to remain in Germany to hunt the Niemeyer brothers down. Like so many other war criminals, however, they were never found and escaped justice.[43]

When 1,800 British PoWs from Soltau arrived at Hamburg docks on the morning of 24 December, they were overjoyed to see a British destroyer and the liner *City of Poona* waiting for them. They were less overjoyed, Private W. Chambers recalled, by the attitude of the German guards who began 'wagging their fingers at us'. A Royal Navy petty officer then bawled at the Germans that he was now in charge. A great relieved cheer went up from the prisoners. 'What a thrill it gave us,' wrote Private Chambers,

> when that burly guard subsided when the sailor yapped at him. For nearly four years, they had ordered and controlled our every action and this was the first time one of our own side was the top dog. Freedom, what a sweet taste it had.[44]

*

Chambers spent Christmas at sea. He had tobacco and a pipe and some pudding as a present.

Benjamin Muse, the American who fought for Britain, sailed for Blighty from Warnemunde, where the 'natives were obsequiously polite to the *Engländer* now'. What really caught Muse's attention, as many times before, was the 'unfailing humour' of Tommy Atkins, his adopted countryman. As the British mounted the gangplank they sang the popular parlour song 'A Perfect Day'.[45] And they sang it right ironically.

They sang. What songs they sang.

> When you come to the end of a Perfect Day
> And you sit alone with your thoughts
> While the chimes ring out with a carol gay
> For the joy that the day has brought.
> Do you think what the end of a Perfect Day
> Can mean to a tired heart
> When the sun goes down with a flaming ray
> And the dear friends have to part?

VIII

HOME, UNSWEET HOME: RETURN AND AFTERMATH

Whether a man highly strung feels it more than a duller and more animal type, or less, I cannot tell, but with a little more than two years' experience of it, I can say with certainty that it is by far the worst thing that ever happened to me, and a thing from which I shall possibly never recover.

Lieutenant Will Harvey, Gloucestershire Regiment
on being a prisoner of war
From *Comrades in Captivity*, 1920

They arrived back as prisoners as they had departed as soldiers. In fanfare.

The ships bringing the prisoners home were met by flotillas of little boats blaring foghorns, and cheering crowds on the dockside waving Union Jack flags. Private William Tucker came across the Channel on the liner *France*, in the very first batch of the repatriated. Those who could manage it stood on the deck wanting to see the white cliffs of Britain. Longing for home was mixed with apprehension in Tucker's mind because: 'All prisoners, or all those with normal reactions, suffer a sense of humiliation for having been captured and, if only for that reason we did not look for or expect any tumultuous reception on our return home.'[1]

But they got a reception fit for heroes. They were the boys who had stuck out the camps.[2] So overawed were Tucker and his fellow prisoners by their frenzied greeting that they could not respond. 'None of us even waved.' Their disbelief continued; to meet them as they disembarked at Dover was the Prince of Wales. The King himself sent each and every one of them a parcel containing a pipe, tobacco, cigarettes, chocolate and toffee. They were conveyed in private motors through streets lined with people to Canterbury dispersal camp, where they were given wool mattresses to sleep on. Corporal Anthony Newman, another of the men returned on the *France*, recalled that soft mattress as the highlight of a day of delights. 'Oh, the joy.'

Dover, along with Hull and Leith were the principal ports of arrival for the repatriated prisoners. But wherever they landed prisoners were greeted by wild, waving crowds and were dispensed 'comforts' of food and drink by the ladies of the Prisoners' Reception Committees. Lance-Corporal Thomas Higgins arrived back in Blighty a month after Private Tucker:

We climbed the mast and anywhere we could get to see the first sight of England. There were now ships of every description round us: warships, destroyers, submarines, steamers, and fishing smacks. When they saw our signal Repatriated Prisoners, it was like New Years Eve at home. They blew foghorns, buzzers and anything to let us know how they welcomed us home, and as we got close to Grimsby the buzzers on land took up the chorus. It was such a noise.

At last we got to Hull about 6 p.m. on December 26. We disembarked with crowds of folks cheering us, and shaking our hands. We were given a mug of tea, a sandwich and a bag of cakes by some ladies, the first English women I had seen since leaving Southampton.[3]

The Holzminden contingent sailed into Hull to a local band playing 'God Save the King' and Admiral Beatty was there 'waving his hat like a schoolboy'.[4] Private Cecil Bacon, arriving at Leith on a hospital ship from Copenhagen, was met by no less a dignitary than Princess Alice. 'I hope you will be alright soon, my boy,' she said to him.

Lieutenant Basil Willey also arrived at Leith:

As we entered the harbour, ship after ship greeted us with every noise-making device it could muster: bells, fog-horns, sirens and human voices. On the quayside where the ship was berthed stood a

throng of ladies dressed in the brightest colours, waving and shouting their welcomes to us.

The men were disembarked before the officers, and the sick
were taken away in motor-ambulances. When we landed we went
straight away into a vast quayside storeroom full of long tables laid
for a meal. This place was a riot of colour: huge festoons of flags
stretched from side to side, and the tables were covered with vases
full of paper-flowers of every hue. Everywhere moved the ladies –
angels we thought them – in purples and greens, carrying plates and
cups and telegraph forms to us all as we sat down at the tables. They
were assisted by a number of very small boy-scouts, whose Scotch
accent would surely have been music even to the ear of a Johnson or
Elia, had they been returned prisoners-of-war. We each had a plate
of steak-and-kidney pie, potatoes, three buns, and tea. As we filed
out to go to the train, each of us received three packets; two containing biscuits, cheese, chocolate, butter-scotch, a pork-pie, cigarettes,
a pipe and tobacco; the third being a souvenir of Leith; a handkerchief, a piece of soap, a pencil and a stamped picture-postcard of
Edinburgh. Everyone was also given a small Union Jack; these we
fixed outside the windows of the train. All the way along the line
from Leith through Portobello and out into the country, people
waved and hurrahed to us – from the windows, from the streets and
from the fields. We roared back in reply with our whole selves, until
at last, as darkness came on, we sank into blissful torpor, overcome
by excitement and exultation.[5]

All returning *Kriegsgefangene* were handed, usually as they
stepped off the gangplank onto the sacred soil of the Promised
Land, a copy of a handwritten note from the King:

The Queen joins me in welcoming you on your release from the miseries and hardships, which you have endured with so much patience
and courage.

During these many months of trial the early rescue of our gallant
Officers and Men from the cruelties of captivity has been uppermost
in our thoughts.

We are thankful that this longed for day has arrived, & that back in the Country you will be able once more to enjoy the happiness of a home & to see good days among those who anxiously look for your return.

George RI

The note was cyclostyled, but nonetheless much appreciated.

Such high hopes, so quickly dashed. Happiness and good days would be limited in the lives of the returned prisoners. The dark notes were already there amidst the euphoria of homecoming, because the prisoners kept dying. Every ship home had someone too diseased and enfeebled to survive the voyage. Sergeant Hawtin Mundy recalled:

> One of the very weak lads died. It was a very sad thing. He had to be buried at sea. The band came on deck, and one of the former prisoners who was a parson in peacetime said he would conduct the service, then the men gently slid the coffin over and it went plop into the sea. Then the band started to play. Even years later it upsets me to talk about it.[6]

Then there were men who, after years of starvation, died of over-eating. They were killed by kindness. Colma Campbell was a VAD nurse tending disembarked prisoners:

> Our prisoners coming through just make your heart bleed, they look at you with such pathetic eyes and say, 'You're a woman, we could not even begin to tell you the things we have suffered.' Many of them are in such a weak condition that the first food which people give them out of the kindness of their hearts knocks them over. Their stomachs are too weak to stand anything.[7]

Some prisoners died as their ship docked. Some had to stay in France and Holland to convalesce, but still died in the crossing of the sea. Some landed in Britain, and were whisked away on ambulance trains and died in hospital, as did the very last two repatriations in March 1919.

On the quayside and at the railway station, mingled among the happy mob, were the lost women. Hardly anyone could bear to catch their eye as they walked up and down holding photographs of missing husbands, sons and brothers. 'Have you seen this man?' 'Anyone here from Döberitz? Please is there anyone from Döberitz?' 'This is my son, a corporal in the Bedfordshires – do you know him?' Private Jack Rogers wanted to give the poor mothers 'a little hope' and say something positive, but he had not seen any of the missing men. Neither had anyone else.

They seemed to be everywhere, those women with the strained faces and the pictures. They would be the most faithful of all in meeting the repatriation ships. Indeed, they would not miss the mooring of a single one.

It was when the ex-prisoners were transported to the Reception (dispersal) centres at Ripon or Canterbury that they knew they were back in the Army as well as back in Britain. Red tape and parades were the order of the day. After a shower to get rid of lice, prisoners walked between tables where they were handed vests, shirts, socks, shoes, suits or new uniform, a kit bag, and coat. ('I used that long after the war,' recalled Hawtin Mundy.) Back pay was sorted, ID documents and travel passes issued. Leave for two months was granted. Then came the blizzard of forms. Officer prisoners were asked to write a report on the circumstances of their capture; capture after all was a taint on an officer's honour, only to be eradicated by proof it was due to chance and the fortunes of war. Officers and other ranks alike were interviewed on behalf of the Government Committee on the Treatment by the Enemy of British Prisoners of War and asked to provide a 'Statement of Extraordinary Experiences in German Internment Camps'. One of the questions was: 'Were you treated brutally yourself or did you see anyone else treated brutally?' In the words of Sergeant Hawtin Mundy, it was 'a bloody silly question to ask!'

The prisoners were impatient. Few could be bothered with the repatriation forms, and not enough could be troubled to apply for a pension, which entailed waiting two or three days for a medical board. Sergeant Mundy took the alternative: a gratuity of £2, a disclaimer to the effect that the prisoner was not suffering any war-related disability, and off home a.s.a.p.

Having taken the £2, Sergeant Mundy spent a lifetime regretting his decision. As did thousands of others.

Bureaucracy. They were British soldiers. So of course they groused. The only pleasant aspect of Ripon dispersal camp for Lance-Corporal Higgins was the 'grand feed', yet even this was problematic, because it was so long since he'd used a knife and fork. Although the soldiers grumbled, the repatriation process was intended to take no more than twenty-four hours for straightforward cases, and usually that was the case. Basil Willey arrived at Leith at dawn on 13 December; at 6 p.m. on December 14 he was standing outside his parents' house in North London. After all the flags and shouting at Leith, homecoming

> seemed an anticlimax. I knocked at the front door, and was let in by my parents as if I had just come back from a stroll to Mill Hill. The truth is that our hearts were too full for much speech. And they, poor souls, were worn out, physically and emotionally, by their years of anxiety. Their experience had in most ways been more exacting than mine; and my mother, who was never robust, lived only two and a half years longer.[8]

Private Tucker, another North Londoner, arrived home to be 'impulsively enfolded' by his mother. Like Basil Willey's his mother looked 'care-worn and aged'.

There were prisoners who looked like that too, so altered by emaciation, stress and illness that they were genuinely unrecognizable to their own kin. More than one household had a knock on the door by a ghost, a prisoner long listed as dead.

Will Harvey's overwhelming emotion on being back 'in my own country and my own county' was relief. And his desire was never to leave either again:

> For I am come to Gloucestershire, which is my very home.
> Tired out with wandering and sick of wars beyond the
>   foam.
> I have starved enough in foreign parts, and no more care to
>   roam.

Quietly I will bide here in the place where I be,
Which knew my father and his grandfather,
and my dead brothers and me.
And bred us and fed us, and gave us pride of yeoman
ancestry.
Men with sap of Earth in their blood, and the wisdom of
weather and wind.
Who ploughed the land to leave it better than they did find,
And lie stretched out down Westbury way, where the
blossom is kind;
And lie covered with petals from orchards that do shed
Their bloom to be a light white coverlet over the dead
Who ploughed the land in the daytime, and went well
pleased to bed.[9]

The prisoners had come home, but home was another country. People had changed, so had society, irrevocably and forever. Few ex-prisoners settled in seamlessly. Lieutenant Brian Horrocks was honest enough to admit: 'I was young and physically fit but my nerves were in rags. I was unable to lead a quiet life at home, and was far too restless even to play games. I spent every available moment beating it up in London.'[10] He had four years of pay saved up. He spent it all in six weeks of partying. So many ex-PoWs joined him under the bright lights of London that the Red Cross Prisoner of War Bureau turned itself into a hostel.

'Beating it up', or what psychologists refer to as 'release', was one reaction to home and freedom. Another was retreat, up to and including the construction of an enclosed world like the familiar camps. Unable to stand being accosted by people in the street, Bill Easton began to spend more and more time inside his Norfolk house, engaged in the perennial prisoners' pastime, reading. 'In the end . . . I didn't go out too much, I was a sort of recluse,' he recalled.[11]

Whether the former prisoners erred towards release or retreat, they found home alienating. In a memorable image Lieutenant Horace Gilliland likened being back in British society to seeing 'dancers through a window when you can't hear the music'.[12] Adjusting to liberty after months and years of exile behind barbed wire was no easy task. Alexander Raban Waugh suffered a disorder common among former 'Kriegers', an inability to drop the 'habits of subservience'.[13] Every time Waugh went to the cinema he kept expecting the usher to tell him *'Es ist verboten, Herr Leutnant!'*

Waugh, at least, had a job. His father, a director of the publishers Chapman & Hall, found a position for him in the firm. When 21-year-old Private Norman Dykes, on demob after his two months PoW leave, went to get his old job at Rochdale Library back he found it occupied by a woman. William Tucker's Army Discharge Certificate put 'Prisoner of War' in his list of Military Qualifications, which hardly enticed employers. Not all PoWs were granted demob at the end of their two months leave. With unemployment rising grimly, Ernie Stevens might have been glad of his retention by the Army, except that he was given the most inappropriate possible task: guarding German PoWs in Lewes.[14]

Rifleman Alfred Hall was one of a hundred or so former PoWs who returned to Germany in early 1919 as part of a joint Red Cross and Order of St John mission, supported by the War Office, to provide 'the improvement of the material and moral conditions of Russian Prisoners of War in Germany'. Due to the civil war in the newly established 'Russian Soviet Federative Socialist Republic', 500,000 Russians, unable to be repatriated, were stranded in the camps, mostly round Hannover. There was no shortage of volunteers for the Red Cross and Order of St John Mission; former 'Kriegers' like Hall knew only too well what it was like to starve in Babylon. He went east as an 'Honorary Lieutenant', wearing British uniform with his regimental cap badge replaced by Red Cross insignia. The Russian PoWs were indeed in a desperate state, as another Honorary British officer on the mission, J. Stuart Castle, discovered on entering at Muggenburger Moor camp:

> My first impression was one of filth and utter despair. Ragged men in
> all stages of sickness and that appalling lazaret full of skeleton-like
> beings dying, if not already dead, of tuberculosis ... Together with

malnutrition, these men had to endure the knowledge of their helplessness and, in some cases worse, of the helplessness of their families
now caught up in the Russian civil war. All they wanted to do – if the
urge to do anything at all had survived – was to lie in bed.[15]

Hall, Castle and their colleagues took a leaf out of the British Army
manual. To improve the Russians' minds they got them active,
cleaning up the camps and playing innumerable sporting games.
To keep the Russians' bodies together, the British Red Cross and the
Order of St John donated half a million pounds' worth of supplies,
and redirected a mountain of food parcels in Holland, originally
intended for British PoWs, to Germany.

Seldom has such fine humanitarian effort gone to such wasted
and tragic end. Part of the Red Cross's brief was the repatriation
of the Russians. Eventually, this was arranged, with most Russians
agreeing to evacuation to the new Bolshevik state. Thousands were
shot after crossing the Red border because they were deemed to be
counter-revolutionaries.

One wholly genuine counter-revolutionary was Brian Horrocks
who, during his enforced sojourn in Germany, had shared rooms
with Russians, and perforce learned the lingo. When the War Office
called for volunteers who knew Russian to go and aid the White
Army, Horrocks, after four years of inaction, grabbed the chance
for action. He was captured by the Red Army on 7 January 1919, at
Krasnoyarsk. Once again Brian Horrocks was a prisoner of war; he
spent ten months in a Bolshevik jail, somehow surviving a particularly virulent strain of typhus.

Notwithstanding his canine nickname, Dog Horrocks had
the constitution of an ox. Back in Britain, other former prisoners
of the Kaiser fared less well in resisting early twentieth-century
bacilli and viruses. On and on went the hidden death toll of the
Great War. Captain Leefe Robinson VC was merely the most high-
profile PoW to die in the war's wake. Sadistically mistreated by Karl
Niemeyer in Holzminden, the flyer-hero was reduced by the time
of his repatriation to a sickly wraith propped up by a walking stick.
On 31 December 1918 while staying with friends at Harrow Weald,

Robinson contracted Spanish flu. Already weak, he died within hours, succumbing to cardiac arrest around midnight. Reportedly,

> During the delirium which preceded his last moments, Captain Robinson was haunted by the vision of the archbrute. He imagined that Niemeyer and sentries with fixed bayonets were standing by his deathbed. Several times he called out to be protected from the fiend.[16]

The mortality rate of ex-prisoners in the Twenties and Thirties was five times higher than that of other veterans. In particular they suffered a greater tendency to gastro-intestinal problems, bronchitis, skin rashes, and enervation.[17] No real attempt was made by the government to address the medical problems endemic among prisoners whose health had been wrecked by disease, short rations and long hours of labour. One soldier recalled that the only medical advice given to him was 'Eat Sparingly, Eat Often'.[18]

Mentally, ex-prisoners were prone to irritability, depression, and suicide. Here is the story of Corporal Alfred Schofield, Machine Gun Corps, captured 25 March 1918. On his return home, Schofield suffered depression and memory loss. He was killed when he walked in front of a train at Swinley Bridge outside London on 23 February 1922.

Schofield's widow applied to the government for a pension to support herself and her two children. She carefully collected affidavits from those who knew Corporal Schofield, confirming his breakdown in mental health on his return to the land fit for heroes. One witness statement, from Mr C.A. Gillett who worked with Schofield, read:

> I as a fellow workman (Regulator on Trains) of the late AH Schofield, do hereby declare that having worked with him for years before he entered and after he left the Army, on returning to us after periods of service, I noticed the marked difference in health and character. At periods he was quite lost, memory failed him, it was apparently impossible to express what he wanted to say, there was tremor and twitch noticeable at times in limbs and face. I believe he was suffering

from what is called Neuresthenia. Myself and his other chums have often noticed it and often remarked about it.[19]

The widow Schofield's application was rejected, because in February 1919 Corporal Schofield had signed a statement at the Reception Camp to the effect that he was not suffering any disability due to his military service. Like other Tommies, Corporal Schofield had been in a hurry to get home.

An appeal by Mrs Schofield was also rejected, despite medical evidence that her husband was under treatment for insomnia and derangement at the time of his death. So destitute was Schofield's family that he was buried in an unmarked grave. Only to the Schofield family, however, was Corporal Alfred Schofield's suicide a tragedy. Determined to cut the costs of war pensions, the government turned down hundreds of applications by Britain's Mrs Schofields.

There were men with broken minds who were shuffled from asylum to asylum. In France, a returned native prisoner was found wandering the station at Lyon. He did not know his own name. His mind was missing. He was the living dead. 'Anthelme Mangin' as he was re-christened, became the international symbol of the citizen soldier made mad by war and captivity. A dozen desperate families claimed him as their missing son. He was the inspiration for the amnesiac soldier Gaston in Jean Anouilh's *Le Voyageur Sans Bagage*.[20]

If any ex-prisoner believed the fine words of the government that the Kaiser's guards would be brought to book for their misdeeds, he was destined to be as disappointed as Mrs Alfred Schofield. Oh, the search for justice began well enough, with Article 228 of the Versailles Peace Treaty stating that:

> The German Government recognises the right of the Allied and Associated Powers to bring before military tribunal persons accused of having committed acts in violation of the laws and customs of war.

The Attorney-General went further, suggesting to the Foreign Secretary that while the latter was at Versailles he proposed

As part of the terms for enlargement of armistice, a condition to be inserted requiring certain enemy officers who may from time to time be named, to be handed over and placed in safe custody with a view to their being dealt with for breaches of laws of war and humanity. The first set of such names will be transmitted within a few days.

High on the 'Black List' of offenders were the names of Karl and Heinrich Niemeyer. But the German authorities were unable or reluctant to find them. One British newspaper reported in 1923 that Karl shot himself dead in a Hannover restaurant; another report said he had committed suicide at his flat in Dresden. A persistent rumour whispered that the twins had fled to South America.

The British government's desire to prosecute German war criminals vanished as quickly and as effectively as Herr Charlie Niemeyer. Initially, the Allies submitted a list of 853 people to the German government under Article 228. Then the list was dramatically guillotined; the British proceeded with just seven cases, these relating to submarine warfare and the maltreatment of British prisoners in the Kaiser's camps. All the big names were dropped; none of the three Germans charged with brutality towards prisoners was anything other than an inconsequential Imperial minion. No Beetz, no Niemeyer, no Von Hanisch. Now absolutely overcome by half-heartedness, the Allied governments decided to allow the cases to be tried before the German's own 'Supreme Court of the Empire'.

No one could be beastly to the Hun in 1921, because it was feared that proper prosecution of war crimes would increase instability in Germany and open the door to Communism.

Some sixty British ex-prisoners travelled to the *Reichsgericht* in May 1921 for the so-called Leipzig War Crimes Trials. The first British case relating to maltreatment was that of Karl Heynen, a *Landsturm* NCO who had been in charge of British prisoners at Friedrich der Grosse coal mine in Westphalia. Heynen was alleged to have used the butt of his rifle, his fists and boots to make prisoners (who were on strike) labour for Germany. The Court accepted that Heynen had used rifle butt, boot and fist – but had been correct to do so, and he was acquitted of the associated charges. By its own risible lights the Court could do little else because, as General von Fransecky argued in Heynen's defence, the NCO's physical methods of securing discipline were 'in keeping with the German Army's finest traditions'. Heynen was more eloquent still, pointing out that as a recruit he had been stoned by his own sergeant. In a tokenistic nod to the disapproving gallery of international observers, the Court found Heynen guilty of other charges of brutality, notably the thrashing of a PoW called Cross. The judges gave Heynen a derisory sentence of six months in a civilian jail, the period of detention pending and during the trial to be considered as part of the sentence.

The second British case involved Captain Eric Müller, the Karlsruhe barrister and Reserve officer who, in April 1918, had taken command of the prison camp at Flavy-le-Martel, where despite the dysentery outbreak the Allied prisoners had been made to work; in one month alone as many as five hundred prisoners had died, the majority of them French. The Court determined that the worst of the dysentery epidemic occurred after Müller's tenure as commander and he was acquitted. As with Heynen, Müller was found guilty on other charges of gratuitous deliberate personal cruelty. His personal photographs of the sick and dying were not, however, held to be incriminating. He was given six months' imprisonment. The lightness of the sentence was pleasing to a courtroom floor packed with seething members of the nationalistic German public.

Case three was against Sergeant Heinrich Trinke and Private Robert Neuman in relation to alleged offences against British PoWs employed in a chemical factory at Pommerensdorf. Like any reasonably competent war criminal of standing, such as Beetz of Bad Colberg, Trinke could not be found; the lesser criminal Neuman was found guilty on twelve out of seventeen instances of assault. His sentence, predictably, was six months' imprisonment. The definition of 'imprisonment' here, as with Müller and Heynen, was generous, being a sort of loose arrest in a furnished room with visitors to-ing and fro-ing. Equally, the Supreme Court's understanding of 'six months' was distinctive, with at least two of the defendants serving four or less months.

The Times correspondent described the trials as a 'scandalous failure of justice'. Legal experts of the Inter-Allied Commission were of the same mind, and proposed that, given the evident bias of the German Court, the remaining cases be handed over to Allied governments for trial. The British government strenuously demurred, oleaginously claiming that the Leipzig trials were fair and satisfactory. This opinion was for public consumption only; Sir Eyre Crowe, the Permanent Under Secretary at the Foreign Office, admitted off the record that 'a mistake had apparently been made by the Allied Governments . . . agreeing to the trial of the culprits by a German court'.[21]

Such were the joys of Realpolitik in the 1920s; in order to normalize relations with Germany the British government pretended that injustice was justice and betrayed its own 'harshed' and murdered soldiers. A motion in the House of Commons for debate on the trials was defeated. By 1923, as far as the government was concerned, war crimes were off the agenda. By 1933 as far as British society was concerned, the former prisoners were a forbidden topic. Pacifism was the mood of the people, and the probing of old wounds to do with prisoner maltreatment seemed suspiciously akin to war-mongering. Friendliness with Fritz was the official order of the era; a series of BBC talks by First World War escapers in 1931 included three Germans. It was these talks transcribed and edited that became the book *Escapers All*, introduced by J.R. Ackerley.

But what really hampered the former prisoners in seeking justice or obtaining help was guilt. Guilt at surviving the war, guilt at being captured, guilt at surviving the camps. How could the ex-prisoners dare to complain when other soldiers of the Great War were lying pale and rotting below the fields of Flanders and the rocky waste of Gallipoli? Or, when disabled veterans begged on the streets of Depression Britain? Will Harvey, the Gloucestershire Lad, suffered badly from the guilt of the *Gefangener*:

I am smelling the smell of the old brown river,
And hearing the bumble of bees:
Half-blind I stand with the shine and shiver
Of waving willow-trees.
These were a dream when that I wandered
Beyond the seas afar; But now so much of life lies
    squandered.
Less than a dream, they are.

Death, you have robbed the Earth of her glory!
You have robbed the Sun of his fire! And because of my
    brothers' pitiful story
My heart is robbed of Desire
Would I were there in the wind and weather
Of your dark Flanders sky!
Would we were sleeping there together.

My brothers you and I.
A colour is on the rose, and the clinging
Clematis, never before I saw: the colour of blood!
And the singing
Of birds may charm no more.
Oh, would I were slumbering, sleeping blindly,
Beneath those wet-eyed stars.
With the heavens to shelter us bending kindly
Above us till the end of wars!

Never a bitter man, there is nonetheless a detectable note of dis-enchantment in Harvey's reaction to the arrival of the certificate from the War Office testifying that the circumstances of his capture had been investigated. No blame was to be attached to him. 'Many thanks!'[22]

Will Harvey, as he feared, did not recover from his two years' caging in the Kaiser's camps. Or, at least, he was altered funda-mentally by it. He returned to legal practice in the Forest of Dean, but recklessly gave away his services for free (particularly to those requiring defence), and eventually had to sell his practice. He yearned too for the comradeship of the trenches and of prison. He was unable to find it.

Small was the ex-prisoners' voice in post-war Britain. A British Association of Ex-Prisoners of War established in 1926 organized a dignified march of six hundred former PoWs to the Cenotaph. A wreath was laid by the mother of a soldier who died in captivity. For the best part of a decade the Association marched yearly to the Cenotaph, issued newsletters and arranged social events, before it faded away for lack of members. Clubs of officer escapers fared a little better; a reunion of former Holzminden prisoners at Hotel Cecil on the Strand in December 1927 led to the formation of the Holzminden Dining Club five years later; a dinner in 1938 at Ye Olde Cheshire Cheese in Fleet Street to celebrate the twentieth anniversary of the tunnel breakout was enlivened by some wag sending a spoof telegram which read: GREETINGS STOP I KNOW DAMN ALL ABOUT YOU AND YOUR DINNER STOP CHARLES NIEMEYER STOP. (The same year saw the release of a film based on the Holzminden escape, *Who Goes Next?*, directed by Maurice Elvey.) In turn, the Holzminden Dining Club became the Officer Prisoners of War Dining Club, its aim 'to maintain the fellowship formed by Officer Prisoners of War during captivity'.[23]

*

They were soldiers once, and young. They were soldiers twice, the second time middle-aged. The prisoners of the Great War did better for Britain than Britain did for them. Many of the prisoners came back in 1939 for the second round against Germany, still imbued with the same love of country and of freedom. And yes, there was the chance to expunge the stigma of surrender by honourable service again. Archer Cust worked for the Special Operations Executive, Surrey Dane commanded 110 Manchester Field Regiment, Royal Artillery (TA), A.J. Evans – an England cricketer after the war – joined the Royal Air Force Volunteer Reserve, James Farrant was a Home Guard officer, Rifleman Hall joined the Home Guard, Jocelyn Hardy led a detachment of Churchill's secret army, 'the Auxilliaries', Duncan Grinnell-Milne re-joined the RAF and flew

Wellington bombers in North Africa, Holzminden escaper David 'Munshi' Gray also rejoined the RAF, as did Marcus Kaye, while Douglas Lyall Grant was officer-in-charge of a troopship at the Sicily landings . . . the list goes on . . .

Major Jack Poole, King's Royal Rifle Corps, fought at Calais in 1940, where he was captured, giving him the unpleasant but unique perspective of imprisonment in Germany in both World Wars:

> The only Germans [in WWII] who showed us any humaneness were those who had been prisoners in England during the First War. They all admitted they had been well fed and correctly treated and many of them were ashamed at our condition.[24]

With admirable perspicacity, the War Office appointed Henry Antrobus Cartwright military attaché in Berne. The post was truly cover for Cartwright's role as an M19 officer charged with organizing the evasions and escapes of British servicemen. Among those he welcomed through the door of the Berne Embassy was Lieutenant Airey Neave, the first Briton to escape from Colditz. Neave knew exactly who Cartwright was, because he had read Harrison and Cartwright's epic escape memoir, *Within Four Walls*: 'As a small boy, I had read it with romantic pleasure, and it played a great part in forming my philosophy of escape.'[25]

Neave's fellow absconder from Colditz, Major Pat Reid, had also been inspired by Cartwright and Harrison's escape memoirs:

> When I was a boy at school I read with avidity three of the greatest escape books of the First World War. They were *The Road to En-Dor* by EH Jones, *The Escape Club* by AJ Evans, and *Within Four Walls* by HA Cartwright and MCC Harrison. These three epics lived long in my memory, so that when the fortunes of war found me a prisoner in an enemy land the spirit enshrined in them urged me to follow the example of their authors.[26]

A golden rope of experience connected the two generations of escapers. Even in publishing their memoirs the great escapers of the First World War were of service to their country.

It fell to Malcolm Hay to provide the most touching, and the most useful of services by the former *Kriegsgefangene*. Hay devoted himself to helping those taken prisoner 1939–45 and their families. He founded the Returned Prisoners of War Association, and established and edited a monthly journal, *Prisoners of War News*. His North-East Prisoner of War Appeal raised a whopping £257,000.[27]

Hay could guess a little of what life was like for the PoWs in Nazi camps.

He'd had a taste of captivity under a German reactionary regime himself.

ENVOI

'Sonnet'

COMRADES of risk and rigour long ago,
Who have done battle under honour's name,
Hoped (living or shot) some meed of fame,
And wooed bright Danger for a thrilling kiss,
Laugh, oh laugh well, that we have come to this!

Laugh, oh laugh loud, all ye who long
Adventure found in gallant company!
Safe in stagnation, laugh, laugh bitterly,
While on this filthiest backwater of Time's flow
Drift we and rot, till something set us free!

Laugh like old men with senses atrophied,
Heeding no Present, to the Future dead,
Nodding quite foolish by the warm fireside
And seeing no flame, but only in the red
And flickering embers, pictures of the past:
Life like a cinder fading black at last.

Lieutenant F.W. Harvey, Gloucestershire Regiment.
Prisoner of War 1915–18

ACKNOWLEDGEMENTS

First and foremost my thanks go to Julian Alexander of LAW and Alan Samson of Weidenfeld & Nicolson for their unstinting commitment and support. And thank you to all the following for help, information, and morale boosts, all well above and beyond the call of duty: Annie Robertson, Hamish Robertson, Figgie Robertson, Joyce Lewis, Nikki Trow, John Ward, Anita and Graham of anitabooks, the Staff of the London Library, the staff of the Imperial War Museum, the staff of the Brotherton Library at the University of Leeds, Betty and Alan Jessop, Kathryn and Nicholas Fox (thanks for the amulet), Dave Stowe, Daniel Kirmatzis (who generously shared the research for his forthcoming book on Emanuel School alumni), Jonathan Ball, Charlotte Zeepvat, Anthony Benn, Conor Reeves, Stephen Cooper, Vera Markova, Leslie Peach, Amanda Jennings, @FathersShed, Mike Edwards, Stephen Barker, Paul Reed, Peter Doyle, Geoff Sullivan, Simon Batten at Bloxham School, Anthony Seldon at Wellington College, Mark Banning, Michael Webb (for pointing out that the Brown RFC who crashed with Knight was *that* Brown, of later Alcock & Brown fame), Mike Stockbridge, Chris Turner, Dawn Monks, the F.W. Harvey Society, Andy Arnold, Paul Hilferink, Dan Jackson, Mary Freeman, @MyLadyCaroline, Alex Tijhuis, David Alton, Rossiter Books, Amarpal Singh Sidhu, @TrufflesP, David Underdown, Andy Keech. Also to Charlotte Heathcote and Nicole Carmichael at the *Sunday Express*, plus of course to Ben Clark, Alice Saunders, and Petra Lewis at LAW, and Lucinda McNeile at Weidenfeld & Nicolson. As ever, I am indebted to my family: Tris (for essential research), Freda and Penny. To the latter, really, should go any praise due.

Lastly, I dedicate this book to the memory of Lieutenant H.W. Medlicott, Captain Joseph Walter and Captain William Morritt. Escapers all. Heroes all.

BIBLIOGRAPHY

Unpublished Sources

National Archives, London: Pte George Agnew WO 161/98/640; Pte Peter Allan WO 161/98/80; Pte Bailes WO 161/98/164; Pte R.S. Baillie WO 161/99/80; Cpt D. Baird-Douglas WO 161/95/63; Cpt Bell WO 161/96/38; Cpt Alan Binnie WO 161/96/42; Cpl R. Burrows FO 383/161; Pte W. Butcher FO 383/161; Pte Chesterton FO 383/161; Pte E. Caine FO 383/161; Pte G. Cox FO 383/161; Pte Charles Davis WO 161/98/80; Pte Robert Evans WO 161/98/80; Flt Lt L.D. Dalzell McLean RN WO 161/96/47; Pte R. Dempsey FO 383/161; Lt T.J. Dobson RNVR WO 161/95/62; Pte W. Elvin FO 383/161; Cpl Alexander Fyfe WO 161/98/1 and WO 161/98/287; Cpt I.M. Henderson WO 161/95/64; Cpt T. Kidson Allsop W 161/96/57; Sgt A.J. Parsons WO 161/100/558; Pte Ernest Thornton WO 161/100/399; Cpl William Walker nr; 2/Lt Ernest Warburton WO 161/96/39; Pte Tulloch WO 161/100/199; Cpt A. Vidal, WO 161/97/30; Lt C.E. Wallis WO 161/91/11; Pte William Wilding WO 161/98/80; Pte A. Wood WO 161/100/199; Lord James Murray FO 383/275; Imperial Foreign Office (Germany) communication re Borsig munitions works FO 383/275

Great War Archive, University of Oxford: 2/Lt C.E. Carr, 2/Lt F. Smith, Pte F. Alexander

Imperial War Museum: N.E. Tyndale-Biscoe 84/9/1, Lieutenant F.N. Insoll 67/392/1, Captain Douglas Lyall Grant 73/175/1, Lieutenant N.A. Birks 73/182/1, J.N. Dykes 76/171/1, Corporal A. Speight 76/206/1, Lieutenant Colonel A.E. Haig 82/35/1, Lieutenant W.C. Blain 83/11/1, Captain P.H.B. Lyon 86/62/1, Lieutenant-Colonel R.J. Clarke 87/62/1, W.T. Kendall 13853, F. Bollen 20332, W.F. Newton, 14135, H.E. Moore 14509, G.D.J. McMurtrie 6796, M.S. Esler 378, Misc. 15/316 (*A Parting Word*), T.C. Rainbird 02/39/1, J.H. Alcock 96/29/1, S.W. Poulton 88/57/1, C.E. Green 83/50/1, W.G. Allen 10875

Liddle Archives, Brotherton Library, University of Leeds: G. & S. Rain,

V.C. Coombs, Reginald Gough, Kenneth Hooper, Richard Milward, H.C. Pattman, George Wells (unpublished ts memoir, 'Recollections of Prisoner of War', 1919), R.H. Harper, Harold Gray, Marcus Kaye (Kaiser).

Mitchell Library, New South Wales, Australia: H. Baker

Published Sources

Magazines, Newspapers, and Journals

Anonymous, 'The Lighter Side of Kriegsgefangenschaft', *Twenty Years After*, ed. Maj. Gen. Sir Ernest Swinton (n.d.)

Anonymous, 'Broomwood Road Prisoner of War: Shot in a Guard Room', *South Western Star*, 26 April 1918

Joan Beaumont, 'Rank, Privilege and Prisoners of War', *War & Society*, May 1985, Vol. 1, No. 1

'Captivus', 'Officers' Prisons in Germany', *Journal of the Royal United Services Institute*, 63, 1918

Brian K. Feltman, 'Tolerance as a Crime? The British Treatment of German Prisoners of War on the Western Front, 1914–1918', *War in History*, Nov. 2010, Vol. 17, No. 4

Niall Ferguson, 'Prisoner Taking and Prisoner Killing in the Age of Total War: Towards a Political Economy of Military Defeat', *War in History*, April 2004, Vol. 11, No. 2

Heather Jones, 'The Final Logic of Sacrifice? Violence in German Prisoner of War Labour Companies in 1918', *The Historian* 65, 2006

Edmund King, '"Books are more to me than food": British Prisoners of War as Readers, 1914–1918', *Books History*, 16, 2013

S.P. MacKenzie, 'The Ethics of Escape: British Officer POWs in the First World War', *War in History*, 2008, Vol. 15, No. 1

Mark Spoerer, 'The Mortality of Allied Prisoners of War and Belgian Civilian Deportees in German Captivity During the First World War: A Reappraisal of the Effects of Forced Labour', *Population Studies*, 60, 2, 2006

Ross Wilson, 'The Burial of the Dead: The British Army on the Western Front, 1914–18', *War & Society*, Vol. 31, Issue 2012

Government and Official Publications

Defence Department, *How the Germans Treated Australian Prisoners of War* (Melbourne, 1919)

Foreign Office, *Reports on the Treatment by the Germans of British Prisoners and Natives in German East Africa* (London, 1917)

Government Committee on Treatment by the Enemy of British Prisoners of War, *Report on the Typhus Epidemic at Gardelegen* (London, 1916)

Government Committee on Treatment by the Enemy of British Prisoners of War, *The Horrors of Wittenberg: Official Report to the British Government.*[2d ed.] (London, 1916)

Government Committee on Treatment by the Enemy of British Prisoners of War, *Report on the Treatment by the Enemy of British Prisoners of War Behind the Firing Lines in France and Belgium*, with two appendices (London, 1918)

Government Committee on Treatment by the Enemy of British Prisoners of War, *Report on the Transport of British Prisoners of War to Germany, August–December, 1914* (London, 1918)

Government Committee on Treatment by the Enemy of British Prisoners of War, *Report on the Employment in Coal and Salt Mines of the British Prisoners of War in Germany* (London, 1918)

London Gazette (Supplement), 16 December 1919

London Gazette (Supplement), 30 January 1920

National War Aims Committee, *Prisoners of Prussia: Official Report on the Treatment of British Prisoners of War by the Enemy during 1918* (London, 1918)

Parliamentary Papers Cd 1450, Vol. 12, *German War Trials Report* (London, 1921)

Parliamentary Papers, Cd 9101, *Report on the Treatment by the Germans of Prisoners of War Taken During the Spring Offensive of 1918* (London, 1918)

Royal Commission on Illegal Warfare Claims for Return of Sequestered Property in Necessitous Cases, *Report of the Commission on Reparations, 1930–1931: Maltreatment of Prisoners of War* (Ottawa, 1932)

War Office, *Statistics of the Military Effort of the British Empire during the Great War, 1914–1920* (London, 1922)

Audio

Helen Macdonald (wr), *Through the Wire*, BBC Radio 4, 30 April 2012

Film

Maurice Elvey (dir), *Who Goes Next?*, 1938
Jean Renoir (dir), *La Grande Illusion*, 1937

Books

J.R. Ackerley (Intro. and ed.), *Tunnelling to Freedom* (Mineola, 2004) [Originally published as *Escapers All*, 1932.]
——*My Father and Myself* (London, 1968)
Charles Altschul, *German Militarism and Its German Critics* (Washington, 1918)
Peter Anderson, *I, That's Me: Escape from German Prison Camp and Other Adventures* (Ottawa, n.d.)
H.C. Armstrong (ed.), *Escape!* (New York, 1935)
Max Arthur, *We Will Remember Them: Voices from the Aftermath of the Great War* (London, 2009)
——*The Road Home* (London, 2009)
L.J. Austin, *My Experience as a German Prisoner* (London, 1915)
Jack Beatty, *The Lost History of 1914* (London, 2012)
S. Bedford, *Experiences of as Prisoner of War, Munster II* (Kingston-on-Thames, 1932)
Henri Beland, *My Three Years in a German Prison* (Toronto, 1919)
Anthony Bird, *Gentleman, We Stand and Fight: Le Cateau, 1914* (Ramsbury, 2008)
Harry C.W. Bishop, *A Kut Prisoner* (London, 1920)
Walter Bloem, *The Advance from Mons: The Experiences of a German Infantry Officer* (Solihull, 2004)
Anthony Boden, *F.W. Harvey: Soldier, Poet* (Stroud, 1998)
R.C. Bond, *Prisoners Grave and Gay* (Edinburgh, 1934)
Joanna Bourke, *An Intimate History of Killing,* (New York, 2000)
A.A. Bowman, *Sonnets from a Prison Camp* (London, 1919)
G.W. Boyce, *A Prisoner of War, and How I was Treated* (Sydney, 1919)
Fred Breckon, *In the Hands of the Hun* (Fort Francis, 1919)

Tom Bridges, *Alarms and Excursions* (London, 1938)

Malcolm Brown, *The Imperial War Museum Book of 1918: Year of Victory* (London, 1999)

Percy Brown, *Round the Corner* (London, 1934)

J.A.L. Caunter, *13 Days: The Chronicle of an Escape from a German Prison* (London, 1918)

Hugh Cimino, *Behind the Prison Bars in Germany* (London, 1915)

A.H.F. Clarke, *To Kiel on the German Raider Wolf and After* (Ceylon, 1920)

George Herbert Clarke, *A Treasury of War Poetry* (New York, 1917)

Israel Cohen, *The Ruhleben Prison Camp: A Record of Nineteen Months' Internment* (New York, 1917)

Arthur Conan Doyle, *The Story of British Prisoners* (London, 1915)

Georges Connes, *A POW's Memoir of the First World War; The Other Ordeal* (Oxford, 2004)

Aidan Crawley, *Escape from Germany* (London, 2001)

W. Ambrose Cull, *At all Costs* (Melbourne, 1919)

L.G.A. Cust, *From Ploegsteert to Graudenz: The Story of a Prisoner-of-War* (London, 1919)

Christopher Danby, *Some Reminiscences of a Prisoner of War in Germany* (London, 1918)

Alfred T. Davies, *Student Captives: An Account of the Work of the British Prisoners of War Book Scheme (Educational)* (Leicester, 1917)

Carl P. Dennett, *Prisoners of the Great War: Authoritative Statement of Conditions in the Prison Camps of Germany* (Boston, 1919)

Wilhelm Doegen, *Kriegsgefangene Völker,* Band 1, Berlin, 1921

Robert V. Dolbey, *A Regimental Surgeon in War and Prison* (London, 1917)

Captain A. Donaldson, *The Amazing Cruise of the German Raider* Wolf (Sydney 1941)

J. Harvey Douglas, *Captured: Sixteen Months a Prisoner of War* (Toronto, 1918)

J.C. Dunn, *The War the Infantry Knew* (London, 1987)

H.G. Durnford, *The Tunnellers of Holzminden* (Cambridge, 1920)

Ralph E. Ellinwood, *Behind the German Lines* (New York, 1920)

Wallace Ellison, *Escaped!* (Edinburgh, 1918)

A.J. Evans, *The Escaping Club* (New York, 1922)

—— *Escape and Liberation* (London, 1945)

Herbert C. Fooks, *Prisoners of War* (Federalsburg, Md., 1924)

A. Forder, *In Brigands' Hands and Turkish Prisons 1914–1918* (London, 1920)

Richard Garrett, *POW: The Uncivil Face of War* (Newton Abbot, 1981)

James W. Gerard, *My Four Years in Germany* (New York, 1917)

Arthur Gibbons, *A Guest of the Kaiser* (Toronto, 1919)

H.G. Gilliland, *My German Prisons* (New York, 1919)

Arthur Green, *The Story of a Prisoner of War* (London, 1916)

H. Gregory, *Never Again: A Diary of the Great War* (London, 1934)

Duncan Grinnell-Milne, *An Escaper's Log* (London, 1926)

Malcolm Hall, *In Enemy Hands: A British Territorial Soldier in Germany 1915–1919* (Stroud, 2002)

Frank Hallihan, *In the Hands of the Enemy* (Australia, c. 1922)

Geoffrey Harding, *Escape Fever* (London, 1932)

J.L. Hardy, *I Escape!* (New York, 1928)

M.C.C. Harrison and H.A. Cartwright, *Within Four Walls* (Harmondsworth, 1940)

F.W. Harvey, *Gloucestershire Friends: Poems from a German Prison Camp* (London, 1917)

—— *Comrades in Captivity* (London, 1920)

M.V. Hay, *Wounded and A Prisoner of War by an Exchanged Officer* (Edinburgh, 1916)

Charles Hennebois, *In German Hands: The Diary of a Severely Wounded Prisoner* (New York, 1917)

H.E. Hervey, *Cage-Birds* (London, 1940)

Thomas James Higgins, *Tommy at Gommecourt* (Leek, 2006)

J.A. Sillitoe Hill, *The Front Line and Beyond It: A Diary of 1917–18* (1930)

Uta Hinz, *Gefangen in Grossen Krieg: Kriegsgefangenschaft in Deutschland 1914–1921* (Essen, 2006)

Frederick Hodges, *Men of 18 in 1918* (Ilfracombe, 1988)

Conrad Hoffman, *In the Prison Camps of Germany: A Narrative of 'Y' Service among Prisoners of War* (New York, 1920)

Richard Holmes, *Acts of War* (London, 2004)

—— *Tommy* (London, 2004)

Charles F. Horne (ed.), *The Great Events of the Great War*, Vol. 4 (New York, 1920)

Hugh Horner, *An Australian Prisoner of War in the Hands of the Hun* (Perth, 1920)

Brian Horrocks, *Escape to Action* (New York, 1961)

Laurence Housman, *War Letters of Fallen Englishmen* (London, 1930)

Keble Howard, *The Quality of Mercy: How British Prisoners of War were Taken to Germany in 1914* (London, 1918)

Robert Jackson, *The Prisoners: 1914–18* (London, 1989)

E.H. Jones, *The Road to En-Dor* (London, 1922)

M.A.B. Johnston and K.D. Yearsley, *450 Miles to Freedom* (Edinburgh, 1919)

Heather Jones, *Violence Against Prisoners of War in the First World War: Britain, France and Germany, 1914–1920* (Cambridge, 2011)

Ernst Jünger, *Storm of Steel* (London, 1929)

Eric A. Keith, *My Escape from Germany* (London, 1919)

Hugh Kingsmill, *Behind Both Lines* (London, 1930)

G.F. Knight, *'Brother Bosch': An Airman's Escape from Germany* (London, 1919)

Donald Laird, *Prisoner-Five-One-Eleven* (Toronto, 1919)

Amanda Laugesen, *Boredom is the Enemy: The Intellectual and Imaginative Lives of Australian Soldiers in the Great War and Beyond* (Farnham, 2012)

Joseph Lee, *A Captive in Carlsruhe and other German Prison Camps* (London, 1920)

V.I. Lenin, 'Zabern', *Lenin Collected Works*, Vol. 19 (Moscow, 1977)

Jon E. Lewis, *True World War 1 Stories* (London, 2001)

Karl Liebknecht, *Militarismus und Antimilitarismus* (Leipzig, 1907)

Brian MacArthur (ed.), *Voices from the First World War* (London, 2008)

Frank MacDonald, *The Kaiser's Guest* (London, 1918)

Clifford Milton Markle, *A Yankee Prisoner in Hunland* (New Haven, 1920)

L.H. Marshall, *Experiences in German Gaols* (Liverpool, 1915)

Fred McMullen and Jack Evans, *Out of the Jaws of Hunland* (Toronto, 1918)

Dwight R. Messimer, *Escape* (Annapolis, 1994)

—— *Escape from Villingen, 1918* (College Station, 2000)

R.R. Money, *Flying and Soldiering* (1936)

J.H. Morgan, *Assize of Arms* (London, 1945)

Desmond Morton, *Silent Battles: Canadian Prisoners of War in Germany, 1914–1919* (Toronto, 1992)

E.O. Mousley, *Secrets of a Kuttite* (London, 1921)

Michael Moynihan, *Black Bread and Barbed Wire: Prisoners in the First World War* (London, 1978)

Claud Mullins, *The Leipzig Trials: An Account of the War Criminals' Trials and a Study of German Mentality* (London, 1921)

Benjamin Muse, *The Memoirs of a Swine in the Land of Kultur, or, How It Felt to Be a Prisoner of War* (Durham, NC, 1919)

Una Pope-Hennessy, *Map of the Main Prison Camps in Germany and Austria* (London, n.d.)

Gilbert Nobbs, *On the Right of the British Line* (New York, 1917)

Pat O'Brien, *Outwitting the Hun* (New York, 1918)

Benjamin G. O'Rorke, *In the Hands of the Enemy* (London, 1916)

William O'Sullivan Molony, *Prisoners & Captives* (London, 1933)

Edward Page, *Escaping from Germany* (London, 1919)

Peter Parker, *Ackerley* (London, 1989)

George Pearson, *The Escape of a Princess Pat* (Toronto, 1918)

G.W. Phillimore, *Recollections of a Prisoner of War* (London, 1930)

H.P. Picot, *The British Interned in Switzerland* (London, 1917)

Arthur Ponsonby, *Falsehood in Wartime: Propaganda Lies of the First World War* (London, 1928)

J.S. Poole, *Undiscovered Ends* (London, 1957)

Pierre Purseigle (ed.), *Warfare And Belligerence: Perspectives in First World War Studies* (Leiden, 2005)

Alon Rachamimov, *POWs and the Great War: Captivity on the Eastern Front* (London, 2002)

P.R. Reid, *The Colditz Story* (London, 1952)

David Rorie, *A Medico's Luck in the War* (Aberdeen, 1929)

Ivan Rossiter, *In Kultured Kaptivity: Life and Death in Germany's Prison Camps* (Indianpolis, 1919)

Paul Routledge, *Public Servant, Secret Agent: The Elusive Life and Violent Death of Airey Neave* (London, 2012)

John Rugg, *A British Soldier's Life As a Prisoner of War* (Stockton-on-Tees, 1915)

Sibylle Scheipers (ed.), *Prisoners in War* (Oxford, 2010)

T.V. Scudamore, *Lighter Sides in the Life of a Prisoner of War* (Aldershot, 1937)

M.C. Simmons and Nellie L. McClung, *Three Times and Out* (Boston, 1918)

R.B. Speed, *Prisoners, Diplomats and the Great War: A Study in the Diplomacy of Captivity* (New York, 1990)

Thomas Stewart, *Nine Months a Prisoner of War* (London, c. 1930)

John Still, *Poems in Captivity* (London, 1919)

—— *A Prisoner in Turkey* (London, 1920)

Claude Templer, *Poems & Imaginings* (Paris, 1920)

Cecil Thomas, *They Also Served: The Experiences of a Private Soldier as Prisoner of War in German Camps and Mines, 1916–1918* (London, c. 1939)

John C. Thorn, *Three Years a Prisoner in Germany* (Vancouver, 1919)

W.A. Tucker, *The Lousier War* (London, 1974)

Bernd Ulrich and Benjamin Ziemann (trans. Christine Brocks), *German Soldiers in the Great War: Letters and Eyewitness Accounts* (Barnsley, 2010)

Jonathan F. Vance, *Objects of Concern: Canadian Prisoners of War through the Twentieth Century* (Vancouver, 1994)

C.B. Vandeleur, 'German Mistreatment of Prisoners', *The Great Events of the Great War*, Charles F. Horne (ed.), Vol. IV (New York, 1920)

Richard van Emden, *Prisoners of the Kaiser: The Last POWs of the Great War* (Barnsley, 2000)

—— *The Soldiers' War: The Great War Through Veterans' Eyes* (London, 2008)

—— *Tommy's Ark* (London, 2011)

A.L. Vischer, *Barbed Wire Disease: A Psychological Study of the Prisoner of War* (London, 1919)

Ann Warin (ed.), *Dear Girl, I Escaped: Experiences of the Great War 1914–18* (Bristol, 1989)

Ernest Warburton, *Behind Boche Bars* (London, 1920)

Andre Warnod (trans. M. Jourdain), *Prisoner of War* (London, 1916)

Alec Waugh, *Prisoners of Mainz* (London, 1919)

—— *The Early Years of Alec Waugh* (London, 1962)

Edward Wigney, *Guests of the Kaiser: Prisoners of War of the Canadian Expeditionary Force, 1915–1918* (Ottawa, 2008)

Basil Willey, *Spots of Time* (New York, 1965)

—— 'A Schoolboy in the War', *Promise of Greatness,* George A. Panichas (ed.) (New York, 1968)

Samuel R. Williamson & Peter Pastor (eds), *Essays on World War I: Origins and Prisoners of War* (New York, 1983)

Barry Winchester, *Beyond the Tumult* (London, 1971)

Neville Wylie, *Barbed Wire Diplomacy: Britain, Germany, and the Politics of Prisoners of War 1939–1945* (Oxford, 2010)

John Yarnall, *Barbed Wire Disease: British and German Prisoners of War, 1914–19* (Stroud, 2011)

Websites

www.purley.eu/H142P/P354-05.pdf

http://www.rhf.org.uk/Books/Wittenberg.pdf

www.vlib.us/medical/pow/pozieres.htm

www.dublin-fusliers.com/Pows/dubliner-pows.html

www.bbc.co.uk/history/worldwars/wwone/humanfacesofwar_gallery_07.shtml

www.worcestershireregiment.com/wr.php?main=inc/pow_tucker

http://www.fam.medlicott.uk.com/HEM_files/7_HWMedlicott.html

http://www.canadiangreatwarproject.com/searches/soldierDetail.asp?Id=80789

http://www.worcestershireregiment.com/wr.php?main=inc/vc_w_l_robinson_page1

www.westernfrontassociation.com/great-war-on-land/78-cas-med/800-pows-western-front.html

ENDNOTES

Prologue

1 'Thomas Perry' is an amalgam of several British escapers of the 1914–18 vintage.

Introduction

1 See Alon Rachamimov, *POWs and the Great War: Captivity on the Eastern Front*, 2002, pp. 1–5; also Heather Jones, *Violence Against Prisoners of War in the First World War: Britain, France and Germany, 1914–1920*, 2011, pp. 319–26.

2 Determining the exact number of British PoWs taken by the Germans and their allies is fraught with difficulty; this is the official figure given by the War Office's *Statistics of the Military Effort of the British Empire during the Great War, 1914–1920*. The figure includes the Royal Navy and Royal Naval Division. The official War Office figure for PoWs from Britain and Empire combined in all theatres is 192,848. On top of these figures there were upwards of 115,000 French, British and Empire PoWs who were unregistered by Germany and her allies.

3 The overall death rate for Britons on the battlefields of the Great War was 12 per cent.

4 Rachamimov, pp. 1–5.

5 The British Association of Ex-Prisoners of War established in 1926 lasted a mere decade.

6 Quoted in Michael Moynihan, *Black Bread and Barbed Wire: Prisoners in the First World War*, 1978, p. 157.

7 R.B. Speed in his *Prisoners, Diplomats and the Great War: A Study in the Diplomacy of Captivity* repeats the same canard of equivalence in treatment, viz, 'Likewise the conditions to which German prisoners in France were subject would be similar to those of British prisoners in Germany', p. 186.

8 Arthur Ponsonby, *Falsehood in War-Time: Propaganda Lies of the First World War*, 1928, p. 22.

9 See page 285.

10 Among the notable British exceptions are to be counted Michael Moynihan, *Black Bread and Barbed Wire: Prisoners in the First World War*, 1978; Robert Jackson, *The Prisoners: 1914–18*, 1989; Richard van Emden, *Prisoners of the Kaiser: The Last POWs of the Great War*, 2000; Heather Jones, *Violence Against Prisoners of War in the First World War: Britain, France and Germany, 1914–1920*, 2011; John Yarnall, *Barbed Wire Disease: British and German Prisoners of War, 1914–19*, 2011; Neil Hanson, *Escape from Germany*, 2011.

11 Joan Beaumont, 'Rank, Privilege and Prisoners of War', *War & Society*, May 1985, Vol. 1, No. 1, p. 67.

12 Neil Hanson, p. 24.

13 See *Statistics of the Military Effort of the British Empire during the Great War, 1914–1920*, pp. 329. The figure for combined British and Empire successful escapes from Germany is 573.

14 Invariably, the Germans treated 'colonial' PoWs as though they were British PoWs, and generally the Canadians, Newfoundlanders, Australians, Indians et al. described themselves as 'British'. A significant number of volunteers from Empire were actually born in Britain; Princess Patricia's Canadian Light Infantry was raised from British expatriates living in Canada.

15 The number of British PoW escape attempts in World War I literature is woefully underestimated; Dwight R. Messimer in *Escape from Villingen, 1918*, claims that 500 British officers and other ranks made escape attempts. This figure is only 8 more than the 492 British soldiers and sailors who actually did make escapes to neutral countries from all theatres.

16 In *Acts of War*, 1985, Richard Holmes estimates the chances of surviving close-quarters fighting and then surrendering as no more than 50:50. This is too pessimistic a figure, at least for the Great War; anecdotal evidence suggests that prisoners surrendering on the Western Front, from whatever side, were more likely than not to be granted quarter.

17 Hague Convention number IV, *Convention Respecting the Laws and*

Customs of War on Land, October 18, 1907, http://avalon.law.yale.edu/20th_century/hague04.asp

18 Carl Dennett, *Prisoners of the Great War: Authoritative Statement of Conditions in the Prison Camps of Germany,* 1919, p. 13.

19 *Statistics of the Military Effort of the British Empire during the Great War, 1914–1920,* p. 329. This is the figure for British servicemen, including the Royal Navy and Royal Naval Division, who died in Germany and occupied France and Belgium. The figure for PoW fatalities for British and Empire PoWs combined in Germany/France is 12,425. Of these, 447 were officers, and 11,978 other ranks.

20 See Heather Jones, *Violence Against Prisoners of War in the First World War: Britain, France and Germany, 1914–1920,* 2011, p. 21.

21 Alec Waugh, *Prisoners of Mainz,* 1919, p. 142.

22 Frank MacDonald, *The Kaiser's Guest,* 1918, p. 84.

23 Government Committee on the Treatment by the Enemy of British Prisoners of War: *Report on the Employment in Coal and Salt Mines of the British Prisoners of War in Germany,* 1918, p. 2.

24 Peter Anderson, *I, That's Me: Escape from German Prison Camp and Other Adventures,* n.d., p. 166.

25 See p. 202. Medlicott was born in 1893.

26 See Robert Jackson, *The Prisoners: 1914–18,* 1989, passim.

1 In the Bag: Capture

1 M.V. Hay, *Wounded and A Prisoner of War by an Exchanged Officer,* 1916, p. 68.

2 Hay, p. 70.

3 See Wilhelm Doegen, *Kriegsgefangene Völker,* Band 1, 1921, p. 28.

4 Doegen offers an approximate guide to the rate of prisoner-taking, p. 28.

5 See David Payne, 'British Prisoners of War on the Western Front in the Great War', www.westernfrontassociation.com/great-war-on-land/78-cas-med/800-pows-western-front.html

6 All Canadians taken prisoner were, regardless of rank, required to report on the circumstances of their surrender following repatriation.

7 A number of officers, NCOs and other ranks kept an unofficial note

of the their capture, including the number of wounded in their unit. Consistently this 'anecdotal' record shows up a wound rate of about one third among those taken captive throughout the course of the war with the wounds being considered sufficiently serious by their bearer to prevent further fighting. There is, however, no absolute and direct correlation between wound rates and surrender rates; Scottish regiments famously bled buckets and yet were among the least likely to 'Hände hoch'.

8 See Richard Holmes, *Tommy*, 2004, p. 537.

9 Thomas James Higgins, *Tommy at Gommecourt*, 2006, p. 83.

10 Alon Rachamimov, p. 5.

11 See Alan Kramer, 'Surrender of Soldiers in World War I' in *How Fighting Ends*, Holger Afflerbach and Hew Strachan (eds), 2012, p. 267.

12 Quoted in Malcolm Brown, *The Imperial War Museum Book of 1918: Year of Victory*, 1999, p. 47.

13 Richard Holmes, *Acts of War*, p. 380.

14 Quoted in Jon E. Lewis, *True World War 1 Stories*, 2001, p. 419.

15 A.A. Bowman, *Sonnets from a Prison Camp*, 1919, p. 10.

16 Quoted in Richard Van Emden, *The Soldier's War: The Great War Through Veterans' Eyes*, 2008, pp. 331–1.

17 See Anthony Bird, *Gentlemen, We Stand and Fight*, 2008, and Richard Holmes, *Acts of War*, 1985 for overviews on Mainwaring's infamous surrender.

18 Robert V. Dolbey, *A Regimental Surgeon in War and Prison*, 1917, pp. 117–18.

19 Quoted in John Sadler and Rosie Serdiville, *Tommy at War*, 2013, p. 317.

20 F.W. Harvey, *Comrades in Captivity*, 1920, p. 2.

21 Harvey, *ibid.*, p. 8.

22 Harvey, *ibid.*, p. 7.

23 Gilbert Nobbs, *On the Right of the British Line*, 1917, p. 115.

24 Nobbs, p. 30.

25 H.G. Durnford, *The Tunnellers of Holzminden*, 1920, p. 13.

26 W.A. Tucker, *The Lousier War*, 1974, p. 42.

27 Quoted in Richard van Emden, *Prisoners of the Kaiser*, 2000, p. 18.

28 Quoted in Jackson, p. 36.

29 Geoffrey Phillimore, *Recollections of a Prisoner of War*, 1930, p. 2.

30 W. Ambrose Cull, *At all Costs*, 1919, p. 90.

31 Quoted in van Emden, *Prisoners of the Kaiser*, p. 21.

32 The whole of the 28th Czech Division voluntarily surrendered to Russia in April 1915.

33 Alec Waugh, *Prisoners of Mainz*, p. 18.

34 See Holmes, *Acts of War*, pp. 380–1 on the 'postures' of surrender.

35 Richard Holmes, *Tommy*, 2004, p. 549.

36 Infamously, Joanna Bourke suggests that the killing of German captives by British soldiers was routine, and 'an important part of military expediency'; Niall Fergusson argues that the take-no-prisoners culture generated 'exaggerated impression on both sides of the risk of surrender' without which 'the war might conceivably have ended sooner, and not necessarily with German defeat'. Fergusson's claim is undermined by his own admission that 'there were relatively few such incidents in comparison with the thousands of captures which proceeded smoothly'. A dispassionate overview of the topic is offered by Brian K. Feltman, 'Tolerance as a Crime? The British Treatment of German Prisoners of War on the Western Front, 1914–1918', *War in History*, Nov. 2010, Vol. 17, No. 4.

37 In an unguarded moment at Bremerhaven docks, addressing troops about to depart to China to suppress the Boxer Rebellion, the Kaiser had urged them to conduct themselves 'like the Huns under their king Attila', adding: 'Should you encounter the enemy, he will be defeated! No quarter will be given! Prisoners will not be taken!' http://german-historydocs.ghi-dc.org/sub_document.cfm?document_id=755. There is also evidence that Prince Rupprecht of Bavaria ordered the whole Bavarian Army to take no uniformed prisoners in early 1915. See *The Story of British Prisoners*, Arthur Conan Doyle, p. 22. Neither was the Kaiser's regime squeamish about race-hatred; it had already committed genocide against the Herero in S.W. Africa. Conversely the British were remarkably loathe to sanction the killing of prisoners, with the *British Manual of Military Law* stating: 'A Commander may not put his prisoners to death because their presence retards his movements or diminishes his means of resistance by necessitating a large guard, or by reason of their consuming his supplies, or because it appears

certain that they will regain their liberty through an impending success of their own army.'

38 Jackson, p. 6.

39 Ernst Jünger, *Storm of Steel*, 1928, pp. 277–8.

40 Walter Bloem, *The Advance from Mons*, 2004. Bloem's autobiography was originally published in German as *Vormarsch*.

41 Quoted in Bernd Ulrich and Benjamin Ziemann (trans. Christine Brocks), *German Soldiers in the Great War: Letters and Eyewitness Accounts*, 2010, p. 65.

42 Heather Jones, *Violence Against Prisoners of War in the First World War*, p. 77.

43 Ibid.

44 On 19 August 1915 HMS *Baralong* sank U-27, and summarily shot the survivors as they swam towards and boarded a nearby merchantman. The justification offered by the captain of the *Baralong* for the killings was that he feared the German submariners would seize control of the merchant ship.

45 Cust, *From Ploegsteert to Graudenz*, 1919, p. 11.

46 Arthur Gibbons, *A Guest of the Kaiser*, 1919.

47 Quoted in Richard van Emden, *The Soldier' War*, 2008, p. 338.

48 Quoted in Richard Holmes, *Acts of War*, p. 382.

49 Quoted in Barry Winchester, *Beyond the Tumult*, 1971, p. 214.

50 Quoted in Holmes, *Acts of War*, p. 382.

51 Waugh, *Prisoners of Mainz*, p. 19.

52 Quoted in van Emden, *Prisoners of the Kaiser*, p. 39.

53 'His Scared Majesty, Chance, decided everything', Voltaire.

54 Quoted in Matthew Hall, *In Enemy Hands*, 2002, p. 45.

55 Quoted in Holmes, *Acts of War*, p. 383.

56 Ibid.

57 *General Annual Report of the British Army 1913–1919*, 1921, xx, Cmnd 1193.

58 See Lewis-Stempel, *Six Weeks*, p. 183 and passim. According to the *Statistics of the Military Effort of the British Empire during the Great War, 1914–1920* 6.59 per cent of officers imprisoned under the Kaiser died in captivity, compared to 7.09 per cent of other ranks. This figure excludes unregistered deaths of other ranks PoWs, which takes the

total percentage of other ranks' deaths to c.10.05 per cent. In 1922–3, the bodies of all British PoWs who died in Germany were taken from individual camp cemeteries and re-interred in four principal cemetries: Niederzwehren, Berlin South-Western, Cologne Southern, Kassel.

59 Quoted in Jackson, p. 9.

60 Higgins, p. 82.

61 Gibbons, pp. 120–1.

62 Ibid., p. 120.

63 Cpt I.M. Henderson TNA WO 161/95/64.

64 Cull, pp. 92–3.

65 Pte Ernest Thornton TNA WO/161/100/391.

66 Quoted in Desmond Morton, *Silent Battles: Canadian Prisoners of War in Germany, 1914–1919*, 1992, p. 31.

67 M.S. Esler IWM 378.

68 Quoted in Moynihan, p. 3.

69 Quoted in Lewis, pp. 413.

70 Quoted in John Sadler and Rosie Serdiville, *Tommy at War*, 2013, p. 318.

71 Milburn played for Ashington AFC; he was the patriarch of a footballing dynasty, the crowning jewels of which were grandsons Jackie and Bobby Charlton.

72 Tucker, p. 47.

73 Quoted in Moynihan, pp. 142–3.

74 See Ross Wilson, 'The Burial of the Dead: The British Army on the Western Front, 1914–18', *War & Society*, Vol. 31, Issue 1, 2012.

75 TNA WO 161/100/199.

76 Quoted in J.C. Dunn, *The War the Infantry Knew*, 1987, p. 244.

77 Defence Department (Australia), *How the Germans Treated Australian Prisoners of War*, 1919, p. 62.

78 A.A. Bowman, *Sonnets from a Prison Camp*, 1919, p. 8.

79 Gilliland, p. 9.

80 Joseph Lee, *A Captive at Carlsruhe and Other German Prison Camps*, 1920, p. 8.

81 Waugh, *Prisoners of Mainz*, p. 24.

82 Cpt I.M. Henderson TNA WO 161/95/64.

83 Defence Department (Australia), *How the Germans Treated Australian Prisoners of War*, p. 20.

84 For instance Sergeant Betts declared in his interview before the Government Committee on Treatment by the Enemy of British Prisoners of War, 27 May 1918, 'I, Betts, on the day of my capture [27 May 1918] saw some of our wounded, about five of them . . . killed by Germans, who bayonetted them'. TNA WO

85 2/Lt Ernest Warburton TNA WO 161/96/39.

86 Cpt T. Kidson Allsop WO 161/96/57.

87 See Morton, p. 34.

88 http:/www.ouc.ox.ac.uk/ww1lit/gwa/document/9066

89 C.E. Carr, Great War Archive, Oxford University.

90 J. Harvey Douglas, *Sixteen Months as a Prisoner of War*, 1918, pp. 41–52.

91 Tucker, p. 45.

92 Quoted in Moynihan, p. 143.

93 Quoted in van Emden, *Prisoners of the Kaiser*, p. 39.

94 Basil Willey, *Spots of Time*, 1965, p. 215.

95 RAMC doctors played an indispensable role in saving British and Allied lives in the typhus epidemics in the Kaiser's camps of 1915. See p. 79

96 Cpl Alexander Fyfe TNA WO 161/98/1.

97 Lt T.J. Dobson RNVR WO 161/95/62.

98 Gibbons, p. 131.

99 Horrocks, p. 17.

100 Waugh, *Prisoners of Mainz*, p. 19.

101 Quoted in Winchester, pp. 219–220.

102 Quoted in Morton, p. 37.

103 Higgins, p. 83.

104 Quoted in Hall, p. 22.

105 Richard van Emden, *The Soldiers' War*, p. 120.

106 H.E. Hervey, *Cage-Birds*, 1940, p. 8.

107 Tucker, p. 53.

108 Ibid., p. 52.

109 Quoted in van Emden, *Prisoners of the Kaiser*, p. 45.

110 MacDonald, p. 80. See note xv for the tendency of the Canadians and other 'colonials' to define themselves as 'British'.

111 Benjamin Muse, *The Memoirs of a Swine in the Land of Kultur, or, How It Felt to Be a Prisoner of War*, 1919, p. 7.

112 Tucker, p. 54.

113 G.W. Phillimore, *Recollections of a Prisoner of War*, 1930, p. 6.

114 Tucker, p. 54.

115 Muse, p. 7. George Wells was equally struck by the sight of an old man handing out barley sugars at Bohain to the Tommies marching past. When a venerable *madame* tried to give the passing milk to drink her bucket was 'kicked ruthlessly into the street' by the guards. See George Wells' 'Recollections of a Prisoner of War', unpublished ms, Liddle Collection, Brotherton Library.

116 Quoted in Winchester, p. 215.

117 The British accused the Germans holding a white flag of shooting at troops taking the surrender. Quoted in van Emden, *The Soldiers' War*, p. 55.

118 Tucker, p. 82.

119 Dolbey, p. 137.

120 G.D.J. McMurtrie IWM 6796.

121 Cust, p. 13.

122 Muse, p. 8.

123 Quoted in Moynihan, p. 4. One British soldier told the Government Committee on Treatment by the Enemy of British Prisoners of War that between 1,300–1,500 PoWs were housed in the church at Salome in April 1918. See *Prisoners of Prussia: Official Report on the Treatment of British Prisoners of War by the Enemy during 1918*, 1918, p. 2.

124 www.vlib.us/medical/pow/pozieres.htm

125 Higgins, p. 84.

126 Quoted in Lewis, pp. 413–14.

127 Ibid., p. 414.

128 Lee, p. 25.

129 By the end of the war British PoWs were convinced that almost every German guard could be 'bought'; see p. 243 for bribery of guards to secure escape kit.

130 Pte Ernest Thornton TNA WO 161/100/391.

131 Sgt S.W. Poulton IWM 88/57/1.

132 Quoted in Lewis, p. 419.

133 Ibid., p. 415.

134 Hervey, p. 9.

135 Knight, p. 34.

136 Quoted in Moynihan, p. 83.

137 Ibid.

138 Jack Poole, *Undiscovered Ends,* 1957, p. 18.

139 See note p. 290.

140 Harvey, *Comrades in Captivity,* p. 12.

141 Harvey, ibid., p. 14.

142 Harvey, *Gloucestershire Friends,* 1917, p. 31.

II The Iron Road: The Journey to the German Babylon

1 Quoted Charles F. Horne (ed.), *The Great Events of the Great War,* Vol. 4, 1920, pp. 406–7.

2 See Yarnall, p. 85.

3 Basil Willey, 'A Schoolboy in the War', *Promise of Greatness,* (ed.) George A. Panichas, 1968, p. 329.

4 Jack Evans and Fred McMullen, *Out of the Jaws of Hunland,* 1918, p. 40.

5 Quoted in Government Committee on Treatment by the Enemy of British Prisoners of War: *Report on the Transport of British Prisoners of War to Germany, August–December, 1914,* 1918, p. 12.

6 Quoted in Moynihan, p. 4.

7 A.J. Evans, *The Escaping Club,* p. 10.

8 Quoted in van Emden, *Prisoners of the Kaiser,* p. 47.

9 Quoted in Winchester, p. 216.

10 Heather Jones, *Violence Against Prisoners of War in the First World War,* p. 59.

11 See Yarnall, p. 85.

12 W.F. Chambers, a signalman with 13th Battalion Canadian Expeditionary Force, spent four days and nights travelling, during which his ration was one piece of bread and one or two cups of coffee per day. See Morton, p. 40.

13 Hay, p. 190.

14 Defence Department (Australia), *How the Germans Treated Australian Prisoners of War,* p. 50.

15 Cull, pp. 107–8.

16 Cpt I.M. Henderson WO 161/95/64.

17 Letter in author's collection.

18 See W.S. Baer 'The Treatment of Chronic Osteomyelitis with the Maggot (Larva of the Blow Fly)', *Journal of Bone and Joint Surgery*, 1931.

19 The instances of British troops dying on the trains east for lack of medical attention are numerous; a private in Peters' carriage bled to death for want of proper dressings in November 1914.

20 Anderson, p. 85.

21 Lt C.E. Wallis TNA WO 161/95/61. Wallis had also been imprisoned with what the Germans called 'nigger prisoners'; French Caucasian officers were housed with German officers.

22 Keble Howard, *The Quality of Mercy*, 1918, pp. 4–5.

23 Quoted in Government Committee on Treatment by the Enemy of British Prisoners of War: *Report on the Transport of British Prisoners of War to Germany, August–December, 1914*, 1918, p. 12.

24 TNA 161/96/57.

25 TNA WO 161/95/62.

26 Quoted in John Sadler and Rosie Serdiville, p. 313.

27 Page, p. 40.

28 L.J. Austin, *My Experience as a German Prisoner*, 1915, p. 37.

29 Heather Jones, *Violence Against Prisoners of War in the First World War*, p. 60.

30 Quoted in Government Committee on Treatment by the Enemy of British Prisoners of War: *Report on the Transport of British Prisoners of War to Germany, August–December, 1914*, 1918, p. 12.

31 Gibbons, p. 153.

32 Gilliland, pp. 22–3.

33 Quoted in Government Committee on Treatment by the Enemy of British Prisoners of War: *Report on the Transport of British Prisoners of War to Germany, August–December, 1914*, 1918, p. 12.

34 Quoted in Government Committee on Treatment by the Enemy of British Prisoners of War: *Report on the Transport of British Prisoners of War to Germany, August–December, 1914*, 1918, p. 42.

35 Howard, p, 15.

36 Gilliland, p. 25.

37 Quoted in Winchester, pp. 217–8.

38 Ibid., p. 220.

39 James W. Gerard, *My Four Years in Germany*, 1917, p. 125.

40 Knight, p. 35.

41 Hervey, p. 13

42 Horrocks, p. 19.

43 Dolbey, p. 147.

44 Cpt I.M. Henderson WO 161/95/64.

45 TNA WO 161/96/39.

46 TNA 161/96/39.

47 Willey, *Spots of Time*, p. 222.

48 Ibid., p. 228.

49 Quoted in Government Committee on Treatment by the Enemy of British Prisoners of War: *Report on the Transport of British Prisoners of War to Germany, August–December, 1914*, 1918, p. 12.

50 Gilliland, p. 17.

51 Horrocks, pp. 18–19.

52 Dolbey, p. 147.

III The Wire World: Life and Death in the Kaiser's Camps

1 R.C. Bond, *Prisoners Grave and Gay*, 1934, pp. 33–45.

2 Quoted in van Emden, *Prisoners of the Kaiser*, p. 84.

3 Quoted in Government Committee on Treatment by the Enemy of British Prisoners of War: *Report on the Transport of British Prisoners of War to Germany, August–December, 1914*, 1918, p. 12.

4 Cpl R. Burrows TNA FO 383/161.

5 Quoted in Van Emden, *Prisoners of the Kaiser*, p. 16.

6 Joseph Lee, p. 76.

7 Quoted in Moynihan, p. 84.

8 Harvey, p. 137.

9 Gilliland, p. 29.

10 Horrocks, p. 21.

11 Austin, p. 143.

12 Beds were usually built on a slant so the higher end served as a pillow. See Sergeant George Wells, 'Recollections of a Prisoner of War'.

13 Sergeant George Wells, imprisoned at Kassel, recalled of the NCO's lot: 'All manner of punishment was threatened if one of our section

was found guilty of misconduct. And as the men were not prepared to carry out orders . . . our task was most trying.'

14 Quoted in Jackson, p. 28.

15 Quoted in Richard Garrett, *POW*, 1981, p. 103.

16 Douglas, p. 99.

17 Cust, p. 23.

18 Quoted in Jackson, p. 28.

19 Dolbey, p. 199.

20 McLean was the only British officer in the fortress. Flt Lt L.D. Dalzell McLean RN WO 161/96/47.

21 Flt Lt L.D. Dalzell McLean RN WO 161/96/47.

22 See p. 148.

23 Lt T.J. Dobson RNVR TNA WO 161/95/62.

24 Higgins, p. 96.

25 Pte W. Butcher FO 383/161.

26 Quoted in Matthew Hall, *In Enemy Hands,* p. 45.

27 Cust, p. 49.

28 Government Committee on Treatment by the Enemy of British Prisoners of War: *The Horrors of Wittenberg: Official Report to the British Government*, 1916, p. 44. See TNA WO 161/97/30 for Vidal's personal report on Wittenberg.

29 Government Committee on Treatment by the Enemy of British Prisoners of War: *The Horrors of Wittenberg: Official Report to the British Government,* 1916, p. 44.

30 Dolbey, p. 183.

31 Cpl R. Burrows TNA FO 383/161. Rifleman Alfred Hall, sent to work on a farm near Limburg in 1917, found the village doctor equally Anglophobic: 'Herr Doctor shares the general hatred against the Englishmen. He said today they vare all too cheeky and proud, and goodness alone knows what he would do with them if he had his way etc etc.' See Malcolm Hall, *In Enemy Hands: A British Territorial Soldier in Germany 1915–1919*, 2002, p. 87.

32 Defence Department (Australia), *How the Germans Treated Australian Prisoners of War,* p. 50.

33 The German post-war historian of the camps, Wilhelm Doegen, suggested that 2,735 British PoWs died of disease during their incarceration

by the Kaiser. The figure is an underestimate since it does not include proper figures from the *Arbeitskommandos* behind the front line. According to Doegen, 1 British PoW died from smallpox, 42 from rigid cramp, 24 from abdominal typhoid, 67 from typhus, 23 from relapse fever, 485 from tuberculosis, 244 from dysentery, 2 from cholera, 1,389 from pneumonia, and 1,679 from other illnesses. See Doegen, pp. 56–7.

34 Government Committee on Treatment by the Enemy of British Prisoners of War: *Report on the Treatment by the Germans of Prisoners of War Taken During the Spring Offensive of 1918*, 1918, p. 16. The experience of British PoWs captured in 1918 gives the lie to German claims that ill treatment of PoWs in 1914 was due to inexperience; the Germans well knew in 1918 that large-scale offensive action was likely to bring a big 'bag' of prisoners, and overcrowding and starvation in camps would result in the deaths of the incarcerated. The survival rate of British PoWs under Hitler was c. 3 per cent – or 300 per cent better than under the Kaiser's regime.

35 Morton, p. 44.

36 Pte E. Caine TNA FO 383/161.

37 Waugh, *Prisoners of Mainz,* p. 51.

38 Higgins, p. 91.

39 Quoted in Garrett, p. 103.

40 Cust, pp. 34–6.

41 Quoted in Jackson, pp. 24–5.

42 Quoted in Lewis, p. 420.

43 Quoted in Jackson, p. 256.

44 Page, p. 45.

45 MacDonald, p. 89.

46 Higgins, p. 85.

47 Cust, p. 21.

48 G.E. Waymark IWM 76/96/1.

49 John Yarnall, *Barbed Wire Disease*, 2012, p. 111.

50 www.vlib.us/medical/pow/pozieres.htm

51 Cust, pp. 48–9. Lieutenant N.E. Tyndale-Biscoe reckoned he put on 5lbs in weight in a week after the commencement of parcels. IWM 84/9/1.

52 Lee, p. 95.

53 Quoted in Jackson, pp. 64–5.

54 The majority of those who starved to death did so behind the German lines in France and Belgium. Figure reflects deaths attributable only to withholding of food.

55 Pte E. Caine TNA FO 383/161.

56 Quoted in Moynihan, p. 85.

57 Pte R.S. Baillie TNA WO 161/99/80.

58 Pte George Agnew TNA WO 161/98/640.

59 Georges Connes, *A POW's Memoir of the First World War; The Other Ordeal*, 2004, p. 46.

60 See Charles Altschul, *German Militarism and Its German Critics*, 1918, passim.

61 Cpl William Walker TNA (no catalogue number). McGraa died on 8 December 1914.

62 Pte W. Elvin TNA FO 383/161.

63 Pte G. Cox TNA FO 383/161.

64 Hall, p. 77. At Döberitz Private T.C. Rainbird somewhat lost count of the homicides and simply took to entering in his diary 'another shocking shooting'. IWM 02/39/1.

65 See p. 283.

66 Phillimore, p. 183.

67 Muse, p. 42.

68 Quoted in Morton, p. 81.

69 Lee, p. 76.

70 Phillimore, p. 12.

71 Higgins, pp. 90–1.

72 Caunter, p. 20.

73 Lee, p. 76.

74 See www.dublin-fusliers.com/Pows/dubliner-pows.html for the experience of Irish PoWs at Limburg.

75 Cpl R. Dempsey TNA FO 383/161.

76 Ibid.

77 MacDonald, p. 158.

78 Gilliland, p. 144.

79 Lt T.J. Dobson RNVR TNA WO 161/95/62.

80 Cust, p. 43.

81 Quoted in Moynihan, p. 124.

82 Nobbs, pp. 216–17.

83 See p. 234

84 Quoted in Moynihan, p. 137.

85 Cust, p. 50.

86 Yarnall, p. 123.

87 Higgins, p. 96.

88 Ibid.

89 Hall, p. 76.

90 Ibid., pp. 96–7.

91 Higgins, p. 105.

92 Government Committee on Treatment by the Enemy of British Pris-
    oners of War: *Report on the Employment in Coal and Salt Mines of the
    British Prisoners of War in Germany,* 1918, p. 2.

93 Morton, p. 84.

94 Government Committee on Treatment by the Enemy of British Pris-
    oners of War: *Report on the Employment in Coal and Salt Mines of the
    British Prisoners of War in Germany,* 1918, p. 3.

95 MacDonald, p. 193.

96 Quoted in Moynihan, p. 64.

97 Ibid., p. 63.

98 Government Committee on Treatment by the Enemy of British Pris-
    oners of War: *Report on the Employment in Coal and Salt Mines of the
    British Prisoners of War in Germany,* 1918, p. 6.

99 Morton, p. 87. Any PoW requesting medical treatment would find he
    was expected to pay for it, the fee being stopped out of his 'wages'.

100 Ibid., p. 112.

101 See Mark Spoerer, 'The Mortality of Allied Prisoners of War and Bel-
    gian Civilian Deportees in German Captivity During the First World
    War: A Reappraisal of the Effects of Forced Labour', *Population Stud-
    ies,* 60, 2, 2006. Only 3.04 per cent of German PoWs in Britain died
    over the course of the war. The figure of 10.3 per cent includes 'weight-
    ing' for unregistered deaths of enlisted men behind the frontline in
    1918, and is not derived from Spoerer.

102 Lee, p. 35.

103 Higgins, p. 99.

104 Morton, p. 62.

105 Nobbs, p. 215.

106 King, p. 26.

107 Austin, p. 104. At Döberitz, one of the first camps for other ranks, a tent was quickly pressed into service as a church and drew a congregation of 500 men. See T.C. Rainbird IWM 02/39/1.

108 McMullen, p. 76.

109 Page, p. 176.

110 Ibid.

111 Lee, p. 38.

112 Gilliland, p. 78.

113 Thorn, p. 147.

114 Ibid.

115 Harvey, *Comrades in Captivity*, p. 222; Waugh, *Prisoners of Mainz,* p. 142.

116 Quoted in Lewis, p. 418.

117 Harvey, *Comrades in Captivity*, p. 28.

118 Emile Durkheim, *Suicide: A Study in Sociology*, London, 1963. According to Doegen, 17 British PoWs committed suicide during their captivity in Germany, of which 5 were officers and 12 men. (*Kriegsgefangene Völker*, p. 56). The disproportionately high percentage of officers – who tended to be more freighted by notions of honour than other ranks – in this tally bears the French sociologist out.

119 Connes, p. 57.

120 Carl P. Dennett, *Prisoners of the Great War: Authoritative Statement of Conditions in the Prison Camps of Germany* , 1919, passim.

121 W.G. Allen IWM 10875.

122 Harvey, *Gloucestershire Friends*, p. 14.

123 Harvey, p. 13.

124 Waugh, *Prisoners of Mainz*, 1919, p. 142.

125 Hay, p. 256.

IV Smile Boys, That's the Style:
The War of Resistance Behind the Wire

1 Muse, p. 13.

2 MacDonald, p. 84.

3 See Chapter VI.

4 Quoted in Morton, p. 70.

5 Captain T.V. Scudamore, quoted in Morton, p. 39.

6 Cust, pp. 54–5.

7 Government Committee on Treatment by the Enemy of British Prisoners of War: *Report on the Employment in Coal and Salt Mines of the British Prisoners of War in Germany*, 1918, p. 7.

8 TNA FO 383/161.

9 Prisoners were drilled for hours so they would learn the 'correct', Prussian, way of saluting (with the right hand, and the left stiff by the side). Corporal Edward Edwards, Princess Patricia's Canadian Light Infantry, described the mood of the men during practice as one of 'sullen rebellion'; he received 5 days cells for refusing to salute in Prussian style during drill. At length, for his consistent refusal to order his men to salute German officers in the required manner his corporal's stripes were 'taken down'. See George Pearson, *The Escape of a Princess Pat*, 1918, p. 102. The standard punishment for failing to salute or saluting improperly was 3 days in cells.

10 Connes, p. 42.

11 Horrocks, p. 20.

12 Quoted in Moynihan, pp. 106–7.

13 Harvey, *Comrades in Captivity*, p. 213.

14 Caunter, p. 98.

15 Horrocks, p. 23.

16 As does Hanson, p. 66.

17 Quoted in van Emden, *Prisoners of the Kaiser*, p. 109.

18 Tucker, pp. 86–8.

19 Ibid., p. 59.

20 Ibid.

21 Ibid., p. 60.

22 George Pearson, *The Escape of a Princess Pat*, 1918, pp. 96–7.

23 Page, p. 205.

24 Quoted in Moynihan, p. 24.

25 Ibid., p. 144.

26 Ibid., p. 41.

27 Moynihan, p. 41.

28 The informal arrangement was codified in January 1916 when Britain and Germany agreed that all non-commissioned officers 'shall be privileged to the extent that they will not be required to work . . . except in the capacity of overseer'.

29 Quoted in Moynihan, p. 39.

30 Yarnall, p. 137.

31 Quoted in Jackson, p. 29.

32 See Morton, pp. 112–13.

33 Quoted in Morton, p. 113.

34 Cpl R. Burrows TNA FO 383/161.

35 See James Farrant in Moynihan, p. 19. Also Sergeant A.J. Parsons TNA WO 161/100/558. The incident occurred in May 1916. According to Parsons 343 men, out of 2,000 initially refused to work, before roughing up and threats (including the stopping of what meagre food was being doled out) reduced the numbers to the hardcore 34.

36 Page, p. 54.

37 Morton, pp. 72–3.

38 Higgins, pp. 97–8.

39 Page, pp. 252–3.

40 Hall, p. 89.

41 Figure derived from Doegen pp. 56–7.

42 Quoted in van Emden, *Prisoners of the Kaiser*, p. 69.

43 Government Committee on Treatment by the Enemy of British Prisoners of War: *Report on the Employment in Coal and Salt Mines of the British Prisoners of War in Germany*, 1918, p. 3.

44 Page, pp. 178–9.

45 Tucker, p. 63.

46 This version is taken from *The Works of James Thomson*, published 1763, Vol. II, p. 191.

47 Cust, p. 57.

48 Poole, p. 19.

49 Templer, p. 7.

50 In the words of Colonel Stokes' adjutant, Hugh Durnford: 'For the Senior British Officer to disclaim authority over his own brother officers implied, legally speaking, that he regarded the conditions of the imprisonment as too monstrous to be covered by the accepted rules of

the Hague Convention, and that in fact he looked upon the Commandant not as his sentinel in an honourable capacity, but as his gaoler in a common gaol, where international conventions did not apply.' Durnford, p. 148.

51 Harvey, *Comrades in Captivity*, p. 102.

52 Evans, *The Escaping Club*, p. 83. Other ranks displayed the same intentional insouciance when faced with German discipline. Private T.C. Rainbird recorded in his diary that he took all German 'brutality with stolid indifference'.

53 Cust, p. 55.

54 See Durnford pp. 30–6 for the struggle against *Appells*.

55 Knight, p. 81.

56 Ibid., p. 89.

57 Ibid., pp. 95–6.

V The Barbed-Wire School: Passing the Time of Day Upon Day

1 Harvey, *Comrades in Captivity*, p. 28.

2 Higgins, p. 110.

3 Cpl Fyfe TNA WO 161/98/1.

4 Tucker, p. 65.

5 Quoted in Moynihan, p. 102.

6 D. Lyall Grant IWM 73/17/1.

7 TNA WO 161/96/38.

8 Gilliland, p. 29.

9 Ibid.

10 Hay, p. 252.

11 Waugh, *Prisoners of Mainz*, p. 198.

12 Knight, p. 85.

13 Austin, p. 143.

14 Hervey, p. 14.

15 Quoted in Moyhihan, p. 10.

16 Muller's guide to physical fitness sold over 2 million copies, and was translated into 25 languages. Muller's system became the official fitness regime of the British Army.

17 Evans, *The Escaping Club*, p. 128.

18 Lt T.J. Dobson RNVR WO 161/95/62.

19 Ibid.

20 Pte R.S. Baillie WO 161/99/80.

21 Lt T.J. Dobson RNVR WO 161/95/62.

22 Cpt D. Baird-Douglas WO 161/95/63.

23 Austin, p. 84.

24 Cust, p. 52.

25 Hall, p. 85.

26 Gilliland, p. 156.

27 Knight, p. 44.

28 Quoted in Moynihan, p. 125.

29 Quoted in Moynihan, p. 126.

30 M.C.C. Harrison and H.A. Cartwright, *Within Four Walls*, 1940, p. 269.

31 Quoted in Moynihan, p. 87.

32 Cpt D. Baird-Douglas WO 161/95/63.

33 Caunter, p. 54.

34 Evans, *The Escaping Club*, p. 142.

35 Cust, p. 39.

36 Yarnall, p. 133.

37 Flt Lt L.D. Dalzell McLean RN WO 161/96/47.

38 Durnford, p. 29.

39 Quoted in Moynihan, p. 92.

40 Harvey, *Comrades in Captivity*, pp. 150–1.

41 Caunter, p. 40.

42 Knight, p. 86.

43 Harvey, *Comrades in Captivity*, p. 65.

44 Lt T.J. Dobson RNVR WO 161/95/62.

45 Lee, p. 158.

46 Harvey, *Comrades in Captivity*, p. 67. According to Wilhelm Doegen's semi-official (and almost wholly propagandistic) history of the Kaiser's camps, 17 French prisoners were found guilty of the crime of cruelty to animals between 1914 and 1918. No 'English' were found guilty of the same crime. See Wilhelm Doegen, *Kriegsgefangene Völker,* Band 1, 1921, pp. 138–9

47 *Ducks and other Verses* was published in 1919. The poem is dedicated to 'E.M., Who drew them in Holzminden prison'.

48 Hervey, p. 101.

49 Caunter, pp. 47–8.

50 Thorn, p. 32.

51 Quoted in Jackson, p. 38.

52 Quoted in Edmund King, '"Books are more to me than food": British Prisoners of War as Readers, 1914–1918', *Books History*, 16, 2013.

53 Hervey, p. 67.

54 Quoted in Moynihan, p. 13.

55 Lee, p. 37.

56 Evans, *The Escaping Club*, p. 134.

57 Quoted in Moynihan, p. 95.

58 See Lewis-Stempel, *Six Weeks*, 2010, p. 135.

59 Nobbs, p. 122. Lieutenant J.H. Alcock in Furstenburg held dinners 'on the slightest provocation!' IWM 96/29/1.

60 Douglas, pp. 125–6.

61 Quoted in Jackson, p. 38.

62 Quoted in Hanson, pp. 77–76.

63 Quoted in Sadler and Serdiville, p. 320.

64 Quoted in Moynihan, p. 7.

65 Ibid.

66 Ibid., p. 91.

67 Higgins, p. 100.

68 Quoted in Moynihan, p. 28.

69 Harvey, *Comrades in Captivity*, p. 84.

70 Harvey, *ibid.*, p. 79.

71 Tucker, p. 101.

72 Harvey, p. 180.

73 Knight, p. 43.

74 Quoted in Garrett, p. 104.

75 Quoted in Moynihan, p. 93.

76 Quoted in van Emden, *Prisoners of the Kaiser*, p. 105.

77 Several members of the Paris Opera were incarcerated in Dulmen, with the result that performances in the camp theatre were always sold out. See van Emden, *Prisoners of the Kaiser*, p. 106.

78 Higgins, p. 105.

79 Hall, p. 84.

80 Quoted in Moynihan, pp. 106–7.

81 Harvey, *Comrades in Captivity*, p. 238.

82 Tucker, p. 100.

83 Quoted in Moynihan, p. 92.

84 Dolbey, p. 190.

85 Quoted in van Emden, *Prisoners of the Kaiser*, p. 96.

86 Tucker, p. 73.

87 Ibid., p. 76.

88 Ibid., pp. 76–7.

89 Only senior officers enjoyed any degree of privacy in the camps, since they were entitled to (though did no always get) their own single room. Soldiers and officers in dormitories and barracks fequently erected curtains and 'walls' of cardboard around their bunks in an attempt at privacy. Such arrangements, of course, were not soundproof.

90 Percy Brown, *Round the Corner*, 1934, p. 277.

91 Douglas, p. 95.

92 Quoted in Moynihan, p. 9.

93 M.S. Esler IWM 378.

94 Caunter, p. 10.

95 Evans, *The Escaping Club*, p. 119.

96 Bowman, p. 32.

97 Harvey, p. 80.

98 Waugh, *The Early Years*, pp. 133–4.

99 Lt T.J. Dobson RNVR TNA WO 161/95/62.

100 Quoted in Edmund King, '"Books are more to me than food": British Prisoners of War as Readers, 1914–1918', *Books History*, 16, 2013, p. 25.

101 Cust, p. 44.

102 Cull, p. 179.

103 Quoted in King, p. 1.

104 H.A. Cartwright, 'Beginners', in *Escapers All*, (ed.) J.R. Ackerley, 1932, p. 43.

105 Gilliland, p. 213.

106 Quoted in King, p. 7.

107 See King, p. 7.

108   Ibid., p. 18.

109   Ibid., p. 19.

110   Harvey, *Comrades in Captivity*, p. 207.

111   Waugh, *Prisoners of Mainz*, pp. 65–6.

112   Gilliland, p. 86.

113   Ibid., p. 13.

114   Nobbs, p. 213.

115   Quoted in Oliver Wilkinson, 'Captivity in Print: The Form and Function of PoW Camp Magazines' in (ed.) Gilly Carr, Harold Mytum, *Cultural Heritage and Prisoners of War: Creativity Behind Barbed Wire*, Abingdon, 2012. See Wilkinson passim for an analysis of British PoW journals.

116   Cust, p. 6.

117   Bowman, p. 3.

118   *The Living Age*, 1 November 1919.

119   http://allpoetry.com/J_M_Rose-Troup

120   Claude Templer, *Poems and Imaginings*, 1920, p. 37.

121   Quoted in Winchester, p. 123.

VI Escapers All: The Escaping Habit

1   H.E. Hervey, pp. 81–2.

2   J.H. Hardy, *I Escape*, p. 11.

3   T.V. Scudamore, *Lighter Episodes in the Life of a Prisoner of War* (Aldershot, 1933), p. 27.

4   S.P. MacKenzie, 'The Ethics of Escape: British Officer POWs in the First World War', *War in History*, 2008, Vol. 15, No. 1, p. 3.

5   Thorn, pp. 40–1.

6   MacKenzie, p. 6.

7   Out of which 1 in 100 Canadians got 'home', compared to 1 in 350 British Army soldiers. The disparity is somewhat accounted for by the shortness of time most Britons were held, the majority being captured in 1918, leaving them relatively little time to make and plan escapes.

8   A.J. Evans, 'Exploits of the Escaping Club', in *Escapers All* (Intro. and ed. Ackerley), 1932, p. 89.

9   A.J. Evans, *The Escaping Club*, p. 67.

10 Horace Gilliland, p. 125.

11 Quoted in MacKenzie, p. 6.

12 Quoted in Moynihan, pp. 64–5.

13 A.J. Evans, *The Escaping Club*, p. 25.

14 Harvey, *Comrades*, p. 26.

15 Page, pp. 54–5.

16 M.C.C. Harrison and H.A. Cartwright, p. 214.

17 Duncan Grinnell-Milne, 'Inveterate Escapers' in *Escapers All* (Intro. and ed. Ackerley), 1932, p. 108.

18 Waugh, *Prisoners of Mainz,* p. 124.

19 Hervey, p. 93.

20 Horrocks, p. 21.

21 The figure is calculated from the age of those escapers who were interviewed by the Government Committee on Treatment by the Enemy of British Prisoners of War.

22 Quoted in Heather Jones, *Violence Against Prisoners of War,* p. 188.

23 Coney quoted in National War Aims Committee, *Prisoners of Prussia: Official Report on the Treatment of British Prisoners of War by the Enemy during 1918,* 1918; Tucker, p. 68.

24 Quoted in Moynihan, p. 57.

25 Hanson, p. 133.

26 Harvey, *Comrades*, pp. 236–7.

27 See Dwight R. Messimer, *Escape*, p. 199.

28 A.J. Evans, 'Exploits of the Escaping Club', in *Escapers All* (Intro. and ed. Ackerley), 1932, p. 93.

29 Evans, *The Escaping Club,* pp. 121–4.

30 Quoted in Moynihan, p. 64.

31 A.J. Evans, *Escape and Liberation,* 1945, pp. 16–17. Kaye's real name was Kaiser. Unsurprisingly, he changed it.

32 freepages.genealogy.rootsweb.ancestry.com/-bathonia/ EdwardOslerBath.htm

33 Durnford, p. 178.

34 Harvey, p. 239.

35 Harrison and Cartwright, p. 214.

36 Horrocks, p. 27.

37 Harvey, *Comrades in Captivity*, p. 30.

38 freepages.genealogy.rootsweb.ancestry.com/-bathonia/
    EdwardOslerBath.htm

39 Durnford, p. 67.

40 Caunter, pp. 24–5.

41 H. Baker (letter), Mitchell Library.

42 Cust, p. 65.

43 Pearson, p. 170.

44 Harvey, *Comrades*, p. 218.

45 Cust, p. 27.

46 Knight, p. 114.

47 Page, p. 111–14. Private Ernest Pearce, 14/Yorks and Lancashire, found
    a ready-made tunnel out of Fortuna Grube mine. The camp sewer. By
    widespread agreement he deserved his Military Medal for escaping.

48 Harvey, *Comrades in Captivity*, p. 67.

49 Morton, p. 100.

50 Harvey, *Comrades in Captivity*, pp. 143–4.

51 W.C. Blain IWM 83/11/1.

52 Quoted in Durnford, pp. 159–61.

53 Durnford, p. 139.

54 See Hanson, p. 229.

55 MacDonald, pp. 102–3.

56 Thorn, p. 123.

57 Hanson, p. 180.

58 Quoted in Winchester, p. 53.

59 Lawrence Wingfield 'Hazards of Escape', in *Escapers All* (Intro. and
    ed. Ackerley), 1932, p. 297.

60 One gramophone dispatched to a British prisoner in Holzminden by
    the War Office, probably with the connivance of the manufacturer, the
    Columbia Gramophone Co. of Wandsworth, London, had false sides
    and bottom. These hid: 6 compasses (5 of which also had magnifying
    glasses and luminous dials), maps, pens and water-resistant ink in four
    colours for the reproduction of the maps, wire cutters, and torches.
    With replacement batteries. Doegen, p. 152.

61 Hervey, p. 59.

62 Phillimore, p. 185.

63 Harvey, *Comrades in Captivity*, p. 146.

64 M.C.C. Harrison, 'What a Skeleton key will Do' in Escapers All (Intro. and ed. J. R. Ackerley), 1932, p. 152.

65 Harrison and Cartwright, p. 94.

66 Quoted in Hanson, p. 87.

67 Hervey, p. 65.

68 Hervey p. 66.

69 Thorn, p. 39.

70 Durnford, p. 175.

71 Harrison and Cartwright, p. 47.

72 Hervey, p. 21.

73 Harvey, *Comrades in Captivity*, p. 170.

74 Evans, *The Escaping Club*, p. 10.

75 Phillimore, p. 141.

76 Later Sir Robert, Chair of Anaesthetics, University of Oxford.

77 Hervey, p. 33.

78 J.L. Hardy, 'A Winter's Tale', in *Escapers All* (Intro. and ed. Ackerley), 1932, p. 123.

79 Pearson, p. 107.

80 Hervey, p. 33.

81 Phillimore, p. 220.

82 Horrocks, p. 33.

83 Evans, 'Exploits of the Escaping Club', in *Escapers All* (Intro. and ed. Ackerley), 1932, p. 100.

84 Page, p. 341.

85 MacDonald, p. 232.

86 Knight, p. 124.

87 Caunter, pp. 126–7.

88 *London Gazette,* 30 January 1920.

89 Jack Evans, p. 6.

90 Harrison and Cartwright, p. 139.

91 Morton, p. 185.

92 Gilliland, p. 245.

93 Lawrence Wingfield, 'Hazards of Escape', *Escapers All* (Intro. and ed. Ackerley), pp. 301–2.

94 H. Baker, Mitchell Library, New South Wales, Australia.

95 Quoted in Moynihan, p. 146.

96 Pte Tulloch TNA WO/161/100/199.

97 Phillimore, p. 110.

98 Ibid.

99 Thorn, p. 56.

100 Quoted in Moynihan, p. 65.

101 Gilliland, p. 248.

102 Page, p. 360.

103 Pearson, p. 186.

104 Evans, *The Escaping Club*, p. 229.

105 Durnford, p. 196.

106 Gilliland, p. 251.

107 See H.P. Picot, *The British Interned in Switzerland*, for an overview of internment. Also Jonathan Vance, *Objects of Concern*, 1994, for attitudes of 'fire-eater' Canadian PoWs on repatriation, esp. pp. 60–8. The quote from the PoW on p. 246 is from Vance, p. 60.

108 Ackerley in *Prisoners of War* offers one perspective on the officer experience of the gilded cage.

VII Goodbyeeeee: Last Days, Armistice and Liberation

1 Tucker, p. 68.

2 Quoted in van Emden, *Prisoners of the Kaiser*, p. 146.

3 Quoted in Jones, *Violence Against Prisoners of War in the First World War, 1914–1920*, p. 213.

4 Waugh, *Early Years*, p. 135.

5 Willey, *Spots of Time*, p. 188.

6 Cust, p. 51.

7 Quoted in Jackson, pp. 123–4.

8 Tucker, p. 118.

9 Jackson, p. 120.

10 Willey, *Spots of Time*, p. 137.

11 Cust, p. 70.

12 Captain McMurtrie, quoted in Malcolm Brown, *The Imperial War Museum Book of 1918*, 1998, pp. 324–5.

13 Horrocks, p. 24.

14 Quoted in Jackson, p. 117.

15 Waugh, *Prisoners of Mainz*, p. 246.

16 Quoted in Max Arthur, *We Will Remember Them* , 2009, pp. 31–2.

17 Ibid., p. 32.

18 Quoted in Jackson, p. 122.

19 Higgins, p. 113.

20 Quoted in Brown, pp. 324–5.

21 Ibid., p. 325.

22 Quoted in Arthur, *We Will Remember Them*, 2009, p. 70.

23 Quoted in Jackson, pp. 124–5.

24 Ralph Ellinwood, p. 153.

25 Ibid., p. 157.

26 Quoted in Garrett, p. 126.

27 Cust, p. 64.

28 Hall, p. 108.

29 Papers of Pte F. Alexander, Great War Archive, Oxford University.

30 Prisoner quoted in Morton, p. 134.

31 http://www.worcestershireregiment.com/wr.php?main=inc/
    pow_tucker

32 Quoted in Jackson, pp. 120–1.

33 Ibid, pp. 126–7.

34 Quoted in Arthur, *We Will Remember Them*, pp. 32–3.

35 Lee, p. 211.

36 Waugh, *Prisoners of Mainz*, p. 246.

37 IWM Misc 15/316.

38 Great War Archive, Oxford University, misc.

39 The very last PoWs were not repatriated until the first week of March
    1919. They were 'in medical charge'.

40 Waugh, *Prisoners of Mainz*, p. 257.

41 Waugh, *Prisoners of Mainz*, pp. 56–7.

42 Willey, *Spots of Time*, p. 239.

43 Quoted in Arthur, p. 43.

44 Quoted in Morton, p. 135.

45 Muse, p. 47.

VIII Home, Unsweet Home: Return and Aftermath

1 W.A. Tucker, p. 122.

2 The phrase is Richard van Emden's.

3 Thomas Higgins, p. 116.

4 Returned Holzminden PoW quoted in Hanson, p. 252.

5 Willey, *Spots of Time*, p. 242.

6 Quoted in Arthur, *We Will Remember Them*, p. 31.

7 Ibid., p. 34.

8 Willey, *Spots of Time*, p. 243.

9 Harvey, *Comrades*, p. 319–20.

10 Horrocks, p. 35.

11 Quoted in van Emden, *Prisoners of the Kaiser*, p. 206.

12 Gilliland, p. 257.

13 Waugh, *Prisoners of Mainz*, p. 265.

14 Van Emden, *Prisoners of the Kaiser*, p. 197.

15 Quoted in Garrett, p. 126.

16 http://www.worcestershireregiment.com/wr.php?main=inc/vc_w_l_robinson_page9

17 Morton p. 151.

18 Jonathan Vance, *Objects of Concern*, 1994, p. 81.

19 Quoted in van Emden, *Prisoners of the Kaiser*, p. 201.

20 In a final tragedy, Anthelme Mangin died, probably of starvation, in a mental institution in France in 1942. Anouilh's play *Le Voyageur Sans Bagage* was first published in 1937.

21 Yarnall, p. 196.

22 Harvey, *Comrades in Captivity*, p. 318.

23 The Officer Prisoner of War Dining Club continued to exist until 1977.

24 Poole, p. 136.

25 Quoted in Paul Routledge, *Public Servant, Secret Agent*, 2012, p. 198.

26 P.R. Reid, *The Colditz Story*, 1974, p. 9.

27 *Glasgow Herald*, 28 December 1962.

28 M.V. Hay, *The Foot of Pride*, Boston, 1951.

INDEX